Savonarola

SAVONAROLA

The Rise and Fall of a Renaissance Prophet

DONALD WEINSTEIN

Yale UNIVERSITY PRESS

New Haven & London

Yale University Press books may be purchased in quantity for educational, business, or promotional use. For information, please e-mail sales.press@yale.edu (U.S. office) or sales@yaleup.co.uk (U.K. office).

Set in Adobe Caslon type by Keystone Typesetting, Inc., Orwigsburg, Pennsylvania.
Printed in the United States of America.

Library of Congress Cataloging-in-Publication Data

Weinstein, Donald, 1926–
    Savonarola : the rise and fall of a Renaissance prophet / Donald Weinstein.
        p. cm.
    Includes bibliographical references and index.
    ISBN 978-0-300-11193-4 (cloth : alk. paper) 1. Savonarola, Girolamo, 1452–1498. 2. Dominicans—Italy—Florence—Biography. 3. Reformers—Italy—Florence—Biography. 4. Florence (Italy)—Biography. 5. Florence (Italy)—Politics and government—1421–1737. 6. Florence (Italy)—Church history. 7. Catholic Church—Italy—Florence—History. I. Title.
    DG737.97.W43   2011
    282.092—dc23
    [B]
                                                                                2011032980

Catalogue records for this book are available from the Library of Congress and the British Library.

This paper meets the requirements of ANSI/NISO Z39.48-1992 (Permanence of Paper).

10 9 8 7 6 5 4 3 2 1

To Giles Constable

Contents

Illustrations follow page 104

Acknowledgments

My greatest debt is to my wife, Beverly Parker. Her moral support, editorial acumen, technical skills, and intelligence have been with me all the way. I could not have written this book without her. Four friends have been extraordinarily helpful. Lorenzo Polizzotto placed his unmatched knowledge of Savonarola and his movement at my disposal and has been a precise, constructive, and sympathetic reader and critic; Alan E. Bernstein has taught me much about medieval religion over the years, and I have benefited greatly from his suggestions, counsel, and friendship; Stefano Dall'Aglio has been unfailingly generous in responding to my countless calls for help with archival and bibliographical problems, caught a number of slips, and readily shared his expertise on sixteenth-century Savonarolism; Jim Banker, my old companion in the Florentine archives, has read the book with his sharp eye for detail and sense of style.

Other friends and fellow scholars who have provided critical assistance are JoAnne Bernstein, Alison Brown, Gene Brucker, Cornelia Carlson, Mel Carlson, Giles Constable, Gail Eifrig, Christopher Fulton, Richard Goldthwaite, Sarah Blake Hamm, Valerie Hotchkiss, Howard Kaminsky, Kate Lowe, Lauro Martines, Julia O'Faolain, Olga Zorzi Pugliese, David Price, Fr. Fausto Sbaffoni, O.P., Piero Scapecchi, Herbert Schneidau, Ludovica Sebregondi, Fr. Armando F. Verde, O.P., Mark Zucker.

Warm thanks to the editors at Yale University Press who have enthusiastically and skillfully guided the book through the stages of publication, especially to Eliza Childs, copy-editor *senza pari*, with whom collaboration has been a pleasure. The manuscript she returned is far more presentable than the one she received. Even so, senior editor Margaret Otzel found still more room for improvement. A special thanks to the skilled, dedicated members of the Interlibrary Loan staff at the University of Arizona Library. Their cheerful cooperation and efficiency in tracking down remote scholarly items has been indispensable.

A Note on Usages

Time

The year. In fifteenth- and sixteenth-century Florence the new year began on March 25, the Feast of the Annunciation. Since this may cause some confusion to the reader, I have adjusted dates from January 1 through March 24 to conform to the current system.

The day. In Savonarola's time the hours were counted from sunset in a twenty-four-hour sequence. The first hour was an hour after sunset, the second two hours after sunset, and so on. In converting to the modern system I have taken into account the seasonal changes of sunset, but times are only approximate. Thus the hour of Savonarola's execution is given as 13, approximately 8 a.m.

Money, Weight, Measures

Money. The *fiorino*, or *scudo*, contained about thirty-two grams of gold and equaled seven *lire*. The *lira* contained twenty *soldi*, each equivalent to twelve *denari*. Three, later four, denari made up a *quattrino*. (The average wage of an unskilled worker was eight to ten soldi per day. Skilled construction workers were paid about two–three times as much.) (On wages I follow Richard A. Goldthwaite, *The Building of Renaissance Florence: An Economic and Social History* [Baltimore, 1980] app. 3, "Workers' Wages.")

Dry measure. The *staio* was equivalent to about three-quarters of a modern bushel.

Linear measure. The *braccio* (plural *braccia*) equaled about two feet.

Bible Citations

I have supplied key biblical references where I can identify them. Because the numbering system for Psalms 10 to 147 differs between Catholic and Protestant versions, I have supplied the numbers used by each. Thus Psalm 10 in the Vulgate is Psalm 11 in the Revised Standard Version, and I write it as (Ps. 10/11).

Also note differences in numbering of the books of Samuel and Kings:

Catholic (Vulgate, Douai)	Protestant (Revised Standard Version)
1 Sam. (also 1 Kings)	1 Sam.
2 Sam. (also 2 Kings)	2 Sam.
3 Kings	1 Kings
4 Kings	2 Kings

Except when noted or when quoting from a published translation, the translations are my own.

Prologue

On the morning of May 23, 1498, Girolamo Savonarola and two fellow Dominican friars, Domenico da Pescia and Silvestro Maruffi, were hanged and burned in the main square of Florence, the city they had hailed as the New Jerusalem (*see Fig. 1*). Relentless interrogation and bone-breaking torture had wrung incriminating admissions from each of them, most devastatingly from Savonarola, the triumvirate's leader. In a written statement read by an official to a perplexed and uneasy public, fra Girolamo declared that his prophecies of Florentine glory and Christian renewal were bogus, inspired not by God but by his own ambition for worldly glory and political power.

One of his admirers, the apothecary Luca Landucci, heard the confession and recorded his feelings in his diary. "I was there to hear the statement and I remained dumbfounded and bewildered. I was grief stricken to see such a grand edifice come crashing to earth because it had been built so wretchedly on a single lie. I was expecting Florence to become a new Jerusalem out of which would come the laws and splendor and example of the good life, and to see the renovation of the Church, the conversion of the infidels, and the consolation of the righteous. Instead, I realized, everything was just the opposite. So I had to swallow the medicine: 'All things, O Lord, are in thy will' [Eph. 1.11?]."

Many who came to witness the execution, Landucci reported, hoped for a sign that would prove the truth of Savonarola's glorious prophecies. But no sign was forthcoming; he went to his death without a word and their remaining faith was shattered. Still, "a few good people" had so much faith that they braved official displeasure by secretly gathering the ashes that had been ordered thrown into the Arno.

The two contrasting faiths of Landucci's account still shadow every telling of the Savonarola story. The hawk-nosed, raspy-voiced little mendicant preacher who briefly captivated the first city of the Renaissance with his gospel of republican liberty, civic empire, and universal Christian renewal—was he a God-intoxicated visionary or a thrusting opportunist? The trial record provides no universally satisfying answer. Savonarola's devotees, his leading modern biographers among them, dismiss the confessions as concoctions of inquisitorial torturers and dishonest notaries and esteem him as a prophet and saintly martyr. Skeptics accept the same evidence as substantially genuine, proof of the corrupt motives that drove him.

But Savonarola is a protean figure who refuses to be confined to such theological pigeonholes as "saint" or "sinner." I have followed him as he moved through the various phases of his spiritual odyssey, from world rejection to world reform, and have tried to understand the circumstances of each juncture. To deny that ambition played a role in Savonarola's rise to prominence would be pointless. It is more fruitful to consider to what ends he directed his ambition and to what extent he remained true to those ends as he moved into the limelight and discovered his charismatic powers.

"Prophets," wrote Henry Mayer in his fine biography of William Lloyd Garrison, the prophet of the abolition of American slavery, "however little they are honored in their time, are nonetheless connected to it." J. H. Hexter in his introduction to the *Utopia* of Thomas More referred to Savonarola, in Machiavellian vein, as the most successful and unsuccessful prophet-without-arms of his time and place. Taken together the two observations sum up a main truth about prophets: not only do they profoundly connect to their time and place, they operate in profound tension with them. This explains both their spectacular success and their ultimate failure.

Savonarola's bold engagement with the ills of his time and his radical vision of a New Heaven and a New Earth mesmerized the people of Florence and made devotees of philosophers, humanists, more than one reigning prince, and even a few Roman prelates; yet to achieve his vision was beyond the power, or the will, of an imperfect humanity. Savonarola came to grief not, as Machiavelli declared, because unarmed prophets are bound to fail, but because like all prophets, armed or not, he mistook his own vision for the fulfillment of history—or, as he would have said, for God's design. It follows that a biography of Savonarola must be, as his first great modern biographer, Pasquale Villari, understood, a "life and times" in order to explain how he came to this vision, why it captivated so many, and why the society that acclaimed him as a prophet ultimately rejected and killed him.

Savonarola lived during the Renaissance, a period named for its fascination, bordering on obsession, with the culture of classical antiquity. There had been earlier classical revivals—since the time of Charlemagne we can count almost one a century—but none of them was so passionate to know and emulate everything about the ancient Greeks and Romans or went about it so methodically. The operatives in those earlier revivals were predominantly clerics in monastic and cathedral centers across Europe who justified their study of pagan philosophy, science, and literature by claiming that this helped them articulate and defend the theology and tenets of their Christian faith. But the protagonists of this new Renaissance were for the most part laymen— notaries, lawyers, scribes, teachers, government officials, physicians, business- men, makers of the new civic culture of thirteenth- and fourteenth-century Italy—who regarded a knowledge of classical Latin language and literature as enhancing their professions as well as opening new horizons of human art and experience.

The chief spokesman and ideologue of the new classical sensibility was Francesco Petrarca (1304–74), or Petrarch, to call him by his Latinized name. Although Petrarch also advanced the cause of Italian literature by continuing the practice of writing his sonnets, canzoni, and other forms of love poetry in the Tuscan vernacular, he believed that to enter the higher thought world of the writers and thinkers of antiquity it was first necessary to master their language. He and his fellow enthusiasts promoted a method of Latin study that began with the fundamentals of classical grammar, syntax, and vocabulary and advanced to the reading of ancient texts and training in rhetoric, the mastery of literary and oratorical styles. Like explorers of lost continents, classical scholars hunted for copies of ancient writings, identified lost or for- gotten authors, compared and edited texts, and established rules for determin- ing the authenticity, accuracy, and primacy of variant manuscripts, thus creat- ing the discipline of philology. They copied inscriptions, studied ancient coins, and excavated and sketched Roman buildings and sites. They also prized ancient science and technology and recovered many influential texts on medi- cine, geography, agriculture, astronomy, mathematics, and military science.

Until the fifteenth century, humanists (as teachers of *studia humanitatis* came to be called to distinguish them from teachers of religious studies) had little access to the faculties of those strongholds of intellectual conservatism, the universities. Since they were obliged to find other means of earning a living and alternate outlets for their intellectual wares, this exclusion had the effect of furthering the dissemination of classical studies in the broader society. Humanists established new schools of the arts and taught in established grammar schools, served as tutors in wealthy households, worked as editors and translators, and dedicated their writings to patrons who could reward them with an honorarium or employment. For their schools they promoted an expanded liberal arts curriculum that included Latin grammar, rhetoric, poetry, music, arithmetic, and history.

By the second half of the fifteenth century the new arts curriculum was established in every Italian city from Milan to Palermo, in the Roman curia, and at princely courts in Italy and north of the Alps. In addition to their belated reception into university arts faculties, humanist-trained professionals served as official historians and biographers, private secretaries and public functionaries, propagandists and public orators. The "orator," or ambassador, who, as the famous English quip had it, "goes to lie abroad for his country," had to be competent enough to deliver a formal address in eloquent, polished Latin replete with references to classical writers and ancient history. Familiarity with the ancient poets and historians as well as competence in "good Latin" was expected of high Church dignitaries.

With the spread of humanist education among laymen (and sometimes among their sisters and daughters), preachers hoping to find favor among elite church congregations adopted techniques of classical rhetoric and sprinkled their texts with classical allusions. Ancient philosophy entered the cultural mainstream too, with the growing availability of Latin and vernacular translations of Plato, Aristotle, and others in the new medium of print. Petrarch's call for the revival of Greek was also answered when the city of Florence offered the Byzantine envoy Manuel Chrysoloras a three-year professorship of Greek in 1397. He was followed by other learned diplomats and churchmen of the Byzantine Empire who came to Italy seeking help against the Turks and remained to initiate a solid revival of Greek language and thought.

The Renaissance was a time not only of new knowledge and linguistic sophistication but also of major changes in taste and aesthetic sensibility. Classical styles and motifs, never entirely absent from medieval culture, now increasingly dictated the forms and decorative details of churches, public and private palaces, monuments, and country villas. In art, classical style came irresistibly into its own in the fifteenth century. Taking their cue from antiquity, artists drew, painted, and sculpted the nude human form, going far beyond ancient art in their observation of anatomy and nature, rendered with new techniques of linear and aerial perspective.

Ancient myths, historical episodes, erotic scenes, and other "profane" subjects took their places in Italian art and literature alongside Christian ones as authors, often now writing in the *volgare*, or vernacular, drew upon classical comedy, romance, satire, and tragedy and adapted ancient forms to native traditions and experience. Niccolò Machiavelli (1469–1527) is a good example of this fusion: his ribald Italian comedies were inspired by Plautus and other ancient authors, but his plots revolved around the complications of everyday life and his characters were the crafty friars, hypocritical priests, grasping merchants, flirtatious young wives, and randy lovers whom he observed in the streets of Florence.

Religious conservatives worried that the rising tide of classical culture was drowning Christian morals and values in a sea of "paganism" and blamed it for everything from the clergy's fixation on money and power to the spread of sexual license. With little comprehension of such historical realities as the rise of an entrepreneurial economy, the demographic catastrophe of the Black Death, and the spread of secular culture, they applied simplistic moral dichotomies—greed vs. charity, ambition vs. humility, luxury vs. austerity, piety vs. worldliness—and called for a return to a "primitive Christianity" every bit as idealized as the classical antiquity of the humanists.

At the beginning of the fifteenth century the influential Dominican preacher and future cardinal Giovanni Dominici (1356–1420) mounted a public attack on the humanists, charging that they were perverting Christian youth by replacing the authority of the saints with that of the ancients. Dominici was no obscurantist but a sophisticated Thomist theologian, and he made his argument on a philosophical level, challenging humanist assumptions about the primacy of will over reason and questioning the rhetoricians' faith in the correspondence between words and things. Coluccio Salutati (1331–1406), the eminent classical scholar and first secretary of the Florentine Chancellery, replied for humanism. All knowledge, including *studia divinitatis*, begins with communication, Salutati memorably declared, and his thesis was elaborated by his successors into a humanist credo: language is the link to reality, the basis of human community and of the connection between past and present. Through language, therefore, we draw both upon our own knowledge of the world and upon the experience of all mankind and gain the information we need to make decisions and to act. Thus the study of language is central to all of human life, to religion as well as to government.

Such claims for language, history, and literary study may seem routine to us, for they have entered the mainstream of Western cultural tradition, but many conservatives viewed them as contradictory to Church teachings, which stressed human depravity and the need for divine revelation and saving grace. Penitential preachers thundered against "pagan" literature and "lascivious" art as provoking unbelief and godless license, and many were convinced that these were signs that Antichrist was at hand. Girolamo Savonarola was one of this chorus of apocalyptic doomsayers. If he had remained only that, however, he would have earned a mere footnote in the history of the era along with such other great fifteenth-century preachers and cultural reactionaries as Saint Bernardino da Siena, Giacomo delle Marche, Giovanni Capistrano, Vincent Ferrer, and Giovanni Dominici himself. How he found his distinctive voice with a message that fused spiritual and moral renewal with social justice and political liberty and, most remarkably, how he—outsider, mendicant preacher, crusader against "worldliness" in all its guises—persuaded Florence, first city of the Renaissance, to embrace him as its prophet are key questions of this biography.

CHAPTER 1

The Making of a Moralist

The man hanged and burned as a false prophet in Florence in 1498 was born in Ferrara on September 21, 1452, and christened Girolamo Maria Francesco Matteo Savonarola. He was the third of the seven children of Niccolò Savonarola and Elena Bonacossi. Niccolò and his four brothers had moved to Ferrara from Padua in 1440 when their father, Michele, accepted an invitation to become court physician to Niccolò d'Este. Although most of the Savonarola men were merchants, physicians, lawyers, and clerics, the family had a slender connection to old Paduan aristocracy through Antonio Savonarola, a military captain in the thirteenth-century wars against Ezzelino da Romano, the infamous son-in-law of Holy Roman Emperor Frederick II. The Porta Savonarola, still standing in Padua, was said to be a monument to the family's former prominence. Mother Elena brought some distinction to the union through her family's claim of descent from the former rulers of Mantua. Girolamo's father, Niccolò, became a merchant and money changer who never found the ticket to prosperity. When he died in 1485 he left Elena with scant means to provide dowries for their two daughters, one of whom remained unmarried.

The most successful and distinguished member of the family was grandfather Michele. Before becoming the d'Este court physician he had taught in the medical faculty at Padua's famous university and was the author of a widely used textbook, the *Pratica medicinae*, as well as a string of treatises on fevers, pulse, urine, purgatives, physiognomy, pregnancy, and pediatrics. As devout as he was learned, Michele wrote religious and moralizing treatises too, among them *On Penitence and Confession* and *In Praise of John the Baptist*, in which he held up the forerunner of Jesus as a model of penitence and sanctity for the wayward clergy of his day. In *On the Treatment of Apathy Due to Illness* he discussed the power of meditation and resignation to God's will, and his treatise on pregnancy and pediatrics contains a chapter on the moral education of children.

Grandfather Michele took his patriarchal responsibilities very seriously. For Niccolò and Elena and their growing family he provided a house across the street from his own, where he could take a direct hand in the education and moral formation of his grandchildren. Grandfather Michele was Girolamo's first instructor in *grammatica,* or Latin letters. He and Niccolò agreed that the boy showed promise and should go on to study logic and philosophy preliminary to enrolling in medical school. Girolamo was fourteen when his grandfather died, by which time he may have already been attending a school in the city, probably the school of liberal arts directed by Battista Guarino and founded by Battista's father Guarino da Verona, whom Michele had praised as "the first of all humanists . . . worthy of great respect for his life and teaching."

At school Girolamo became proficient in humanist Latin, read classical poetry, and wrote sonnets in the manner of Petrarch. Years later fra Girolamo responded to the charge that he was ignorant of poetry. Not true, he said: he had once frequented the schools of the poets and the versifiers and taken their raps on the knuckles; that was before the love of God opened his eyes and he abandoned those barren forests to savor the fruits of the vineyards of the Church.[1] God also turned him from his early enthusiasm for Plato, he recalled. ("Look, today all you hear out there is 'Plato, that divine man.' I was in that same misapprehension myself and I studied Plato's dialogues a lot, but then, when God gave me light, I tore up everything I had written about them.")[2]

Girolamo's early biographers make a point of saying that he displayed his religious affinities quite early.[3] Often, they say, he would leave his games with other children to go off by himself to play at being a priest by constructing little altars. Such stories perhaps tell us more about the aura of sainthood that began to envelop Savonarola soon after his death than about his actual childhood; manifestations of childhood piety and a preference for solitude were among the clichés of medieval hagiography. Reared by conventionally pious parents, Girolamo also imbibed more than a little of his grandfather's dour moralism along with his Latin lessons, Bible studies, and Saint Thomas.

The same biographers tell us that he found great men and their courts "abominable," especially the court of his own prince of Ferrara (but since he visited it only once, with his grandfather, the antipathy was mainly second-hand: grandfather Michele had had plenty of experience with courts and courtiers and wrote about them, usually disapprovingly). Young Girolamo, according to an early biographer, preferred solitary walks in the country and the company of his lute and sketchbook to socializing with people. This might be another hagiographical topos, but it may also hint at an internal struggle, for Girolamo seems to have liked the world well enough. Reminiscing to some Florentine youth in 1496, he recalled, "When I was in the world I said a thousand times that I would never become a friar; yet I had to go when it pleased God. I couldn't eat and I was going around in circles. When a person gets the idea [of becoming a friar] he can't sleep; then once he arrives there he lives entirely contented."

How long this argument with himself had gone on is impossible to say. We know little about his ambitions just before his life-changing decision other than that he was a student in the Arts faculty of the University of Ferrara,[4] apparently pursuing the medical career decided for him by his father and grandfather. By becoming a physician he would have been fulfilling his obligation to satisfy their ambitions—a dutiful son striving to add distinction to the family name and also to help relieve its chronic money problems. To take that road meant striving for success, plunging into the world's business, marrying and begetting sons to carry on the Savonarola name. To choose a life in religion, on the other hand, was to declare his independence from the tutelage of parents and grandfather. It offered both freedom and quiet, two things, he later told a congregation, he had longed for more than all others and in pursuit of which he had arrived at his present threshold. In the contest between the pressing claims of family and the call of God, God had the victory. For the sake of his freedom, he later said, he had never wanted to take a wife; for the sake of peace he had fled the world and entered religion.[5]

What disturbed his peace he did not explain, although in linking it with the rejection of a wife he may have been intimating that sexual desire had some part in it. Savonarola's earliest biographers cite reports from his superiors and confessors that attested not only to Girolamo's virginity ("as virgin as when he came out of his mother's womb") but even to the absence in him of any venial sin, that is, sexual desire. But here again hagiographical mythmaking is at work, as well as some refashioning by fra Girolamo himself. There is no reason to doubt that he remained a stranger to sexual activity, but he did admit to being troubled by physical desire. In the farewell letter he wrote to

his father after he had left home, he declared that he too was made of flesh
and that although his reason found sensuality repugnant, he had to fight
"cruelly" to keep the devil off his back.

It is also conceivable that disappointment in love played a part in his
decision to renounce family and world. According to fra Benedetto Luschino,
an early biographer who had this story from fra Mauro Savonarola, Girolamo's brother, he had become acquainted with a young woman named Laudomia Strozzi, illegitimate daughter of Roberto di Nanni Strozzi, an exiled
member of one of the great Florentine families.[6] One day as the two were
talking from their windows, across the narrow street separating their two
houses, Girolamo asked Laudomia whether she would consider becoming his
wife; if so he would speak to her parents. "She, regardless of the well-known
shame of being born in adultery, replied arrogantly and offensively: 'Do you
think that the blood of the great house of Strozzi would deign to be united
with the house of Savonarola?' Whereupon Girolamo immediately retorted,
'And do you think that the house of Savonarola would care to give one of its
legitimate sons to a bastard like you?'"

"And so," fra Benedetto writes, "Girolamo's love turned into hatred—not
hatred of the girl herself," he piously hastened to add, "but of her defect."[7] An
argument for the authenticity of the story of spurned love is that neither
brother Mauro nor biographer Benedetto could have had any hagiographical
or aggrandizing purpose for telling it. On the contrary, it breaks with the
hagiographical convention of steadfast unworldliness and shows Girolamo
giving way to unholy anger and pride, not the typical stuff of most early saints'
lives. Perhaps, then, it was the anger and humiliation Girolamo suffered from
Laudomia's rejection that he poured into complaints against a sinful world
and its shameless stewards. In a canzone entitled *On the Ruin of the World*,[8] he
addresses God almost reproachfully:

> Although it's true, and I believe, Rector of the world, that your provi-
> dence is infinite (nor could I not believe it, since it's proved to me by
> experience) sometimes, when I see the world turned upside down and
> every virtue and good practice fallen to the ground, it seems colder than
> snow. I found no light, or even anyone who shows shame for his vices.
> Some deny you; some say you are sleeping. But I believe you are only
> waiting, O Eternal King, to deliver greater punishment for the world's
> sins. Perhaps, then, it is near, and you await the Last Day when hell will
> tremble. For us virtue is finished for all time. Cato goes begging. The
> hand of the pirate has grasped the scepter. Saint Peter falls to the ground.

... Do you not see the mad satyr, how proud, how like a river of vice, how my heart consumes me with its great indignation? Oh, look at that catamite and that pimp robed in purple, a clown followed by the rabble, adored by a blind world! Do you not scorn that lascivious pig? He pleasures himself and usurps your high praises with sycophants and parasites while your followers are exiled from country to country. The world is so oppressed with every vice that it will never rid itself of its burden without help: Down falls Rome, its capital, never again to resume its great office. Oh, Brutus, how you will grieve, and you Fabricius, learning of this second great ruin! Not only Catiline, or Sulla, Marius, Caesar, or Nero, but every man seeks to do some sort of harm. The time of reverence and purity has gone.

The poem concludes:

> My song, take care not to put your trust in the color purple
> Flee palaces and balconies
> And take care to share your thoughts with few,
> So that to the whole world you will be hostile.

This is the work of an apprentice poet. It owes its opening line to another versifier from Ferrara, Antonio Beccari, and its canzone form and some of its phrasing to Petrarch.[9] But if the classical allusions are the obligatory dues the author is paying to his humanist education, the condemnation of a world hopelessly drawn down by vice, the warnings against purple-robed prelates and princes and the urging to flee from princely courts and balconies (of nubile Strozzi maidens?) are more in the spirit of Isaiah and John the Baptist. At twenty, the astringent moralist is beginning to find his voice. He boldly decries the passage of the papal see into the hands of "the pirate," an obvious reference to the simoniac pope Francesco della Rovere (Sixtus IV, 1471–84). The certainty that God would soon bring his punishment down upon this dark world formed the bedrock of apocalyptic expectation upon which he would elaborate his full prophetic vision.

Two years passed during which Girolamo's gloom about the state of the world deepened, although he still hesitated to quit it. When at last he broke away, Girolamo wrote a short tract and left it tucked behind some books stacked against the window of his room. "Read it," he told Niccolò, it "will tell you something about me."[10] What it tells *us* is that Girolamo's mood had darkened, his agony intensified.

"What are we doing?" he asks. "Simple folk and women teach us, more by example than by words, to reject human affairs and follow Christ alone. They take possession of heaven while we, with our learning, sink to Hell. We tell ourselves we have become wise, although we have become fools."

Having established the paradox of worldly wisdom and spiritual simplicity—a theme he would pursue more deeply in years to come—he expands the catalog of the world's sins he had commenced in his poem of 1472. We behave like swine and Epicureans. Everyone praises vice and ridicules virtue. We argue over superficial virtues and consider bodily pleasures to be the highest good. If someone is zealous for philosophy and the fine arts, he is a dreamer; if someone lives chastely and modestly, he is unfeeling; if pious, he is called unjust; if he wishes to be just, he is held to be cruel; if he believes and has faith in the greatness of God, he is crass and ingenuous; if he puts his hope in Christ alone, everyone makes fun of him; if he has charity, he is regarded as effeminate, while those who expropriate widows and orphans are called prudent. He who knows how to squeeze out lucre is considered wise, and he who is shrewdest in coming up with fraudulent schemes is venerated. Only he is manly who knows how to produce wickedness and cruelties and great blasphemies, who murders his neighbor and spreads sedition and conflict. All is violation and adultery, sodomy, murder, and envy; all ambition and pride, hypocrisy and falsity, wickedness and evil.[11]

One of Savonarola's early biographers called this work *On Contempt for the World*, but it has little in common with other examples of the medieval ascetic genre that goes by that name, and the difference is instructive. Most of the great monastic moralists, including Saints Anselm, Peter Damian, and Bernard of Clairvaux, addressed themselves to the theme. The classic treatment was by Cardinal Lotario dei Segni, the future Pope Innocent III. Innocent more accurately called his work of 1195 *On the Misery of the Human Condition*, for like the earlier models on which it was based, it was a discourse on human frailty, a bleak assessment of the squalor, uncertainties, sorrows, and brevity of life and the terrors of death. Man was conceived "from the itch of the flesh, the heat of passion and the stench of lust, and worse yet, with the stain of sin. He was born to toil, dread, and trouble; and, more wretched still, was born only to die. . . . He would become fuel for those fires which are forever hot and burn forever bright, food for the worm which forever nibbles and digests; a mass of rottenness which will forever stink and reek."[12]

Young Girolamo's contribution is of a different spirit. Innocent had composed a meditation on the limitations of human nature and happiness, whereas his is intensely personal and censorious, a venting of disgust for the unrelieved human wickedness he saw filling every worldly space. Compassion for human weakness and gratitude for divine mercy are the appropriate responses to Innocent's catalog of human weakness whereas Girolamo's screed expresses only indignation and scorn—and justifies his coming flight from society. "O flee these cruel lands, flee this shore of greed, flee the lands of Sodom and Gomorrah, flee Egypt and the Pharoahs, flee this most vile and proud people, these greedy youth, lascivious old men, fawning paupers."[13]

"Sometimes," fra Girolamo told a congregation many years later, "a word will penetrate you, so that it enters your heart and sends you your salvation."[14] The word that had penetrated his own hesitant heart and which he still recalled almost a quarter century later was spoken by an Augustinian preacher in Faenza, where he had gone on a pleasure jaunt: it was the call, he later told his biographer, to leave the world.[15] In the meantime, still debating what course to follow and still beset by "imaginings," he dreamed one night that ice cold water had been poured over him. He awoke, "the desires of his flesh checked, the youthful heat that had so often tormented him extinguished." Whereupon, feeling these marvelous effects in himself, he decided he had to follow Christ and leave behind all worldly glory.[16]

On the morning of April 24, 1475, giving his family to believe that he was attending the celebrations for the Feast of San Giorgio, Girolamo set out on foot for Bologna, fifty kilometers from Ferrara. Knocking at the door of the Convent of San Domenico, Order of Friars Preachers, he asked to be accepted into the Order. Two days later, April 26, Girolamo and another aspirant, Lodovico di Bologna, underwent the questioning of motives required of everyone who applied to the Order, then divested themselves of their worldly goods. The two postulants were accepted by fra Giorgio Vercelli, the convent prior, received the tonsure, and put on the Dominican habit. This consisted of the *caligae,* an undergarment that covered the legs from groin to ankle; the monastic cord worn day and night around the waist next to the flesh; a white tunic secured at the waist by a leather belt; a white scapular consisting of two strips of cloth, one falling over each shoulder; and a black hooded mantle, or *cappa.*

Even before he reached Bologna Girolamo had written to his father to ask for his understanding and blessing. He had caused his family grief, he knew, especially since he had left in secrecy. But his decision was no childish whim. His father, "a real man" (*omo virile*), rational and a lover of truth and seriousness, not a silly woman guided by emotion, would understand this. He was leaving a world full of iniquities, of defiled virgins, adulteries, thieving, pride, and idolatry. The cruel blasphemies had reached such a level that "there is no good person to be found." Unable to bear the blind wickedness of the Italian people he had cried out (with Aeneas) "Ah make haste to flee these coasts of avarice, this land of savagery!"[17] and prayed that God rescue him and give him guidance. At last, when it pleased him, God, in his infinite mercy, answered him. Was it not a great virtue to flee the filth and wickedness of this wretched world and to choose to live a rational life rather than a bestial life among the pigs? And since God deigned to show him the right way, would it not have been enormously ungrateful not to follow it?

Instead of weeping, his sweet father should give thanks to God for giving him a son and excellently preserving him until making him "a militant knight," "a cavalier of Jesus Christ" at the age of twenty-two. Either his father loved him or he didn't, he said, and if he did, surely it was his soul he loved, not his body, the vilest part. "And if you love my soul, why then do you not seek what is best for my soul? Rejoice then in this great victory!" Never has he, Girolamo, suffered greater pain than in having to leave his own flesh and blood, to sacrifice his body for Jesus Christ and subordinate his will to that of strangers. But he remembers that Christ himself "did not disdain to make himself a slave among us worms" (cf. "did not disdain to make himself a slave among us humans," Phil 2.7–8). And he had had to go in secrecy, "as if I were running away from you," because if he had told his family of his decision beforehand their lamentations would have broken his heart and rendered him unable to bear it. He begged Niccolò, as the man of the house, to comfort his mother, and he asked both parents for their blessings.[18]

The letter is a case study in mixed emotions as well as mingled rhetorical styles. Savonarola's affection for his father and his understanding of what he must be suffering seem genuine enough, if tinged with artifice (that "real man" with superior gifts of wisdom and reason). From pathos he turns to reason (if you love me you must love my soul, and if you love my soul you will want what is best for it), although he fears that Niccolò will not grasp his logic. He tries self-pity, calling his father's attention to his own pain; he is ripping himself away from a loving family to place himself under the control of strangers. But all this is overcome by his disgust and repulsion for "the world" in general and his fellow Italians in particular.

No such humane balance graces his second letter, written to his family after the first reaction from home had reached him. Patience and sympathy give way to an indignation that fairly scorches the page. He admonishes his whole family: "without light, blind, insensate, and without a ray of faith."

Plainly, in spirit as well as body, he has already left parents, brothers and sisters, and his former life and has passed into the world of the cloister. The Prince of Princes has called him, Girolamo, to buckle on his sword and become one of his knights, but instead of rejoicing for him, he complains, his parents lament and pretend that they do so because they love him. But they are his main enemies—enemies of all virtue—and he says with the Psalmist, "Depart from me, all ye workers of iniquity: for the Lord hath heard the voice of my weeping" (Ps. 6.8). "Since the soul is more precious than the body, rejoice and exult that glorious God is making me physician of souls, even though I might wish to become a physician of the body."[19]

His repudiation of his family was cruel as only youthful rebellion can be cruel, but the zealot who aims to renounce the world must first tear the bonds of family affection that hold him to it. Christian exemplars are legion—Jesus' admonition to his disciples, "He that loveth father or mother more than me, is not worthy of me" (Matt. 10.37); Saint Francis in the cathedral square of Assisi stripping off the clothes his father had bought for him[20]—but the compassion and shared suffering evident in the earlier letter to his father was real too, if for the time being suppressed. Once his independence is secure there will be other letters in which he will be able to express softer feelings again, but never will he allow family feeling to interfere with the claims of his hard-won vocation.

CHAPTER 2

The Making of a Preacher

The genius of the Dominican Order lay in its potent fusion of *vita contemplativa* and *vita activa,* thought and action.[1] The friars lived under a modified form of the Augustinian Rule, taking the triple vow of poverty, chastity, and obedience and following a daily liturgical round of prayer and choir song, but unlike most monks they did not support themselves by the labor of their hands or shut themselves inside cloister walls. Their main mission, as their official title, Order of Friars Preachers, indicates, was to go forth into the world to preach.

In 1203 the Castilian canon regular Dominic Guzman, accompanying his bishop, passed through Toulouse where they were shocked to find thriving Cathar and Waldensian communities. They resolved to organize a preaching mission to oppose heresy with the Gospel. After limited success, Dominic and a few comrades took a leaf from their older, more successful counterparts, the Franciscans, and expanded their mission to the cities of France, Germany, Spain, and Italy. In those centers they found both eager recruits and ready audiences.

The Order of Friars Preachers, or Dominicans, lived on charity; wore simple, even shabby, robes; ate no meat; fasted often; and handled no money, owning nothing but a few books for private devotions. Reflecting their Augustinian influence, the brothers developed a form of systematic worship and prayer, which gave their preaching vocation its meaning and ardor. Seven times daily they gathered in choir to chant the canonical round of offices, including the Night Office midway between midnight and dawn. In those sessions they renewed and reflected on their personal and collective bonds to the mysteries of their faith—to the Incarnation, Passion, and Resurrection and to the Blessed Virgin who was the special protectress of the Order.

Brothers also came to understand and perhaps to share Dominic's conviction that the Order of Friars Preachers had resumed Jesus' own preaching mission —in a certain sense, that the Order had been founded not by Dominic but by Christ.

The inspiration and power of Dominican belief, together with new opportunities for preaching the Gospel, explains the exponential spread of the Order within its first half century. Before Francis and Dominic, preaching had been the duty of local diocesan clergy regulated by their bishops. Orders of preaching specialists living under a constitution of their own making and electing their own leaders, at the service of, but not under, the episcopate or subject to the absolute rule of a monastic abbot, was a major departure for the Church, but Rome, recognizing the immense promise of a semi-autonomous, disciplined corps of militant gospelers, gave its approval.

The friars evangelized non-Christian peoples on the northeastern borders of Europe, converted Jews and Muslims in Spain and Portugal, and eventually carried the Gospel to Asia and the New World. Their main effort, however, was in Christian Europe's new population centers. With diocesan clerics unable to keep up with the pastoral needs of the fast-growing towns, the Dominicans, Franciscans, Servites, and other mendicant orders moved in to fill the gap. Soon they were founding convents and building churches, hospitals, and schools in newly urbanized areas. A Third Order of Dominican lay penitents took form in the late thirteenth century. Women played an important role in the movement from the onset, with Dominic organizing a Second Order of Dominican sisters to provide women with spiritual and vocational outlets. Dominican sisters practiced contemplative prayer, served as teachers, and ministered to the poor and sick. Most famously, the charismatic gifts of Saint Catherine of Siena (1347–80) won her great authority among popes and princes, which she did not hesitate to use in the cause of Church unity and reform.

Aware that sound preaching required educated and trained preachers, Dominic had insisted that each priory must have its lector, or resident teacher, and sent able recruits to enroll in university courses.[2] Within a generation a three-tier system was taking shape: the local school, the provincial *studium*, and the university-level, interregional *studium generale*. Dominican masters taught in the secular faculties of the universities of Paris, Oxford, Bologna, Cologne, and Montpellier and in their own *studia*, welcoming lay as well as clerical pupils. (Dante Alighieri, for example, studied theology at the Order's studium in the church of Santa Maria Novella in Florence.) Using the newly available translations of Aristotle as well as those of Muslim and Jewish philosophers, Dominicans, most notably Albert the Great at Cologne and Thomas Aquinas at Paris and Bologna, achieved renown as systematizers of Christian doctrine.

But while Dominicans became specialists in doctrine and arbiters of orthodoxy, their main mission, as that of Franciscans and other mendicants, was preaching. The crowds who filled mendicant churches on Sundays, saints' and feast days, through Lent and Advent, came to hear doctrine explained and applied to the problems and questions of everyday life. They came to be stirred, directed, admonished, consoled, and amused, to be briefly taken out of themselves, to hear about the world beyond their street and city wall. They also came to admire and applaud, to evaluate the artistry and invention of the preacher himself, compare preachers, rate performances. For fourteenth- and fifteenth-century society the church was a central space for cultural and social interaction and the preacher its prime catalyst.[3]

Rapid growth brought many changes, and change brought problems: insubordination, unauthorized moving about, and "evil familiarity" between friars and nuns. The Order's growing complexity demanded structural reforms that centralized authority, weakening the democratic and egalitarian principles of the founders. The original ban on the use of money and the requirement of absolute poverty were also compromised. Nature too had its say: the Black Death of 1347–48 thinned the ranks of the Order and made it difficult to find recruits. One solution was to relax Dominican austerity. Dispensations for eating meat, wearing better clothing, and trimming the amount of time spent in choir became more frequent; so did calls for reform.

In a longer view, apostolic poverty was a casualty of the Order's success. Initially dependent on the laity for alms, the friars needed, and became accustomed to, a grander scale of patronage. Pious donors funded church buildings and chapels; commissioned paintings, sculptures, stained-glass windows, and liturgical objects; and made bequests of property. Dominican convents and churches such as Santa Maria sopra Minerva in Rome, Santa Maria Novella, and San Domenico in Bologna became showplaces of art and repositories of precious books as well as centers of urban life, catering to the intellectual, aesthetic, and social—in addition to the spiritual—needs of their lay constituencies.

With calls for a return to apostolic simplicity and poverty and full performance of the canonical liturgy (the rising for the Night Office had been almost eliminated, for example), the Order pulled in opposite directions. A small group of die-hard conservatives refused any compromise with the original austerities. A larger faction of Observantist reformers made some concessions but drew the line between institutional and individual property and insisted on full restoration of the liturgy. These reformers also complained that the preaching and pastoral functions so central to the Dominican vocation had been overshadowed by the Order's preoccupation with sophisticated philosophical and theological studies. The Conventuals, by far the most numerous group, held that the Order could not function without holding of property and that this could be reconciled with the ideals of the founders; moreover, intellectual life was one of the glories of the Order. Still, the ideal of the apostolic life was a counsel of perfection increasingly difficult to sustain. By the time Savonarola entered San Domenico, the Order had gone through repeated cycles of decline and reform, while Observantists and Conventuals continued to vie for recognition (and lay support) as the legitimate heirs of their founders.

For Girolamo Savonarola, resolved to flee the world and yet serve both as a physician of souls and a militant knight of Christ, the Dominican Order was an inspired choice, however anguished he had been when he made it. The Order's union of vita contemplativa and vita activa mirrored his own complex religious aspirations. As he later told his biographer Giovanfrancesco Pico, he had hesitated before becoming a friar, afraid that the ascetic life he yearned for was no longer so easily to be found in the cloister. Entering a religious order, he feared, would only be to pass from one kind of worldliness to another. Besides, he mistrusted the Dominicans' vaunted scholastic intellectualism. Between pedantic laymen and disputatious friars, both inordinately devoted to Aristotelian philosophy and to science, Girolamo saw little to choose. He was, he said, familiar with that kind of learning; he had been nourished on it and was afraid that the Order would want him to get more of the same.

The learning Girolamo had been nourished on was, of course, his grandfather's. If we can trust this recollection long after the fact, it adds a dimension to the spiritual crisis that had first taken him to San Domenico's door: in formulating a more authentic, apostolic spirituality it seemed to him necessary to repudiate Michele Savonarola's more conventional piety. (Although he also had grandfather Michele to thank for kindling his love of Scripture and setting him on the path of liberal studies, he never acknowledged this, perhaps because doing so would have offset his sense of having made a conscious break with his past.) What that struggle for independence cost him emotionally may be gauged by the angry impatience with which he dismissed his family's objections to his flight. It also helps explain his passionate search for an alternate form of spirituality. If this reading is correct, we can understand his hesitation about entering "religion," as the ordered life of a monk or friar was known. He was paying a high price for leaving the world; would he find his soul's satisfaction with the Dominicans?

Although Ferrara had its own Dominican priory, Santa Maria degli Angeli, Girolamo chose to enter the Convent of San Domenico in Bologna. After his novitiate, or trial year, he would, in the regular course of things, become a *filius,* or son of that house, with voting rights. Besides offering the advantage of distancing him from his family and other hometown distractions, San Domenico was one of the jewels in the Dominican crown, famous for its learning and austerity. Saint Dominic had died in Bologna, and his body reposed in a splendid tomb in the convent church, where it was an object of formal reverence by the friars. Fra Girolamo later said that he would have preferred to become a *converso,* or lay brother, working in a garden, sewing clothes for the friars, or performing some other humble labor, but that as soon as he was received into the convent he forgot such notions so completely as to be unable to recall any part of them. Whereas he had once intended to become a physician of the body, he now hoped God would make him a physician of souls.

Despite his initial misgivings, the life of a Dominican friar suited him. Before he entered the convent, he recalled, he was like a young man who went fishing and found his boat being carried out to sea. When he cried out that he had lost sight of land, he heard a voice saying, "Come, depart from your house and your country and leave all behind" (Gen. 12.1). Then, led into the port of religion, he found safety, that is, salvation, tranquility, and liberty. Liberty, he explained, meant being able to do what one wanted to do. In the convent he wanted to do nothing other than what he was told and commanded to do, so he was free. Had he merely cultivated his new-found tranquility he would never have wanted to become a priest, but now he "allowed" himself to be led into the priesthood so that he could minister to others. "And thus, having entered into this happy port, I looked into the waters of the sea of this world and I saw many fish swimming through its waters. So I conceived a desire to go fishing, and I began to catch some little fishes with love, that is, to draw some souls into port and into the way of salvation by preaching."[4]

In this new outgoing spirit, and zealous to preach, he went through his novitiate. Novices were instructed in basic matters, such as how friars should walk in the convent, conduct themselves at meals, and behave toward their peers and superiors. They learned the proper way to make their confession and to perform the daily rounds of the Divine Office—choir singing and prayer. Besides memorizing the Psalter, or book of psalms, and the constitution of the Order, they learned how Dominicans practiced devotions to Mary and how they performed "the discipline," the mortification of the flesh through self-administered whippings. Each novice was also obliged to take his turn in the kitchen, serving meals, cleaning, and doing the other menial jobs that were the main work of the lay brothers. All this they did in strict silence. Even before they began their course of studies, a novice was seldom to be seen without a book. Lives of the saints and the desert fathers were high on the reading list as were the devotional writings of Saints Jerome, Bernard, and other masters of the communal life. John Cassian, the great fourth-century chronicler of the desert fathers and advocate of the ascetic life, became one of fra Girolamo's lifelong favorites.

Freedom, happiness, tranquility, love, salvation—these had been unfamiliar words on Girolamo's tongue, absent from the lexicon of alienation and despair in which he had written the canzone *On the Ruin of the World* and the treatise known as *On Contempt for the World*. Reflecting on it some twenty years after the event, he saw his flight from Ferrara to Bologna as both exodus and arrival, a passage from darkness to light. "Light" and "illumination" were also new words in his spiritual vocabulary, and henceforth he used them frequently when talking of God's grace. The more positive mood is discernible in an unfinished canzone in praise of Saint Catherine of Bologna, which he began during these early years in the convent. Although she had not been formally canonized, Caterina Vigri's body, intact and fragrant with the odor of sanctity, was on view for the veneration of the faithful, and it may have been a visit to her tomb that moved Girolamo to write his poem. While it maintains the same dark view of the world we encountered in his earlier writings ("O wretched mortals and blind people / Do you not yet realize that the world is nothing / and that all your thoughts are vain?"), the tenor of the canzone is more hopeful. Through her holy life Catherine shows the way to personal redemption. By venerating her bodily remains we are led to believe in the afterlife, and through her example as through her intercession we too may achieve the exalted state.

> Virgin, thus with hope I come
> With hands pressed together and knees bent

Though I am but a worm and mere mud
Your lofty, singular virtues
Will bear some fruit in me, I know.[5]

When he had completed his novice year Girolamo made his profession and took final vows. He also entered the priory's school and began his studies for the priesthood, becoming a subdeacon in September 1476 and a deacon on May 1, 1477. Some parts of the elementary curriculum, heavy in Aristotelian logic, natural sciences, ethics, and metaphysics, he was able to skip—thanks to his grandfather's earlier tutoring and to the arts course at Ferrara; but there was no question of bypassing Bible studies. As "men of the gospel," Dominicans regarded the Bible as their essential source and gave it a central place at every level of the curriculum. Girolamo could have had no objection; Scripture was ever his fundamental inspiration to the ascetic life, with the early fathers his revered guides. Gianfrancesco Pico wrote that in turning away from philosophy with its (excessive) subtleties, Savonarola found much in the lives of the early fathers as set forth by Cassian, Jerome, and Augustine in his meditations to nourish his devotion to Christian simplicity. But wanting "even better food," he found it in sacred scripture where saintly men were illuminated and taught by Christ himself. Students would hear the literal sense of the Bible expounded by a *cursor biblicus* and the spiritual sense by the *lector bibliae*, or *lector principalis*, the title indicating the importance of his material. Studying the Bible day and night, he learned it almost by heart, although the limiting qualifier is dropped by another early biographer who says Girolamo learned *all* the canonical books by heart.[6]

Friars began their training as preachers by delivering their first sermons to the other brothers of the priory or to some nearby lay or clerical congregation. Girolamo, concerned about his speaking abilities, was soon seeking advice from an expert rhetorician. Giovanni Garzoni, lector in medicine and philosophy at the University of Bologna with close ties to the Convent of San Domenico, had studied with the great humanist Lorenzo Valla in Rome and was much sought after as a public orator and composer of polemical tracts.[7] Approached by the young friar on how to become an effective preacher, Garzoni replied:

> I am delighted that you wish to learn eloquence: I can think of no more
> excellent undertaking for you. You have come to the city of Bologna as to
> a market of the good arts; if you persevere in your determination I have

no doubt that you will become a great orator. If you add philosophy and theology to eloquence you will achieve immortal praise. Had they lived, Vincent of Ferrer and Bonifacio da Casale, whom I assisted in learning eloquence, would have been great preachers and earned much praise. . . . For, to be sure, people commonly admire a preacher who speaks fluently and wisely, while his wisdom is thought to be not human but rather due to divine enlightenment. So if you persevere, I will do whatever I can on your behalf, even though I personally may not be endowed with eloquence. Be well; and accept my regards.

Girolamo must have responded to this offer with a more explicit description of what he was aiming for; perhaps he sent Garzoni a sample of a sermon he was preparing. Whatever it was it provoked an angry and dismissive reaction from Garzoni. "From your letters, delivered to me by some messenger," sniffed the great man, "I learn that you have declared war on the grammar of Priscian [sixth-century author of the standard classicizing Latin textbook]. While you have been fighting and wounding him, I have consulted Apollo. He tells me that there is no way Priscian can come out of this unharmed, nor that you yourself, wounding him, can emerge unscathed, just as it happened when Achilles thrust his sword into Beliphus. Farewell."[8]

Savonarola's letters to the pompous Garzoni have not survived. We can only wonder why he asked advice from such a well-known practitioner of humanist eloquence in the first place, since he seems to have been already adverse to drinking from the fountain of ancient pagan wisdom or wrapping his sermons in rolling Ciceronian periods. In the fussy constructions and ostentatious classical citations exhibited in Garzoni's two letters he must have seen the seductive frivolities of the world he had just rejected. Neither, on the other hand, was he enamored of the traditional scholastic sermon with its elaborate divisions, logical demonstrations, and philosophical propositions. Spurning both the traditional and the humanist way of preaching, he set himself a radically different goal: he would use unadorned language informed by the divine Word. Eventually he would find a personal style better suited to his biblically based spirituality, but only after he had experienced failure in the pulpit and not until he had begun to find himself as a prophet.

Girolamo's rejection of Garzoni's advice on preaching styles was symptomatic of his general discomfort with the intellectual trends he encountered, although he seems to have forgotten this in his later happy recollections of these early days. After his first flush of enthusiasm at being received into the Order, his initial reservations about worldliness in the convent were reviving.

If he deplored humanist influence with its near-cultic veneration of classical literature and eloquence, he was also uncomfortable with the convent's general preoccupation with "Aristotle, disputations, and debate." Not by words, not by human learning, but by deeds, by the simplicity of ignorant men and women, is heaven possessed, he had insisted in *On Contempt for the World*.

The deeds were to his disliking, too. Even as a novice he perceived a growing laxity of ascetic practice among his fellow friars.[9] His anonymous sixteenth-century biographer/hagiographer known as Pseudo-Burlamacchi put it more emphatically. "After Girolamo had observed the practices and behavior of his fellow friars for some time, comparing these to the Christians of the primitive Church, the most holy monks of Egypt and the early fathers of the religion, it seemed to him that there was no similarity between the present and that old holy life." The friars, he worried, occupied themselves in all sorts of vain projects and acquisitions, and they devoted more effort to studying Aristotle than to "the books of blessed Jesus Christ."[10]

The criticism was—characteristically—extreme, but Girolamo's conviction that the friars were abandoning their primitive ideals was timely and, to some extent, justified, however unpolitic it must have been coming from so junior a brother. Particularly at that moment: just two and a half months after Girolamo knocked on the door of San Domenico, Pope Sixtus IV issued his bull *Considerantes* granting Observant houses the right to hold property communally. This was a great victory for the friars, probably the majority of whom argued that the rules of strict poverty were out-of-date and unworkable. But to Girolamo, who regarded poverty as an indispensable condition of the mendicants' life, the papal decision was bitterly disappointing. About the time the bull appeared he wrote his poem *On the Ruin of the Church*. He addresses himself to the "Chaste Virgin, the uncorrupted Church of ancient times" in a highly symbolic language. ("Where, ah me, are the gems and fine diamonds? Where the ardent lamps and lovely sapphires?") He laments the passing of the early saints, the great preachers and contemplatives, the holy virgins and clerics, saintly bishops armed with the Old and New Testaments, who once vanquished the Church's enemies. Pride, he observes, has entered Rome, avid for ecclesiastical dignities and carnal pleasures, committing grave sins in the confidence that God will take no revenge, although earth, air, and sky cry out for it.

Preaching the Old and New Testaments is neglected because modern doctors are stuffed with philosophy and logic and divided by a thousand different opinions. The doctors and preachers are full of pride, and clerics think only of ancient rhetoric and philosophy. The Church is stung by secret heretics and seduced by the devil. False friars pretend to fly high and live as Christians, but they are earthbound, stifling the flowering of goodness and choking the roots of grace. And so the Church falls and her holy works go to ruin. Meanwhile infidel dogs excoriate her, saying that if Christianity were the true faith, Christians would not live as they do. The poet (the soul) appeals to the Blessed Virgin to tell him whether it is possible to break those grand wings (remove the spiritual and temporal power of the Church from the hands of the wicked). She tells him that neither mortal tongue nor arms can do it. When the blind say that these things are not true and that there will be no tribulations, say nothing; do not dispute them. Remain in peace.[11]

It is unlikely that Girolamo voiced his misgivings to his peers or superiors. "Tell your thoughts to few because everyone will be your enemy," he had written three years earlier in *On the Ruin of the World*, and in this new poem, although intimating that the Church will suffer divine retribution for its sins, he concludes that mortal speech can do nothing. "Weep and be silent, this seems best to me." If his superiors had any inkling of his criticism there is no sign. While most young friars received only two or three years of instruction in the Bologna studium before moving on to other teaching and preaching duties, the more intellectually promising were advanced to the higher course of theology in preparation for an academic career. Fra Girolamo was one of these select few. Since the San Domenico school was a studium generale, associated with the University of Bologna and authorized to grant the bachelor and master of sacred theology degrees, fra Girolamo would be able to pursue his studies without moving away from the mother convent. In his second year in the program, on July 3, 1478, he was designated *studens formalis*, signifying his matriculation in the theological faculty of the university, on course for a higher degree.[12] Among the teachers at the studium were Pietro da Bergamo, compiler of a comprehensive guide to the works of Saint Thomas Aquinas;[13] Niccolò da Pisa, who was to become known for his writings on asceticism; and Vincenzo Bandelli, in the early stages of his own important career as theologian, professor, and, ultimately, general of the Order.[14] Whatever Girolamo's reservations about scholastic disputations and overemphasis on Aristotelian logic, he would participate in weekly disputations and teach the logic, ethics, and philosophy of "the Philosopher" to beginning students as well as attend lectures in theology and Bible.

At the end of his second year as studens formalis, either in late 1478 or early 1479, Savonarola was assigned as junior lector to the priory of Santa

Maria degli Angeli in Ferrara, where he most likely taught logic to the novices. (His *Compendium logicae,* published a few years later, probably originated as a textbook in the Ferrara course.) The Ferrara posting was a normal excursus from the academic pathway; every two or three years, to break the long, demanding grind of the theology course, students would be sent on temporary assignment to one of the Order's other houses where they would teach and probably do some preaching.[15] They would then return to the Bologna studium to continue their studies, although there would be further interruptions along the way. Ultimately their superiors would decide whether to bring them back to the studium to complete work for the master's degree and, presumably, to get their license for a university teaching post or, alternatively, to reassign them to a different convent, a posting which signified the end of the candidate's academic career. Only a few would be selected to continue, and this decision was final. In the case of fra Girolamo, still in the early stages of his studies, that critical decision was yet to be made.

Ferrara was the venue for the 1481 provincial chapter meeting of the Lombard Congregation. Savonarola undoubtedly attended the disputation staged for the occasion and would have heard his former teacher Vincenzo Bandelli deliver his celebrated attack on the doctrine of the Immaculate Conception.[16] Dominicans, following the lead of Albert the Great and Saint Thomas, uniformly opposed the doctrine, so no one would have been surprised when Bandelli took the Dominican line, especially since he had already published a maculist, or anti–Immaculate Conception, tract in 1475. Whether the later antagonism between Bandelli and his former pupil had its origins in their early differences is difficult to say. Bandelli was a skilled but traditional scholastic theologian, while the young fra Girolamo already inclined toward a more spiritual theology nourished by sacred scripture and the writings of the Fathers.[17] In the ongoing controversies over Dominican reform Bandelli took the view that the rules on poverty should be relaxed, supporting the move toward the holding of communal property. If he knew anything about fra Girolamo's austere views on Dominican life and learning at this point, he could hardly have been pleased, although there is no evidence that the young friar had publicized his desire for such reforms while he was Bandelli's student in Bologna or in the years immediately following. Two years later he wrote a brief summary of Bandelli's arguments against the doctrine of the Immaculate Conception, which suggests, at least, that he still regarded his former professor with respect.[18]

In April 1482 fra Girolamo attended the chapter meeting and apparently took part in a formal disputation together with Bandelli and other Bologna teachers and companions. He seems to have performed well: it is reported that Count Giovanni Pico della Mirandola, then a student at the University of Padua, attended and was mightily impressed. Eight years later, when Pico had attained fame as a philosopher, his admiration for fra Girolamo was to have important consequences for both of them.[19]

After the Reggio chapter meeting fra Girolamo was assigned to the Convent of San Marco in Florence as master of novices, another byway before the final decision on his academic status. Fra Placido Cinozzi, author of the earliest biographical sketch of Savonarola, says that in 1481 the San Marco prior—none other than Vincenzo Bandelli—sent for fra Girolamo because he admired "his doctrine and the goodness of his life."[20] The assignment was actually made by the chapter, not by the convent prior, but it is unlikely that Savonarola would have been sent to San Marco over Bandelli's objections. In any case, in April 1482 thirty-year-old fra Girolamo, aspiring physician of souls, assertive Observantist, would-be knight of Christ, eager to do battle with worldliness both within the convent and without, made his way down the Via Bolognese to arrive at one of the worldliest cities of the age.

CHAPTER 3

The Making of a Prophet

The friars of San Marco, went the cliché, ate the bread of the Medici. Vespasiano da Bisticci, the Florentine book dealer-biographer, wrote that Cosimo's patronage of San Marco began with a midlife crisis of conscience. When Cosimo asked his friend Pope Eugenius IV how he might earn God's pardon for his sins and still keep his worldly possessions the pontiff replied that he should spend 10,000 florins on alterations to the Convent of San Marco, transferred by papal decree to the Dominicans of the Observance in 1436.[1] Cosimo agreed, and after the first building project was completed Eugenius duly issued a bull of expiation. To make sure that everyone knew his gift of bread had come back to him as spiritual profit, Cosimo had the text of the bull inscribed over the door of the church sacristy.

The Medici had actually become involved in the affairs of San Marco some years before Cosimo's belated attack of conscience. Even before he came to power in 1434, Cosimo and his brother Lorenzo had been supporting efforts to bring a reformed Dominican community to central Florence.[2] An obvious location was the Convent of San Marco, occupied for over a century by a Silvestrine congregation of Benedictine monks that had fallen on hard times. A report of 1420 showed just nine monks in residence, only one a native Florentine. Fire and other disasters had wrecked the convent roof and caused structural problems, which the monks were too poor to have repaired.

A few minutes' walk from the Cathedral and Baptistry and almost within sight of the Medici palace and the basilica of San Lorenzo, San Marco was on the vital axis of Florentine religious, social, and ceremonial life. Several lay confraternities, including the Medici's favorite, the Magi, had quarters there, and it was associated with important women's religious groups. San Marco also served as a parish church, so, with several Medici households in the neighborhood, it was already within the family's orbit.[3]

As with most lay patronage of ecclesiastical foundations, the Medici had reasons in addition to those of conscience and piety to assist the Dominican takeover of San Marco. Besides enhancing their visibility as benefactors, by promoting new Observantist houses they would offset the influence of older Conventual foundations, which took direction from their regional headquarters in Milan or Rome. A wholly Tuscan congregation of reformed houses dependent on local patronage and populated by local sons would be more malleable and singularly responsive to Florentine territorial interests. (This advantage would be realized sixty years later when Savonarola established a Tuscan Congregation with enthusiastic Medici support.)

In 1418 Cosimo and Lorenzo de' Medici joined with the friars of San Domenico of Fiesole in a petition to the Council of Constance to replace the Silvestrines with a priory of Observant Dominicans. The monks, they charged, lived scandalously, "without poverty and without chastity." The Silvestrines denied the allegations and vigorously resisted expulsion. A papal investigation found no evidence to support the charges, but local lay and ecclesiastical influence prevailed against them. In January 1436, Pope Eugenius, living in exile in Florence and thus a beneficiary of the Medici's hospitality as well as financial backing, issued a bull ordering the Silvestrines, "for civic utility," to trade places with the Dominican Observants of San Domenico of Fiesole who had been provisionally installed at the Convent of San Giorgio on the south bank of the Arno. The transfer was messy. Monks and friars squabbled over books and property rights until an accommodation was reached in 1437.

Cosimo ultimately spent far more on San Marco than his expiatory 10,000 florins.[4] Since the hapless Silvestrines had failed to maintain the buildings properly, the Dominicans spent their first two years in unhealthy, damp, semi-ruined cells, and primitive wooden huts. Cosimo put his favorite architect Michelozzo Michelozzi in charge of renovating the cloisters and living spaces. From San Domenico of Fiesole came fra Angelico to paint an altarpiece for the church and decorate the convent interiors. On the wall of each cell he painted a luminously mystical scene from the life of Christ for the private meditations of the occupant. The still unfinished church was consecrated in 1443 in the presence of the pope, the College of Cardinals, numerous bishops and, as the San Marco chronicler put it, "a great concurrence of people."

Dominican San Marco brought benefits to the city as well as to the friars. The Observants encouraged new confraternity activity, revitalized San Marco's function as a parish church, and preached in the city and surrounding towns. But Cosimo also aspired to make San Marco famous as an intellectual center. From the estate of the late humanist Niccolò Niccoli he bought more than 400 codices and continued to add rare philosophical and patristic texts, making the convent library one of the finest of its time. The library, re-designed in elegant Renaissance style, was open to all qualified readers and even had a lending system. Just as San Marco's revitalized spiritual functions and new aesthetic magnificence helped it connect with the Florentine community of believers and worshipers, so its new intellectual treasures, liberally shared, made it a favored resort of humanists, philosophers, and literati. And throughout the convent, the frescoes on its walls, the books in its library, the very fabric of its buildings reminded friars and visitors that these treasures were gifts of the Medici.[5]

"I invoke God's curse and mine upon the introduction of possessions into this order," concluded Saint Dominic in his legendary admonition to observe chastity, humility, and voluntary poverty. In 1448 plague carried off some of the San Marco brothers and an earthquake struck the city on the night of September 29, the Feast of Saint Michael the Archangel. The convent had suffered "*horrenda ruina*" to buildings and life.[6] Some friars died, others took flight. Repairs, paid for by Cosimo and his son Piero, went on for at least another five years.

When a second earthquake devastated San Marco in 1453 the friars might have reflected upon Saint Dominic's curse, for they must have known that holy poverty had been compromised in the very founding of the convent. In addition to the huge outlays for reconstruction and furnishing, the friars depended upon weekly Medici remittances for their basic necessities, since their preaching, study, and pastoral duties made begging impossible and revenues were inadequate. Prior Antonino Pierozzi, an Observantist who had moved from San Domenico of Fiesole, was obliged to recognize that strict poverty was no longer tenable. In 1450, Antonino, or Antoninus as he came to be known, now archbishop of Florence, had with Medici backing petitioned Pope Calixtus III to allow San Marco to receive gifts of property and retain the income. A papal bull granted the petition in 1455.

If San Marco could not live without Medici patronage, living with it brought its own problems. The relaxation of austere rule seems to have led to a drop in lay donations, although Antoninus blamed this on economic depression. With little incentive to favor a backsliding Observant community, lay donors tended to redirect their generosity to Santa Maria Novella, the older and intellectually more distinguished Conventual house. San Marco's decline in revenue made it even more dependent upon the Medici and consequently more compliant. Recruitment continued to falter. In 1456 San Marco had only two novices. To counteract its losses, the convent decided to detach itself from the Roman Province and join the wealthier and larger Lombard Congregation.[7] Thus began a period of shifting allegiances for San Marco, San Domenico of Fiesole, and other Tuscan houses, each trying to attract recruits and reignite the inspiration for greater austerity. San Marco's rigorists were unhappy with what they perceived as the relaxed austerity of the Lombard Congregation. By the time Savonarola joined San Marco in May of 1482, they were already enlisting powerful emissaries to negotiate at the papal court for a new separation.

As lector, fra Girolamo instructed the novices in the basic disciplines of logic and philosophy. He also wrote textbooks, *Compendium logicae* completed in 1484, followed by *Compendium philosophiae naturalis* and *Compendium philosophiae moralis.* As school manuals, none make any claim to originality, but they show the thoroughness of his reading in the ancient philosophers (whose dangerous influence on Christian minds was to become a frequent complaint in his sermons). Aristotle was his chief authority, an Aristotle—unsurprisingly, given his grandfather's influence and his training in the Dominican studium— "filtered, as far as logic is concerned, through Thomist commentary" and scarcely aware of "the disturbing warnings of the new [more empirically grounded] logic or of the more up-to-date circles of physical science."[8] His exposition of logic is mainly descriptive and heavily oriented toward the construction of syllogisms, although aware that his pupils would have to meet challenges to the traditional logic, he added an eleventh book of the *Compendium of Logic* in which he raised one hundred of "the more subtle questions of logic in order that I might lift undiscriminating minds [*mentes insipidium*] so that they may have an easier passage to the other doctors of logic and to philosophy."[9] In examining the nature of logic, for example, on the hotly argued question of the nature of universals he came down on the side of the pre-Occamite traditionalists.[10] Whatever distaste for scholastic culture he may have been harboring, in these instructional texts he follows the traditions of his Order.

The last book of the *Compendium of Morals* is entitled *On Politics and Government* (*De politica et regno*). Brief and succinct, it appears almost an afterthought, but it gives some insight into Savonarola's thinking about government and society long before he set foot on the political stage and even longer before his ideas about government came to be part of the canon of Renaissance political thought.

In good Thomist-Aristotelian fashion, Savonarola begins with a definition: a state, or political community (*civitas*), is a natural association of households and other small groups of humans organized for the purpose of living
well. To this end the community makes laws to prevent ignorant and wicked
people from oppressing others and doing evil, for without law people are
more libidinous and voracious than the brute animals, and if heavily armed
and without the restraint of law, they are a danger to others. A well-ordered,
virtuous community promotes the human arts by which people live well.
Moreover, it helps them to pursue their highest good, which is the contemplation of God. Thus community helps us attain that highest blessedness
in the next life. As for material needs, it is better that citizens farm their own
land than to pursue wealth by commerce. Fueled by greed, commerce cor-
rupts the community with venality, fraud, and contempt for the public good,
while the wealth of the few enables them to rule over the many. Besides,
businessmen who frequently travel abroad are more likely to be corrupted by
alien ways. And since merchants are not familiar with military arts the community becomes dependent upon mercenary armies, which have no loyalty to
it. As the examples of Florence and Venice show, mercenaries fight for money
not for the love of country.

A community lives by its *politia*, its structure of governance. Polity thrives
when citizens are neither very rich nor very poor. Citizens of the middling
sort tend to be more reasonable and function as a countervailing force against
either of the extremes. For the best form of government God, prince of the
universe, is the best model. A single ruler is most able to maintain unity and
peace among the many. On the other hand, a tyrant is the very worst, for he
sows discord and disunity. To resist or depose a tyrant, however, is not the
prerogative of private persons but of a legitimate public authority, someone
who holds his place from God. If the founder of the regime was a high
nobleman, it is he who decides. If the regime has been founded by the people,
they may depose a tyrant on the grounds that he has not kept the founding
covenant, but a tyrant who cannot be deposed by these means is best left to
God or to "some other better means." It is preferable to tolerate a tyrant than
to rise against him, particularly if he is not too repressive, for a popular rising,
especially an unsuccessful one, incurs many dangers and foments much dissension.

To look ahead ten years to when Savonarola endorsed the revolt against
the Medici, excoriated tyrants, and campaigned for popular republicanism is
to appreciate the practical changes he was to undergo. These earlier views are

both authoritarian and abstract: he argues for monarchy, disapproves of popular revolution, and omits any discussion of political liberty. And although he was living in one of the wealthiest, culturally vibrant, and (despite the decline of freedom during the Medici years) proudly republican city-states in all Italy, in these works he has next to nothing to say about Florence, yet he must have had Florence in mind when he expressed strong distaste for commerce on both moral and political grounds. Unlike some earlier Dominican preachers in the city, most notably Archbishop Antoninus,[11] this enemy of materialism in all its forms had no praise (either then or later) for the vaunted Florentine talent for industry and banking, certainly none for the notion that the Florentines had an imperial destiny.

At San Marco Savonarola also preached to his fellow friars, and from this time we can follow his thinking in sermon drafts and notes. They show him intensely cultivating the inner life, examining "the reasons of faith," and seeking affirmations of the divine through contemplation and love. The great writers on Christian spirituality—Pseudo-Dionysius, Saint Augustine, John Cassian, Saint Thomas, Saint Bernard of Clairvaux, and Nicholas of Lyra—were his principal masters, although the Bible was his main love. Scriptural study, spiritual detachment, meditation, and contemplation dominate his thoughts about preaching as well. Six months after his arrival he wrote these lines for his own instruction: "The preacher should be completely dedicated to God, full of the grace of the Holy Spirit, of love and of divine Wisdom. He should take himself outside himself, be wholly involved in what he is expressing. . . . And he should separate his mind from human arts, neither employing any human mode of speech or doctrine, nor be guided by eloquence or human philosophy, but only by what he is able to justify according to Scripture."[12]

He followed his own advice. He expounded Scripture to his fellow friars with such fervor, says one admiring biographer, that his eyes often filled with tears as he spoke. Another declared that he transported his listeners to a new world where they could comprehend scriptural books previously inaccessible to them "with seven keys."[13] His earliest extramural audience seems to have been the congregation of Benedictine nuns at the Convent of the Murate. There his sermons, as he noted, consisted largely of meditations on such themes as death, the name Jesu, (a devotional motif deriving from Pseudo-Dionysius and popularized by Bernardino da Siena and Giovanni da Capistrano), and "inflammatory" mystical conversations with Jesus.[14]

In his sermon for the Feast of the Circumcision at the Murate, January 1,

1483, he explored the symbolic meanings of circumcising the heart: cultivating obedience, humility, and charity; taming the senses (vision, hearing, smell, taste); repressing anger and controlling desire—liberating the soul for the contemplation of Christ. A mystical dialogue with death follows: "Death, stay here among us! I want to dispute with you. You have been overcome in the victory. In what victory? In the victory of Christ. What is Christ's victory? The death of the Cross. Why? Because it destroyed sin, overcame the prince of darkness, and [citing Zech. 9.1] liberated the prisoners."

That year he preached his first Lenten sermons in Florence, making them do double duty for the nuns of the Convent of the Murate and for his first predominantly lay audience in the church of Orsanmichele. As his principal text he chose the first book of Lamentations, a harrowing outpouring of grief over the sorrows of Zion, which provided him with rich opportunities for moral and allegorical applications to contemporary religious and temporal institutions. He deplored the avarice that flourished in the Church, and he touched on the need of the civitas to serve the common good. Sinners should seek divine forgiveness and earn redemption through penitence, meditation on Christ, and moral improvement.

Afterwards he recorded summaries of each sermon, commenting on his performance and audience reaction. On one he curtly noted, "I was not pleased"; and at another, "pretty enough"; and after telling a story from the *Dialogues* of Gregory the Great, "This was very pleasing." Of one he remarked that he was pleased with his exposition of the moral, but not with the allegorical, sense. On still another: "I liked both [the allegorical and moral] parts, but not my manner of speaking."[15]

The self-criticism reflected real difficulties. His first audiences in Florence were put off by his "foreign," that is Ferrarese, speech and his gravelly voice. Besides, they—and increasingly he himself—were impatient with the pedantic scholastic style of preaching in which he had been trained, the complex division and subdivision of the text into numbered sections, and the systematic propounding of the various senses—literal, moral, allegorical, and so on—in turn. Adopted two centuries earlier by university-trained mendicant preachers to convey abstruse theological ideas, it was a method and style prone to fossilization, a labored academic exercise, overly complicated and abstract, easily caricatured. By the fifteenth century itinerant preachers were beginning to adopt a popular, less formal approach, some by dramatizing themselves and their texts, others, most famously Saint Bernardino da Siena, with a folksy, conversational manner, homely vignettes from everyday life, and simple moral instruction. Folksiness was never Savonarola's forte, nor, at least in his early days, was self-dramatization, but already in some of these early sermons there are inklings of the direct, artful, deceptively spontaneous style he subsequently mastered.

As he liberated himself from the scholastic sermon he also found more dramatic ways to present his message. (The dialogue with death already mentioned was one example.) Concluding the second of five planned sermons for the Feast of Ascension and Pentecost of 1483 he comments, "Note that I have not divided this sermon nor the two following, but I said that I wanted to talk as though the Spirit was leading me, just as the Bride cried, 'Let him kiss me with the kiss of his mouth.'"[16] That quotation is from the Song of Songs (1.2), which he was beginning to study with the guidance of the great mystical commentary by Saint Bernard of Clairvaux. Such was his enthusiasm that for Pentecost "I changed my theme to 'Kiss me with the kisses of your mouth' and prepared new, sweet preaching for those three days." He also chose the first book of the Song of Songs for his Lenten sermons in San Lorenzo the following year.[17] Following Bernard, he treated the erotic imagery of the text as the expression of the soul's search for God's illuminating love. ("What, then, is the kiss of the mouth if not the subtle penetration and delectation of divine things, not the knowledge of words but the experience of celestial light?")[18]

For Savonarola, however, even this highly personal exercise had its social purpose. Whereas Bernard's focus was on the mystical experience of divorcing oneself from the world, fra Girolamo treated spiritual union as the foundation of Christian life in the world and the keystone of humanity's redemption.[19] Achieving divine illumination through the love of Christ was the ultimate remedy for the world's corruption—that melancholy preoccupation of his youth that had impelled him into the convent. He catalogues, again, the sins of "this wicked century," its pursuit of riches, glory, and the pleasures of the flesh, its evil prelates and corrupt priests, thieves and knaves, the pomp of the Church, false apostles, heretics, and worldly philosophers with their vain pretensions to wisdom. "When will the day come when I enter your presence, filled with peace, and out of that evil and most wicked world? . . . It sickens me not only to live in it but even to see it. My lord I would like to be with you always, to live with you and sweetly to embrace you. Lord, these are the words of the bride inflamed with the love of Jesu."

The response to the sermons on the Song of Songs was dismal. Fra Placido Cinozzi attended from hopeful start to disappointing finish and said that fra

Girolamo's gestures and pronunciation pleased almost no one; by the time
Lent was over fewer than twenty-five men, women, and children remained. In
Florence a preacher who failed to master the worldly arts of eloquence courted
popular apathy. Worse, he would almost certainly be shunned by the people
who "counted," the literati and intellectuals of the Medici circle; by their
presence or absence they signaled who was "in" and who was "out." Discouraged by his dwindling audience and by the criticism he was hearing, says
fra Placido, he intended to abandon preaching, return to Lombardy, and
concentrate on teaching.[20]

In thrall to his preaching vocation, Savonarola did not, in fact, return to
Lombardy. He probably could not have done so had he wanted to. His
assignment to Florence had not yet run its course. Instead, he reacted to these
setbacks in his characteristic way. He found a new source of inspiration in the
discovery of his apocalyptic voice. The connection between defeat and new
inspiration was made by fra Girolamo himself. In a sermon of 1496 he recalled, "Everyone who knew me ten [actually twelve] years ago knows that I
had neither voice nor breath nor preaching style, in fact everybody disliked
my preaching; but when God gave me this gift [of prophecy] I accepted it
willingly for love of him."[21]

In August 1484 the death of Pope Sixtus IV, that tenacious old enemy of
Medici Florence, initiated a prolonged fight over a successor, reviving fears
that there would be a new schism and the shattering of a tenuous Christian
unity. In his *Prayer for the Church,* Savonarola trembles at the prospect of a
world become a battleground between God and the devil with control of the
Church as the prize. The devil foments dissension over the choice of a successor; God graciously extends his hand over Rome and peace is restored with
the election of a new pope, but this is only a temporary reprieve. Without a
great renewal, demonic forces will prevail and the Church will suffer.[22]

The apocalyptic scenario of the *Prayer for the Church* soon found its way
into his preaching. That same year, while composing a sermon during a visit
to the Convent of San Giorgio, he suddenly thought of "about seven reasons"
why the Church was soon to be scourged and renewed. From that time on, as
he later recalled, he began to think about such things a great deal and to
search in Scriptures for further confirmation of these "conclusions." In 1485 he
went to San Gimignano as Lenten preacher and delivered a series of blistering sermons on sin, especially vanity, excoriating the bad pastors who corrupted their flocks and deploring the "tepid," Christians who were lukewarm

and superficial about their faith. With the Psalmist he invited his congregation to come to the Lord for enlightenment and so avoid the confusion that befell the builders of the Tower of Babylon, misguided seekers of false knowledge (Gen. 11.4). If they did this, they would forestall the scourging that awaited them.

When he returned to San Gimignano as Lenten preacher in 1486 he was more emphatic about coming tribulations. He begins his fifth sermon with John the Baptist's piercing call to do penance for the Kingdom of Heaven is approaching (Matt. 3.2) and warns that a scourge is coming soon, "either of Judgment or of Antichrist or war or plague or hunger." Protesting like Amos that he is no prophet (Amos 7.14), he cites Saint Thomas: "We conjecture much from Scriptures and from what has happened in the past, for by remembering past events and understanding present ones we make provision for the future" (Aquinas, *Summa theologica* I. 22. 1). Although fifteen years later he was to tell his interrogators that it was in San Gimignano that he first prophesied the great renewal of the Church, there is no evidence for this; the dominant tone of these sermons is pessimistic, their outlook for the future indeterminate.

After Easter he returned to Florence and to his regular teaching and preaching duties. In his sermon notes for this period there is no mention of the San Giorgio episode nor any reference to the prophecies of renewal, no reports of them by observers, no entries in the San Marco chronicle. When he left the city in 1487 for a new assignment, Florence had heard nothing of his preaching of coming tribulations or the renewal of the Church.[23]

The illumination in San Giorgio and the San Gimignano sermons, however tentative and conjectural, were Savonarola's first ventures into eschatological preaching. Convinced that the world and the Church were corrupt and determined to make himself heard as a preacher of penitence, he found his apocalyptic scenario in Scripture. War, famine, pestilence, and mortality, the four horses and their ghostly riders, galloped ceaselessly through the pages of the Book of Revelation, terrifying generations of Christians who saw them as heralds of Antichrist and the End Time. Saint Augustine, the great meditator on human destiny, had discouraged eschatological speculation, and after him it was marginalized, condemned, sometimes punished. But in a society that viewed itself through the lens of sacred history, speculation about the divine design and Last Things was irrepressible, especially in times of crisis and change. The Muslim threat, both real and imagined, spurred Christians to search apocalyptic texts for clues on the place of the Great Infidel in the Last Things. Islam was seen as the instrument of divine wrath for Christian sin, but it had another more promising role to play: once the Muslims were defeated—as Christians believed they were destined to be—they would accept the True Faith and together with Jews and all other unbelievers would be enclosed in the single sheepfold ruled by one shepherd envisioned by the prophet (Ezek. 34).

The most innovative late medieval eschatological thinker was Gioacchino, or Joachim, of Fiore, the Calabrian abbot who challenged eschatological orthodoxy as never before.[24] Claiming the gift of "spiritual intelligence," Joachim declared that he had grasped Scripture's divine design: time was unfolding in three "states" each corresponding to a person of the Trinity. The first, the state of the Father and of the Old Testament, had ended with the coming of Christ, which opened the present, or Second State, of the Son and his New Testament. Already, however, the tribulations predicted in the Book of Revelation were at hand; Antichrist was in the world or soon to be born. His defeat would bring an end to the tribulations and usher in the Third State, the reign of the Holy Spirit. By the time Joachim died in 1202 his writings were circulating throughout Italy and the rest of Christian Europe. Other works falsely claiming his authorship gave his ideas an even more radical coloration.

One of the more extreme Joachimite spin-offs was *The Introductory Book* of the Franciscan Gerard of Borgo San Donnino, which introduced the idea that in the Third State both the Old and New Testaments would be supplanted by an "Eternal Gospel." The condemnation of Gerard's teachings in 1255 tainted Joachimism with heresy,[25] although many continued to read the abbot's works. Dante encountered Joachim in paradise (*Paradiso* XII) and hailed him as gifted with the spirit of prophecy, and Boccaccio acclaimed him (*On Famous Women* CIV.4.9).

A majority of Dominicans, including Thomas Aquinas, rejected Joachim's prophecies and condemned his views on the Trinity as heretical. Mainstream Franciscans did the same, although extremist Spiritual Franciscans identified with his vision of an order of poor monks who would dominate the coming Age of the Spirit. Fra Bernardino da Siena railed against apocalyptic heretics: "If you cut them open you'd find Antichrist in their own hearts." "When I was a boy, some fifty years ago," he said in a sermon in 1439, "the delusion about the multitude of revelations and visions was running wild and people were asking if Antichrist had already been born." When these turned out to be false, Bernardino concluded that the Serpent encourages demonic illusions so that when the real Antichrist comes people would not believe it.[26]

In the climactic struggle between Papacy and Empire for dominance in thirteenth-century Italy, papalists and imperialists alike exploited Joachimite and other prophecies to prove that God and history were on their side. Prophetic texts continued to be "newly discovered." Some of these, notably the Second Charlemagne, the Last Emperor, and Angelic Pope prophecies, were to have a very long career. And poor people found their places in this great scheme of things too. Disaffected peasants and workers—the Ciompi wool workers in Florence, for example—rallied to leaders promising the speedy fulfillment of Joachim's vision or were inspired by variations of their own. Some envisioned a spiritualized church or millennial kingdom, some the end of lordship, the freeing of the serfs, or the redistribution of property. One such movement was "the Great Alleluia," which brought friars and laymen together in the belief that Joachim had calculated the beginning of the Third Age for the year 1260. In that year Antichrist, in the person of the Holy Roman Emperor Frederick II, would die and the Age of the Holy Spirit begin. But Frederick, uncooperative to the end, died in 1250.

Failed prophecies were soon forgotten and skeptics ignored; the need to know God's plan was ineluctable. Prophetic and oracular texts circulated everywhere. Some were anonymous, some pseudonymous, claiming the paternity of Joachim or the prophet Daniel, Methodius, the Roman Sibyls, Merlin the Prophet, the Oracle of Cyril the Carmelite, Hildegard of Bingen, or Antonius of Spain. A few, as the so-called Toledo Letter, were "miraculously" transmitted and disseminated or, like the fifteenth-century tablets of Saint Cataldus, "found by chance."[27] The seed of apocalyptic fantasy was implanted in the common culture. Laid down in a complex stratification of announcements and predictions,[28] deploying an ever more familiar vocabulary of symbols and signs, and constantly being revised to "predict" new events, millenarian apocalypticism was a key feature in the propaganda of princes and the manifestos of popular leaders, a resource for penitential preachers, and a pervasive element of civic and political discourse. Even that pillar of orthodoxy Archbishop Antoninus cited Joachim as having given a special role to Saints Francis and Dominic as preachers of the new spiritual age.[29] As one historian succinctly put it, "[Joachim's] doctrine gave shape to the fears and hopes of humanity for centuries."[30]

Prophecies circulated by word of mouth as well as print. There were many rhyming texts, perhaps intended for, or invented by, people who were illiterate.

Printed and handwritten prophecies circulated in both Latin and vernacular, sometimes in a mixture of the two. Astrology was also brought into play to lend its "scientific" authority to "revealed" prophecies. On the basis of astrological theories derived from Albumasar, the ninth-century Arab astronomer, some Western thinkers and reformers predicted that a conjunction of Jupiter and Saturn would occur in 1484 signaling radical change in Christendom. This was the contention of the astrologer Paul of Middelburg, a correspondent of Marsilio Ficino. (Ficino himself was not without "a touch of the apocalyptic.")[31] Another who expected 1484 would be a year of great events was the popular German pamphleteer Johannes Lichtenberger. The sixteenth-century astrologer who cast Luther's horoscope and misdated his birth to 1484 instead of 1483 was surely a believer in the Great Conjunction. In 1484, although he abhorred astrology, Savonarola wrote apocalyptic verse and preached catastrophe for a wicked Christendom.

The arrival of the printing press in Italy in the 1460s made it easier to disseminate prophetic texts and astrological prognostications. In 1479 the busy press run by the sisters of San Jacopo di Ripoli in Florence offered two vernacular prophecy collections, each numbering a few pages, at a very modest price. Sold at bookstalls and by stationers, such texts were also recited by itinerant storytellers. Florence was to become Italy's leading center for the diffusion of printed prophecies.[32] Prognostications bearing the name of Saint Bridget, the Swedish noblewoman who died in Italy in 1373, were among the most influential.[33] She left a large collection of *Revelations*, which also became the inspiration for many forgeries bearing her name, one of these the Ripoli press collection of *Profezia di Santa Brigida*. Typically these regarded the leaders and events of the day in moral and religious perspective. Some of the Bridget prophecies found in Florentine texts, for example, hailed Florence's election to leadership but warned against the excessive coveting of new territories. In this respect the prophecies formed a notional link with the old Guelf tradition, recalling Florence to her religious and moral responsibilities toward the Christian community.

Savonarola later took pains to deny that he had more than a passing acquaintance with the prophecies attributed to Joachim of Fiore, Saint Bridget, or others of that kind. There is no reason to disbelieve him; his own apocalyptic vision was based on Scripture and remained rooted there. At the same time, defending his apostolate, he acknowledged prophecy of a more recent vintage. "Many have been prophesying this scourge of Italy for a hundred years, many holy preachers in past times, for a hundred years until today, have said, 'Woe to you, Italy and Rome, the wrath of God and the scourge are coming to you.'"[34] "Arriving in Florence," one historian has observed, "Savonarola did not invent prophecy, rather he set foot on terra profetica."[35]

CHAPTER 4

Florence and the Medici

A fifteenth-century traveler entered Florence through one of its massive gates, made his way through noisy, malodorous streets walled in by multistoried houses with overhanging roofs and teeming with people of every class and calling: gentlemen in doublet and hose, silk-gowned ladies with retinues of servants and exotic slaves, long-robed, sandaled clerics, grimy laborers, beggars, hawkers, cutpurses, flesh peddlers, and gangs of rowdy youths. Passing shops, street corner tabernacles, churches, and formal residential doorways, he soon neared the city's monumental center. In just twenty or thirty minutes the visitor would have retraced in the city's dense fabric more than two centuries of history, from medieval provincial town to proud Renaissance capital of near-mythic fame.

The fame was duly earned, the myth consciously cultivated. Poets sang the city's beauties, orators lauded it as a new Athens, chroniclers and historians declared it "Daughter of Rome," and painters depicted it as a garden of delights in an enchanted landscape. Graceful spires and towers, white and green marble church facades, beige-toned palaces with graceful loggias, all presided over by Brunelleschi's brick-red, white-ribbed cathedral dome—largest in Christendom—tipped with Verrocchio's golden orb. The visitor who examined public inscriptions, studied church frescoes, or turned a page or two of a local chronicle could not fail to be impressed by the artful way the Florentines blended history and myth in a constant visual and verbal fashioning of their collective self-image. Florence, declared an inscription in the Palace of the Captain of the People, is full of riches; her rule brings happiness to Tuscany; she will be eternally triumphant over her enemies; she reigns over the world.[1]

History and myth were intertwined in the Florentine civic identity even before it emerged in the late eleventh century as a self-governing commune electing its own consuls. A twelfth-century chronicle glorified Florence's modest origins as a Roman colony by claiming that Julius Caesar had founded the city *ex flore hominum Romanorum,* from the flower of Roman manhood (hence *Florentia*) after defeating the traitor Catiline and destroying his stronghold at Fiesole. The chronicle dates from the time Florence had begun extending her reach by destroying rival Fiesole in 1125. As *parva Roma,* a little Rome, she had a special destiny for greatness.

Florence shaped its destiny more by economic than military prowess.[2] By the mid- to late-twelfth century the little market town on the Arno had begun to quicken with the effects of a commercial revolution that had already begun to transform other parts of Italy and western Europe. Immigrants flocked there from the Tuscan countryside to find work in its shops, foundries, and mills. Cheap woolen cloth made up the bulk of its early industrial production, but by the thirteenth century Florence was also exporting fine woolens, silks, leather, paper, soap, glass, and objects crafted of wrought iron, gold, and silver. Florentine merchants were establishing trading networks throughout Italy, the Mediterranean, France, and northern Europe. With their accumulated capital they doubled as bankers, branching out into exchange and lending operations in domestic and foreign financial markets. By the end of the thirteenth century they had become the principal money men of the papacy and had a near monopoly as collectors of church revenues as far afield as England. The finely made gold florin, stamped with the lily and a portrait of John the Baptist, the city's patron saint, surpassed all rivals as the international monetary standard.

Commercial and financial profits paid for churches as well as government palaces. Three buildings embodied the religious heart of the city: the Baptistery, "il bel San Giovanni" as Dante called it, an octagonal masterpiece of Tuscan-Romanesque; the grandiose cathedral of Santa Maria del Fiore, rebuilt in fourteenth-century Gothic style, its rough unfinished facade a reminder of an earlier incarnation when it was known as Santa Maria Reparata, but more familiarly as the Duomo; and Giotto's freestanding, elegant campanile, or bell tower, on the Duomo's south flank, its white marble sheath "coloured like a morning cloud and chased like a sea shell" with rose and green accents.[3] A few minutes' walk from the ecclesiastical center was the Piazza della Signoria, locus of secular power, dominated by the Palazzo della Signoria, the giant town hall, familiarly known as the Palazzo Vecchio, or Old Palace. Built of a ruddy brown, rough-cut local stone in the fourteenth century, the fortress-like palazzo, with its scowling, teeth-like ramparts and lofty tower lording it over the city and countryside, was the proud statement of a communal government that had come through a century of domestic violence and launched an era of regional expansion. The vast piazza that opened in front of it served as marketplace, social venue, and ceremonial theater as well as open-air council chamber. In moments of crisis male citizens were herded into the great square where they were designated a *Parlamento,* or General Assembly, and constrained to shout their yeas to reforms and emergency measures proposed to them by the Priors and Standard Bearer of Justice who made up the Signoria.

Building Florence was a collaborative effort involving government, clergy, aristocrats, wealthy gildsmen, skilled artisans, and laborers, and the sense of communal—if often fractious—participation and accomplishment remained a fundamental part of the Florentine republican identity.[4] Important contributors to the urban landscape were the Dominican, Franciscan, and other mendicant friars who had begun arriving in the second quarter of the thirteenth century. With financial help from the commune they built great hall-like churches—Santa Croce for the Franciscans, Santa Maria Novella for the Dominicans, Santa Maria del Carmine for the Carmelites, and Santissima Annunziata for the Servites—to hold the crowds who came to hear their famous preachers. Mostly confined to the new working-class districts outside the first circle of walls, these peoples' churches were a major force for integrating new neighborhoods into the fabric of the city and extending religious and cultural life outward from the old ceremonial center.

The mendicants were keen to depict the lives of their founders and saints on church doors, walls, windows, chapels, and crypts. Bishops and civic officials affixed their motifs and family crests; lay religious confraternities and merchant and artisan gilds contributed stained glass, altarpieces, and statuary. Families purchased church space for chapels and tombs and presented silver and bronze candlesticks, chalices, embroidered clerical vestments, and altar cloths, often bearing their monograms and crests. Humbler parishioners contributed their pennies for candles and donated their labor to clean, dust, sweep, polish, and make repairs.

Inevitably, Florence's economic and territorial expansion had profound effects upon its political life. Wealthy bankers and international merchants had been merging with old landowning *grandi* families to form a new elite, which by the thirteenth century seemed to threaten the more egalitarian ways of the old commune. Increasingly referred to as *ottimati,* they were energetically and, to a considerable degree, successfully opposed by the master craftsmen, skilled artisans, lawyers, and notaries who made up the middle socioeconomic levels of society and identified themselves as *il popolo,* or *popolano,* exercising their influence through their gild organizations. The situation was complicated by the borrowing of political identities from the struggles between popes and emperors. Old landed gentry tended to sympathize with the pro-imperial Ghibellines while the arriviste popolani generally favored the supposedly more progressive pro-papal Guelfs, although political loyalties were likely to be as much a matter of family tradition and opportunity as of ideology.

The control of Florence alternated between Ghibelline and Guelf until 1293 when a new set of ordinances established the principle of representation by occupation rather than party. To be eligible for a council or administrative post a male citizen had to be enrolled in one of twenty-one officially recognized gilds of bankers, wool and silk merchants, lawyers, doctors, notaries, and master craftsmen, be wealthy enough to pay a substantial property tax, and pass scrutiny by an electoral committee. The names of the approved candidates (*veduti,* or "seen") were written on slips and deposited in electoral bags. A designated number of these were drawn and took office (*seduti,* "seated"). Terms of service were strictly limited: Priors sat for two months, most other magistrates for six. Members of the lesser gilds, journeymen, and gild-ineligible wage laborers (*popolo minuto*) were excluded, as were members of the old landed aristocracy (*magnati*).

The Ordinances of Justice of 1293 were the Magna Carta of Florence's gild republic. With some adjustments they remained in force, at least formally, until the sixteenth century. Guelfism survived the early conflicts, but Ghibellinism, associated with the foreign empire and its magnati supporters, did not, at least in Florence. The Guelf Party possessed great tax-exempt wealth and exercised conspicuous ceremonial, charitable, and honorific functions, such as the conferring of the title of knight, a dignity much prized in this society of merchants. It also participated in the selection of the well-paid officials who administered Florence's expanding territorial state. Long after the Ghibellines had been defeated and the Guelf alliance with the papacy was no longer the keystone of Florence's security, the highly select members of the Guelf Party regarded themselves as the keepers of the republic's values. The chronicler Giovanni Villani recalled that during a visit to Rome in 1300 he was inspired to write the history of Florence, for he noted, while Rome was in decline, "Florence, the daughter and creature of Rome, was in the ascendant."

In Villani's view, Florence's Roman-Guelf legacy stood for republican government, prosperity, and the charity and culture of her citizens, not territorial aggrandizement.[5]

But Florentine expansionist ambitions were eroding such salutary restraint. In the next half century, by a combination of military conquest, subversion, and outright purchase, Florence absorbed Prato, Pistoia, Colle, and San Gimignano, stepped up her pressure on Arezzo (purchased in 1384), conquered Pisa (1406), and tried repeatedly, although unsuccessfully, to conquer Lucca.

Hand in hand with the expansion of the territorial state went image building. Writers forged a new version of Florence's history, reworking the old myth of Florence, the daughter of Rome, heir to Rome's imperial mission. In the second half of the thirteenth century a pseudo-prophecy of French origin predicted that a king named Charles would rule the empire, reform the Church, and conquer the infidel in the East, uniting the world into one sheepfold under a single shepherd (Ezek. 37.24) before laying down his crown on the Mount of Olives.[6] In the next century Florentines adjusted both myths to their own legend. That their city had been rebuilt by Charlemagne after its destruction by the barbarian Totila reflected the reality of their strong economic and political ties with France. On Easter Sunday, as Villani recounts it, after rebuilding the city, the emperor granted it independence and communal privileges. Thus, by moving Charlemagne forward several centuries they made him a hero of the renewed republic and agent of its future glory. Two poems by the Ghibelline poet Fazio degli Uberti (d. 1370) proclaim the new triumphalist ideology.

> Rome acted as long as she was strong;
> And in that happy and not-far-off time,
> Gave birth to a young maiden such
> As to be considered her equal.
> She was called "Flower" [Florentia], which was truly her name,
> And I shall tell of her deeds.
>
> .   .   .   .
>
> Of her who descended from my descendant
> Florence, flower of every good root,
> To make herself empress
> As her mother had been in past ages.[7]

Florentine triumphalism soon clashed with the reality of a papacy bent on reasserting its temporal power in Italy after years of exile at Avignon. Between 1375 and 1378 Florence and the Church fought over conflicting interests in southern Tuscany.[8] Civic humanists celebrated this so-called War of the Eight Saints as a struggle for republican liberty against tyranny. When Pope Gregory XI placed an interdict on the city Florentines responded with an outpouring of religious fervor which, especially among the popolo minuto, thrived on Joachimite millenarian fantasy and the leveling ideals of the Spiritual Franciscans. Shortly after the war the wool workers, or Ciompi, revolted to form a government of workers' gilds, but they were quickly dispersed by an association of twenty-three gilds of masters and artisans. Four years later this popolano coalition was itself forced to give way to the resurgent ottimati, members of industrial, banking, and merchant families who were to dominate the city's political life for the next hundred years. Still, their deeply ingrained civic ideology as well as fear of revolution from below induced them to maintain the appearance and manipulate the symbols of republican liberty.

While mending fences with the papacy Florence faced the even greater threat of expansion into central Italy of Milan under its feared duke, Gian Galeazzo Visconti. Communal leaders took strong measures to discourage further social and religious ferment. One domestic troublemaker, the radical Franciscan Spiritual preacher fra Michele da Calci, was burned at the stake in 1389.

After Florentine forces defeated the Milanese in 1397 the poet Bruscaccio da Rovezzano urged the city to grasp the opportunity God and Fortune had given her:

> You are Rome, and the Duke is Hannibal.
> If you will, transmit
> To the people the light of freedom in their state.
> This rejected dog
> Ought to be destroyed; it will please God,
> And peace for all Italy will follow.
>
> . . . .
>
> But above all, Florence is such
> That in her power
> I have my hope, as in a mighty tower.[9]

Preachers and publicists stressed the need to put patriotism above family loyalties and self-interest. Stefano Porcari, the humanist who served as captain of the people in 1427, exhorted the Florentines to fulfill their destiny by acting for the common good: if they did so they would see their rule continually flourish, "the triumphant name of Florence grow in the world in ever more honored fame to earn the veneration of all peoples."[10] In his famous oration in praise of Florence, the humanist chancellor Leonardo Bruni assured the Florentines that their founder was the Roman people, lord and conqueror of the world.[11]

Beneath this bracing rhetoric of empire simmered the hard reality of debt. The members of the ruling class who could follow Latin orations would have understood that when Porcari and Bruni appealed to their sense of civic unity and the common good they were calling not only for harmony within the ruling group but greater financial sacrifice. Florence had been able to absorb the smaller towns and petty signories of the upper Arno with citizen militias, but the larger-scale campaigns of the fourteenth century required hired professionals—companies of mercenary soldiers recruited from everywhere and captained by *condottieri* whose loyalty to Florence, or whichever state paid them, did not extend beyond the terms of their *condotta,* or contract.[12] How to meet the costs of war became the most pressing problem of the commune. Import duties and consumption taxes were levied on everyone but fell most heavily on those least able to pay. The *estimo,* or forced loan, based on an estimate of wealth by a supposedly neutral third party, was the particular bane of the business and landed classes, provoking resentment, invidious comparisons, and jealousy, not to mention fraud.

After years of debate, two reforms were adopted, both particularly beneficial for the propertied classes. The first, in 1425, was the communal Monte delle Doti or dowry fund. On behalf of a newborn daughter a family could buy shares in the Monte, redeeming them with substantial interest for a dowry at the time of her marriage. After some modifications, the Monte delle Doti became a fixture, with reciprocal advantages for the government and for citizens burdened by the sharply increasing price of dowries.[13] The second major reform was the *Catasto* of 1427 which dispensed with the hated estimo and required heads of households to make their own inventory of assets and pay taxed based on their declaration.[14] This did not solve all the commune's money problems, nor did it eliminate squabbling or cheating, but it was a significant expression of political maturity, implying a degree of citizen responsibility and mutual trust that made the ideal of *governo civile* something more than self-congratulatory rhetoric.

From 1347 to 1348 Europe had been devastated by the Black Death, a bubonic plague pandemic which killed between a third and a half of its people.[15] Florence's population fell from ninety to forty thousand. Industrial exports dwindled. Critical food imports dropped. Wage workers were left jobless, hungry, and fearful. In some industries the scarcity of labor caused wages to rise sharply, and the shortage of farm workers may have hastened the demise of personal bondage, already giving way to *mezzadria*, the classic Tuscan sharecrop system.[16] By the early fifteenth century Florence was showing definite, if uneven, signs of recovery despite recurrences of plague every decade or so, although not until about 1600 did the population regain its pre-1348 level.

The psychological and emotional impacts of the Black Death are harder to gauge than its effects on the economy. No plague was needed to make Italians pious: private and public life were already leavened by Catholic belief, practice, and ceremony.[17] In Florence hundreds of clergy, scores of houses of worship, monasteries, convents, and shrines gave the Church a felt human, physical, and spiritual presence undiminished by the Black Death or by the War of the Eight Saints with its accompanying papal interdict later in the century. Revenues from church properties in the city and the provinces were an important part of the economy, especially since the more lucrative and influential benefices—the canonries, deanships, abbacies, and priories—were considered the birthright of important families who importuned and intrigued for them on behalf of their sons and daughters.[18] Since persuasion and negotiation usually worked better than strong-arm methods, the roads from Florence to the papal curia were plied by diplomats, special envoys, and couriers. Money bought favor: a friendly cardinal could whisper the name of a generous client into a papal ear; an obliging papal secretary could tunnel through the curia's mountain of requests. The pontiffs themselves were not immune to temptation: permission to levy an "emergency" tax on the Florentine clergy, for example, might be more forthcoming if His Holiness were guaranteed a share of the proceeds. In short, even before the War of the Eight Saints eroded the old Guelf patron-client relationship, a new symbiotic partnership between Rome and Florence was well on the way to replacing it. Mutual interests operating at every level of church and secular society held the partnership together, although with so many parties and personalities involved, and so much at stake, the relationship sometimes overheated and meltdown occurred, as in 1378, and again in 1478, when Florence was attacked by the pope and Naples in the Pazzi War. But Florence and Rome needed each other too much to allow relations to deteriorate beyond the possibility of reform.

At the peak of the Florentine ecclesiastical pyramid was the archbishop (elevated from bishop in 1420). Appointed by the papacy upon local recommendation, this prince of the Church came with increasing frequency from one of the city's patrician families. The archbishop's relationship with the city was symbolized in Florence's elaborate welcoming ceremony.[19] Wearing his episcopal miter and robes and riding a white palfrey, the new prelate approached the city with a stately retinue and was met at the Porta Romana by a delegation of local notables. After a formal greeting, His Eminence and his party proceeded to the Convent of San Pier Maggiore, where the abbess was waiting to receive him. The archbishop dismounted and placed a wedding ring on her finger. After Mass in the convent church with the nuns in attendance, the "bride" and "groom" dined together; then the abbess led her guest to a convent chamber where the nuns had prepared a bed for him. The next morning the archbishop formally took his seat in the Cathedral, then crossed the square to his official palace.

Like all marriages, the union between Florence and her archbishop functioned on various levels. He was the chief authority in matters regarding the clergy. He presided over the ecclesiastical court, exercising jurisdiction over the laity in important matters such as marriage and faith. From the revenue-producing properties under his control he dispensed patronage, most of it to the city's influential families. A successful archbishop had to know how to balance the interests of the local clergy with those of the curia. He had to speak for the laboring classes without aggravating their masters. He had to be a skillful administrator, a student of canon law and theology, a diplomat mediating between the interests of the republic and the hierarchy, and also, as shepherd of his flock, an effective preacher and doctor of souls.

The man who met and famously exceeded these specifications was Antonino (Antoninus) Pierozzi, archbishop from 1446 to 1459.[20] Born into Florence's high professional class (his father was a notary), Antonino was a protégé of Pope Eugenius IV and the chief disciple of fra Giovanni Dominici, the founder of the Dominican Observance in Venice and Florence.[21] As a champion of Catholic orthodoxy, Archbishop Antonino banned offensively profane civic festivals and issued a death sentence to a member of the radical Franciscan sect of *Fraticelli*. At the same time, in his sermons and writings he set forth an ideal of republican life that amalgamated the civic ethos of Florentine humanists with the political thought of Saint Thomas Aquinas. He promoted the idea that service to the common good (*bene comune*) was a Christian as well as a civic virtue, especially relevant to life in a communal polity such as Florence.

Like some earlier mendicant preachers, Antonino was sensitive to the quandary of this city of bankers and traders, namely, how to reconcile proto-capitalist practices, such as the taking of interest, with the Christian condemnation of usury.[22] He made some concessions on interest charging, but more important, he taught that the pursuit of wealth was justifiable, even necessary, so long as it was employed for the common good in the form of public works, aid to the poor, and other charitable purposes. To that end, he extolled "magnificence" and generosity, not merely as means of atonement for individual sin but, more positively, as essential urban virtues. As Peter Francis Howard has put it, Antonino demonstrated that "there was a convergence of purpose between the humanists' civic orientation and the mendicant mission of salvation to the city."[23] (But he omitted the neo-Roman imperialism that was the other side of the coin of humanist civic ideology.)[24] In 1523, just sixty-four years after his death, with the support of the Medici and to general rejoicing in Florence, Antonino was elevated to sainthood.

When Antonino became archbishop of Florence in 1444 the party of Cosimo de' Medici had been in power for a decade and the civic virtues Antonino preached were already an endangered species. (Leonardo Bruni, civic humanism's main ideologue, died the same year.) Although the Medici made a point of their simple rural origins, they had built one of the largest and most sophisticated trade and banking businesses in Europe.[25] They had also assembled a party network, consolidated political and marital alliances among the ruling elites, and forged bonds of clientage with lesser citizens by means of favors and gifts with a liberality made possible by their enormous wealth.

In 1433 the dominant Albizzi faction, seeing Cosimo as a dangerous rival, had contrived his exile, but in less than a year his party was in the ascendant and he returned with a mandate to "reform" the government. In establishing his primacy Cosimo mainly used proven party methods, but he exploited them on behalf of himself, family, and friends more effectively than any of the aspiring oligarchs who preceded him.[26] A general open-air assembly, or Parlamento, duly granted special powers to an emergency commission (*balia*). Leaders of the previous regime were expelled, others stripped of political rights. Medici loyalists were appointed to the principal executive offices. In filling the minor magistracies only names of approved candidates were placed in the electoral bags. Medici partisans dominated the Councils of the People and the commune. Some criticism was tolerated, but persistent dissenters could expect retaliation ranging from increased tax assessments to banishment. Every failed coup provided the regime with an excuse for more stringent controls. In 1458, after an extended crisis, a Council of One Hundred

(*Cento*) was established that gave the Medici party control of legislation and candidate selection.

Cosimo was fond of the conceit that he was a plain Florentine of the old school. He seldom held public office, preferring to exert his will behind the scenes and through surrogates. His patronage of the arts, by contrast, was personal, open, and princely in scale. He was an avid builder of palaces and churches, employed the finest painters and sculptors of his time, and retained agents who traveled far and wide hunting for rare manuscripts and books. He sponsored Greek and Latin scholars and philosophers, most notably Marsilio Ficino, the son of his physician, setting him up with the income from a farm at Careggi and a house in town, where he translated and commented on Plato and taught his brand of Neo-Platonism to leading citizens and their sons.

While the more creative of Cosimo's encomiasts praised him as a kind of republican philosopher king who had little personal ambition and exercised his influence through his wisdom and magnanimity, he also liked to be seen as a benevolent father figure who embodied the traditional Florentine virtues of the pious Christian, shrewd pragmatic merchant, and republic-loving patriot. He played on the symbolism of the family name: the Medici were the republic's *medici*, physicians protecting the health of the polity. In art he was often represented as Cosmas, the ancient doctor-saint, and the Medici as Magi, fabled wise men of Christian tradition.[27]

Cosimo wielded his monopoly of power most exclusively in his conduct of foreign relations. Sensing that the era of Florentine expansion was waning, he understood that the survival of his regime depended upon his ability to keep Florence independent as well as prosperous. As a man of business as well as a political realist he knew that the city had more to gain from peace than from war, and to that end he strove to maintain a balance of power among Italy's notoriously contentious states. He also knew how to enhance the prestige of both the city and its first citizen. In 1439 he brought to Florence the ecumenical council which had convened in Ferrara to consider the union of the Latin and Greek Churches. Florence thus played host to the pope, the Greek emperor, and the greatest prelates of East and West. Benozzo Gozzoli's fresco in the Medici palace chapel memorialized the event, showing the members of the Medici family in splendid procession, their beauty, elegant dress, and even the elaborate trappings of their horses and costumes of their retinues betokening royal splendor rather than republican egalitarianism.

In 1451, concerned about the resurgence of papal expansion on the borders of Tuscany, Cosimo led Florence in a diplomatic revolution. By supporting the mercenary captain Francesco Sforza in his takeover of the Duchy of Milan, then formalizing an alliance between the two states, he converted Florence's longtime rival into its principal ally and chief enforcer, while the Medici bank helped keep the Sforza afloat with subventions passed off as loans. (Those unpaid loans were a huge drain on the bank, whose decline began around this time.) The price for this reversal of alliances, however, was war. When the Angevins set out to reconquer the Kingdom of Naples for France, they were supported by Milan and Florence, while the pope and the Venetians took the side of the Angevins' rival, Alfonso of Aragon. But increasing concerns about French and imperial intervention in Italian affairs, and about the Turks' conquest of Constantinople in 1453, led the states to negotiate. At Lodi, in Lombardy, they made a historic peace, pledging a crusade against the infidel and founding a *Lega Italica* for collective security. Members pledged to repel foreign invaders as well as to intervene against any Italian state that attacked its neighbors.[28] The Peace of Lodi of 1454 suggests that Italians were becoming more aware of themselves as a collective entity greater than the sum of its parts, but whether the sense of interrelatedness did more to reduce friction among them or to intensify it is a moot point.

CHAPTER 5

The Magnificent Lorenzo

Cosimo died in 1464, hailed as *Pater Patriae*, Father of His Country and defender of its liberty.[1] Although his operatives expected a smooth transition of power to his son Piero, they were caught off guard by a group of citizens "who were having second thoughts about how this land is to be governed."[2] Two years of ineffectual wrangling over control of offices and the expensive alliance with Milan induced a group of 400 citizens led by the patrician Luca Pitti to swear an oath to uphold republican freedoms. Amid rumors of an anti-Medici conspiracy, Pitti insisted that a Parlamento be called, whereupon Piero de' Medici surrounded the meeting in the piazza with 3,000 troops. The show of force cowed the assembly into passing measures consolidating his regime. Many opposition leaders were banished.

Galloping to the scene on horseback, seventeen-year-old Lorenzo, son of Piero de' Medici, burnished his image as a leader. Three years later, when the sickly Piero died, seven hundred citizens hastily met and decided to offer Lorenzo the dignity of "first citizen." Lorenzo and his younger brother Giuliano were glittering stars in the Florentine social and cultural firmament—expert horsemen and falconers, soccer players, swordsmen, jousters, musicians, and dancers. They attended Mass and took active part in several of the city's important religious confraternities. That they were no ordinary Florentine youth, however, was underlined by Lorenzo's marriage to Clarice Orsini, the daughter of an old, important family of Roman and Neapolitan nobles, in a princely wedding. Whereas Florentine burghers traditionally took spouses within the city and from their own social class, the Medici were now allying themselves with old Italian aristocracy, a shift with important consequences for future policy making, as will be seen.

If the Orsini marriage suggested the tensions between republican values and Medici ambitions, the era of Lorenzo stretched those tensions to the limit. Lorenzo himself shared many of his compatriots' republican sensibilities, but, bred to rule, he protected and extended his near monopoly of power.[3] Just four months after his accession the discovery in Prato of an exiles' plot to overthrow him led to the hanging of fifteen citizens, including the son of a former Standard Bearer of Justice. Expulsions, confiscations of property, and official warnings narrowed the governing circle to a still narrower circle of favorites and fostered a culture of clientage. Lorenzo, not only party head but Florence's patron-in-chief, was constantly importuned for money and jobs, called upon to mediate quarrels, settle disputes, find marriage partners, and render judgment in aesthetic questions.[4] Like Cosimo and Piero, Lorenzo dealt directly with ambassadors, provincial administrators, and heads of Italian and foreign states while continuing to honor the fiction that he was only a private citizen. Lorenzo showed his ruthless side when a revolt in Volterra in 1472 endangered Florence's management of the papal monopoly of alum (an indispensable ingredient in cloth dyeing). At his orders, the condottiere Federico da Montefeltro put down the revolt by sacking the city, an atrocity for which Lorenzo, as *il maestro della bottega,* master of the shop, received heavy blame.[5]

Medici enemies at home and abroad soon precipitated a greater crisis. When the Duke of Milan was assassinated in 1476, King Ferrante of Naples, fearing that the French would try to exploit this disruption of the Italian balance of power by mounting a new invasion of their former Angevin kingdom, drew closer to Pope Sixtus IV. King and pope assumed that the Medici government would support the French. When members of the Pazzi and Salviati families revealed to the pope that they had formed a plot to assassinate the Medici brothers, Sixtus IV, smarting from recent quarrels with Lorenzo, either gave his approval or turned a blind eye.

On Easter Sunday Lorenzo and Giuliano de' Medici accompanied a party of distinguished guests, including Archbishop Salviati, to Mass in the Florentine cathedral. At the appointed moment the conspirators struck. Giuliano was stabbed to death. Lorenzo had just time to draw his sword and deflect the blows of the two priests who had been hired to kill him. Bleeding from a neck wound, he barred himself behind the doors of the north sacristy. Archbishop Salviati led a force to take over the Palazzo della Signoria, but the guard was alerted to arrest them. Jacopo Pazzi rode through the streets at the head of a troop crying "people and liberty!" Medici loyalists countered with shouts of "palle, palle" (the iconic balls of the Medici coat of arms) and rallied the crowd for Lorenzo. By this time Lorenzo had made his way to the Medici palace and stood at a window to show that he was safe. Florentines ran through the streets hunting conspirators, torturing suspects, mutilating corpses, and displaying body parts on the tips of pikes or tossing them into the streets. Most of the Pazzi and Salviati participants as well as the two priest-assassins were killed.

Altogether about eighty people were slaughtered and many others beaten, imprisoned, fined, exiled, and stripped of their property. According to Poliziano, the execution of Francesco Pazzi and Archbishop Francesco Salviati concluded with a particularly gruesome bit of savagery. As the two conspirators, naked and bleeding, were hanging side by side from the window of the Palazzo della Signoria, the archbishop lunged toward Pazzi, fixed his teeth into the other man's breast, and held on as both men strangled to death.[6]

It is a comment on the moral condition of the Renaissance papacy, as well as on the obtuseness of Sixtus IV, that neither murder nor the profanation of the Mass aroused the fury of His Holiness as much as the Florentines' violation of clerical immunity in dealing with the Pazzi conspirators. In the bull excommunicating Lorenzo and the chief members of the Florentine government the pope listed his grievances and promised a plenary indulgence for anyone taking up arms against Florence. On June 22, he placed Florence and its satellites Fiesole and Pistoia under an interdict, and in July he and King Ferrante sent troops into Tuscany. If the Florentines would expel the tyrant Lorenzo, the pope promised, all would be forgiven.

As the coalition troops looted and burned their way through Tuscany, the pope arrested Florentine businessmen and closed their offices in Rome with further devastating effects on the city's economy. Bread riots erupted and in the heat of the summer came plague. Milan, the city's main ally, appeared to be edging toward rapprochement with King Ferrante of Naples. In a move of near-desperation Lorenzo decided to go in person to the king, the mainstay of the papal coalition, and try to deal for peace. If he failed, he would be in Ferrante's power; if he prevailed he would be the city's savior.

After negotiating a truce to hold off the invading troops and satisfying himself that the king was prepared to talk, Lorenzo set out for Naples, sending an open letter to the Signoria once he was on his way. In Naples, after two months of intense bargaining, with generous gifts and entertainments, promises of friendship, and displays of his personal charm, Lorenzo persuaded King Ferrante and his advisors that a rapprochement with Florence would neutralize the French threat. At the point of success he received reports of anti-Medicean agitation in Florence. He sailed for home, leaving agents to conclude the peace treaty which was now assured.

Lorenzo returned to Florence a hero, his critics confounded, his main enemy, Sixtus IV, outmaneuvered. Abandoned by Naples, the pope was forced to accept the peace, although he refused to lift the excommunication or the interdict unless Lorenzo came to Rome to do penance. Lorenzo had no wish to put himself at the mercy of the angry pope, so the stalemate continued until overtaken by events. In August 1479 an Ottoman Turkish fleet swooped into the port of Otranto in the heel of Italy and occupied it with surprising ease, killing thousands and carrying thousands more into captivity. To mount a joint campaign to extirpate this new Muslim incursion into the heart of Europe, Ferrante and Sixtus were forced to patch up their differences. When the pope informed Lorenzo that he might make his amends without a personal appearance in Rome, Lorenzo sent a delegation which obtained absolution for him and the lifting of the excommunication and interdict on the city. Meanwhile he negotiated the departure of the coalition forces from Tuscany, agreeing to send fifteen Florentine galleys for the campaign against the Turks. Medici artistic patronage also played its part in restoring cordial relations. In 1481 a contract was signed committing the Florentine painters Domenico Ghirlandaio and Sandro Botticelli to go to Rome and help decorate the Sistine Chapel.[7]

Admiration for Lorenzo now took on a certain awe: in snatching victory from the jaws of defeat he had shown himself brave, brilliant, ready to sacrifice himself for his country. Even more crucial for a popular hero, he was successful, "greatly loved both by fortune and by God," as Machiavelli put it. The grievous loss of his charming and handsome brother also had a positive side: as co-heir to the family fortune and a popular favorite, Giuliano had been a potential rival; in martyrdom he became a sentimental asset.[8] Once again conspiracy gave Lorenzo a plausible motive for extending his control over Florence. While leaving the old councils and magistracies in place, a powerful new Council of Seventy was stacked with Medici loyalists. Restrictive, secretive, monolithic, and subservient, with sole power to initiate legislation and control appointments to the Signoria,[9] the Seventy became the negative emblem of the Medici-dominated republic.

Other plots followed, but republican protest grew feebler. Conspirators were henceforth charged with lèse-majesté "as if Lorenzo held the status of a titled prince."[10] In a sense he did: "Il Magnifico," the honorific customarily bestowed on high public dignitaries, came to be peculiarly his own. Gone was the egalitarian pretense: like a lord, he went about the city accompanied by armed bodyguards, summarily dispensing justice and favors.[11] Gone were most of the old civic festivals, replaced by others that projected Lorenzo's image at the charismatic center of the city.[12] Abandoned, too, was the fiction that Medici power was not hereditary; Lorenzo spared no effort to assure that primacy would pass to his eldest son Piero. By securing Piero's marriage to Alfonsina Orsini he renewed the connection to that noble and militarily powerful family. Lorenzo also arranged the marriage of his daughter Maddalena to Francesco Cibò, son of the new Pope Innocent VIII (1484–92), which was not only a political coup but gave him access to ecclesiastical benefices for members of his family as well as to coveted Church properties for himself.

Whether it was prudence or residual loyalty to Florentine republicanism that deterred Lorenzo from establishing a formal principate is hard to say. We cannot know what he might have attempted if death had not taken him at the age of forty-three, although having his second son, fourteen-year-old Giovanni, made a cardinal in 1489 was a master stroke in promoting his legacy. As Pope Leo X (1513–21) Giovanni would use his great powers to complete the transformation of the Medici from city bosses to hereditary princes.

In 1482, the year Savonarola arrived in Florence, Vespasiano da Bisticci wrote that thanks to an "infinite" number of the most excellent and learned men, as great as any of the Ancients, Latin, Hebrew, Greek, and the seven liberal arts were flourishing in the city.[13] Resident sage Marsilio Ficino spoke of Florence as the center of a golden age where, from near extinction, the liberal arts had been restored to light and music and painting flourished.[14] In 1482 the city could boast the greatest concentration of artistic talent in Christendom. Leonardo da Vinci was just departing for Milan, leaving behind his unfinished *Adoration of the Magi*. Andrea del Verrocchio, who could count among his former apprentices Sandro Botticelli, Lorenzo di Credi, Pietro Perugino, and Leonardo, was completing his dramatic sculpture *The Incredulity of Saint Thomas*, and Domenico Ghirlandaio (in whose workshop Michelangelo would begin his apprenticeship in 1488) had just completed his *Last Supper* for the refectory of the convent church of Ognissanti. Botticelli, after his interlude in Rome to work in the Sistine Chapel, undertook a series of mythological paintings, including *La Primavera* and *Birth of Venus*, with its daring nude figure of the goddess.

Religious confraternities and works commissions for churches and public buildings provided opportunities for cultural sharing across class lines. "A whole range of citizens, from little-known major guildsmen through artisans and small businessmen to widows, and even a handful of wage laborers"[15] commissioned religious and secular objects. That same year, 1482, Andrea della Robbia inherited his uncle Luca's workshop and his technique of ceramic glazing, and "introduced virtual mass production" into the making of finely modeled polychrome terra-cotta sculpture and reliefs.[16]

White, blue, green, and yellow della Robbia Madonnas and saints found their way into dozens of Florentine and Tuscan chapels and churches as well as private homes. There was a lively market for cheap paper copies of religious pictures, and many objects were executed in wax, wood, and plaster. Still another opportunity for popular cultural production was in the design and decoration of temporary structures for saints' days, carnival festivities, and civic ceremonies. The disappearance of most of these ephemera has left us with the false impression that art was the monopoly of governments and the wealthy. Often portrayed as living in a world insulated by classical education, exquisite taste, and extreme wealth, the sophisticated Florentine upper classes were actually a product of a civic and religious culture that included "ordinary" people.

Many of Florence's wealthy families patronized the arts; some, notably the Rucellai and Strozzi, had been at it a lot longer than the Medici.[17] But like everything connected with the Medici (and perhaps for the very reason that as relative newcomers they had more to prove), their patronage was on a grander scale and played an outsize part in shaping the physical and cultural environment in which Florentines lived, thought, and worshiped. Their neoclassical residence on the Via Larga designed by Michelozzo set the trend for a generation of splendid Florentine private palaces. Despite the declining profitability of the Medici bank and many other obligations, Piero's two sons, Lorenzo and, until his violent death in 1478, Giuliano, patronized the arts almost compulsively, heirs to the family's passion for the classical aesthetic.

By the early 1480s, with the Florentine economy again going strong, commissions for civic and ecclesiastical projects were increasing and wealthy citizens were striving to outdo each other in the grandeur of their private residences. The Pazzi crisis behind him, Lorenzo was preparing to launch the high-energy phase of his building career by immersing himself in Leon Battista Alberti's *Ten Books on Architecture.* To amass capital for projects like the rural villa at Poggio a Caiano, he began selling some family properties and using his influence at the papal curia to acquire certain others.[18] (According to some sharp-eyed contemporaries, he was also "borrowing" from communal funds.)[19] Lorenzo's aesthetic influence went beyond personal patronage; as a member of countless civic committees and works commissions he was involved in most of the republic's major projects. (He also intervened in other people's private building plans—sometimes by invitation, sometimes not.) Princes and governments asked him to recommend artists and workmen, sent him models and designs for their projects, and begged to see his own.

This intense activity was all the more remarkable because, although still in his thirties, Lorenzo's health was beginning to fail. Frequently in severe pain, he was sometimes bedridden and often recovering at one of his several country estates or taking the waters at a spa. The trials of domestic and foreign politics and the multiple shocks of his brother Giuliano's murder, followed by the deaths of his mother, daughter, and wife, all within a decade, may have taken their toll on his strength; certainly they contributed to the darkening of his mood and gave special meaning to a favorite theme of his love poetry, which he had continued to write all through his youth and under the heavy pressures of public life:

> Time flees, taking flight
> my youth and the happy age pass away.[20]

As with the arts, fifteenth-century humanist and philosophical culture in Florence was the product of diverse influences and an astonishing number of creative minds. Lorenzo's personal endorsements and discriminating patronage guaranteed the success of trends that were in step with his own intellectual and spiritual itinerary. As a youth he had been more interested in cultivating the poetry of Dante and Petrarch than continuing the scholarly and philosophical patronage of his father and grandfather. Lorenzo himself wrote sonnets, love songs, and pastoral, dramatic, and religious poetry much praised by fellow writers and the literary public. With a taste for satirical and erotic verse, he had been a friend and patron of the notorious Luigi Pulci, whose irreverent, bawdy mock-epic *Morgante* delighted many and scandalized others (notably Savonarola who, shortly after his arrival in Florence, began using the *Morgante* as a prime example of the evil effects of "pagan" poetry).[21]

After mid-century, classically educated Florentines had begun to open their minds to philosophy of a more speculative nature. As autocracy transformed citizens into subjects, the old humanist ideal of *vita civile*, active political engagement in a self-governing republic, was losing its relevance, along with the rationale for liberal studies as the education of free, politically engaged citizens.[22] Humanism had absorbed Latin culture and was turning increasingly to Greek thought. Reading Greek texts, debating in symposia, and attending lectures on Plato and Aristotle, some from learned Byzantine exiles, patricians and burghers deliberated on the attractions of a life of contemplation and the search for "the highest good."[23] Platonism was particularly welcomed as providing a balance with the concerns of public life. As an intellectual pursuit that required leisure and a grounding in the liberal arts, the Platonic search for wisdom symbolized aristocratic refinement and offered an alternate way for the ruling class to define itself.

In 1455 Donato Acciaiuoli, one of Florence's leading patrician intellectuals, made the case for philosophical study. "There is too much stupidity, too little wisdom; without the latter no republic has ever been able to last long. If republics are happy, as Plato, the greatest philosopher, believed, when wise men rule, those must be miserable when fools govern rashly."[24] Not that classical literature was to be dropped from the humanist curriculum or that the ideal of the politically engaged life should be made to disappear from Florentine discourse,[25] but the intellectual climate now favored "wisdom" over "action."

This gave center stage to Marsilio Ficino. As the organizer and guiding spirit of the group of philosophy enthusiasts known as the Platonic Academy, he brought Platonism to the center of intellectual discourse in Florence.[26] Ficinian Platonism, an eclectic admixture with Neoplatonic and Neo-Pythagorean texts, Augustinianism, and Christian scholasticism, offered a means of self-perfection through mastery of the "ancient wisdom." This was based on the Neoplatonic idea that the universe was a great chain of being stretching downward from divine unity to the lowest levels of animal existence. Midway in the ontological hierarchy is man, part creature, part god, endowed by his creator with reason and will, who by proper use of his gifts strives to live a moral life and to find his way back to the One. But reason is not powerful enough to make this return journey by itself. The universe has been willed by divine love and it is by love, the handmaiden of will, that humans find their way upward. Love begins in the visible world; in loving other creatures we discern the first traces of our divine maker and are carried upward toward the contemplation of the One and ultimately to union with the divine essence.

Ficino, who took holy orders in 1473 and became a canon of the Cathedral of Florence, professed to see only harmony between Christian revelation and the teachings of the ancient seers. Christ was the latest and highest avatar of divine wisdom; the way of self-perfection was the way of Christian salvation. Love, the highest Platonic virtue, in its metaphysical form held the universe together, in its social form it manifested itself in harmony and brotherhood. Such unifying ideals had at least a theoretical appeal for members of a contentious ruling class as well as for those troubled by the apparent disharmonies of Christianity and "neo-pagan" culture. To his circle of initiates, with whom he kept up a lively, didactic correspondence, Ficino was, in Pythagorean mode, the priestly guardian and interpreter of the divine mysteries. "Pagan" learning was part of the cultural unity of humankind, Eros but the outer husk of Agape.[27] But to understand this a reader had to know how to lift the veil of allegory protecting truth from the profane gaze of the uninitiated.

The elitist implications of such ideas are evident: the sacred mysteries more easily yielded their secrets to those who had leisure, education, and refined sensibilities. Still, Ficino himself did not think they should be restricted to the socially privileged. He popularized his "ancient theology" during a long busy career of lecturing, tutoring, translating, and composing treatises on various aspects of his thought, and there are some indications that he found an audience beyond the liberally educated elite, since there was a demand for Italian translations of his major works.[28]

Lorenzo de' Medici had begun to turn to philosophy after the death of his father in 1469, a change of direction that may have quickened when his beloved mistress Simonetta Vespucci died in 1473. In that year he had a well-publicized encounter with Ficino at Careggi, which he memorialized in his poem *De summo bono* (On the Supreme Good). Whether or not this was a sincere conversion from his earlier, irreverent ways (he distanced himself from Luigi Pulci, for example, playing Prince Hal to Pulci's Falstaff) or a calculated, image-creating move, it had important implications for Lorenzo, for Ficino, and for Florence. Entering into a master-disciple relationship with Ficino was a way for Lorenzo to legitimize his succession to the Medicean intellectual legacy, of assuming Cosimo's mantle of the philosopher-ruler, possessor of esoteric wisdom, united with his people in Platonic love. Lorenzo defended his love sonnets against the charge of carnal sensuality with the Ficinian argument that romantic love properly understood was the longing for the divine.[29] As for Ficino, Lorenzo's endorsement confirmed him as Florence's chief philosophical guru. In the next two decades intellectual and aesthetic discourse in the city became permeated with his Neoplatonic, Hermetic, and Orphic teachings, heavy with mystical ideals of self-perfection and messianic hopes of a new era.[30] The idea of the transformative power of beauty and love ran through the work of the Laurentian poets and humanists, and Botticelli's *Venus* seemed the very embodiment of ethereal love.

The theme of Platonic transformation into a higher love inspired the canzoni and sonnets of another member of the Laurentian circle, the poet Girolamo Benivieni, who based his *Song on Divine and Celestial Love* on Ficino's commentary on Plato's *Symposium.* But Ficino's theosophical marriage of Platonism and Christianity did not always run smoothly, especially for one of Benivieni's anxious temperament. Perhaps because he was depressed by the murder of his friend and patron Giuliano de' Medici in 1478, Benivieni began, as he told his readers, to worry about eternity. When the young philosopher-prince Giovanni Pico della Mirandola first came to Florence in 1484 Benivieni asked him to write a commentary on his love poems. Pico complied, but afterward, according to Benivieni, both men "began to lack some of that spirit and fervor" for the work and decided it was unfitting that "one who professed the laws of Christ should write of divine love as a Platonist and not as a Christian." The love poems and commentary were set aside. Pico himself, settling in Florence in 1489 after clashes with both the Church and civil authority, was resolved to live a more austere Christian life and was writing religious poetry and studying the Bible. When Savonarola returned to Florence in 1490, Pico and Benivieni were impatient to hear him preach and highly receptive to his penitential message. If Benivieni needed any further sign that he must abandon his profane affections it came with the shock of Pico's sudden death on November 17, 1494. God, he decided, must have had a purpose in allowing him to outlive his great friend, and he resolved to make every use of his life for that divine purpose. From then on, Benivieni put his talents as a poet at the service of the Savonarolan crusade.

Pico's haven in Florence had been provided for him by his admirer Lorenzo de' Medici. Savonarola's reassignment to Florence was also due to Lorenzo who, at Pico's request, had intervened with the Dominican authorities. Perhaps, in view of his illness and preoccupation with mortality, Lorenzo wanted the presence of this great preacher on his own behalf as well. Whatever his motive, Il Magnifico once again—and perhaps for the last time—played a key role at a fateful turning point in Florentine culture.

CHAPTER 6

Bologna to Florence

When Savonarola looked back over his prophetic apostolate, each phase seemed to flow smoothly into the next to form a coherent whole, its central meaning his God-appointed mission to Florence. Yet his actual progress was more complicated. During the time he was struggling to improve his preaching skills, and even as he was taking his first apocalyptic soundings, he was expecting to return to Bologna to resume his preparations for an academic post. When he left Florence in 1487 it was not, as some of his myth-making hagiographers had it, because his prophecies had angered Lorenzo de' Medici. Neither Lorenzo nor anyone else in Florence seems to have paid the slightest attention to what fra Girolamo had been saying in San Gimignano. He left Florence because he had been recalled to the Bologna studium to resume his course toward the degree of master of sacred theology.[1]

For a friar aspiring to an academic career this was the decisive year. In addition to his own studies, as master of students in San Domenico of Bologna he would conduct theological disputations and guide his charges through cases of conscience and scriptural interpretation. Meanwhile he would be observed and evaluated by his superiors, who would decide whether he was to be retained in the studium. If the evaluation was favorable, he would continue his studies for the master of sacred theology degree, the next rung on the academic ladder; if not, he would be reassigned to more routine convent duties elsewhere. Fra Girolamo was not retained. In the spring of 1489 he left the studium for a new assignment. He had, apparently, been evaluated and dismissed. This is puzzling, since he was certainly well-prepared, and his selection as studens formalis by his superiors had been a vote of confidence in his academic promise.

The best available clue for solving the puzzle lies in the relations between Savonarola and his superior, Vincenzo Bandelli. Their paths crossed and intertwined inevitably and fatefully. As regent master of the Bologna studium in 1478–79, Bandelli was Savonarola's professor in theology. He was prior of San Marco when fra Girolamo arrived there in 1482, although he left the following year. When Savonarola returned to the studium in 1487 to continue his studies, Bandelli was again there as regent master. As already seen, master and pupil held divergent views on such important issues as the question of Dominican poverty, Savonarola favoring a return to the rigorous austerity of the Order's early years, Bandelli arguing for easing the ban on holding communal property. Fra Girolamo, although a dedicated Thomist, was openly critical of the heavy emphasis on Aristotle and on scholastic disputation in the training of friars. Bandelli, on the other hand, was one of the Order's most prominent practitioners of scholasticism. We can only speculate that Savonarola antagonized Bandelli during that critical year at the studium, 1487–88, for his academic career was terminated at the Lombard Congregation chapter meeting in Milan. Bandelli's recommendation would have been crucial. Perhaps this rejection by his Bologna superiors helps explain why four years later, as soon as he was in a position to do so, he moved to withdraw San Marco from the Lombard Congregation altogether and abandon its heavy emphasis on scholasticism in favor of "an affective, spiritual theology nourished by Sacred Scripture and the writings of the Fathers of the Church."[2] In that parting too Bandelli was to be a principal antagonist.

Separated from the Bologna studium in the spring of 1488, fra Girolamo was reassigned to Santa Maria degli Angeli in his native city of Ferrara. After five years and infrequent exchanges of letters, he saw his family again. But the reunion brought its own strains, some related to his preaching career. Both his father and his maternal uncle Borso had died in the previous two years, and Elena Savonarola was hard-pressed to support the family and to provide dowries for her marriageable daughters. Unreasonably perhaps, she expected some material help from Girolamo and complained that his preaching assignments took him away from Ferrara too much of the time. A long letter he wrote to her reveals something about these discontents, his earlier insecurities and his feelings about his preaching vocation.

Honored Mother,
May the peace of Christ be with you. I know you are surprised that I have not written to you for many days, but . . . there have been no messengers . . . except one of ours who came after Christmas, but then I

was so busy with the holidays that I forgot to write. . . . Afterwards fra Iacopo da Pavia, prior of Sant'Angeli . . . came to us and talked about you and how grieved you were. . . . So, as I am being sent to Genoa to preach this coming Lent and have reached Pavia I write to you . . . to tell you that I'm well, content in mind and healthy in body, although tired of traveling, with yet a long way to go to Genoa. . . . I can well imagine your difficulties for which I continuously pray God for you. . . . If there were some other way I could help you I would do so, but once having freed myself I made myself a slave for the love of Jesus and this love has made me take on the condition of a slave in order to be free.

So, most beloved Mother, do not grieve if I go far from you and hold forth in various cities, because I am doing all this for the salvation of many souls, preaching, exhorting, confessing, teaching, and counseling. . . . If I were to remain always in Ferrara, believe me, I wouldn't reap such fruit as I do elsewhere, because no religious, or very few, reaps the fruit of a holy life in his own land. . . . Thus our Savior says a prophet is not accepted in his own land. So, since God has deigned to elect me, with all my sins, to such an office . . . you should be satisfied that I am in the vineyard of the Lord. . . . If I were [in my own country] and tried to do what I do in other cities I know they would say of me what Christ's countrymen said of him when he preached: "Isn't this the carpenter, the son of the carpenter and the son of Mary?" and they wouldn't listen to him. And of me they would say, "Isn't this master Ieronimo who used to commit the same sins that we do? Well, we know all about him," and they wouldn't pay any attention to what I had to say. . . . But outside my home country such things are not said to me; on the contrary, when I am about to leave, men and women weep and greatly esteem my words. . . . And so, my honored Mother, do not be sad about this because the more I please God, the more my prayers for you will count with him. And don't think he has abandoned you to your tribulations. On the contrary, you should think that you have abandoned him rather than he you, and therefore your scourges [*flagelli*] should compel you to return to him.

Finally, know that my heart is more than ever set on venturing my soul and body and all the knowledge and grace God has given me for the love of God and the salvation of my neighbor. . . . So I beg you not to hinder my course and to be assured that when I can help you in some way I will, and if need be I won't mind coming to Ferrara. . . . I wish you to be patient in all things and comfort our sisters; they should be aware that God has provided for them better than they believe, and that if he had treated them differently, giving them possessions and honors and marrying them off, they would have fallen into various grave sins, worse than they can possibly know, and they would be more caught up in the world than they are. Let them open their eyes and recognize the grace God has given them. . . . Today, after I've eaten I will take the road for Genoa. Pray God to guide me there safely and that I have great results among that people. Greet our uncle and aunt and our cousins.

Written in Pavia in haste, the day of the Conversion of Saint Paul the Apostle 25 January 1490

Your son frate Hieronymo Savonarola.[3]

The advice to his mother and sisters to ignore their material problems and embrace the life of religion is the counsel of a zealot who regards his family's tribulations not only as just punishment for their sins but as a distraction from his own all-important mission.[4] A note of self-satisfaction creeps in as well: his current success compensates for the humiliations he has suffered on account of the family's mediocre social standing (the point of the story of his rejection by Laudomia). And however disappointed he may have been with his dismissal from the Bologna studium, he has found renewed inspiration for his preaching mission. Christ has called him to go out to prophesy in strange lands.

Years later, during his prison interrogation, Savonarola recalled, "I also preached in this manner in Brescia and the same, sometimes, in many other places of Lombardy where I stayed about four years." The "manner," which he recalled as continuing what he had preached in San Gimignano, was apocalyptic. By the time he preached at Brescia he was much more explicit about the coming of the great scourge.[5] One friar reported that he preached after dinner, "explaining the chapter of the Apocalypse which tells of the twenty-four elders [Rev. 4–8] . . . he said that God had sent these twenty-four elders through the world and that one of them had come to him to tell him that he should say that a great scourge was coming to Italy, particularly to Brescia, and that he should call everyone to penitence, for fathers would see their children killed, horribly and pitilessly torn apart in the streets of Brescia, and this in the lifetime of people who were then living and present. This was completely fulfilled in 1500 when the people of Brescia rebelled against the French. The French entered the fortress and staged a great massacre. People waded in blood to their knees, and they sacked the city."[6]

The story of the Brescia prophecy and its misdated confirmation (the sack actually took place in 1512) is told by Pseudo-Burlamacchi who also reports that in the early morning after Christmas, while the Brescia friars recited the Divine Office, they observed Savonarola rapt in ecstasy. For five hours his body did not move, his mind and emotions totally absorbed in the contemplation of God, his face so resplendent that as the brothers returned from chanting the Office they saw the entire church illuminated.[7] Hagiographical enhancement aside, we may assume that fra Girolamo was in a highly charged religious state, which puts his indifference to the mundane troubles of his mother and sisters in deeper context. (It was also at Brescia, according to the same source, that he received a letter from a devout local matron who prophesied the events of his coming career and death in Florence and that he was so terrified that he threw the letter into the fire.)[8]

From Brescia fra Girolamo moved on to Genoa where he preached during Lent. With his appointment as *socius,* or full-fledged member, of the Dominican priory at Mantua, he might reasonably have thought the peripatetic phase of his career had come to an end, but this was not to be. At the chapter meeting of the Lombard Congregation in Como, which he attended, the delegates were asked to decide on a request that fra Girolamo Savonarola be reassigned to San Marco in Florence. That the request had been pending for a year is surprising, considering that it had been made by none other than Lorenzo de' Medici. Master General Gioacchino Torriani seems to have passed Lorenzo's petition on to Vicar General Bandelli, who then referred it to the chapter. In the meantime, he assigned Savonarola to Mantua. Whether this was bureaucratic bumbling or Bandelli's way of muffling Savonarola's growing fame as a preacher can only be guessed.[9] But the chapter granted the request (presumably Savonarola himself voted in favor of it), and he set out for Florence almost immediately.[10]

In the eight years that Savonarola had been absent from Florence, the Magnificent Lorenzo had further dissipated the city's republican legacy. Dazzled, manipulated, and bullied, the citizens had traded the balance of their freedom for the splendors and stability, although not the name, of a hereditary principate. Medici placemen chose the members of the all-important commissions (balie) controlling the selection of candidates for government offices. The Council of Seventy, put in place after the Pazzi conspiracy, gave the regime a semblance of representative government, but the majority of its members were Medici loyalists.

For the routine work of government Lorenzo mainly employed men of modest means and social backgrounds.[11] Lacking the wealth and prestige of the old ruling class, its pretensions and client networks, and dependent on Lorenzo for their careers, the obedience of these functionaries could presumably be counted on. But the price paid was incessant grumbling: the once-proud citizens' republic now appeared to be in the hands of hirelings. More-over, these "upstarts" were no faceless bureaucrats but men from the city or nearby towns, many of them notaries, known by sight and name and more readily demonized than their lofty patron.

The more Lorenzo deprived the old elites of what they considered to be their right to govern, the more reason he had to distrust and fear them. Ottimati resentment sometimes broke through the facade of solidarity. One patrician, Alamanno Rinuccini, had the courage to write a diatribe against Lorenzo's abuses of power after the Pazzi crisis. In his dialogue *On Liberty*, Rinuccini looked back to a quasi-mythical era of republican liberty as it had been portrayed in the rhetoric of the civic humanists employed by the pre-Medicean oligarchy. As an exposé of Lorenzo's tyranny, however, it was no less valid for that.[12] Whether Rinuccini (who lived in self-imposed exile on his country estate) spoke for a substantial number of his cohort is hard to say; most of them expressed their disaffection more discreetly. Conspirators were punished by death or banishment and confiscation of property. Those whose lives were spared to go abroad joined the "contrary commonwealth" already peopled by the exiles of Cosimo and Piero, living restlessly for the day they could return home to reclaim their birthright and take their revenge.[13]

That Lorenzo should have been the instrument of the return to Florence of the very person whose name would become synonymous with the revolt against "Medici tyranny" was an irony of history which Savonarola devotees regarded as providential. It is generally believed (by Pseudo-Burlamacchi among others) that Lorenzo acted to please his guest, the philosopher prince Giovanni Pico, Count of Mirandola—that, in fact, Pico composed the letter of request which was then copied by Lorenzo's chancellor Ser Piero Dovizi da Bibbiena. As previously mentioned, Pico probably met Savonarola at the Dominican disputation in Reggio Emilia and had been impressed by his piety and learning. Both men were in Florence between 1483 and 1485, where they had opportunities to renew their acquaintance. Pico then moved on to the University of Paris where he took the first of a series of missteps that led to imprisonment and spiritual crisis. "With strange imprudence" he composed a set of philosophical propositions incorporating some doctrinally suspect views of the Paris Aristotelian school and announced he would defend them publicly in Rome.

In May 1486 Pico stopped in Arezzo where he committed another impru-dence: he made off with a certain "genteel Florentine lady"—against her will according to the official reports, voluntarily according to Pico's sister-in-law. The lady, Madonna Margherita, not only had a husband, the husband was Giuliano Mariotto de' Medici, an Arezzo tax official and cousin to Lorenzo de' Medici. Messer Giuliano and a company of armed men gave hot pursuit and caught up with the party at the Sienese border. In the fracas that followed eighteen men were reportedly killed and Pico was wounded. Pico was shut up in an Arezzo prison; Margherita was restored to her husband. While Lorenzo expressed sympathy for the affronted husband, he also did what he could to downplay the gravity of the incident and secured Pico's release.[14]

Pico's misadventures continued. After a brief respite in Florence he went to Perugia to study Arab philosophy, magic, and Kabbalah with Elia del Medigo and other Jewish teachers. In November 1486 he arrived in Rome and prepared to defend his *Conclusions,* now expanded to nine hundred. In his preface he asserted that all philosophies tended toward a single, unified truth and declared that unlike all other natural creatures, humans were endowed with the freedom to choose their own place in the universe.

The manifesto, known as the *Oration on the Dignity of Man,* regarded as one of the classic texts of Renaissance humanism, failed to appease the Roman authorities.[15] Allegations about Pico's defense of natural magic and Jewish Kabbalah and suspicions about his enthusiasm for Arab philosophy had already filtered into the curia and aroused the ire of Pope Innocent VIII. The pope suspended Pico's public disputation and appointed a clerical commission to examine the *Conclusions* he proposed to defend. Seven of these were condemned, six others declared suspect. When Pico refused to retract, the commission condemned all thirteen. In May 1487 Pico published an *Apologia* (dedicated to Lorenzo de' Medici) reaffirming his admiration for Kabbalah and his belief in natural magic. He accused his critics of ignorance and boldly invoked the right of freedom of thought in matters not defined by Christian doctrine.

In August the Church responded: a papal bull condemned all nine hundred propositions and sent out an order for Pico's arrest. Pico fled, eluded capture, and headed for Paris; but in January 1488, near Lyons, he was stopped and imprisoned in the fortress of Vincennes. This time it was not local officials but the pope himself who had to be appeased. Influential admirers and supporters set diplomatic wheels in motion and won his release. Among them was Lorenzo de' Medici who, although engaged in delicate negotiations with Rome to secure a cardinal's hat for his second son Giovanni, took the risk of displeasing the pope by interceding and offering Pico a haven in Florence via a letter from Marsilio Ficino. "To a strong man any country is fatherland," Ficino wrote, "but Saturn destines you to cleave to ours. Once before, under that great conjunction [of Saturn and Aquarius] he commanded you to live in Florence and you came. So, be happy and be Florentine."[16]

"The Count of Mirandola has come to stay with us here," wrote Lorenzo to the Florentine ambassador in Rome, "where he lives a very holy life and is like a monk. He has written and continues to write excellent works of theology, comments on Psalms and on other worthy theological matters. He recites the priest's ordinary office, observes the fasts and strictest continence, lives without much of a household or pomp, and takes only what is necessary. In my opinion he is an example to other men."[17] Lorenzo obviously intended these assurances to reach the ears of the pope and his court, so he may have exaggerated the conventionality of Pico's studies as well as his monk-like austerity (Pico was later reported to have been keeping a concubine). Still, Pico's new mode of life was decidedly more subdued. Settling into Lorenzo's villa in Fiesole, he worked on his biblical commentaries and pursued his lifelong project of reconciling Platonic and Aristotelian philosophy. It was during this period that Lorenzo wrote his letter to Dominican General Torriani, presumably at Pico's instigation, requesting that fra Girolamo Savonarola be reassigned to Florence.

Lorenzo too had been on his spiritual odyssey, less sensational than Pico's and decidedly less picaresque. Often crippled or bedridden by his painful illnesses, he composed lauds for Holy Week, revised his Carnival songs to eliminate profane passages, and began a commentary on his earlier sonnets, exploring their metaphysical and religious meanings. In general his poetry took on "a loftier and more thoughtful tone."[18] At the same time, in what has been described as a choice for "concrete and solid . . . erudition" over the "ambiguous veil of beautiful poetic images," he moved closer to his sons' former tutor, the great humanist philologist Angelo Poliziano, whom he elevated to the coveted professorship of rhetoric and poetry in the Florentine studium in 1480.[19]

Neither illness nor concern for his spiritual well-being distracted Lorenzo from his worldly interests. By providing a haven for Pico Lorenzo not only acquired a scholarly guide for his own religious quest, he also enhanced his reputation as a generous and powerful patron and sent a signal to Rome that although he was a loyal son of the Church he held Florence's philosophical culture under his personal protection. Rome, however, was not to be so easily put off. After the condemnation of Pico's *Nine Hundred Theses* and the rejection of his *Apologia,* Innocent VIII threatened action against his latest work, *Heptaplus,* an unconventional exploration into Genesis which appeared in 1489. Lorenzo was furious and charged that certain ignorant and malignant devils at Rome were using the pope as a shield to persecute an innocent and pious man. Even as his envoy in Rome was employing all his talents to ward off this new threat, however, there was a new provocation. Members of the curia were shocked by Marsilio Ficino's new book, *De vita* (Concerning Life), a sober treatment of astrology, natural magic, and the occult, and were considering prosecuting him for heresy. Ficino, an icon of Florentine culture as well as a priest and canon of the Florentine cathedral, was obliged to enlist powerful friends to intervene on his behalf.[20]

While Lorenzo resisted outside interference in Florence's intellectual life, other culture wars were raging on the home front. Angelo Poliziano in the preface to his *Stanze* of 1489 (dedicated to Lorenzo de' Medici) complained of the malignant and philistine preachers speaking from local pulpits who "defame humanistic letters to unwary, ordinary folk; they bluster . . . emboldened by their own crass uncouthness which, as Saint Jerome said, they deem to be the only sanctity; they fulminate against literature and its devotees, not even hesitating to proclaim their disapproval of those famous Greeks . . . Basil, Chrysostom, the Gregories, and among the Latins Cyprian, Ambrose, Augustine, and Jerome."[21]

One of the preachers who had been haranguing the "unwary, ordinary folk" of Florence was the Franciscan Bernardino da Feltre. Like his mentor, Bernardino da Siena, he attacked the everyday vices—vanity, pride, anger, avarice, and lust—in unabashedly graphic terms. ("Woman, God gave you breasts so you could nourish your children; instead your breasts feed the eyes of men!") Bernardino kept his theology simple: humans had free will and could earn salvation by availing themselves of the sacraments and by doing good. He warned against intellectual sophistication: the more science and learning, as at Padua, the more sin, he declared. A colorful showman and master manipulator of crowds, Bernardino adopted his namesake's technique, staging bonfires of vanities to dramatize the conquest of sin. Into the fire went jewelry, pagan books ("Each time we read the ribald Ovid we crucify Christ!"), and lewd pictures. But as a Franciscan, Bernardino's asceticism was informed with the communal values of late medieval Italy, not those of the Egyptian desert: Christian virtue was as much a civic as an individual responsibility. To combat avarice he urged the establishment of a communal loan fund, or Monte di

Pietà, and its corollary, the expulsion of the Jews. As patriotic citizens, he argued, Christians had the responsibility to sacrifice their individual well-being to the good of the entire community. Thus, Florentines should contribute to a Monte di Pietà which would make cheap loans to the poor, and Jews would no longer be able "to suck the blood of Christians with their usury." In March 1488, a mob of boys burst out of the cathedral, where they had been listening to a sermon by Bernardino, and attacked a nearby Jewish pawn shop, desisting only after an hour's struggle with the communal police. Bernardino was arrested and, to the great resentment of the populace which lauded him as a saint, expelled from the territory. Dire punishments were forthcoming for the magistrates of the *Otto di Guardia* (Eight of Security) who carried out the sentence, according to Landucci; one broke his head in a fall from his horse, another died insane.[22] A few years later Bernardino was readmitted.

Another Franciscan agitator constantly on the verge of expulsion was Domenico da Ponzo, a supporter of Bernardino, rumored to be a spy for the Duke of Milan. (Machiavelli later referred to him as the stereotypical crafty friar.)[23] In contrast to these populist icons, Poliziano's model preacher was the Augustinian Mariano da Genazzano. Mariano has been portrayed, mainly by Savonarola's partisans, as a shallow aesthete and flatterer who catered to the rhetorical tastes of the Laurentian circle and sometimes resorted to theatrical gestures, such as pretending to collect his own tears and throwing them out to his audience. But the intellectually discriminating Poliziano regarded him as "second to none in theology, among all the preachers we have heard not only the most prudent but the most eloquent . . . and, while not professing a forbidding and rigid austerity [he is] praiseworthy for the exceptional severity of his morals and his appreciation of the ornaments of poetry and the lovely variety, splendor and pleasures of literature." Perhaps also because Mariano supported Lorenzo's political interests in his sermons, Lorenzo built the Augustinians a new monastery just outside the San Gallo Gate.[24] There Lorenzo, Poliziano, Pico, and other men of letters gathered as if it were an "academy of Christian Religion."[25]

Neither Bernardino nor Mariano complicated his sermons with heavy doses of formal doctrine or abstruse theology. Faith in Christ's redemptive sacrifice was sine qua non; the sacraments were indispensable as sources of grace; the will was free to perform good works and avoid the devil's incitements to riches, pride, earthly glory, and fleshly pleasures. Confession was required once a year—more often only if one's conscience demanded it. The more populist Bernardino especially railed against greed and the mistreatment of the poor, but neither he nor Mariano challenged existing social and political institutions or had much to say about clerical corruption or the need to reform the Church. Nor, as far as we can tell, were these star preachers assiduously working the apocalyptic vein. Bernardino and Domenico da Ponzo occasionally warned that signs indicated the end of the world was near —Ponzo increasingly, perhaps in competition with Savonarola—but neither ventured very deeply into eschatology.[26] Mariano's elegant sermons contained no eschatology at all, at least not enough to find its way into the diary of Margherita Soderini, the patrician woman who attended and assiduously recorded what she remembered of them.[27] Rather than from its preachers, the rich loam of prophecy in late fifteenth-century Florence was seeded by the anonymous and pseudonymous texts and prophecies, astrological predictions, poems, letters from Toledo, Bridget of Sweden and Second Charlemagne prophecies, and Sibylline pronouncements that circulated and even gained a new lease on life with the introduction of the printing press.

The preacher Pico and Lorenzo had been looking for was not to be found among the rabble-rousing likes of a Bernardino da Feltre, a Domenico da Ponzo, or the learned, polished Mariano da Genazzano. To help him through his religious crisis and accompany him in his biblical and theological studies, Pico needed a mentor of exceptional spirituality and deep Christian learning, one who could not be accused of partiality to the poets and pagan authors or known for crass anti-Jewish incitements. Besides pleasing his princely guest and allaying the unpopularity of his expulsion of Bernardino da Feltre, Lorenzo had his own reasons for inviting Savonarola: a preacher who boldly denounced the moral rot in Rome and publicly called upon the Church to reform itself might serve as a counterweight to a politically interfering pope to whom Il Magnifico owed the elevation of his son to the College of Cardinals and did not wish to oppose openly.

A preacher of such lofty austerity could also be a useful ally in Lorenzo's patronage of mendicant reform. Two years earlier Il Magnifico had enlisted a delegation of Observantist friars to introduce reform into the Convent of Santa Caterina of Siena in Pisa, which until then had remained outside the reform movement. Now he turned his attention to Florentine San Marco, which had been lagging in reputation and failing to recruit an adequate number of novices. Especially needed were new friars from wealthy and influential families.[28] With new, inspired leadership San Marco might rise above the lax jurisdiction of the Lombard Congregation and become once more the vital spiritual and cultural center his grandfather Cosimo had intended.

CHAPTER 7

Lo, the Sword of God!

Plodding the dusty mountain road to Florence in the heat of early summer, fra Girolamo stopped, exhausted, at the Apennine town of Pianoro. There an angel in the form of a man helped him to rest and refreshment, then accompanied him on his journey. At Florence's San Gallo Gate the mysterious stranger left him with this charge: "Do what God has sent you to Florence to do." (Pseudo-Burlamacchi said he heard this story from Savonarola's devoted colleague fra Bartolomeo da Faenza who said he had it from fra Girolamo himself.)[1]

After his arrival, in May or June of 1490, Savonarola resumed his old office of lector at San Marco, teaching philosophy and explaining biblical texts to his fellow friars. But this rising star in the northern constellation of Italy's preachers, a champion of austere reform with a riveting apocalyptic message of divine wrath and punishment, had not been brought back merely to teach elementary logic and philosophy to novices. Although not a popular hero on the order of a Bernardino da Feltre or a silver-tongued rhetorician in the mold of Mariano da Genazzano, he came—if not escorted by an angel—at least at the behest of two of the city's illustrious men. Pseudo-Burlamacchi describes him idyllically surrounded by admiring friars and laymen—"not ignoramuses but the learned, and men of letters"—who came to the convent garden to sit at his feet and hear his "celestial teaching."[2] In less than three months he needed a larger venue and announced that he would move to San Marco's church. There, on August 1, he began a course of evening "lessons" on the Apocalypse, which ran until early January. Beginning October 31, on feast day mornings he also preached on the First Letter of John. From this time on he was seldom out of the public eye.

What the public saw was a man of thirty-eight, slight of build, short to

middling height. Dark bristling eyebrows, bright eyes, and a broad, readily
furrowing brow gave him an intense, severe look, further accented by a prominent beaked nose. His jaw was swarthy and his lips full, the lower slightly
pendulous.[3] He would speak "new things in a new manner," he announced,
meaning that he intended to replace the cerebral intricacies of the scholastic
sermon with a plainer, Scripture-based exposition.[4] One who heard him said:
"He introduced an almost new way of speaking the word of God, that is,
apostolically, without dividing the sermon, not starting with a question,
avoiding the singing of eloquent embellishments. His only purpose was to
expound something of the Old Testament and introduce the simplicity of the
early Church."[5] We have already seen him experimenting with a new preaching style during his first stay in Florence. Still, years of scholastic training
hardened into habit did not let go of him easily. Although he promised to
leave out "divisions and arguments, irrelevant digressions and excessive citations of authorities," some of these features of the scholastic *sermo modernus*
remained with him always.[6]

In still another sense the Apocalypse sermons were unequivocally new: he
delivered them with a conviction and an authority he had previously hesitated
to claim, drawing upon the capital accumulated in years of studying and
teaching Scripture and poring over the commentaries and glosses of the
masters—Augustine, Gregory the Great, Pseudo-Dionysius, John Cassian,
Nicholas of Lyra, Albert the Great, and Saint Thomas, among others. All
these he had assimilated into his own prophetic message and practiced in the
pulpits of northern Italy. Now he spoke the message in a voice with the
sureness of a seasoned guide, taking his rapt listeners through the Christian
drama of sin, divine punishment, and penance and unveiling the mysteries of
renewal and Last Things.[7]

In fact, he did begin with a traditional scholastic *questio:* how do we know
that the time is near? And his answer: "not because of the diverse prophecies
of Joachim [of Fiore], Saint Vincent [Ferrer], and others, which simple folk
are prone to believe, not by visions, which, as Ecclesiastes says, only fools are
quick to trust, but by the evidence of reason and the revealed truth of Scripture."[8] Seeing that good prelates are lacking, that religion has become nego-
tiable and the sacraments polluted, that the world abounds with lukewarm
faith and sinfulness, he has turned to the Apocalypse where, in the first
chapter, he reads: "this is the revelation of God to Christ . . . the hour of
fulfillment is near."[9]

In Savonarola's medieval worldview society was a moral community, united in the search for God's grace. Ordered hierarchically, like creation itself, its leaders held their power from God and were answerable to him for the spiritual and material welfare of their people. To these leaders, then, he addressed his harshest words: officials "great and petty" grasp for payoffs; in their subservience to rulers they search ceaselessly for new taxes; they undermine statutes, condemn innocent men, and let the guilty go free; with their oppressive tax burdens governments force usury upon the people. He was equally unsparing of his own kind: prelates contaminate all of society with their pride and lust for power; clerics flatter princes, read Scripture with a blind eye, and "sacrifice to demons." Avaricious and wanton, they commit unspeakable crimes and cause endless scandal. The regular clergy (monks and friars), who are lukewarm in their vocations, vie with each other for the money of the wealthy and treat themselves to the fruits of greed. Avoiding frequent confession and communion they violate their vows of chastity and contaminate everything with their lust. Everyone keeps silent and lets evil grow; as Saint Thomas wrote, our minds and feelings are dulled by gluttony and lust (*Summa theologica* II.II. 15.3). As Matthew says, woe to the world that such scandals arise! Princes will hang or be killed in other ways (Matt. 18.7). Some will be made clean by fire or water (Num. 31.23).

Of the world's seven ages we are living in the fourth, but now, almost 1,500 years after the birth of Christ, the Fifth Age is approaching, the age of Antichrist, universal evil, and divine judgment. Demonic clerics, prelates, and all the wise and powerful of the earth will be scourged: "I have given [Jezebel, false prophetess] time to do penance but she refuses to repent of her fornication. Therefore I will fling her on a bed of pain and visit her lovers with terrible punishment unless they do penance for their actions, and I will kill her children. All the churches will know that I examine all thoughts and all hearts, and that I will give to each one of you according to your works [Rev. 2.21–24]." After great destruction the Church will be renewed—changed spiritually, not materially—and the conversion of the Turks and of all other pagan and infidel peoples, the Jews among them, will follow.

The surviving outlines and notes for these sermons do not tell us precisely what Savonarola said in the pulpit or how he said it—the gestures, intonations, asides, silences, and improvisations that were so effective a part of his pulpit oratory. Fra Giovanni Caroli, a learned theologian of the Conventual Dominican Convent of Santa Maria Novella and as such virtually programmed to be unfriendly to the "foreign" preacher of upstart San Marco, had this to say about fra Girolamo's performance:

He began to read the Apocalypse, in which there are great mysteries, hidden from common knowledge and perhaps not yet revealed. The common people liked what he made of it . . . visions of ruin, voices, candelabras, trumpets, precious stones, terrible thrones, and marvelous damsels, dragons, angelic battles, and many other things, all loaded with spiritual and sacred meanings. Gates and walls and lightning bolts and hail over the earth he described so elegantly and aptly as to persuade all doubters, but especially people devoted to such things and curious about them. Thus his sermons inflamed everyone's mind. It seemed as if it was not he who was talking, nor was it organized in the usual way. It was as if the spirit was talking through his mouth. So the fame of his teaching and of his uprightness grew and the people fell in behind him, as you know.[10]

There were those who, seizing upon fra Girolamo's criticisms of the rich and powerful and his championing of the poor, sneered that he was the "preacher of the desperate." His followers were mocked as *Piagnoni* (Wailers), and the name stuck—a label of scorn to his critics, a badge of pride to his devotees. Public corruption, unequal taxes, selective application of the laws, and harsh penalties for worker protest were common grievances in the oligarchic regimes of fourteenth- and fifteenth-century Italy, and any mendicant preacher who aimed to attract a popular following had to project sympathy for them. Savonarola did likewise, but he was preaching the Apocalypse, not social revolution. A good Christian, he often declared, did not aspire to leave the station in which he was born. For the failure of the rich and powerful to do justice, God, not man, would exact the price. Still, the more evils he could cite, the more it strengthened his case that divine retribution was near.

What God had in store for humanity after the universal cleansing and conversion, whether a millennial reign of Christian peace and love on earth or the Day of Judgment and the end of the world, was and remained ambiguous. Two centuries after Joachim of Fiore had revived early Christian expectations of a New Age of the Spirit, what Savonarola called "the diverse prophecies of Joachim, Saint Vincent, and others" were so deployed in popular belief that he had to begin his Apocalypse sermons with a disclaimer: he was not basing his certainty of the coming divine scourge on such prophecies but on Scripture and the ruinous state of the world. Whether this was a blanket rejection of millenarian expectations or simply an assertion that his own prophecies had scriptural authority is not clear. Nowhere in these sermons does he say that an earthly millennial reign of the Spirit would come before the Day of Judgment and the end of time. His liberal use of apocalyptic phrases and images—a New Heaven and a New Earth, the New Jerusalem, the coming renewal of the Church, and the conversion of the infidel—does not resolve the matter; Christians had been arguing over the meaning of these same texts and images for centuries. It seems likely that Savonarola still followed the non-millenarian reading of Nicholas of Lyra, whose Apocalypse commentary was one of his main authorities. But on one point he was certain: the divine scourge was coming and soon.

Pico, Ficino, Poliziano, Girolamo Benivieni, and others of the Laurentian circle who had expected Savonarola to be an ally in the battles against ecclesiastical censorship must have heard the Apocalypse sermons with some unease. Fra Girolamo denounced poets, clerics who read [pagan] poets, and artists who painted "nude Venuses." His insistence that philosophy and science had no claim to true wisdom rendered Ficino's grand synthesis of Neoplatonism and Christianity and Pico's reconciliation of the biblical and Aristotelian accounts of creation not only futile but sacrilegious. Where Laurentians celebrated the renaissance of classical antiquity as the glory of the present golden age, Savonarola saw it as one of the signs of the coming of Antichrist. Nevertheless, they, and with them a significant part of Florence's intellectual elite, greeted Savonarola with respect, even with reverence, attesting not only to the life-altering power of his preaching but also to the need to keep in step with their common patron, Lorenzo de' Medici.[11] If any of them harbored a contrary opinion they kept it to themselves, at least for the time being. Although Ficino must have been offended by Savonarola's attacks on magic and astrology, even he was briefly "seduced" by the preacher's "diabolical powers."[12]

Ficino's discomfort reflected the strains already beginning to trouble the Medici "brigade." Lorenzo's own turn toward a more conventional piety weakened his ties with Ficino, although there was never an open break. Relations between Ficino and Giovanni Pico also were growing tenuous. Pico offended Ficino by openly criticizing his Neoplatonism and by writing against astrology, and Lorenzo's partiality to his princely guest made Ficino feel that he was being supplanted as the Medici's star philosopher. Other members of the Laurentian circle could not avoid being affected by these tensions. Some followed Ficino; others, notably the great classicist Angelo Poliziano, the Franciscan theologian fra Giorgio Benigno Salviati, poets Ugolino Verino and Girolamo Benivieni, and Domenico Benivieni, sometime professor in the studio and canon of San Lorenzo, accompanied Pico into the camp of "the Frate," as everyone had begun to call him.

Lorenzo himself kept his counsel and his distance. If he attended any of the sermons there is no record of it. (Savonarola frequently complained that princes and magnates seldom came to hear him preach and when they did come they wanted to hear only pleasant things.)[13] Il Magnifico could not have been happy about the denunciations of despotic rulers, corrupt officials, and exploiters of the poor. Eight years later, in his farewell sermon of March 18, 1498, fra Girolamo recalled that in the early days of his preaching five leading citizens had come to warn him against talking about such things. Although they denied they were on a mission from Lorenzo, he sent them back to their master with the advice that he do penance for his sins. Whether the message had reached Lorenzo he did not know. Many others, the Frate said, had given him the same advice, warning that he could be expelled. His reply, as he recalled, had been to assert that he had no fear of exile: Florence was but a grain of sand in a vast land, and in any case he, the foreigner, would remain while the citizen would be the one to go.[14]

A more detached appraisal of relations between Lorenzo and fra Girolamo came some years later from Francesco Guicciardini, whose father, Piero, had been a leading Piagnone. In his *History of Florence,* Guicciardini wrote that Lorenzo had not been pleased with Savonarola's preaching but took no action because it "did not touch him in a vital part."[15] Apparently so long as the preacher's attacks on the rich and powerful were generic (Savonarola named no names), and so long as he started no riots, Lorenzo could afford to shrug them off. With his health deteriorating alarmingly, Lorenzo was preoccupied to confirm the succession of his eldest son Piero and could not risk another unpopular and divisive move.

Meanwhile the apocalyptic whirlwind moved from San Marco to the Cathedral where Savonarola was invited to preach for Lent.[16] On February 16, Ash Wednesday, 1491, he mounted to his new pulpit. Filling the vast nave with the sound of prophecy, he exhorted the congregation to penitence for "the end will come quickly." Every day until the Wednesday after Easter, fifty sermons in all, he drew upon his rich fund of biblical texts, passing easily between literal and moral meanings. Like Elijah, he has come to accuse King Ahab and his family of bringing drought and famine to the land by forsaking the Lord's commandments (3 Kings 18). Like Amos, he declares that the famine was not of the body but of the spirit, a hunger and thirst to hear the word of the Lord (Amos 8.11–12). Yet, with Paul, he understands that people demand to hear bizarre, extraordinary things and that preachers, in their desire to please, cater to them, whereas to hear the true word of the Lord they must shut their ears to the professors and their so-called authorities, their "gentile" books, their refinements, and new way of speaking, for as Isaiah said, they bring dismay to the carders and weavers, the spinners and artisans (Isa. 19.9). If they do these things they can turn to the true wisdom, the knowledge that the purpose of life is to render honor and glory to God, and to do penance—for this is the time! He knows that this is not easy for them, but the very fact of his own presence among them signals that it is the beginning, therefore he will adopt a new kind of preaching, for as Isaiah says, "The spirit of the Lord God is upon me, for the Lord has anointed me [Isa. 61.1]."

It was a bold start, sparing no one. Claiming a divine mandate, he chastised "the king" and his family for impiety, dismissed "the doctors" with their pagan books and their rhetoric, and pointedly heaped scorn on crowd-pleasing preachers.[17] Would the city's mighty continue to tolerate him? Although he claimed in his final sermon eight years later that he had had no fear, at the time he had observed that preachers who tell intolerable truths are silenced by decrees or corrupted with rewards and honors, victims of a soul murder worse than the killing of their bodies.[18] Midway through Lent, he assessed his situation in a letter to fra Domenico da Pescia.

(March 10, 1491)

Most beloved brother in Christ Jesus,

Peace and joy in the Holy Spirit. Our cause goes well, for God is doing wonderful things, although there is strong opposition among the mighty. But I'll tell you all about that in detail when you return; it's not wise to write about these things now. Many feared, and some still do, that the same thing will happen to me as to fra Bernardino [da Feltre]. Certainly our position here has its dangers, but I have always put my trust in the Lord, knowing that the heart of the king is in the hand of God and he turns it whichever way he wills [Prov. 21.1]. You also must take heart and be steadfast. . . . Don't worry if there are many in this city who do not come running to hear us preach; it's enough to announce such things to a few.

I often announce the renovation of the Church and the coming tribulations, not categorically, but always with the support of Scripture so that no one can reproach me, unless it is someone who doesn't wish to walk in the right path. The Count [Pico della Mirandola] grows steadily more devout and often comes to hear me preach. I can't send you any alms, for although there has been money from the Count, you must wait a little, for good reasons.[19]

Even as he attempted to encourage his devotees he had his own doubts and fears. As he later reported, he was finishing work on the sermon for the next day, the second Sunday of Lent (February 27, 1491) when he suddenly put the text aside, vowing to preach on (apocalyptic matters) no more. All that day and night he struggled with his decision, unable to find a way open to him. The next morning, exhausted, he heard himself say, "Fool, don't you understand that it is God's will that you preach in that manner?" Whereupon he entered the pulpit and preached a "terrifying sermon."[20] He was like Jeremiah, who, though mocked, chained, and beaten, felt compelled to preach the word of God in his heart, to prophesy to the princes of Judah and to Jerusalem the terrible destruction that would be visited on that place (Jer. 19–20). He was like Jonah who despite all obstacles fulfilled his mission to prophesy destruction to the great city of Ninevah (Jon. 3.3–4). After hesitating all through the previous day and night he was constrained to promise that God would smash the vessel that was Italy, especially this part of it.

With a vehemence unusual even for him, Savonarola lashes out at the intertwined ills of Church and city. Like the people who sacrifice to alien gods, so Christians, even bishops and priests, have replaced the worship of God with reverence for money. Families steer their sons into the priesthood in exchange for benefices, consuming the Church's substance. Even the most minor saints have their church bells and their feasts. New altars and new (statues of) the Virgin Mary are constantly "discovered." For money anything is available, but not to the poor; indeed, if a poor man earns fifty he has to pay a hundred. Widows and the poor are told, "Pay! Pay!" Murderers go free while the innocent are blamed. Young girls are exploited. Filthy sodomites— even some who have wives—have boys brought to them in their storerooms and shops. Women use the church as a brothel; the streets are full of whores. To the poor he can only say, be patient, bear up, wait for God. To the rich, however, the Lord said, "Woe to you patricians. . . . I will bring affliction upon you! No longer will the city be called Florentia, but [a place of] turpitude and blood and a robbers' cave [Jer. 7.11]." The Last Days are almost upon them. After six days, that is, after all have transcended the body, solid in faith in the Holy Trinity, they will be led up to a secret place on the great mountain of contemplation where Christ will be transfigured among them (Luke 9.28–29). But let the disciples be warned not to speak of this vision until after the Resurrection when Christ will come in glory and all will be fulfilled. For now we cannot understand; we can only pray.

On May 16, 1491, the brothers of San Marco elected fra Girolamo their prior.[21] Pseudo-Burlamacchi would have us believe that one of his first acts was to assert his independence from Lorenzo de' Medici. Newly elected heads of religious houses were expected to pay a ceremonial visit to the city's first citizen to offer their homage, but "the servant of God" refused, preferring to give private thanks to God. When some friars urged him to reconsider, he replied. " 'Who elected me prior, Lorenzo or God?' 'God,' they answered. 'Well then it is my Lord God whom I want to thank. Not any mortal man.' And he arose and left." Hearing this, the account continues, Lorenzo complained to his intimates, "A foreign friar has come to live in my house and doesn't deign to come to visit me." But he continued trying to win Savonarola over with acts of generosity.[22] If the story is true (Pseudo-Burlamacchi is our only source), it subverts its hagiographic intention: Savonarola comes off as more churlish than principled, Lorenzo more forbearing than tyrannical.

The same biographer tells another story of these early days of Savonarola's priorate. He himself was present, he says, when Savonarola announced to the brothers that they would be abandoning San Marco for Montecavo, deep in the chestnut forests above Careggi. There they would build a new convent and pursue a more austere and spiritually rewarding life. The land had been donated, plans were set, and the monies in hand. The younger friars were enthusiastic but the "bad older" brothers objected, arguing that the move would be a disaster for all of them and its religious benefit nil. They gave the alarm to the families of the young friars and persuaded them to intervene. Greatly disappointed, Savonarola abandoned the venture.[23] It is hard to believe that a prior of San Marco, even one as independent as Pseudo-Burlamacchi's Savonarola, would have defied the convent's chief patron by planning to abandon it. Perhaps, at the distance of a quarter century, the hagiographer's memory promoted what had been no more than a rumination into a full-blown enterprise. If there is any truth to the story, it is that Savonarola's reforming ambitions were still tentative and that as yet he had not conceived that his prophetic mission was divinely linked with the destiny of Florence.

The account of the aborted move, fanciful or not, prompts a closer look at the San Marco community under Savonarola's leadership. In the more than quarter century since the death of its founder patron, Cosimo de' Medici, the convent had lost some of its luster both as an intellectual center and model of Observantist spirituality. Recruitment was modest, with an average of six novices per year, few from the important families whose money and influence were critical, and few whose piety earned more than routine praise. As Savonarola's magnetic presence began to be felt, that trend was reversed. Slowly at first, then with increasing momentum, a stream of new vocations came to San

Marco and its sister house in Fiesole. In the next few years the spate would swell to a flood, causing alarming shortages of living space and funds for construction. Savonarola turned all misgivings aside with prophetic confidence:

> Some years ago, when we were about seventy, someone complained that we were too few. I told them . . . the time will come when the prophecy of Isaiah will be verified in us: "Lord, the place is small, give me room that I may live" . . . and now so many have come that there is no room for them, and every day they din in my ears that there is no room. . . . Now we're about 200. . . . "O frate, how will you handle the expense of so many people?" But I know what I'm going to do. One of these days I'll run out and with the crowd behind me, I'll go into one of those palaces of yours and say, "We want to stay here."[24]
>
> I tell you so many people will come to our religion that it will spread through all of Tuscany and not only Tuscany but as far as the infidels. I'll give you a sign: if it isn't verified you will say I'm a false prophet.
>
> In our religon there are three languages in perfection, that is Latin, Greek, and Hebrew, and we also have Chaldean [Aramaic] and Moresco [Arabic]. Don't think God has sent us this [knowledge] without a reason. So come ahead my son. . . . Come soon because you will have had to learn these languages by the time the sword arrives.

Not all who answered the call were equally welcome, however:

> But some will protest: "Why won't you take me?" Don't complain I tell you; the Lord has greater need for those who are educated. It's true we also take some to do the exterior work, but only as many as we need.[25]

Indeed, some of the newcomers were highly educated, even distinguished. Niccolò Serratico, who took the habit in 1494, was a student of Latin letters. The patrician Zanobi Acciaiuoli, who came in 1496, was an accomplished humanist and future papal librarian; Leonardo Pietro di Colle and Malatesta Sacromoro, entering in 1496, were specialists in church law; and Giorgio Vespucci, a cathedral canon from a prominent family, who received his habit from fra Girolamo in 1497 at age sixty-four, was a Greek and Latin scholar. At least two were Jewish converts; one, Clemente Abramo, was a Sephardic rabbi skilled in Hebrew and learned in Scripture.[26]

Presumably these learned newcomers were expected to enrich the convent culture as well as to prepare younger brothers to go out to preach the Gospel to the unbelievers of the East. Beyond a few glimpses of fra Girolamo himself studying Hebrew and Scripture with his charges, however, there is little evidence that he succeeded in establishing a thriving program of Semitic languages and biblical exegesis. A decade later San Marco's fra Santi Pagnini was to become renowned for his translation of the Bible.[27] But Savonarola's design of forming a cadre of learned preachers who would bring the word of salvation to the infidel "at the time of the sword" appears to have died with him.

Whatever its prospects for universal proselytizing, San Marco's version of "our religion" was already captivating the Florentines themselves. Men and women came to get spiritual counsel, gossip, exchange information, or simply to be near this new charismatic center. In his Lenten sermons of 1491 Savonarola complained of visitors who were coming to see him about "foolish things." This was a kind of honor that didn't please him, he said wryly; he would be available to visitors after Easter, but let them see to it that they come for a useful purpose.[28]

Rapid growth and intense involvement with the lay community made new demands on convent leadership. A preaching, writing, reforming, and politically engaged prior needed assistants to relieve him of routine duties and confidants with whom he could share private thoughts. Inevitably the favored brothers drew off criticism meant for fra Girolamo himself and became the focus of certain resentments. After Savonarola's downfall fra Roberto Ubaldini, who served for a time as his secretary and as the convent chronicler, voiced some of these feelings:

> Three great masters had been created in the house, he [fra Girolamo] and fra Domenico [da Pescia] and fra Silvestro [Maruffi] [who] usurped all the power. . . . Everything was decided and set among those three, although they also consulted a good deal with a fourth, a German, fra Antonio d' Olanda, the father (supervisor) of religious life. All that was left to the other padri and frati was to say yes to everything they did.[29]

Savonarola seems to have chosen his two principal aides more for their loyalty and enthusiasm than for subtlety of judgment or intellect. Fra Domenico Buonvicini da Pescia's admiration for him had begun when both were at San Domenico of Bologna. He was at San Marco when fra Girolamo returned there in 1490 and quickly enlisted in the cause. He served as a confidential envoy on missions and as fra Girolamo's alter ego in the pulpit. Fra Roberto scorned fra Domenico's credulity, saying he believed "women's revelations and dreams," and opined that he had "a thick head," a judgment that seems to have been widely shared if his nickname, "il fattoraccio" (the

feckless steward) is any indication. Still fra Domenico was generally acknowledged to be "pure" and devoted to his leader.

Savonarola's other lieutenant, fra Silvestro Maruffi, was the son of a Florentine cobbler who at fourteen had followed his uncle into the convent.
There he was discovered to be a sleepwalker, a dreamer, and visionary. He was
said to perform prodigious feats of memory, reciting the Letters of Saint Paul
and the Divine Office and repeating whole sermons, including one that had
been preached in German the previous day. Imprisoned after Savonarola's
downfall, he testified that when in those early days he had told the Frate that
nocturnal spirits were warning him that his prophecies were demonic decep-
tions, Savonarola had simply advised him to pray for better guidance. When
the ghostly warnings persisted fra Girolamo had confided that sometimes
during prayer God imprinted the image of the cross and the name "Jesu" on
his chest. This had won fra Silvestro over; his apparitions had become friend-
lier, and despite occasional twinges of doubt he had embraced the Piagnone
cause.[30]

Besides going out to spread the message of penitence and reform fra
Silvestro taught in San Marco's school and served as confessor and spiritual
counselor to the convent's steadily increasing stream of lay visitors, which
made him the principal conduit for news and gossip between the convent and
the city.[31] Fra Silvestro's own visions became an occasional resource for fra
Domenico and for Savonarola himself, although he later told his inquisitors
that while he had encouraged Silvestro to believe they were godly, he really
thought this was a sickness that would fade in time.[32] One night in his sleep
fra Silvestro saw the air filled with good and evil spirits. Armed with daggers
and torches they battled each other until the good spirits prevailed. He related
this to fra Domenico who passed off the vision as his own in a sermon he
preached to the Signoria, confident that he, fra Girolamo, and fra Silvestro
spoke with one prophetic voice. In another dream Silvestro saw the three of
them bound together with a golden chain by angels who explained that God
wanted them to be united as one heart and one soul. The angels admonished
him that the revelations were not for his own salvation but for fra Girolamo
and the good of the Church. At the pain of being stripped of God's grace,
Silvestro was not to disclose that he was the source of these revelations.[33]

The more timely and lurid fra Silvestro's dreams, the more excitedly they
were received by friars and laity alike. Savonarola might condemn false
prophets, inveigh against the diabolical divining arts, and deplore the popular
fascination for astrologers, necromancers, palm readers, and other adepts
with claims to special powers, but his exchanges with fra Silvestro show that

even for him the distinction between legitimate and illegitimate, godly and demonic, ways of knowing the future was not altogether clear-cut.

Visionaries and oracles, male or female, were no rarity. Some found their way to San Marco, among them three matrons of distinguished local families, Camilla Rucellai, Vaggia Bisdomini, and Bartolomea Gianfigliazzi, who shared their own revelations with fra Girolamo, some of which, he would later confess, he had incorporated into his own prophecies. Camilla Rucellai, né Bartolini, twenty-five years old at the time of the friar's Apocalypse sermons, became an ardent Savonarolan, as did her husband, and her prophecies took on a Piagnone coloration. (One of the more notorious was her alleged prediction that Giovanni Pico, Count of Mirandola, would take the Dominican habit at "the time of the lilies," which was understood to refer to the fleur de lis of the French monarchy. As it happened, Pico seems to have been considering entering the Order when he died on November 17, 1494, the day the French entered the city.) After her husband took his vows in San Marco, Camilla became a Dominican tertiary, and eventually she and her colleagues founded the Convent of Santa Caterina di Siena on Via Larga, near to San Marco and closely affiliated with it.[34]

During Lent of 1492 Savonarola preached in the basilica of San Lorenzo, the Medici parish church. Genesis, which he had begun to expound the previous year, continued to serve as his main text. Even in the attenuated form in which the sermons survive, the intensity of his emotion is palpable.[35] There are the usual targets: sodomites, philosophers, and scientists who vaunted their irrelevant worldly knowledge; corrupt and tepid churchmen; writers of obscene books (Luigi Pulci was a convenient example); and clerics who polluted the temple by introducing pagan authors. "They tell me, don't say such things in the pulpit . . . but I am speaking only generally." But in at least one instance he named names, singling out Filippo Strozzi as one of the wealthy Florentines who were buying up the houses, shops, and lands of the poor in order to build lavish palaces.[36] (Perhaps it was only a coincidence that Laudomia, the young woman who was said to have rejected Girolamo's marriage proposal, was a Strozzi of the exiled branch in Ferrara.)

He directed his greatest outrage against the unholy alliance between temporal magnates and church prelates trafficking in ecclesiastical benefices and for clerics who flattered princes and lived soft lives. Instead of guiding the bark of Peter, these miscreants rejected any criticism of the Church. As for the regular clergy (monks and friars), avarice, lust, and pride had replaced charity, purity of heart, and contemplation. The *tiepidi*, by now one of his favorite

tropes, made their appearance as well. Steadily more confident of his prophet's brief ("I was fairly certain; then I was certain; now I am more than
certain"), he turned again and again to the Apocalypse, including lengthy
excerpts in his marginal notes.

The Fifth Age is approaching; the fifth angel is about to blow his trumpet
announcing the great tribulations of the Church. This is the time of the
terrible beast (Job 40.15), of false saints and false religion, of the persecution
of truth-speaking preachers. All must confess and pray and amend their lives,
for the sheep are about to be separated from the goats, the grapes crushed by
the winepress of God's wrath. The star that has fallen from heaven to earth
(Rev. 9) is the devil; he will unlock the shaft into the abyss and release a swarm
of locusts to torment the people who do not have the seal of God on their
foreheads. The devil recruited his troops among the wicked and the tepid, for
like attracts like: false preachers, hypocritical and worldly prelates, the powerful, the avaricious, the proud. Against such as these the righteous must arm
themselves, for the wild boar threatens to destroy the vineyard.

Still, the Church will be renewed, and in the next age the infidel will
convert to Christ. When this will happen he cannot say, nor can he say how
much time will pass between the conversion and the next era, when Antichrist appears. But he knows that Christ is the chief of the righteous and that
Antichrist will lead the impious. These two giants will lead their armies—
white against black—in a terrible climactic battle. What the nature of this
battle will be, with what weapons it will be fought, he remains in the dark
(although in another sermon he declared himself opposed to those who believed that faith would be spread by the sword).[37] But this is certain: the battle
will be won by Christ and his legions after which will come the final age, the
time of the Last Judgment.[38]

No longer was Savonarola the lone prophetic voice crying in the wilderness. Crowds were also flocking to the Cathedral to hear the Franciscan fra
Domenico da Ponzo (perhaps energized by his Dominican rival) also prophesy the coming scourge: God was sending his punishment for their sins,
especially sodomy; if they did not amend their ways by August, the streets
would run with blood. Whoever refused to heed this warning should have his
head cut off. "All of us, 'the whole brigata,' is terrified," wrote Niccolò di
Braccio Guicciardini, "especially me. God help us."[39] Niccolò was frightened
not only by the threat of the coming scourge: he was worried about a new
roundup of sodomites (which seems to have also caught Angelo Poliziano in
its net).[40] A preacher of Santa Maria Novella, San Marco's rival Dominican

church, was delivering a like message. Everyone was running to these three churches, reported Niccolò, while the preacher of Franciscan Santa Croce was drawing barely ten people and the preacher of Augustinian Santo Spirito even fewer.[41] Presumably they were offering less sensational fare.

Even as Savonarola and other Lenten preachers were working audiences into apocalyptic frenzy, they must have known that a domestic disaster was imminent. For months Lorenzo de' Medici had been suffering intense pain from "stomach ills, gout, kidney disease, and other acute ailments which brought on fever." By April 1492 he lay dying in his villa at Careggi. Heaven sent portents. An elderly woman was heard to scream in Santa Maria Novella: in the heavens she saw a raging bull destroying a massive temple.[42] During the night of April 5, out of a cloudless sky, a lightning bolt struck the lantern surmounting the great dome of the Cathedral. Marble shards and bricks came hurtling off, crashing heavily into the roof. Amazingly, no one was hurt. The Piagnone diarist Luca Landucci wrote that if it had happened during the morning sermon—preached by fra Domenico da Ponzo with some fifteen thousand people in attendance—it would surely have killed hundreds.[43] Niccolò Guicciardini was sure it was a miracle.[44] From his sickbed Lorenzo asked where the damage had occurred and when told it was on the side facing Via de' Servi, remarked, "Well, that's the side toward my house; I'm a dead man."[45]

Attended by the faithful Poliziano, Lorenzo was visited by his eldest son Piero, Giovanni Pico, and—whether summoned or on his own initiative has never been explained—"fra Girolamo of Ferrara, a man eminent in both learning and sanctity and a superb preacher of heavenly doctrine."[46] Poliziano's description of the deathbed scene might have served as a model for the "good death" prescribed by contemporary preachers including the same fra Girolamo. Savonarola exhorted Lorenzo to keep the faith and to live blamelessly, but if death was inevitable, to endure it with equanimity. According to Poliziano Lorenzo assured Savonarola that his faith was unshaken and his determination strong and asked for and received the Frate's blessing. (That Savonarola demanded the dying Lorenzo restore the liberty of Florence and declined to bless him when he refused is an apparently ineradicable legend that seems to have originated in the overactive imagination of fra Silvestro Maruffi.)

The night after his visit to Lorenzo, Savonarola had struggled to find ideas for his next sermon. It would be Sunday, the Feast of Lazarus, and he wanted to retell the story of that miraculous triumph over death. Uncertain how to proceed and unable to rest, he found himself reciting these words,

"Lo, the sword of the Lord, soon and swiftly!" The following morning he repeated the warning to a rapt audience. That night, April 8, Lorenzo died. Within a few hours Medici family men and friends escorted his body into the city and deposited it in San Marco where it remained through Monday. On Tuesday, April 10, a funeral cortege, which included San Marco friars, escorted Il Magnifico to the basilica of San Lorenzo for burial in the family tomb.[47] The same night brought more portents: a bolt of fire was seen crossing the sky and Florence's two caged lions, symbols of the city's might, attacked each other. One was so badly mauled it had to be put to death.[48]

"Every day," worried Niccolò Guicciardini, "fra Girolamo assures us that we will be visited by God's scourge; the sentence is unalterable." Fra Domenico da Ponzo took the lightning bolt as confirmation of the coming scourge repeatedly prophesied by "this holy man." Savonarola himself would revisit these Lenten sermons three years later in one of the defining moments of his apostolate and elaborate their prophetic and visionary content beyond anything to be found in the Latin summaries he made at the time. The Cathedral strike, the celestial vision of God's avenging sword, and Lorenzo's death following so closely upon each other would seem prophetically related, harbingers of coming tribulations and ultimate triumphs.[49]

Penitential preacher, convent prior, reformer, spiritual counselor, author: the affective sources of Savonarola's extraordinary energy must be found in the mounting conviction of his divine mission. The mystical awe, the compulsion to enlighten corrupt humanity about the true end of existence and the certainty of imminent cataclysm, all of these drove him to preach and work to the point of exhaustion and ill health. By this time he had brought his apocalyptic refrain of the coming divine scourge, penitence, and renewal and its terrifying coda "soon and swiftly!" to every important pulpit of the city. Invitations came to him to preach in Prato, Lucca, San Gimignano, Pisa, and other neighboring towns; he accepted as many as he could, sending fra Domenico or fra Silvestro when he could not. When absent from San Marco on convent business or preaching he sent back affectionate letters of pious instruction to his friars; when present he rallied them to the task of building "the new city."

In his sermon of October 21, 1492, on the psalm "I place my trust in God" (*In te Domine confido*, Ps. 10/11), he reminded them that it has been two years and three months since he began preaching to them on the Apocalypse "in a new manner." What real fruit this has brought, only God, who sees into our hearts, can say, while we who judge from external appearances can only conjecture. However, having received new light from God we have progressed in our understanding and have become united in faith. We are now better able to distinguish good from evil and to see that what we thought to be works of perfection are only a beginning. Despite many setbacks and contradictions, we have labored to build a new city. Some have challenged and derided him, questioning what he was about, and predicting failure, but he simply responds "in God I place my trust" and continues building. The task is both external and internal. The outward part is easy—perform good works, go to Mass, confess, listen to the word of God—but the internal task is difficult, for it consists in trying to know God. Philosophers can tell us what the good life is, but they cannot help us achieve it; this comes only through the light of faith. Through faith we understand God's goodness, why he was crucified, and as the Apostle says, his face is revealed to us (2 Cor. 3.18). And this, according to Augustine, generates love (*Confessions*, bk. V, 4). But shedding the habits of the exterior life is not easy, first because there are so many earthly attractions, second because superficial ecclesiastical ceremonies hinder our inner progress. We must, therefore, begin with the children, teaching them to resist earthly temptations and many of the ecclesiastical ceremonies, for as the proverb says, "set a youth on his path and he will not leave it even in old age [Prov. 22.6]." We must pray and avoid despair, avoid the temptations and seductions of the learned, the philosophers and astrologers, the false clerics and false religious, the soothsayers, diviners, and prophetesses and seek the truth only in the right reading of Scripture.[50]

Fra Girolamo allowed neither preaching or convent politics to interfere with his steady output of pastoral and devotional letters and tracts, many in response to requests from clerical and lay admirers, some elaborating on a theme from a previously delivered sermon or from his earlier notes. A few titles indicate the range of subjects: *The Life of the Widow*, the *Exposition of the Sacrament and Mysteries of the Mass, Some Very Brief and Useful Rules Pertaining to the Lives of the Religious, Treatise on Humility, Treatise in Defense and Commendation of Silent Prayer*, and *Treatise on the Love of Jesus Christ*.[51] Each tract was a variant of his central concern, how to live righteously and mindfully, how to achieve divine grace and through it the knowledge of God. Each was based on his conviction that true religion demanded a deeper, inward spirituality than the conventional "ceremonial" piety—the superficial piety of the "tepid."

In another sense, these treatises were companion pieces to his apocalyptic preaching, for they instructed Christians in the conversion of life which must accompany the coming renewal. For example, in *The Life of the Widow,* fra Girolamo regards a woman's loss of her husband as an opportunity for personal renewal, a second chance for her to cultivate the inner life while remaining in the world. By not remarrying a woman frees herself from obligatory service to a husband and to the many "works of the flesh" incumbent upon a wife. She not only renounces sexual activity but also the distractions of rearing children and involvement in family matters. She dresses simply, without ornamentation, and avoids conversation and familiarity not only with men but with women. Like the prophetess Anna, she spends her widowed life in the temple, praying, honoring, and worshiping God day and night (Luke 2.36).

The severe asceticism of the treatise on widowhood is balanced by the erotic mysticism of the *Treatise on the Love of Jesus Christ.* Adapted from his Good Friday sermon of a decade earlier, it combines a Thomist's rational argument for loving God with a mystic's rapturous account of the accompanying beatitude. Drawing upon such masterpieces of medieval contemplative literature as Pseudo-Bonaventura's *Meditations on the Passion of Christ,* he describes how contemplation of the love of Christ makes a believer dissatisfied with mere knowledge of the visible world and more avid for knowledge of God himself.[52] Such a love of God makes him worthy of receiving the grace of God's love in return, and so the lover is elevated to mystical union with Him: "In this beatitude [enjoyed by lovers of Jesus Christ] the rational creature is elevated so high as to be able to unite with the infinite good by means of intelligence and love. Everything is transformed, and the eye of his intellect becomes so strong that he can look safely into that inaccessible light and fearlessly contemplate the infinite, all-powerful majesty. With the greatest security he embraces it, not as his Lord, but as his friend, indeed as the sweetest of spouses."

Having described the journey from love to mystical union, he imagines the Christian who contemplates the grief and despair of living without the love of Jesus, then experiences the rapture of finding it: "O, sweet Jesus, what force, what pity has persuaded you to provide such medicine for my iniquities? O kind Jesus, what love convinced you to wash me in your blood? . . . You have gently pierced my ungrateful heart. You have shattered every hardness. Jesus, now make me die. Jesus, make me languish. Jesus, make me come to you!"

Visualizations of the Passion close the meditation: he imagines Jesus washing the feet of his disciples, suffering on the way to the place of his execution, in agony as he is being nailed to the cross, more agony as the cross is raised upright; the words he speaks as he suffered and died. Finally: "You, Jesus, have broken rocks, you have pierced fine diamonds, you, Jesus, have melted ice, you have shattered our hard hearts; you, Jesus, have penetrated our cold minds; you have made us enamored of your infinite love, so that I want to die for love of you. . . . O sweet love, o gentle scar, o honeyed wounding, how sweetly it leads to eternal life!"[53]

CHAPTER 8

The New Cyrus

On October 13, 1492, a Genoese sea captain named Cristoforo Colombo, sailing under the royal flag of Spain, reached the Western Hemisphere, soon to be called the New World. His countrymen, preoccupied with events closer to home, scarcely noticed.[1] The deaths of Lorenzo de' Medici the previous April and of Pope Innocent VIII in July, followed in August by the notoriously corrupt election of Cardinal Rodrigo Borgia as Pope Alexander VI, were being seen as auguries of evil times. Whether those evils would be self-inflicted or come from abroad was a matter of opinion, depending upon one's location on the checkerboard of Italian politics. Forty years earlier, when the Turks had conquered Constantinople and seemed poised to overrun Christian Europe, the warring Italian states had signed the Peace of Lodi and historically joined forces to forestall attacks on each other and maintain a common front against foreign invaders.

In retrospect "the spirit of Lodi" was part of that golden age celebrated by Marsilio Ficino. But long before Ficino wrote, the league had been unraveling, the separate states turning on each other, vying for the support of the same "barbarians" whose intervention they had sworn jointly to resist. In 1490 Pope Innocent VIII called upon Charles VIII to pursue the old French claim to the Neapolitan Regno and rid him of the detested Aragonese usurpers. In France exiled Neapolitan barons had been urging the same course upon Charles since 1488, while visionaries and prophets called upon him to fulfill his destiny as the New Charlemagne by going to Italy to reform the Church, then to the East to conquer the infidels. To lead a crusade was part of the legacy Charles inherited from his father, Louis XI, whom he succeeded in 1483. The fourteen-year-old Charles had also inherited Louis' close advisor, the Calabrian hermit Francesco da Paola, a tireless advocate of the crusading enterprise.[2]

Five years after his succession, Charles took a tentative first step by helping Lodovico Sforza, the regent of Milan, to occupy Genoa in return for
which he secured harbor rights for French ships. But before he could undertake a foreign venture he had to secure his throne, pacify his fractious subjects,
and buy off potential enemies. In 1491 Charles announced his intention to
exercise the French claim to Naples. Lorenzo de' Medici's death the following spring removed another obstacle. Il Magnifico had been a strong advocate
of maintaining the Lodi balance of power, and he exercised a moderating
influence on his Milanese ally. Free of that restraint and confident that he
could turn a French invasion to his own advantage, Lodovico now collaborated openly with the French to offset the anti-Milanese coalition of Pope
Alexander VI and his former Neapolitan enemies. He pressed Charles to
commence his Italian adventure.[3]

Two months after Lorenzo's death Piero Parenti complained that Italians
were asleep to the ominous portents of radical change occurring every day. At
Pietramala, in the mountains to the north, there had been reports of phantom
armies passing in the night. At Taranto, in the south, tablets said to be eight
hundred years old bearing oracular messages had been unearthed. (These
were probably some version of the legendary Saint Cataldus prophecy of
Charlemagne's imminent restoration of Florence.) Even the spring figs in
Florentine markets were cited by Parenti as a bad presage because they were
covered by rust.[4]

In his last sermon for Advent of 1492, Savonarola reported that he had
again seen the hand in the sky holding a sword with the inscription "the Sword
of the Lord over the earth quickly and soon." Above the hand was the legend:
"True and just are the judgments of the Lord." Three faces coming out of a
single light spoke warnings of coming punishments for human iniquities, then
all in a single great voice announced: "I the Lord speak in my holy zeal: Lo, the
days come and I will unsheathe my sword over you. Therefore turn to me
before my anger is exhausted, for then, when terrible trouble overtakes you,
you will want peace and it will not come." He saw angels in white holding red
crosses descending from heaven and offering white scarves and crosses to
everyone. Some accepted them, others refused. Still others, the tiepidi and
worldly-wise, refused them and tried to dissuade those who wanted to take
them. There followed terrible images of war, pestilence, and hunger. Angels
offered the cup of penitence, and those who took it recited, "How sweet is thy
promise in my mouth [Ps. 118/119]," while those who had refused now tried to
drink the dregs but could not, nor were they able to do penance or lift up their

eyes to see God. The great voice issuing from the three faces said that the worst of the sinners, those who blocked others from going to Heaven, were the "wicked prelates and preachers of philosophy" who put the Church in a bad way. Their punishment would be far worse than bodily suffering.

"Then I said, still illuminated by God, that one like Cyrus was going to cross the mountains, [he] of whom Isaiah wrote: 'Thus says the Lord to my Christ Cyrus, whom he has taken by the hand that he might subdue nations before him and undo the might of kings, and open the gates before him, and no gates would be shut: I will go before you and humble the proud of the world. I will break down the bronze gates and cut through iron bars. I will give you hidden treasures laid up in secret places, so that you may know that I am the Lord, the God of Israel who calls you by name, for the sake of Jacob my servant and Israel my chosen' [Isa. 44.1–4]." Italy, he warned, must not put its trust in castles or fortresses; God will capture them with no difficulty. And he predicted that the Florentines, that is, those who governed at the time, would take advice from the losers; like drunkards they would be heedless of any good counsel.

The Advent sermons of 1492 not having survived, Savonarola's later claim to have predicted the coming of a New Cyrus cannot be confirmed. In a cycle of sermons on the psalm *Quam Bonus* (Ps. 72/73), reliably dated to 1493, he frequently referred to his other apocalyptic themes—the coming tribulations, the humbling of the *magnati*, the renewal of the Church, and a new heaven and new earth—but made no mention of the New Cyrus, the future troubles of the Florentine regime (or the even more dubious predictions of the deaths of Lorenzo de' Medici and Innocent VIII, which in 1495 he also claimed to have foreseen).[5] Savonarola recalled this 1492 sermon in his famous "Reformation Sermon" of January 13, 1495, and again in the *Compendium of Revelations* of the following August. In both he was vague about sequences and dates.[6] In fact, much of what he preached—and, more crucially, what he prophesied—in those uneasy years of darkening skies over Italy has come down to us through the filter of his own memory. And yet by 1492 it took no divine revelation for anyone scanning the political horizon to see that Charles VIII was preparing to invade Italy. That Savonarola was already referring to him as the New Cyrus is plausible.

While Savonarola was prophesying *novità* for Florence and Italy, he was also personally involved in another upheaval, this one of his own making. Good people, he said, in the sermons for Lent of 1492 (which unlike those for

Advent have been preserved), seek out others of similar virtue while the wicked cleave to those like themselves.[7] The division between Rome and Jerusalem, that is, between the impious and the holy, was everywhere, even in the Dominican Order. The remedy was separation. If in 1491 Savonarola had speculated about taking his friars out of San Marco and out of Florence, in 1492 he was determined to take San Marco out of the Lombard Congregation. The idea had occurred to him and some of his colleagues independently, he later wrote, but he had hesitated for many months while he sought advice and prayed. Finally he determined to go ahead. "And so I was increasingly moved by the Spirit to bring about this separation which more and more seemed useful and necessary, and [I saw] that for the love of God I had to leave my fatherland, family, friends, honor, and glory, and embrace the cross of Christ, as it is written, 'Go out of your land and kindred.'"[8]

The words are from Genesis 1.12; they are the same words he had heard from the preacher in Faenza when he had decided to become a friar. This time too he felt God was moving him to a new course. (If he had been stymied on the move to Montecavo it would have been like him to find divine inspiration to turn that defeat into new opportunity.) In any case, secession was a less radical, more practical plan than a move into the wilderness; by separating San Marco from the Lombard Congregation he would be freer to introduce the austerities he so craved while continuing his work "in the world." To Stefano da Codiponte, a young friar who had written to him of his disappointment in finding so little spiritual zeal in the Dominican Convent of Santa Caterina in Pisa, he replied—perhaps admonishing his own more radical self as much as fra Stefano—"In heaven everyone is good; in hell everyone is evil; but in this world we find both good and evil. . . . My son, to live well is to do well and to suffer evil and persevere unto death. . . . In the world you have lived among scorpions; in the cloister, however, you must live among those who are perfect, those who are progressing and those who are imperfect, but no longer among those who are purely evil."[9] Secession from the Lombard Congregation had its own obstacles, as he was well aware. "I wasn't so blind as not to see that this was a hard thing to do, and that if I did it I'd have everyone complaining of me and I would turn all my friends of the Congregation into my enemies."[10]

In February 1493 Savonarola went to Bologna as Lenten preacher. Pseudo-Burlamacchi says that few people came to hear him at first because he preached only what was "useful and devout to nourish the soul" and expounded sacred scripture simply—not the sort of "curious" and more complex things favored by sophisticated persons. He must have resumed his attacks on Roman corruption, however, for when he left Bologna he was pursued by allegations that he had insulted the pope. (Two years later, after investigation by a papal commission, the charge would be dropped.) Another story, of a confrontation with Ginevra Bentivoglio, wife of the ruler of Bologna, also conveys the impression that he was no respecter of persons and had a sardonic sense of humor. When the great lady, with all her courtly retinue in tow, repeatedly arrived late, disrupting sermon after sermon, he took his revenge, pointing to her and exclaiming, "Look, the demon! Look, the demon, come to interrupt the word of God!" Only divine intervention, the hagiographer tells us, saved him from this Jezebel's diabolical attempt to retaliate by having him assassinated. After the incident his Bologna audiences swelled.[11]

During the Bologna interlude he seems to have pressed his plan for the release of San Marco from the Lombard Congregation. The other member convents were bound to regard secession as not only diminishing the Congregation's standing in the Order but as a rebuke for having relaxed the rules governing communal poverty.[12] Fra Girolamo's old teacher Vincenzo Bandelli, advocate of relaxed austerity and soon to be re-elected to a second term as vicar general, led the opposition. Bandelli's patron, Duke Lodovico "the Moor," would surely have opposed San Marco's withdrawal from the Lombard Congregation as a loss of Milanese prestige and influence. For the time being the secession proposal was tabled. When he still had not secured approval by the conclusion of the spring chapter meeting in Piacenza, Savonarola realized he would need more powerful allies. Returning to Florence in April, he dispatched Tommaso Busini and Matteo di Marco to Venice to plead San Marco's case before Master General Gioacchino Torriani.

Torriani was more favorably disposed to reform than Vicar General Bandelli, but just as he had done with fra Girolamo's reassignment to Florence, he refrained from committing himself. Instead he referred the matter to Oliviero Carafa, the Order's cardinal protector, at the same time forbidding Bandelli to take action on his own.[13] Savonarola immediately sent two envoys to Rome to make the case for withdrawal—"two little friars, one blind" (il fattoraccio Domenico da Pescia, who had poor vision), "the other an old man" (Alessandro Rinuccini who fell and had to return home). Rinuccini was replaced by the younger, more vigorous fra Roberto Ubaldini, who wrote that pitiable description. Ubaldini might have noted that the "two little friars" carried potent weapons—supportive letters from the Signoria of Florence and Piero de' Medici, as well as a letter from Cardinal Giovanni de' Medici—and Ambassador Filippo Valori had been instructed to use his influence at the papal court on behalf of secession. They also brought a notarized letter attesting to the enthusiastic backing of all the San Marco friars.[14]

The cause needed all the support it could muster: Cardinal Protector Carafa was favorable to San Marco's move and could be expected to press the Florentine case as far as he could, but he had to be careful not to anger his royal master King Ferdinand I of Naples, who in turn did not wish to alienate the Duke of Milan (whose support he would need against the French). The anti-secessionists also had a formidable champion in Cardinal Ascanio Sforza, brother of Duke Lodovico and a confidante of Pope Alexander VI. Vicar General Bandelli, ignoring his superior's order to refrain from independent action, sent a delegation of four friars with a letter from the Duke of Milan himself. In this way, what had been dismissed as a commonplace quarrel was elevated to a matter of state and high intrigue at the papal court.

When it seemed that Sforza would successfully block the presentation of San Marco's request to the pope, fra Domenico da Pescia offered to perform a miracle. To prove to His Holiness the worthiness of San Marco's case he would raise a body from the dead! But a courtier's guile, not a friar's miracle, won the day. As Cardinal Carafa bantered with the pope, he drew from his robes a breve he had prepared containing the order of separation and playfully asked Alexander to sign it. When the pope demurred, Carafa, chuckling, took the pope's hand, removed the ring with the Fisherman's seal from the papal finger and laughingly pressed it into the document. He then carried the breve to the antechamber and gave it to fra Domenico to carry to Florence. Vicar General Bandelli had already fired off a letter to Savonarola and his two lieutenants demanding that all three present themselves before him at once, but since this arrived a day after the papal brief, when they were no longer under Lombard jurisdiction, the summons was ignored.

Fra Girolamo promptly wrote a letter of thanks to Piero de' Medici who had succeeded his father as first man of the city.[15] The deference and homage that the Frate was said to have withheld from Lorenzo is here plainly offered to his son:

> Magnificent Piero, I told our fathers that it was my intention and the intention of the convent to do all that Your Magnificence declared you wanted and to do it in the way you wanted, as I understood it.
>
> Ever ready to carry out all your wishes, I recommend to you your convent. The Lord's grace be with you. Amen
> Frate Girolamo.

Bandelli, fortified by the patronage of the Duke of Milan, not only continued to defy the express commands of General Torriani but of the pope himself. Four days after the papal breve, he negotiated an agreement between the Lombard Congregation and San Marco putting Piero de' Medici in charge of the execution of the order of secession for a specified time. Bandelli seems to have hoped that Piero would seek to please the duke, while Savonarola counted on Piero's continued support. In any case, the agreement was a dead letter from the start: San Marco's independence was now a fact.

In late May, General Torriani extended Savonarola's term as prior beyond the constitutional limit of two years, and on June 24, 1493, he assigned both fra Girolamo and fra Domenico as socii, or full-fledged members, of San Marco, a designation that protected them from being transferred out of Florence and made them more secure from Lombard Congregation interference. A week earlier, June 18, in a letter to the whole Order but clearly addressing the members of the Lombard Congregation, General Torriani had written that no one should trouble the San Marco friars further. Five months later he was obliged to repeat his order, this time addressing the Lombard friars alone: he had heard reports that on account of the separation, the brothers of San Marco were being harassed and denigrated, to laymen as well as to other friars. This was intolerable, and he warned that any more such actions would be punished with excommunication. The warning appears to have been effective for a time, but two years later the Signoria twice wrote to General Torriani asking for protection for the friars of San Marco.[16]

Meanwhile, Prior Savonarola moved the reform of San Marco forward by insisting that the convent sell off all its properties and superfluous possessions. In a letter to the prioress of San Domenico in Pisa he denied that these were radical changes. The friars were only eliminating superfluities in dress, diet, and worship that were contrary to the old ways. They wanted to wear robes of coarse, patched old cloth, eat and drink soberly, live in humble cells, keep silence, and devote themselves to contemplation and solitude, avoiding familiarity with the outside world. None of this, he said, was new. What was new was the spectacle of mendicants building marble-columned palaces and rooms fit for lords, owning property, dressing with vanity, praying little, and wandering about. What was new was aspiring to poverty while renouncing nothing. The friars of San Marco, he insisted, had created no surprise or scandal in Florence, only great edification. Besides they had barely begun; it was too early to form a judgment about their exodus from the Lombard Congregation. With prayer and good counsel they would achieve much more.

Shifting into apocalyptic mode, he warned that in this darkened world, where every class of men and women was so depraved as to sicken God himself, it was time for renewal, time to declare war against tepid and false brothers. For this the separation had been helped—indeed it had been brought about—by the hand of God.[17] Savonarola refrained from telling the abbess that (despite official unanimity) some of those "tepid and false brothers" were his own San Marco brethren who worried that separation from the wealthy Lombard Congregation would be the convent's ruin. Some, distraught at having to give up their familiar comforts, had nightmares of being beaten by black-faced, obscenity-spewing evil spirits. Fra Girolamo went among them at night, reassuring them with his own visions and sprinkling their cells with holy water. Others, presumably overzealous in practicing the new austerities, became weak and ill.[18]

What more Savonarola hoped to achieve with Master General Torriani's help soon became clear. On November 15, 1493, during a visit to Florence, Torriani elevated him to the status of provincial of the Roman Congregation, apparently in anticipation of enlarging his San Marco jurisdiction. Ten days later the Signoria wrote to Cardinal Carafa asking him to help bring about the union of the Convent of San Domenico in Fiesole with San Marco and on December 17 extended the request to include Santa Caterina in Pisa. The possibility of including the Convent of San Domenico in San Gimignano was also raised. These requests must have been initiated and coordinated by the new provincial, Savonarola himself. They were immediately resisted by Bandelli and his colleagues in the Lombard Congregation ("the usual enemies," fra Domenico called them),[19] prompting Savonarola to obtain the master general's authorization to send at least two additional friars to Rome without interference from anyone of lesser rank than Torriani,"[20] although he was aware that diplomats experienced in such negotiations would be more effective.

In April 1494 he wrote three times in two days to Agnolo Niccolini and Pierfilippo Pandolfini, Florentine ambassadors to Naples, who had been instructed to stop in Rome and take a hand in the negotiations. Shrewdly, he sized up the state of the negotiations, warning the envoys that with Lombards ranged against Tuscans the enterprise was in great peril. God, he wrote, now entrusted the cause to their Benevolences; if they failed the Tuscan province would be destroyed. They should be aware that the matter depended upon the king (of Naples) and that already certain agents of Duke Lodovico had been at work urging the king to oppose their cause. Confident that he had the support of the Florentine government, he noted that the Magnificent Piero and the Signoria had written on their behalf, but if the envoys needed more letters they had only to inform him.[21] For their part, the priors understood the advantages of bringing the Tuscan houses under local control, although, understandably, they emphasized the spiritual dividends of the move. Everyone, they wrote, was aware how San Marco's separation had enhanced religious observance and worship. Now the friars of San Domenico in Fiesole wanted the same, and the Signoria wished to help them.[22] More months of negotiating, intrigue, deal making, and letter writing were to pass before His Holiness resolved this new request in favor of the Tuscans. On August 13, 1494, he dispatched a brief ordering the separation of the Convents of San Domenico of Fiesole and Santa Caterina of Pisa from the Lombard Congregation and authorizing them to unite with San Marco.

Not all the Dominican convents Savonarola had hoped to include in the new congregation were amenable. A proposal to bring in the San Gimignano convent had been withdrawn some time earlier due to strenuous local opposition. It was led by the San Gimignano prior, Francesco Mei, thereafter one of Savonarola's bitterest enemies. The following June, at the request of General Torriani, fra Girolamo led some of his friars to Siena to help reform the Convent of Santo Spirito. This alarmed many Sienese who regarded them, not unreasonably, as pawns of Florentine imperialism and a threat to their independence. Florentine envoy Alessandro Bracci gave a bathetic account of what happened. "They brought in that poor religious, fra Girolamo, with about twenty friars from San Marco and he was treated, you might say, like a Christian among the Jews—vilified, rejected, and threatened by the whole people. If they hadn't left I think they would have been stoned."[23]

The next attempt was more successful. In late August Savonarola and twenty-four friars went to Santa Caterina of Pisa. Armed with the papal brief, they expelled all the brothers except four who were amenable to the takeover and elected a new prior, Matteo di Marco, San Marco's master of novices. Subsequently, San Marco, San Domenico of Fiesole, San Domenico of Prato, Santa Caterina of Pisa, and Santa Maria del Sasso joined in a new reformed Tuscan Congregation, which received official sanction the following year, with Savonarola as its first vicar general.[24]

The death of King Ferdinand of Naples on January 25, 1494, spurred Charles VIII to action. Assuming command of his army he set off to the south, dispatching envoys to try to secure his investiture with the Neapolitan crown. In March he reached Lyons, but distracted by the city's pleasures, he remained there until the following summer. Meanwhile, at Genoa and Porto Venere, the French were winning skirmishes on land and sea over Neapolitan forces sent to intercept them. In early August Charles arrived in Savoy with an army of more than 40,000 infantry, cavalry, and a fearsome array of artillery, a huge force by any contemporary standard. In September, after meeting with Lodovico il Moro in Asti, he advanced into Liguria. Local defenders were terrified by his enormous siege guns firing iron projectiles. Even more terrifying was the cruelty of his troops; stories of civilian massacres at Rapallo and Mordano preceded the army all along its route.

By late October 1494 Charles and his army reached the northwest border of Tuscany and sacked the fortress town of Fivizzano, slaughtering many of its residents. To the south stood the port of Pisa and the coastal road to Rome. To the east, an easy three-day march through inland river valleys, was Florence, a rich prize and particularly resented by the French for having rebuffed all their appeals for support. Blocking their way were the fortresses of Sarzanello and the great citadel of Sarzana, both recently acquired by Florence from the Genoese and extensively rebuilt. When his first assault on these two strongholds failed, Charles paused to see what he might accomplish by diplomacy and threat.

On Ash Wednesday Savonarola entered the pulpit of the great basilica of San Lorenzo to preach the Lenten sermons. Genesis was still his text, and he resumed at chapter 6: God, deploring the wickedness of men, chose the just man Noah to make a new beginning.[25] The diarist-historian Bartolomeo Cerretani marveled: "In 1493 [1494] he preached in San Lorenzo and began to build an ark, as Noah did in the Old Testament, and in each sermon he wonderfully laid his foundation on four propositions: that the flood would come soon; that soldiers and princes would occupy the cities and fortresses; that Italy would be ruined; and that there would be no remedy. And all this he said on God's authority. The popolo flocked in to hear these sermons as did many very great men, including Messer Marsilio Ficino, Messer Oliviero Arduino, Messer Malatesta da Rimini, and Girolamo di ser Paolo Benivieni, highly distinguished philosophers and theologians, and Count Giovanni [Pico] della Mirandola, the most learned man of his time, as well as many other leading worthies."[26]

Every path was befouled with vice, the Frate complained. Maidens decked themselves out like whores; sodomites ran free; everywhere astrology was being used to divine the future, although no one knew when the Day of Judgment would arrive. Clerics, both priests and friars, were the root of corruption. The Church was a beautiful woman who bore the seed of tepid Christians incurably avid for ceremony. But the sack was full: punishment was coming in the form of plague, hunger, and war. Daniel and Ezechiel had seen the signs of imminent death. Cries of angels were heard every day. *Cito! Cito! Cito!* Soon! Soon! Soon! And the Florentines, when the tribulations arrived, what would they do? There was only one recourse: like those who had found safety in Noah's Ark, they must take refuge in the spiritual Ark of Jesus Christ and do penance.

Figure 1 Hanging and burning of fra Girolamo Savonarola, fra Domenico da Pescia, and fra Silvestro Maruffi in the Piazza della Signoria, May 23, 1498. Early sixteenth century, artist unknown. Museo di San Marco, Florence.

Figure 2 Savonarola's vision of a crown presented to the Virgin
Mary by the people of Florence. Illustration for sermon of April 1, 1495.
In Girolamo Savonarola, *Compendio di Rivelazioni* (Florence: Francesco
Buonaccorsi, post April 1, 1495). Bridwell Library Special Collections,
Perkins School of Theology, Southern Methodist University.

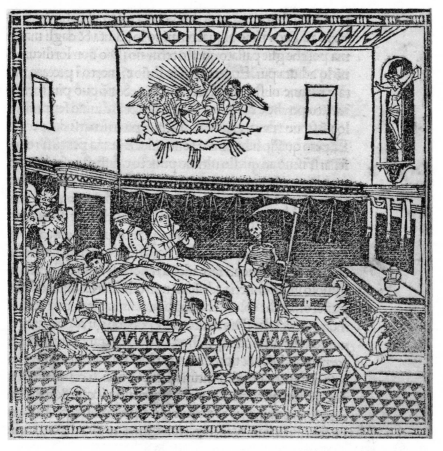

Figure 3 Confessing a dying man. Illustration for Girolamo Savonarola, "Predica delarte del bene morire" (Sermon on the Art of Dying Well), November 2, 1495. In Girolamo Savonarola, *Predica del arte del bene morire* (Florence: Bartolomeo dei Libri, post November 2, 1496). Bridwell Library Special Collections, Perkins School of Theology, Southern Methodist University.

Figure 4a Bronze medal, 1497. Generally attributed to
fra Mattia (Marco della Robbia) of San Marco, Florence. Obverse:
Profile of Fra Girolamo Savonarola, encaptioned HIERONYMUS SAVo[NAROLA]
FER[RARIENSIS] ORD[INUS] PRE[DICATORUM] VIR DOCTISSIMUS (The
Very Learned Girolamo Savonarola of Ferrara of the Order of Preachers).
The Metropolitan Museum of Art/Art Resource, NY.

Figure 4b Bronze medal, 1497. Generally attributed to fra
Mattia (Marco della Robbia) of San Marco, Florence. Reverse: Hand
holding a dagger over a city, encaptioned "GLADIUS DOMINI SUPER TERRAM
CITO ET VELOCITER" (The Sword of the Lord over the Earth Soon and Quickly).
The Metropolitan Museum of Art/Art Resource, NY.

Figure 5 Savonarola's vision of world redemption through
the blood of Christ. Sermon of January 13, 1495. In Domenico Benivieni,
*Trattato in defensione et probatione della doctrina et prophetie predicate da frate
Hieronymo da Ferrara nella citta di Firenze* (Florence: Francesco Bonaccorsi,
1496). Bridwell Library Special Collections, Perkins School of
Theology, Southern Methodist University.

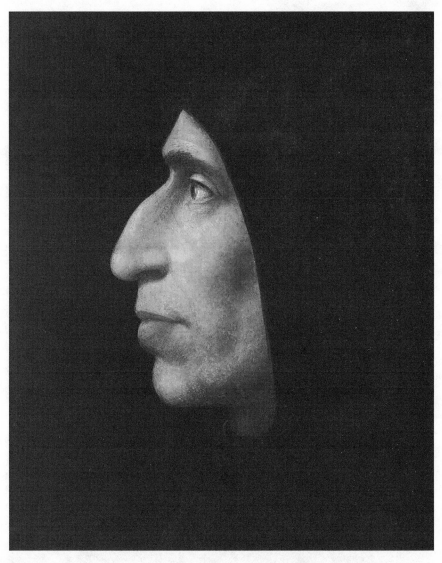

Figure 6 Portrait of fra Girolamo Savonarola by fra
Bartolomeo (Baccio della Porta), post May 23, 1498. Museo di San
Marco, Florence. Photo by Erich Lessing/Art Resource, NY.

Figure 7 The Mystic Nativity by Sandro Botticelli, 1500,
oil on canvas. Savonarola-inspired apocalyptic vision of redemption.
National Gallery, London/Art Resource, NY.

CHAPTER 9

Liberty!

A revenge-minded French king poised with a fearsome army on the border of Tuscany was final proof to the Florentines of Piero de' Medici's disastrous leadership. Piero had disappointed both the ottimati, who had expected to recover some of their power after Lorenzo's death, and the popolo, who had vainly hoped for relief from oppressive taxes. The more his senior advisors urged him to restore the vita civile (for many of them a euphemism for oligarchic rule), the more Piero relied on career bureaucrats—notaries and career officials, many from the provinces. These functionaries were sneered at by aristocrats and common people alike as jumped-up provincials with overweening airs and showy dress, ill suited to republicans with a fading self-image of egalitarianism.[1]

Much of what critics took to be willful tyranny was Piero's inability to cope with problems inherited from his father, compounded by his own inadvertence and hauteur. The twenty-two-year-old "first citizen" preferred hunting and ball playing to the hard work of governance. Typical of his insensitivity was his conversion of a much-used public square into a private jousting field for himself and his friends. When Piero did manage to make a decision it was likely to be ill considered and ill timed. A half-farcical but near-disastrous riot in the spring–summer of 1493 had put some of these defects on flagrant display. Piero had backed fra Giorgio Benigno Salviati, his old tutor in logic and philosophy, as the next general of the Franciscan Congregation.[2] When Benigno was passed over, Piero took it as a personal insult and in an angry confrontation with the retiring general accused him of cronyism, venality, and improperly trying to win a cardinal's appointment. (This from the brother of Giovanni who had won an appointment to the cardinalate at the age of fourteen due to his father's lobbying.) A fight broke out at

Santa Croce between armed supporters of fra Giorgio and his rival, and some friars were wounded. The convent bell sounded the alarm; residents of the quarter seized weapons and headed toward Santa Croce, while the more affluent rode their horses through the streets in an attempt to raise full-scale revolt. The Otto di Guardia (Eight of Security) finally restored order, but not before Piero had embarrassed himself and further exposed the strains in his regime. To many it seemed that the magic of the Medici name had died with Lorenzo the Magnificent.

Citing their common Guelf traditions and strong commercial ties, French envoys had demanded safe passage through Florentine territory for their army. Piero had temporized, bound by his commitments to Naples and his connections to his wife's Orsini clan, powerful lords in the Neapolitan Regno. Besides, the good will of Rome was crucial to the Florentine banking families who shared the farming of papal revenues, and young Cardinal Giovanni de' Medici depended on the benevolence of Pope Alexander VI for preferment in the curia. Under pressure, Piero had signed on to the new anti-French alliance formed by the pope and the new Neapolitan king, Alfonso II of Aragon. In April 1493 Piero Capponi, Florentine ambassador to Charles VIII, had reported that there was talk at the court about a possible revolt in Florence and seems to have suggested that he himself would not be unfavorable. Like many of his fellow ottimati, Capponi had major business interests in France.[3]

The following January and again in March another Florentine envoy, Gentile Becchi, had sent urgent warnings that Piero's cousin Giovanni di Pierfrancesco de' Medici was involved in subversive dealings with the king. In April the Florentine government had imprisoned Giovanni and his brother Lorenzo for collusion with the French. The Council of Seventy had recommended the death sentence. Considering the long-standing financial and political disagreements between the two Medici branches, their recent quarrels, and the increasing evidence that they were lending money to and scheming with the French, it would have been prudent of Piero to follow these plot lines where they might lead. Instead he had pardoned Giovanni and Lorenzo, under French pressure it was said, and allowed them to retire to their country estate north of Florence, where they were able to keep in touch with Charles VIII's court. In such ways were Piero's domestic and foreign enemies brought together in common cause.[4]

In June King Charles had expelled all Florentine merchants and bankers from France, a crippling blow felt almost immediately in Florence in reduced exports, lower returns on investments, and loss of jobs. Leaders of the so-called French lobby now thought to recover their huge investments by cooperating with the king in his invasion scheme. One Medici informant said they were promised special treatment when Charles and his army reached Florence. The overthrow of Iacopo Petrucci, the tyrant of Siena who had been friendly with the Medici, was more unsettling news for Piero. In July fra Domenico da Ponzo, suspected of being an agent of Duke Lodovico of Milan, was forbidden to preach and soon returned to Lombardy.[5] Piero continued to harbor the delusion that his troops could resist the invaders. To the French envoy who had brought a request for cooperation he replied that he was standing firm. With more and more civic leaders advocating a switch to the French side, however, Piero's regime was foundering. Now it was he who looked to the king of Naples for support, rather than, as previously, the king to him.

After his terrifying Lenten sermons, Savonarola had taken a respite from preaching, spending much of the summer working on the plan for the union of Tuscan convents and preparing sermons for the November–December Advent cycle. But with the news of the French advance and apprehension and confusion spreading throughout the city he could no longer keep silent. On September 21 he returned to the Cathedral pulpit and resumed at the point in Genesis where he had left off the previous Lent.[6] The French invasion had not only validated him as a prophet in the eyes of many Florentines, it also strengthened his own conviction that he was speaking with divine inspiration and the authority of the prophets:

> And then, returning to preach in September, the day of Saint Matthew the Apostle, [I expounded] the text where I had left it, that is, "Lo, I will bring the waters over the earth" [Gen. 6.17], it already being public knowledge that the king of France with his people had entered Italy. Terrified at these words, many immediately acknowledged that this reading from Genesis had been guided step-by-step by the secret impulse of God.[7]

The conjunction of the Flood passage with the arrival of the French did indeed seem uncanny. (Pico della Mirandola told fra Girolamo that as he listened he felt his hair stand on end.[8] Michelangelo is said to have heard and fled the city.) Many, including Savonarola himself, believed "he had been led as if by the hand by a secret instinct of God to that place in Genesis." For two years, since Advent of 1492, Savonarola now asserts, he has been predicting that a New Cyrus was coming to cleanse the Church and punish Italy for its wickedness and that instrument of divine wrath is now poised to do its terrible work.

"O, Italy, these adversities have come to you because of your sins! O Florence, these adversities have come to you because of your sins! O clergy, this storm has arisen because of you!" Italy and especially Rome will be turned upside down. "O nobles, O wise men, O people, the hand of God is mighty over you . . . but your God is waiting for you so that he may show his mercy to you. Therefore, turn to him with your entire heart, because he is kind and merciful. But if you refuse he will turn his eyes from you forever."

As the crisis mounted he preached almost every day, laboring to build the Ark of Penitence to ride out the coming Flood. For three straight days, beginning on November 1, All Saints' Day, he called for penitence and urged "everyone in the land" to give themselves to prayer and to fast on bread and water. Overwrought and ill, he drove himself to exhaustion.[9]

On October 20, with Florentines shuddering over the news of French atrocities at Fivizzano, Piero de' Medici appealed to Venice for military help. When no response was forthcoming, he sent King Charles VIII an offer of money, said to be 300,000 francs. The eleventh-hour bribe was rejected, prompting him to try an appeal in person. Without waiting for authorization from the Signoria, which was constitutionally responsible for foreign affairs, Piero and his aides rode off to the French camp. Once out of the city he wrote back to senior officials with an appeal to the citizenry to remain loyal in his father's memory. This was a calculated reference to Lorenzo's famous public letter in the midst of the Pazzi Wars when he went on a peace mission to the court of Naples. The allusion was not missed, but it only made the son's ineptitude the more egregious.

Piero held some strong negotiating cards if he but knew how to play them. Charles VIII was in an uncomfortable situation: the fortresses of Sarzana and Sarzanello were refusing to surrender, winter was coming, the marshy Tuscan coastal area where his army was quartering was unhealthy, and he had no enthusiasm either for laying siege to Florence or fighting in its narrow streets. But Piero threw down his hand before the king's resolve could be tested. Arriving at Sarzanello and ushered into the royal presence, he lost his nerve and gave in to all demands, surrendering the northern border fortresses and giving Charles entry into Pisa and Livorno (Leghorn), the two seaports crucial to the city's defense and commercial life. He was also said to have promised troops and a subsidy of 200,000 ducats for the French expedition, and that in return he received the king's vague assurances that he would be allowed to remain in power.

Piero's secretary, Ser Bernardo Dovizi, wrote the Duke of Calabria, the Neapolitan commander, on October 31, that Florence was now "entirely French." The following day, just as Savonarola was beginning his Advent sermons, the city received the first reports that Piero had traded the independence and security of Florence for his own survival.[10] The Signoria decided to send its own embassy to the French king, then summoned a *pratica*, or consultation, of past Standard Bearers of Justice and all who had been declared eligible (veduti) for that office to consider how to restore "good government" to Florence. Old Medici stalwarts began "to turn their mantle," as Piero Parenti put it.[11] One councilman in the Seventy, a Medici stronghold, declared it was "time to be done with this government of boys!" Hearing the great bell of the Palazzo della Signoria ring out, people streamed into the streets, but they were confused and uncertain what to do next. Inside the palace it was decided that an embassy of four citizens (some sources say five) should go to the king. Savonarola ("who we believe to be a prophet," wrote the diarist Luca Landucci) was chosen to lead it.[12]

Accompanied by fra Domenico da Pescia and two other friars, Savonarola set out in the night of November 5. The other delegates left the next day to join him at the town of Ripafratta, on the border between Lucca and Pisa. There, according to Pseudo-Burlamacchi, occurred another of Savonarola's miracles. The town's *podestà*, or chief officer, sent a servant to catch some fish for his guests' supper. When the man returned to say it was too stormy to fish, Savonarola told him to go out on the river again and cast his net in the name of Jesus Christ. This time the yield was so great that the fisherman needed help to bring in the catch.[13] Thus had Jesus filled the nets of the fishermen at the Lake of Gennesaret (Luke 5.1–8).

On his way back to Florence after his capitulation to Charles VIII, Piero de' Medici stopped at Lucca where he heard that a citizen embassy had been sent from Florence to the royal encampment. He rushed back to the city, arriving in the afternoon of November 8. While Piero's supporters set off fireworks and shouted "palle, palle!" he had sweets and wine distributed in the streets to simulate a triumphal entry. The mock victory celebration continued at the Medici palace on the Via Larga, where his familiars gave him an ostentatious greeting and distributed alms to the crowd outside. With his brother Cardinal Giovanni and a few relatives and friends as well as an escort of pikemen, he went to the church of Santissima Annunziata in a show of pious thanksgiving, then to the Palazzo della Signoria, where he exchanged hot words with city officials who blocked him at the door. Unwilling to try the issue by force, he lamely returned home.

The next morning Piero attended Mass in the Cathedral and in the afternoon returned to the government palace with a detachment of soldiers and demanded entry. Finding that the magistrates were barricaded inside with their own armed men, he turned away, vowing to come back with more soldiers. With the palace bell ringing in his ears, Piero pushed through a hostile crowd that was shouting "Popolo e Libertà!" and made his way back to the Medici palace. In the meantime he had sent for his kinsman Paolo Orsini to come north with more soldiers, but Orsini had not arrived and time was working against him. Government criers were already in the streets proclaiming that any foreigner who did not lay down his arms or who gave aid to Piero was subject to the death penalty. After his brother and Tornabuoni cousins failed to rally a counterforce in the streets with more cries of "palle!" Piero understood that all was lost. Together with Cardinal Giovanni (prudently disguised as a simple friar) and a few followers, he rode out of the San Gallo Gate into exile.

When the Signoria picked Savonarola ("most excellent servant of God . . . reputed to be a prophet since he had publicly predicted such calamities") to head the delegation to King Charles VIII, the Frate's first instinct was to refuse. He had more than enough reasons to disqualify himself: he might be seen to be stepping outside his clerical role; he was a non-citizen, worse, a foreigner; and as prior of San Marco, he was a recipient of Medici patronage, specifically from Piero to whom he had only recently commended himself and his convent. Then, reconsidering, he asked for time to pray and consult with the elder friars of San Marco and certain citizens. Only when these counselors unanimously advised him to go did he accept, he said. Nevertheless, he stipulated that he would not "discuss the status of private persons"; he went only to entreat the king for the safety of the city. In other words, he did not wish to be involved in any effort to remove Piero de' Medici from power but went only as a peacemaker. Perhaps simple prudence played a role: not even a prophet could say what direction this palace uprising would take or whether it would be successful. And yet by agreeing to go on this mission, he not only expanded his role in the affairs of the city, he cast his lot with the rebels against Medici rule.

The envoys found Charles and his entourage at Pisa. An escort conducted them through the French encampment bristling with soldiers and into the royal presence. Fra Girolamo was the first to address the king. He opened with a brief discourse on the nature of divine justice and mercy, then quickly came to the point of his visit: he was a prophet of God, and he was there to instruct the king in his sacred duty. The king should take his words to heart, for this sacred mystery had been revealed to him: for four years, as the people of Florence could bear witness, he had been urging penitence, warning of the great scourge that God was sending to Italy for its sins, and announcing the great renewal of the Church that would follow. God had willed that Charles not be named until now, but at last he, Savonarola, was allowed to confirm that the king was indeed the long-awaited, secretly chosen instrument of this cleansing, and he must now fulfill his mission. The king should be merciful, particularly to his city of Florence where, though there was much sin, were also many of God's servants among the clergy and the laity who would pray for him and help him on his expedition. Charles must defend the innocent, the widows and orphans, the poor, and above all, he must protect the chastity of convents housing their brides of Christ. He must forgive those who had offended him, for they had acted in ignorance, not knowing that the king had been sent by God.

After Savonarola had finished speaking, one of the French barons took him by the hand and conducted him to the royal chamber where, according to Pseudo-Burlamacchi, he had an hour's private conversation with the king. What they said to each other the biographer did not say. When the other envoys returned to Florence they reported that they had received a kind reception from His Majesty and gave their opinion that the prospects for safeguarding the republic's liberty were excellent. Still, they admitted, they had failed to extract any promises that Charles would reconsider his agreement with Piero de' Medici. Moreover, even as they spoke, French advance men were arriving in the city chalk-marking houses they selected as billets for their troops, terrifying residents with the prospect of a brutal occupation.

Still more bad news: on November 9, the day Florence had recovered its own liberty, Pisa, unrestrained by its French garrison, had rebelled against Florentine rule, driving out the hated Florentine officials and merchants. The loss of its principal seaport was a disastrous economic blow to Florence, its trade already devastated by the expulsion of its merchants and bankers from France and the disruptions of the invasion. But the breakaway was more than a matter of profits and losses. Pisa was the jewel in the Florentine imperial crown; its submission in 1406 had been the symbolic as well as tangible validation of Florence's claim to hegemony in Tuscany. It would have been difficult to find anyone in Florence willing to concede to Pisa the same right to liberty the Florentines now claimed for themselves. That King Charles had stood by as the Pisans rebelled against their rule did not reassure the Florentines about his good intentions toward them. Meanwhile, persistent reports that Piero de' Medici had been raising troops and preparing an assault on Florence added to the general anxiety. On November 11, someone reported having seen Piero's soldiers on the road toward Florence. This, the first of many such alarms, some false, some true, prolonged the street violence that had driven Piero out two days earlier, with Medici property and sympathizers equally at risk.

Amidst civic disorder and the frightening prospect of an occupation by French troops, more and more Florentines accepted fra Girolamo not only as a true prophet but as *their* prophet, holy intermediary between Florence and heaven itself. With seeming reluctance at first, then with growing conviction as he was drawn into the revolt against Piero de' Medici, Savonarola came to the same view. In fact, two months later he would claim that on the day Charles VIII was in Pisa he had prophesied to a select circle the revolution and renewal of the state.[14] When he returned from his embassy to the king, he found the city in turmoil. Piero de' Medici and some of his chief supporters had been driven out; a mob had murdered one hated tax official, wounded some of the Medici's Tornabuoni relatives and a few officials closely identified with Piero, and vandalized their homes. What had been a palace coup was turning into violent, popular revolution.

Savonarola could no longer remain aloof. Immediately upon his return he resumed preaching in the Cathedral.[15] The Florentines, he said, were like the man on the road from Jerusalem to Jericho (Luke 10.33–35). For their sins, they had fallen into the hands of robbers and devils who bruised their souls, nor had their fawning priests and tepid Christians offered them any help. Only Christ the Samaritan had given them the healing oil of his mercy and the wine of repentance. He had placed them in the care of the preacher, the keeper of the stable, and the two pennies he gave them were the Old and New Testaments. Now they must board the Ark and shut all the portholes against the coming flood of tribulations; they must do penance, pray, humble themselves before God and do justice. They must fight the devil by giving up the false doctrines of the astrologers, poets, and philosophers and by resisting his libidinous temptations. They must confess and take frequent communion, abandon childish, worldly desires with no tears for the worldly treasure they might lose in their tribulations. They should read the lives of saints to learn how to suffer martyrdom and gain paradise. Women must give up their vanity and their excesses; now, he insisted, was the time to do penance.

The Florentines, he declared, had heeded his preaching by building the Ark with fasting and penance, and God had mitigated their portion of the evils while other cities suffered. Even better, they had achieved a revolution without bloodshed—a thing unknown in other cities or in their own past. If they persevered in their good actions, he could assure them that God would continue to be merciful to them in the tribulations still to come. But now they must give thanks. All religious should sing a solemn Mass in honor of God and the Virgin. And as God has shown mercy to the Florentines, so they must show mercy to others; if not they would provoke his anger and suffer their share of the affliction that was about to befall Italy. He was their father and he ordered them to fast on Lenten food three days a week until Advent and on Fridays to take only bread and water. In every household those who could read should recite the seven penitential psalms, others might substitute seven Pater Nosters and seven Ave Marias. Above all, everyone must confess their sins.

Florence has moved into a central place in Savonarola's apocalyptic vision, and he redefines his mission accordingly. No longer hesitant about joining the revolution against Piero, he embraces it, although at first he conceived it in predominantly moral terms: those robbers and devils and their lackey priests, he says, were the robbers and devils who have abused Florentine souls and kept them from the straight way. By overthrowing Piero's regime they have done God's work. Downplaying the violence of the past few days, he declares that the absence of bloodshed or other "scandal" has been miraculous.[16]

The Florentines looked to their prophet for still more intervention. Barely had he returned from his first embassy to Charles VIII when the Signoria sent him on a second. This time he and the patrician Bernardo Rucellai were "to determine whether His Majesty meant for the Pisans to do what they are doing, and if not, we want his help, because we cannot defend ourselves and recover Pisa without [French] arms." Savonarola's lack of sympathy for Pisa's own aspirations to liberty shows how thoroughly he had adopted the Florentine perspective. For his part, King Charles, now at the Capponi country villa, replied to the Florentines' appeal by reassuring them that they were his people whose integrity he wished to protect and even augment; when he arrived in the city he would take care of everything.[17] With this not altogether reassuring answer, the envoys returned to Florence where residents were hastily, if not whole-heartedly, making preparations to greet His Majesty. Streets and squares were decorated with olive branches, palms, and fleurs-de-lis. Carnival spirit figures soared and giants stomped on stilts around the Piazza della Signoria where, as much in hope as in celebration, a tableau depicting the Triumph of Peace had been erected.

In his Sunday sermon on the eve of the king's arrival, fra Girolamo called upon the Florentines to continue building the Ark to keep them safe in the coming Flood. Like their predecessors in the biblical Ark, they must live simple, communal, chaste lives according to natural law, not guided by the worldly, human knowledge that had ruined both the Church and Florence in the past. God loved this city, which had many hidden treasures, both among the religious and the laity, and was so generous in giving alms to the poor. Over the past four years they had heeded his preaching of Holy Scripture and his prophesying—all of which, he said, had been confirmed—and the Florentines had been spared much suffering as a consequence. He had been given by God as a father to them, and he trusted that God would continue to protect them.[18]

CHAPTER 10

The Ark and the Flood

The Flood reached the city the following day, November 17, about five in the evening. French infantrymen with lance and shield came first, then crossbowmen, pikemen, sappers, mounted crossbowmen, archers, richly costumed and decorated men at arms, and still more archers. Then, in full armor, the king himself, lance on hip and canopy overhead—the pose and symbols of a conqueror. At the San Frediano Gate Charles and his barons were greeted by Florentine dignitaries and prominent citizens, dressed sumptuously "in the French manner." Welcoming speeches were delivered and acknowledged. Although the main French force had gone ahead to Siena, nine thousand troops accompanied the king—so many that it took almost two hours for the procession to weave through the narrow Florentine streets and past cheering crowds to reach the Cathedral.[1]

At the church steps the king and his barons dismounted, then entered the Cathedral and promenaded solemnly down its nave, an angel holding a lighted candle on every pillar. After hearing Mass they rode up the Via Larga, also festooned for the occasion, to the Medici palace, decorated with the royal coat of arms and elaborately prepared to receive the royal party. Some onlookers viewed the king's posture as a conqueror with misgiving, but the diarist Bartolomeo Masi contrasted the magnificence of his display with the meanness of his personal appearance: "a small person, ill-favored, big shoulders, an aquiline nose, splay-footed, web-fingered." On foot, sniffed Landucci, "he seemed to the people less imposing, for he was really a very small man." Parenti noted "a ruddy complexion, longish, wispy beard, and genial expression . . . short, rode a small horse, and was dressed in brocade, his head covered by a gold-bordered white cap decorated with black feathers, tied under the chin so that it nearly covered his mouth." Hardly the image of a conquering New Cyrus or latter-day Charlemagne. Outwardly, at least, the public mood was festive, with cries of "viva Francia" on all sides.

The following day a delegation of three hundred citizens led by members of the Signoria arrived at the palace for an audience with His Majesty. Messer Luca Corsini addressed Charles as the liberator not only of Florence but of all Italy, bringing, it was to be hoped, peace, tranquility, and quiet. His Majesty, whispering his replies into the ear of a spokesman, acknowledged the splendid welcome and promised he would satisfy all requests for his favor, both public and private.

In an effort to promote good will, it was agreed that Frenchmen and Florentines would stand night guard together, and that every house should have a candle in the window so that the streets would be lighted for the length of the invaders' stay. But when it became known that the king was demanding a heavy subvention and that he and his counselors were suggesting Piero de' Medici might be allowed to return, the mood quickly darkened. Nervous citizens murmured that Piero's wife, Alfonsina Orsini, and Lorenzo Tornabuoni, together with other Medici loyalists who had remained in the city, were suborning the royal advisors, perhaps Charles himself, on behalf of the discredited regime.

At the Signoria some *primati* (leading citizens), including Monsignor Francesco Soderini, bishop of Volterra, expressed indignation, declaring that "the king had said one thing and now wanted another," and urged their fellow citizens to resist if he tried to restore Piero. As they spoke, two Frenchmen tried to force their way into the chamber to shout them down. They were suspected of having been sent by Piero de' Medici's cousin Lorenzo Tornabuoni, who was housing some of the French dignitaries. When word came that French troops were headed for the palace, the chamber erupted, councilmen vowing they would die to preserve their liberty. With the return of calm it was decided to send an embassy to His Majesty warning him that Piero's return would lead to many deaths and the ruin of Florence.

Fra Girolamo, by now the revolt's acknowledged spokesman, was chosen to put the Florentine case. On November 21, he and his party threaded their way through citizen crowds and French troops to arrive at the Medici palace to deliver the Signoria's message. Charles replied that he had no intention of disappointing the people or causing the state to be overturned, but he did not think it unjust or outrageous if Piero were allowed to return to defend himself and live in the city as a good citizen. His Majesty gave his personal guarantee that he would behave correctly. But when he understood that the Florentines were adamantly opposed, he agreed not to raise the issue again for four months.

During a long, tense week the Florentines continued to make a show of celebrating the king's presence with masses and festive banquets. Meanwhile they made unsuccessful overtures to the Milanese and the Venetians. The king himself played tourist: he visited churches and monuments and gawked at the civic lions (evidently a replacement had been found for the one killed at the time of Lorenzo's death). Meanwhile, it became known that His Majesty's ministers were conferring with envoys from Venice and Genoa, both avid for a share of the lost Florentine territories.

In this climate of distrust and tension, fear that Charles would put the city to sack alternated with defiance. Minor disturbances escalated to panic; riots erupted; frightened merchants barricaded shops; young protesters pelted soldiers with rocks and paving stones. A detachment of French soldiers filing through Borgo Ognissanti to investigate some incident were met by a hail of stones, tiles, and other missiles and were drenched by boiling water dumped from windows and roofs by stalwart housewives. The soldiers "trembled like women," remarked Cerretani, unaware of the irony. They seized the Arno bridges and the San Frediano Gate to protect their avenues of escape.

Both occupiers and occupied were alarmed by the mounting violence and tried again to negotiate a settlement. According to Cerretani, when the talks reached an impasse the exasperated king threatened, "We will blow our trumpets!" and Piero Capponi retorted, "Most Christian prince, we shall sound our bells if you sound your trumpets, and we will show you this people in arms." Both men were bluffing: Capponi knew that the Florentines would be no match for the French forces and could expect savage treatment if they took up arms, and Charles and his captains must have been aware that an army trained for combat in the field would find a street-by-street, house-to-house battle with citizens fighting for survival very costly.

A settlement was finally reached.[2] King Charles reaffirmed that the purpose of his mission was liberation rather than conquest, and both parties agreed to a two-year alliance during which time neither would support the enemies of the other. Florence pledged a sum of 120,000 florins to the king, the first installment of 50,000 florins to be delivered within fifteen days. The Florentines also agreed to contribute an unspecified number of soldiers to Charles's campaign on condition that he leave Florentine territory promptly. The king further guaranteed that Pisa would remain under Florence's governance, as meaningless a provision as the Florentine pledge that with the agreement of "our Council" Piero de' Medici might return to the city in four months. In the meantime, however, Piero must remain a hundred miles from the city, although his wife, Donna Alfonsina, and his children might stay, providing Medici debts were paid. Piero's brother Cardinal Giovanni was allowed to return without sanctions.

Bell ringing and bonfires and a solemn Cathedral ceremony celebrated the peace, but when it seemed that the king was delaying his departure the Florentines grew uneasy again. Some San Marco friars urged fra Girolamo to intervene once more, and he agreed to seek an interview with the king. What has been written about this meeting is a mixture of sparse fact and Piagnone legend. Savonarola himself reported that the king's guards, suspecting that he had come to prevent them from carrying out their intention to sack the city, at first refused to let him pass, yet, "I don't know how it was, but with God's help, they suddenly took hold of me and led me before the king." Charles and his barons welcomed him cordially. He was asked to read over the terms of the agreement "three times, that is, first in Latin and Italian, then, for those who do not know much of our vernacular, twice more, half in Italian and half in French. In this way everything was confirmed."[3]

When the French marched out on November 28, chronicler Parenti had generous praise for Savonarola. Fra Girolamo, he declared, had worked effectively for our liberty, courageously telling the king that his dishonorable actions in Florence would surely lose him the heavenly favor on which depended the success of his expedition, and he had warned Charles against dishonest governors who were giving him bad advice. But when the king asked him to name these evil governors the Frate had demurred; it was not part of his profession to make such assessments; let His Majesty look into it. And so, Parenti concluded, the city was delivered from a bad situation by a combination of Savonarola's persuasiveness and the bold spirit of the Florentine people who were ready to die to protect their liberty.

Parenti was unable to decide which was the greater miracle: the recovery of Florence's liberty in the revolt against Piero with only one loss of life (a hapless Medicean shouting "palle"), or the death of only ten French and Italians during the occupation. Truly, he thought, the fasts and good works undertaken by the people at the behest of fra Girolamo must have persuaded God not to punish them for their excessive faults.[4] Piagnone Luca Landucci, whose son had been wounded in an encounter with the French, also credited the Frate, "renowned as a prophet in Florence and all Italy," with having persuaded the king to take his leave. Still, he said, an even stronger reason for the king's departure was that the comte de Beaumont, Charles's most trusted captain, had told the king somewhat peremptorily that he must leave at once; bad weather was coming.[5]

On Advent Sunday, November 30, Savonarola preached to thousands of relieved Florentines.[6] Taking as his text Psalm 114/116, "I love the Lord, for he has listened to my prayer," he returned to his Genesis metaphor: by prayer and penance the Florentine people had entered the Ark as he had long called upon them to do, and by closing it just in time, before the arrival of the armies and the onset of the tribulations, they had escaped the worst. Now they must continue to live in the Ark—live in the world yet live according to God, "our Noah." First the clergy, for the tempest had arisen on their account, must pray to the Lord and resolve to do his will. Citizens must renounce their pomp and live simply. Women must give up their vanities and extravagances and affect simplicity in dress, each setting an example, for if the plague should come, those who did not live simply would die like dogs! In a week's time it would be the Feast of the Conception, and everyone should go in solemn procession to honor the Blessed Virgin, and ask her to intercede for the city.

Finally, he called for measures to relieve the sufferings of economic stagnation and joblessness. Public monies that normally went to finance the university should be diverted to support the poor; theirs was the greater need. If this was inadequate, Church paraphernalia should be confiscated and turned into cash for "the poor of Christ"; canon law should not be allowed to stand as an obstacle, "for charity breaks every law." It would also be good measure to open the workshops so that everyone, especially the poor, could support themselves by their labor. Officials should also consider reducing taxes, particularly those that burdened the most needy. But the citizens could discuss this in the government palace if they chose to do so.

With these bold populist proposals fra Girolamo was moving a step closer to the political arena. The events of the next few days were to draw him the rest of the way. On November 30, the Signoria called a pratica for leading citizens. The Priors had already abolished the Council of Seventy, the Council of One Hundred, and other despised agencies of Medicean tyranny, but they left in place the Councils of the People and of the Commune, the traditional legislative bodies that had been effectively deprived of power by the previous regime. Speakers in the pratica insisted that the magistracies and councils had to be purged of men compromised by their service to the Medici regime and replaced with "right-thinking" citizens. Before new men could be selected, however, the electoral bags had to be restocked with a pool of names of "good men and lovers of liberty." The scrutiny was to be carried out by a special commission of twenty citizens called *Accoppiatori*. Since some of these proposals involved constitutional reforms, they would first have to be approved by the citizenry in Parlamento. The Medici, and others before them, had manipulated Parlamento to consolidate their hold on government while preserving the fiction that Florence was still a free republic. Skeptics predicted that this time it would be manipulated to favor the patricians who had led the revolt against Piero de' Medici. As Parenti drily commented, "Past experience is the true schoolmistress of the future."[7]

On December 2, to the ringing of the great bell in the tower of the Palazzo della Signoria, soldiers herded male citizens into the piazza and blocked the exits behind them. The Twelve Gonfalonieri, or Standard Bearers, of the Companies[8] mounted the rostrum and after ruling that two-thirds of the citizenry were present ordered the proceedings to begin. The assembly was asked to ratify the abolition of Medici-imposed councils and magistracies, leaving in place the traditional Council of the People and Council of the Commune, and to authorize the Signoria and its Colleges to select a new twenty-man commission of Accoppiatori. This body would have full power for a year to select the Priors of the Signoria—still limited to two-month terms—and to scrutinize the lists for names to be placed in the electoral bags. After the first year a more permanent electoral system would be put in place, although there was an option for extending the Accoppiatori's prerogative for a second year. The commission would also choose new war ministers—optimistically renamed the Dieci di Libertà e Pace, or Ten of Liberty and Peace— to direct the campaign for the recovery of Pisa and the border fortresses. The Eight of Security was to rescind Medicean decrees of banishment still in force. When all these proposals were read out in the Parlamento "some people shouted yea, and this was considered enough."[9]

No sooner had the crowd dispersed, however, then many who had duly shouted their yeas under the watchful eyes of the guards began to complain that they had been duped. When some citizens returned to the palace to protest that the Parlamento had proceeded "non popularmente," the Signoria had them forcibly removed. It was no surprise that most of the twenty new Accoppiatori elected on December 3 were from the old ruling elite or that in filling vacant posts they gave preference to their peers. Parenti, one of the anti-Medicean ottimati who favored meaningful republican reform, said that "all good citizens" were aggrieved; they had taken up arms for liberty but found that they had merely saved the state for the same old ruling circle, except for those who were too strongly tainted by Medici loyalty. When the new Eight of Security began to punish notaries and tax officials of the Medici regime with imprisonment, torture, hanging, and banishment, even leaders of the revolt against Piero worried that this was going too far.

Tensions increased as political exiles returned. Longtime victims of Medici tyranny wanted retribution against former collaborators who had prospered under the hated regime and now proclaimed themselves lovers of liberty. But with almost all the leaders of the revolt compromised to some degree, blanket retribution was unthinkable. When the Signoria ended the selective weeding out of citizens deemed to have been "too friendly" to the Medici, many took this as further proof that the primati remained Medicean at heart, perhaps plotting to restore the despised Piero. Some, with incurable Florentine cynicism, even put it about that the government was intentionally failing to reconquer Pisa so as to undermine the new republic. The lack of success in restoring trade and employment inspired complaints that the ruling patricians were indifferent to the sufferings of the poor.

To lead the Florentines out of this corrosive thicket of mistrust, score settling, hydra-headed factionalism, and popular unrest, Savonarola preached in the Cathedral almost every day until Christmas. There was reason, he said, for them to rejoice but still much to do. They had overthrown the tyrant and taken shelter in the Ark; the Flood threatening to engulf the city had been rolled back. The uprooting of the Medici regime begun on December 2 was a godly work; the Florentines had transformed themselves in the flesh, now they must transform themselves in the spirit. Florence without the Medici was a new city; it had turned away from paganism to guide itself and others by prayer and right living.

Psalm 149 gave him his theme for December 7: "Sing to the Lord a new song." The Florentines, he now told them, were God's elect! Soon the Flood would come to renew the Church; they, dwellers in the Ark, must be fit to take the lead. Religious renewal and civic liberty were a single cause and must proceed together. For their material and spiritual welfare they must adopt a simpler life, renounce usury, and reduce the duties and taxes that oppressed the poor, for then the people would be content and peaceful, requiring no public festivals to keep them happy, contrary to what many fools have said. They had committed themselves to prayer and right living; now they must also find a way to govern themselves.

That way, he was now convinced, was a governo civile, a representative republic. Despite what the wicked said, it was not true that a state was not ruled by paternosters (a saying famously attributed to Cosimo de' Medici). That was the view of tyrants, not of true leaders; only the mad and the wicked believed it. In the new republic good men would no longer avoid public office but serve willingly. The Grand Council of Venice might provide the city with a model, although if the people came together in their own councils, God might inspire them to something even better. And if the city lived more simply, there would be more money for self-defense and for fighting wars. (What sort of wars would be justifiable in the New Era he did not specify, although he promised that the Florentines would recover Pisa "despite all the world.")[10]

To achieve all this Florence must be governed by good citizens, men who had the well-being of their patria at heart, for Florence was the Lord's. With God's grace they would find their proper form of government in which no person could raise himself up to be sole ruler (*capo*) and where none would have to abase themselves.

In his December 10 sermon Savonarola's prophecy for the city took wing. If the Florentine people wanted to complete the healing work that Christ the physician had begun in them, they would heed him, the preacher, "like the Gospel," and if they did so, then:

> *I announce this good news to the city, that Florence will be more glorious, richer, more powerful than it has ever been. First, glorious with regards to God and to men: and you, Florence, will be the reformation of all Italy and the renewal will begin here and expand everywhere, for this is the navel of Italy, and it will be your counsels that will reform all through the light and grace that will be given to you by God. Second, Florence, you will have uncountable riches and God will multiply everything for you. Third, you will spread your empire; thus you will have temporal and spiritual power, and you will have such abundant blessings that you will say, "We want nothing more." But if you don't do what I have told you, you won't have it.[11]*

With this electrifying threefold promise, so different from the dark tenor of his earlier penitential preaching, Savonarola redefines his prophetic message embracing Florence's own triumphalist New Charlemagne mythology. The ascetic, uncompromising censor of worldly wealth and power now asserted that temporal empire would accompany spiritual renewal. If the Florentines persevered with their reforming mission, he promised, they would not only recover Pisa and the other lost territories, they would extend their dominion beyond all previous limits.

God, he thought, had illuminated him directly as to the meaning of the events of the past two months. Scripture provided him with his models: the Florentines were the ancient Israelites, God's chosen people, delivered from bondage, conquerors of the pagans, idol worshipers, and unbelievers, and inheritors of the Promised Land. The same books of Scripture gave him the prototypes of his own prophetic role; he was Jonah, he was Jeremiah, he was Noah, Haggai, even Moses, according to the circumstance.

"Until now I have been the prophet Jonah, who told the city of Ninevah it must convert; but I tell you that if they do not do what I have told them to do, I will from now on be Jeremiah who predicted so many years in advance the destruction of Jerusalem, then wept for it, destroyed and desolate."[12] No longer was he the preacher of the desperate, the prophet of doom; he now spoke of liberty and hope. He had become the prophet of the Florentines, for like the ancient Hebrews, this people had been chosen by God, just as he the prophet had been chosen to announce their glorious place in the forefront of the coming New Age.

Promises of glorious rewards for spiritual and political renewal notwithstanding, Florentines craved vengeance. At dawn on December 12, after a hasty trial, ser Antonio di Bernardo Dini, the administrator of the Monte, or treasury, who, said Guicciardini, was an honest man but hated for his crude manner, arrogance, and cruelty toward the poor, was hanged from a window of the Captain's Palace, his body left there until nightfall.[13] Another despised official, ser Giovanni Guidi da Pratovecchio, was sentenced to life imprisonment. According to Parenti, Savonarola had intervened to rescue ser Giovanni from hanging because he had been a generous benefactor of San Marco. Parenti's cynicism was unwarranted. Appalled by the savage reprisals and afraid that more disorder would negate the city's new-found freedom, Savonarola was stepping up his campaign for reconciliation. "O Florence, Florence, you have been cruel and have shed blood although you know how many times I have told you not to be cruel to others because the Lord has been merciful to you, but you have done the contrary."[14]

Moral suasion needed political implementation. For his next sermon he requested the attendance of city officials and again specified "no women, only men," a notice that he would be dealing with high matters of state. Three years later, in his statement to his interrogators, Savonarola would testify that he had embraced the governo civile as a means of enhancing his worldly glory and because he saw it as an instrument for effecting his political will.[15] But that was in 1498, in the anguished retrospection that followed public disgrace and self-incrimination. In the autumn of 1494 he had every reason to regard his motives as pure: only a governo civile would engage the massive participation of the people in building the New Jerusalem, and this only with peace and only under his own prophetic leadership.

On Sunday, December 14, Savonarola delivered what has been called his "first great political sermon."[16] It was a brief discourse on political philosophy, a homily on caritas, and in a departure from his earlier school treatise on politics, a prescription for republican government. Still drawing on Aristotle's *Politics* and Aquinas's *On the Government of Princes* for his theoretical underpinnings, he demonstrated why Florence had to have a governo civile. Every community that wishes to live righteously must choose the form of government that suits it best. This may be the government of a single ruler, of a few, or of all the people. Because unity is more easily achieved by the few than the many, the government of a single ruler is best, providing that he be a good person; nothing is worse than a government with an evil head. But in temperate areas like Italy, where both spirit and intelligence are plentiful, people do not easily tolerate a single head; in such places everyone wants to command, and this leads to discord. This has occurred repeatedly, in the time of the Romans as well as in today's Italian cities, including Florence. This is why the holy doctors taught that in these cities the rule of the many is better than the rule of one. And this is especially true of Florence, where men are particularly high-spirited and intelligent. But if a government of the many is not always to be in dissension it must be well ordered; if it is not, the restless will divide into factions, stir up rebellions, and try to drive out their rivals.

"The first thing you must do, is to make a general peace [*una pace universale*] between all citizens and see that all past offenses are forgiven and cancelled out. And so I say to you and command you in God's name: pardon everyone and keep in mind that what these others have done anyone would have done had he been called upon to do so."[17] At stake was more than the rescue of a handful of corrupt or unpopular officials from mob fury; in calling for a general amnesty, Savonarola was asking the Florentines to discard a longtime practice of their political culture, treating defeated rivals as traitors and punishing them with imprisonment, torture, exile, and confiscation of property.

"If you make such a peace, all you citizens together, and stay united, believe me, when they hear of this union all your enemies will fear you and in this way you'll be safer and stronger than they. . . . Why do you flee peace if you are a good citizen? Peace is none other than love and charity, and if you lack charity you are not a good Christian. . . . Peace is what unites you. . . . Peace, I say, peace, Florence!" With daring presumption he claims God's authority for promising redemption: if the Florentines take all his advice with a good will, their sins will be remitted and they will have great glory in Paradise![18] Thus, just as good government and true religion are inseparable, so too are Florentine citizenship and Christian righteousness.

Peace, however, must be accompanied by changes in government, for no one must be allowed to make himself sole head of the state. Tyrants are devoid of God's grace. They manage their affairs with astrology; they are incapable of friendship; they hate and fear virtuous people and confide in none but the worst sort of men. The Florentines should take as their model the government of the Venetians, omitting any features unsuited to their own needs, such as the office of Doge. They must also find a way to make their artisan class eligible for office, for the promise of honors will inspire people to live more virtuously. To this end it would be preferable to have major offices filled by election and minor ones by lot. To begin the political restructuring Savonarola called upon citizens to meet in their sixteen neighborhood companies (*gonfaloni*), each under its respective standard bearer, to discuss the form of government they thought best. The gonfalonieri would then meet to select four of the proposals and deliver them to the Signoria. After the singing of a Mass of the Holy Spirit in the council hall, the Signoria would make its selection and this, he assured them, would be the choice of God. The Venetians' form of government was very good; they had had it from God and since adopting it they had been free of civil dissension. In any case, the Florentines should know, "God has made himself your physician. If you do as I have told you to do you need have no fear of your enemies because you will always be the more powerful, and God, who is blessed in eternity, will protect you. Amen."[19]

Throughout the time of his ascendancy in Florence Savonarola claimed that the idea of a reform on the Venetian model had been his own, that it came to him as an inspiration from God. Contemporary observers attributed it to more mundane sources. Piero Parenti, among others, said that the plan was conceived by some of the leaders who were afraid that unless they acceded to the demands for greater representation they would be swept from power by a popular uprising. Election of magistrates and a new sovereign body on the model of the Consiglio Grande of Venice, they hoped, would satisfy populist critics without endangering the privileges of their ruling class. When their more conservative colleagues rejected the plan, this "Soderini faction," called after its eponymous leader, Paolantonio Soderini, brother of the bishop of Volterra who had spoken out so bravely against the king, found an ally in Savonarola, "who had such authority among the people that whatever he said had to be approved."[20]

Savonarola's biblical eloquence and prophetic authority were crucial in winning support for the Venetian-style reform, and in that sense he had a proprietary claim. But as a reader of the histories of Leonardo Bruni and other Florentine humanists, he must also have been aware that the idea of the Venetian constitution as the embodiment of classical principles of governance was a commonplace among humanist-educated Florentine gentry. This "myth of Venice" was particularly favored among the ruling elite, who regarded the Consiglio Grande with its limited membership as the bedrock of Venice's aristocratic constitution.[21] Government by a Venetian-style Grand Council might appear to be a gain for representative government, but adopting Venice's hereditary principle would preserve the power of the old Florentine ruling class. In proposing the Venetian model, the Soderini faction, ex-Mediceans almost to a man, may have been gambling on this inherent ambiguity.

For his part, Savonarola, while acknowledging the aristocratic nature of the Venetian Grand Council,[22] was confident that such a body, if modified to allow some degree of popular representation, could anchor a broad-based government (*governo largo*).[23] If he foresaw difficulties with his patrician allies, he seems to have been confident that the differences would be resolved in a common striving for the holy cause. Having already embraced the revolution and declared that further constitutional reform was vital to the city's spiritual regeneration, he now put his authority behind the Venetian plan as the way to achieve the common good (il bene comune). If a state could not be governed without paternosters, neither could it be governed by paternosters alone. To build the New Jerusalem in Florence religious and political reform had to advance together under a unified banner of Christ and republican liberty.

Even a prophet could lead his people only as far and as fast as they consented to be led. Parenti (speaking partly for himself) observed: "With Savonarola clamoring from the pulpits it looked as though he was taking the people under his charge and our leaders didn't like it. Secretly they complained that [the city] had fallen under [his] power. It was one thing to have charge of a convent, they said, another a city. . . . Pardoning all the citizens on his say-so was perilous, they thought. On the other hand, they did not dare contradict him. So our city lived in great suspense."[24] Since so many of the current leaders were tainted by their past connections with the Medici regime they might have been expected to welcome Savonarola's call for a general amnesty, but they temporized. Many of these Bianchi, or Whites, were afraid that amnesty would only encourage the remaining Medici loyalists, the Bigi or Grays, perhaps because they lived in the half-light of political disgrace, to work even harder to bring back the old regime.

For the time being at least, reform would have to proceed without the general peace that an amnesty would bring, however much Savonarola continued to insist on it as fundamental to the new Florence. White or Gray, political leaders had their own ideas of how to proceed with the constitutional reform. Ignoring Savonarola's call for citizen involvement through the neighborhood companies, the Signoria entrusted the recommendation of new constitutional reforms to the city's highest ministries, most of them still occupied by former Medici collaborators.[25] The proposals were examined on December 19, and although there was a broad consensus on the main features of a new government, such as the need for a sovereign council, there was considerable disagreement about such a council's functions and qualifications for membership. All agreed that the system of election to public office should be overhauled, but they differed on requirements for eligibility, methods of election, and the powers to be entrusted to each office. The most candidly elitist proposal, mainly the work of the anti-Medicean patrician Piero Capponi, proposed the establishment of a smaller, select council modeled on the elite *Pregadi* of Venice, which would serve as a kind of upper chamber.

One of the more innovative of the draft schemes, probably drawn up by the Piagnoni magistrates who dominated the Ten of Liberty and Peace, reflected both the spirit and substance of fra Girolamo's sermon of December 14.[26] Taking its title from Psalm 120/121, "Whence comes my help? My help is from the Lord," the preamble of this proposal viewed the question of reform *sub specie apocalypsis*. Shedding a past ridden by factional strife and tyranny, the Florentines had been summoned by God through the mouth of his prophet, and they had turned to liberty, equality, and steadfastness. Now they must shed their skin and take up a new form, instructed by their neighbors the Venetians, who have had a powerful state for a thousand years. The basic cause of their political troubles, it said, was the use, or misuse, of the system of choosing officials by lot. At times too restrictive and at times excessively egalitarian, this system had produced officials who were either oligarchic and corrupt or incompetent and unworthy. The Ten's proposal suggested a compromise: election for the more important magistracies, which would favor the more prominent citizens; sortition for the minor offices, which would allow for broader access to office. Eligibility for the new Great Council was to be based upon a combination of service and inheritance: all who had served (seduti, those who had been seated) in one of the three major magistracies (the Signoria, the Twelve Gonfalonieri of the Companies, and the Dodici Buon' Uomini or Twelve Good Men)[27] or who had been declared eligible but had not been selected (veduti, seen), as well as all whose father, grandfather, or great-grandfather had been seduto or veduto, were entitled to a seat in the Great Council.

On the whole, the Savonarolan proposal fell between the more elitist and more populist reform schemes. It favored a broader participation in government than had been the case since the radically democratic Ciompi rebellion of 1378, but it stopped far short of calling for universal male suffrage or equal access to all offices. While it did not endorse Capponi's proposal for a second, select council of notables, he and his fellow conservatives were to prevail on this with the establishment of a Council of Eighty. In the highest matters of state, involving changes in law and the punishment of citizens, the Signoria was not to act without a two-thirds majority in the Great Council. An unspoken but clearly underlying concern was preventing the arbitrary exercise of power that Savonarola and his allies regarded as the most egregious feature of the Medici regime.

From his Cathedral pulpit fra Girolamo, still preaching to men only, continued to press his dual vision of political and spiritual renewal. Florence, he exulted, had become a new city; it had heard the voice of the preacher who was filled with the Holy Spirit. The magistrates of the city had heard it too: almost miraculously the sixty-year Medici regime had been swept away in an instant and a new heaven and a new earth were emerging. Now was the time to protect and consolidate Florentine liberty, for it was God's will that Florence be ruled by the people, not by tyrants.

But liberty did not mean equality. One human must naturally be subject to another—not as slave to master, but as disciple to teacher—for those of superior ability and intelligence govern the others who would not know how to govern themselves. As Saint Thomas said, if all men were good they would be governed by charity and love and live in peace, but since they were not all good there must be law to restrain the rest.

Savonarola's concern for social justice was no mere pulpit rhetoric, but justice was not to be served by political equality. The body politic, he thought, should represent the interests of all, but all did not have an equal right to govern; political power must be reserved to those who had the moral and intellectual qualifications. To prevent a resurgence of tyranny, the Florentines must see to it that everyone remain within his limits, that the great not swallow the small, that offices and honors be fairly distributed to, and magistracies filled with, prudent and wise men. God would give this new city good prelates and pastors and good magistrates, and would fill the land with riches. The fame of Florence would then spread throughout Italy and as far as the land of the Turks, who would become Christians—even, in their simplicity, better Christians than themselves. "O father, when will this be? O, God wants it to be done in two years."[28]

Discussion of the proposals continued behind closed doors. For three days advocates of constitutional reform and defenders of the status quo exchanged heated recriminations and threats. But even as Ambassador Manfredi was predicting to Duke Ercole of Ferrara that the exasperated negotiators were about to become violent, they were in fact reaching a compromise proposal. An advisory council of citizens, about fifty from each quarter, was hurriedly convoked to hear the plan, after which it was passed by the Council of the People on December 22 and by the Council of the Commune the following day. In effect these two bodies, relicts of previous regimes, voted themselves out of existence, merging into the new Consiglio Maggiore, or Great Council, with broad legislative and elective powers. Membership in the Council was reserved for those who had been veduti or seduti for the three major magistracies, or whose fathers, grandfathers, or great-grandfathers had been so designated. The Council would have both legislative and elective functions: members would vote on laws proposed by the Signoria and choose officials in an intricate system of election for major magistracies and sortition for minor offices. Thus far the new reform law of December 22–23 followed the Savonarolan proposals fairly closely. On the other hand, the adoption of the proposal for a Council of Eighty as a second, elite chamber of prominent citizens forty-years-old or more was a major victory for the ottimati, although its functions were more limited and its membership broader than some of them wished.[29] Savonarola accepted it, apparently with little hesitation.

Would the new constitution favor the ottimati or the mid-level popolani? Opinion was divided. Piero Parenti thought that the election system for important offices enabled the notables to regain control of the government, while the system of choosing minor offices by lot offered a sop to the popolo. Still, he conceded, there were misgivings on all sides: "Even beforehand each person thought [the new system] would be bad for him." Many turned "cru-elly" upon fra Girolamo, without whom the reform would not have gone forward.[30]

The very universality of the complaints may have been the best indication that the founding law of December 22–23 was a skillful balancing of competing interests. Still, its innovative features made it something of a leap into the dark. No one knew how many citizens would be eligible for the new Great Council nor how effectively it would function. No one could say whether the oligarchs would give way to a true governo largo.[31] Nor could anyone, not even the prophet himself, predict what role he would play in the new government.

With additional constitutional reforms under consideration and the elec-tion of a new Signoria at hand, the Frate addressed the outgoing government on December 28. "I say that the old Signori have earned a great crown in paradise and another great crown in the society of your fellow men. The angels have helped too. This is no mere human work, but God's too. So these signori deserve to be held in reverence by you and to be written about in your chronicles as an example of right living for others to come." Then, addressing the incoming Priors, he urged them to follow up this work "more divine than human" by passing the amnesty law (*la pace universale*) during their term.[32]

He too was taking his leave, but only from the pulpit and just for a few days. He was exhausted and needed rest he said, having labored on behalf of Florence for four years, foreseen the coming scourge, and worried and prayed for them, as his fellow friars could bear witness. Again he urged the Signoria to enact the general amnesty, the key to civic unity, and to pass other laws to strengthen the new republic. Disunity was the work of the devil; his instru-ments were hatred, discord, and war. Four things the Florentines must do to overcome Satan and his agents, the lukewarm Christians (*tiepidi*). They must love God, love the common good, forgive their enemies, and complete the reform God had given them. If they did these things Florence would become the city of God, glorious in Italy and the world, the wellspring of reform for the whole Church. The renewed Church would lead the way to the Holy Land, would convert the Turk and other infidels. The new Christians would then do battle with the Antichrist and win a glorious victory.[33]

Two days later, on December 31, he interrupted his rest and went to the Palazzo della Signoria to try again to convince the outgoing Priors that they must crown their angelic labors with la pace universale.[34] "And just as I told you of the great glory that God will grant to this city, so will he grant you fullness and abundance of spirit. Lo, the spirit of the Lord over the earth fully and abundantly. And the man born there, Christ, will be born in the hearts of many. The Lord will found his Church with his spirit."[35] But as for the universal peace, the Priors served out their term without taking action.

CHAPTER 11

Toward the New Jerusalem

On November 9 rival ottimati had put their differences aside to join in revolt against the feckless tyranny of Piero de' Medici. They had soon divided over the question of how the freed republic was to be governed. Those determined to preserve the hereditary prerogatives of their class rallied behind Piero Capponi, chief spokesman for a government of notables (*governo stretto*). Others from equally prominent families, including Paolantonio Soderini, Giovambattista Ridolfi, and Piero Guicciardini, variously inspired by republican idealism, religious excitement, and political expediency, decided the time had come for a more extensive distribution of power (*governo largo*). Joining forces with Savonarola and his Piagnoni, on December 22, they had established the Great Council, keystone of a new broad-based constitution. Piero Capponi and his fellow anti-Medicean conservatives now became the nucleus of an opposition party, ever more extreme in its contempt for this government of dreamers in thrall to an alien friar.

A third group nervously harbored their loyalty to the Medici regime and were suspected, in some cases with reason, of plotting to restore it. Hearing calls for retribution against former agents of Medicean tyranny, these so-called Bigi, or Grays, looked to Savonarola for protection and usually gave his *Frateschi* (politically active Piagnoni) their support in Council. This alliance of convenience fueled charges that Savonarola was merely a stalking horse for Piero de' Medici.

Savonarola had promised that under the single great umbrella of the Consiglio Maggiore all such antagonisms would be reconciled. In that fellowship a God-fearing, penitent people, rededicated to charity, political reconciliation, and social peace would pursue the city's messianic destiny. But barely a week after he had saluted the new government and its first Signoria he perceived that the momentum for universal peace was dissipating. On January 6, he cut short his rest and began a new cycle of sermons.[1] Praise, blame, warnings of divine anger, and awkward sentiment ("I am crazy for this people!") poured forth in rich metaphor: after he had left the bark of reform in mid-ocean with his companion fra Domenico on watch, he complained, the sailors had reversed course, fighting off the few who tried to go forward and ignoring the watchman's warnings. In danger of being dashed against the rocks, they were followed by pirates who were amused at the insolence and madness of the sailors and ready to seize control. Two angels had arrived with flares to guide the sailors away from the rocks, but to no avail. The vessel of reform was in jeopardy: many wanted to go back; the few who tried to hold course had been attacked and impeded, and the pirates—the enemies outside the city—rejoiced and waited for them to crash on the rock of their dissension. Those two angels with torches were the two lights he had preached, fear of God and the bene comune, the common good. The failure of the Florentines to perfect their new constitution with the reforms ordained by God violated the divine honor and would rekindle his wrath. Civic discord gave comfort to their enemies and prevented them from recovering Pisa. So he had had to break his rest, to take over the watch from his companion and guide the bark back to its rightful course.

The Florentines must make a new start, he declared, for God had shown them that such a marvelous opportunity might never come again. Amnesty was the first imperative: civic peace meant wiping the slate clean of all political recrimination, neighbor forgiving neighbor. (Surely each of them could recall an occasion when he had betrayed a duty or voted against his conscience?) From this time on, then, no one should be prosecuted for having been a friend or servant of the former regime. Indeed, they should banish White, Gray, and all such divisive party epithets from their vocabulary, setting a fine of ten florins for a first violation, four turns of the rope (*strappado*) for a second, life imprisonment in the Stinche (the city's most fearsome prison) for a third. Torture, then, "turns of the rope," to punish divisive political speech, but not to punish the unfortunates who fell into debt. Debts both public and private must be paid, but payment must not be exacted by torture, for nothing made God angrier than putting innocent people to torment, forcing them to confess to crimes they had not committed, punishing the guiltless.

His next proposal was an even more radical challenge to Florentine notions of punitive justice. With six votes out of nine (eight Priors and the

Gonfaloniere of Justice) the Signoria could impose sentences of death, exile, amputation of a limb, imprisonment, and confiscation of property for so-called crimes against the state. To eliminate, or at least blunt, what had become a vicious weapon of political rivalry, Savonarola insisted that the Florentines institute a right of appeal. Persons convicted of political crimes should be allowed to appeal their sentences either to a select Council of Eighty or to a committee made up of a hundred members of the Great Council. A two-thirds vote would be required to confirm the sentence. Without this reform, promptly dubbed the Law of Six Beans (beans being used as voting counters, black for yea, white for nay), the good work that had been done so far, he warned, would be ruined. Drastic punishments, such as exile, did not reduce internal opposition, they increased it, and he cited the example of Cosimo de' Medici, who had used his year of exile to build up his following, with what consequences everyone knew.

The proposal for a law of appeal was blocked in the Signoria, "corrupted" Parenti charged, "by the first men of the regime," who had no wish to surrender a weapon which from ancient times they had used to such good effect against their enemies.[2] Savonarola's outrage at this unexpected opposition threatened to undermine his own call for reconciliation. His opponents were hateful, proud, stubborn, envious, hypocritical, stupid, insipid—without salt —and foolish, and he mocked them crudely: "I want to teach you how you respond to such as these: take a bushel (staio) of millet, dump it into their laps and tell them, 'go, feed the chickens.'"

Constitutional mandates and legislative reforms were necessary, but Savonarola perceived that the health of the polity required a more fundamental change. Politics in Florence had become a zero-sum game; power came with a warrant to garner spoils, punish enemies, and reward family and friends, thus giving the wheel of hatred and cruel revenge still another spin. His calls for reconciliation through amnesty and a right of appeal were intended to halt this vicious cycle and stemmed from his understanding of politics as the collective pursuit of the bene comune. Saint Thomas had adapted this Aristotelian concept to his ideal of a Christian society. The bene comune thrived on spiritual and practical well-being and depended on forbearance, trust, compromise, and moderation. Further, it required justice: a well-ordered community could not tolerate the exploitation of the less fortunate.

In Florentine tradition and theory, justice was the ultimate responsibility of Florence's chief officer, the Gonfaloniere of Justice, and the eight Priors of the Signoria over whom he presided. But the Signoria sworn in January 1, chosen by the twenty patricians of the Accoppiatori, showed even less enthusiasm for Savonarola's calls for justice through reconciliation than the previous one. As Gonfaloniere of Justice they elected Filippo Corbizzi, a man of very little quality, authority, or virtue, according to Guicciardini. (Savonarola probably had him in mind when he remarked, "You know, it's not always the wisest citizens of the city who occupy that position.")[3] Corbizzi was as much the tool as the leader of the *Arrabbiati* or Mad Dogs, as the Frate and his supporters had begun to call his most intransigent political enemies. ("These are certain mad dogs who don't love the common good but think only of their own advantage and want to catch that hare for themselves. Now I've come and scared off the dogs, not me but God.")[4] Still, the Mad Dogs were not alone in their dislike of proposals for reconciliation. With Piero de' Medici reportedly raising troops for an assault on the city, there was a general fear that la pace universale would bolster a Medici fifth column ready to fling open the gates at his approach. The Arrabbiati exploited these anxieties, insinuating that the amnesty proposal was evidence of fra Girolamo's secret Medicean sympathies.

Amnesty and the right of appeal were important issues, but the Florentine man in the street was more directly affected by the government's powers of taxation. The constitution of December 22 mandated a reform of the tax system, shifting the burden from imposts and consumption taxes to a levy on *beni stabili* (real property). Clerics were to pay as well, provided that their superiors assented. But although fra Girolamo made tax reform a critical part of his program, with men of property still dominant in the Signoria as in the critical magistracies of the Ten of Liberty and the treasury, finding an acceptable way to carry out that mandate became one of the most vexing problems of the new constitution.[5] Savonarola urged the newly elected revenue officials to mend the reputation of their department by practicing impartiality, treating everyone equally, with no preference for relative or friend. The sharp increases in food costs due to higher import and sales taxes (*gabelle*) especially hurt the poor and should be reversed. (Under the previous regime it had also been decreed that imposts be paid in "white money," that is, the new quattrino, a coin with a silver content of four denari, rather than the old quattrino, which had three.) The tax on wine, for example, should be reduced to its previous level, and grain should again be sold to the poor in the marketplace for twenty soldi per staio. Moreover, officials should not accept gifts "from anyone in the world."

Branding the resistance to his reform proposals as the callous self-interest of the ruling elite and a betrayal of the bene comune, Savonarola called for efforts to find employment for workers, lower consumption taxes, and provide cheap grain. Stymied by his formidable ability to exploit popular resentment (even as he deplored its effects), the Arrabbiati tried discrediting him. The half-comical affair of ser Giovanni Guidi's hidden treasure seems to have been such an effort. Ser Giovanni, a Medici Chancellery official, had deposited a cache of jewels, gold, and coins (some said 1,200 florins) in San Marco for safekeeping. Now the Guidi treasure was suddenly "found," and Savonarola's enemies trumpeted the discovery as proof that he had conspired with a corrupt official for personal gain. After he explained that Guidi was one of many who had entrusted their valuables to San Marco for safekeeping during the recent troubles and that he himself had little personal knowledge of the business, the matter was dropped.[6]

A more tenacious challenge came from a former ally, the Franciscan fra Domenico da Ponzo. Two years earlier fra Domenico had praised Savonarola and endorsed his prophetic claims. Having left the city shortly afterward, he now returned as a dedicated enemy, suspected by the Piagnoni to be a secret agent of Duke Lodovico of Milan. Lodovico had initially promoted the French expedition, but his relations with Charles VIII had soured and he now ranged himself with the pope's Holy League. Savonarola's unshakeable support for the Florentine alliance with the French put him at odds with the duke as well as the pope. The strategy of "the crafty Ponzo," as Machiavelli was later to call him, was to attack Savonarola on the issue of his prophetic apostolate. The age of prophecy was over, he now declared, and no one should claim to speak with the voice of God. Ponzo also raised the sensitive question whether a religious ought to intervene in secular politics at all, although he had no qualms about injecting his own strident voice into political discussion, declaring his opposition to amnesty and the reform of the Six Beans.

Florentines of all parties intently followed the furious verbal thrusts and parries of this preachers' duel. In his sermon of January 13 Savonarola responded to Ponzo and his allies with a confident amplification of his prophetic apostolate to the Florentines. The tone is triumphant, magisterial; the mode is visionary. He puts himself at the center of the apocalyptic drama.[7]

The light of prophecy, he says, began in him more than fifteen years ago, perhaps twenty, although he started speaking of what is to come only in the last ten years, first in Brescia, then in Florence, the navel of Italy. Through him, poor little friar, the Florentines have heard with their own ears what they should now report to all the cities of Italy.

The corruption of prelates, the loss of primitive faith, the decay of worship, the absence of justice, the multitude and stubbornness of sinners—all confirm that the renewal of the Church is at hand. Besides, universal opinion holds it to be so: the abbot Joachim [da Fiore] and many others preach and announce that the scourge must come now. Biblical prophets confirm it. Zechariah shows how the two mainstays of the Church, that is, its prelates and secular princes, have collapsed on each other and brought it to ruin (Zech. 2.1–3).

At the time of Pope Innocent's death (1484) he saw, "through the power of imagination," two crosses, one black, over Rome-Babylon, on which was written "the wrath of God," and upon it a rain of swords, knives, lances, and every sort of weapon, with hail and stones and streaks of lightning. Over Jerusalem he saw a gold cross on which was written "God's mercy." Here the skies were calm and limpid. "Wherefore, on account of this vision, I tell you that the Church of God must be renewed, and soon, for God is angry, and afterward the infidels have to be converted, and this will be soon."

Again, he saw a sword quivering over Italy while angels offered everyone a red cross to kiss and white robes to put on. Those who accepted were given sweet wine; those who spurned the gifts twisted and turned, begging to be spared from drinking the dregs. "All of a sudden, I saw the sword that quivered over Italy turn its point downward and, with great storm and scourge, go among them and scourge them all." Those who had taken the white robes suffered less and drank the sweet wine; those who had refused now begged for a share of the robes so they wouldn't have to drink the dregs, but time had run out. "This is why I tell you that the renewal will happen, and soon." (*see Fig. 5*)

> The quivering sword—I tell you, Florence—belongs to the king of France; [that sword] is manifesting itself throughout Italy. The angels with the red cross, the white robes, and the cups are the preachers who announce this scourge to you; they give you the red cross—that is, martyrdom—so that you might bear up under this scourge which must come during the renewal of the Church. The robe signifies the purification of [the Church's] conscience, cleansing her of every vice, so that she may be white with purity . . . those who have taken the robe and cleansed their consciences will drink the sweet wine, that is, they will feel only a little of this scourge . . . will be the first to be scourged, but it will be sweet because they will endure it patiently, and should they die, they will go to eternal life. Those others are forced to drink the very bitter dregs. . . . This sword has not yet turned its point downward, even though it has shown itself throughout Italy, because God still awaits your repentance. Be converted, Florence, for there is no other remedy for us but penitence.
> Remember when I said, three years ago now, that a wind will come,

as in that figure of Elijah and that this wind would shake the mountains [3 Kings 19.11]. This wind has come . . . and it has shaken the mountains, that is, the princes of Italy, and has kept them vacillating for the year between believing and not believing that this king would come. And, behold, he has come, [although] you were saying, "He will not come; he has no horses; it is winter," and I would laugh, for I knew how things had to turn out. See now, he has come, and God has made summer from winter, as I said then. . . . Remember, also, that I said to you that great fortresses and walls would be of no help. . . . Tell me, Florence, where are your fortresses and strongholds? . . . Remember also that I told you that your wisdom and prudence would be of no avail and that you would get everything backwards, you would not know what to do or what to take hold of, like a drunk out of his senses. Now he has come, and it has been verified, and . . . still you do not believe. I say to you, obstinate as you are, you will not believe the rest either, for God will not give you the grace to believe, because your obstinacy does not deserve it. Remember that at times during the past three or four years when I preached to you I spoke with so much force and ardor and vehemence that it was feared I would burst a vein in my chest. You didn't know, my child, why it could not be otherwise.[8]

Three years earlier, on the Feast of Saint Lazarus, when the lightning bolt struck the Cathedral dome, he suddenly found himself repeating, "Lo the sword of God over the earth quickly and soon!" The following morning he had described this in his sermon, explaining its meaning: the wrath of God was at hand. This "soon" is not one of those vague apocalyptic expressions meaning hundreds of years. They should believe him; it will be soon.

Although he has been a father to them, sharply reproaching them as his children and demanding that they convert, he sees that now God wants to be their father and is coming to punish them, so he must be the mother who says gently, "Children, do penance, do penance!"

They will recall that he told them he was giving them an apple, as the mother does to quiet her crying child, but when the child does not stop crying, she gives the apple to another of her children. "And so I say to you, Florence: God has given you the apple, that is, he has elected you for his own; if you don't want to do penance and convert to God, he will take the apple from you and give it to another. . . . So, Florence, do these four things that I have told you and I promise you, you will be richer than ever, more glorious than ever, more powerful than ever."

Some years ago, he says, he foretold the deaths of Pope Innocent VIII and of Lorenzo de' Medici. He also predicted that there would be a renovation of the government of Florence and that the change would take place on the day the king of France was in Pisa, and so it has come about. He said these things privately to some who are here today and can bear witness to it.

The sermon of January 13, 1495, was a consummate performance, worthy of its Old Testament models, Haggai, Zechariah, Daniel, and Isaiah. Quickly printed and distributed, "The Sermon on the Renewal of the Church," as it was called, became the classic manifesto of the Savonarolan apocalypse. If some of his more critical listeners questioned the validity of some of his proleptic claims—the death of Lorenzo and of Innocent VIII, the revolution in Florence, the coming of the new Cyrus—most were inclined to believe, swept by the power of his delivery and the authority he radiated from his lofty Cathedral pulpit, and gratified to hear of their providential role.

The next day, an hour-long tolling of the great bell in the Palazzo della Signoria heralded the first meeting of the new Great Council. The very size of the body must have dismayed the ottimati, who had tried to hold it back, as much as it delighted the popolani, for whom it was concrete proof that the promised new era was about to begin. Since Florence had no council hall that could hold the full membership of some 3,600 eligible citizens, it was decided to divide it into three sections. These would meet in rotation, six months per section, each with full powers to act for the whole. Even these reduced sittings overwhelmed the capacity of the existing council halls and discouraged attendance, making it difficult to find a quorum. It was decided to create a room large enough to hold the entire body, enabling it to return to unified sessions. In August Antonio Sangallo was appointed architect and instructed to combine some of the existing rooms in the Palazzo della Signoria into one large council hall.[9] For Savonarola this was a top priority: neither the fiscal crisis, the expense of the Pisan war, or the huge subvention to Charles VIII was to deter the project. In sermon after sermon he insisted that each succeeding Signoria demonstrate its commitment to the new republic by pressing for the completion of "the Sala."[10] Despite the constant shortage of funds, by April 26 of the following year the project had made so much progress—with the help of God and his angels, Piagnoni believed—that fra Domenico da Pescia was able to say Mass and preach there to the Signoria.[11]

Fra Domenico da Ponzo and other clerical antagonists responded to the sermon of January 13 and the opening of the Great Council as further proofs of Savonarola's improper interference in secular affairs. Gonfaloniere Filippo Corbizzi and his Arrabbiati cohort in the Signoria moved quickly to take up these objections, although mindful of the Frate's popularity, they shied away from an open condemnation. On January 18, they invited two distinguished theologians who were among the Frate's most formidable critics—fra Tommaso da Rieti, regent of the Dominican studium of Santa Maria Novella, and fra Giovanni Caroli, lecturer in the Florentine civic studium—to debate fra Girolamo and fra Domenico da Pescia before an audience of select clerics and laity. To avoid the appearance of using the debate to undermine the Piagnone cause, the highly partisan Signoria directed that the sensitive subject of further political reforms, including Savonarola's call for la pace universale and the Law of Six Beans, not be debated, since this would concede that clerics could legitimately discuss civil matters. Yet by confining the debate to the technical questions of prophetic inspiration and clerical political activity, they reduced the confrontation to a bloodless academic exchange. With no official winners and losers, the contending friars returned to their pulpits, each free to resume the battle on his own terms.[12]

And battle they did. Savonarola was both resigned and defiant: "I have now become the scandal of Florence; nevertheless I am still here," he told his congregation on January 20, and proceeded to defend his political activism. Those fellow Dominicans who protested his concerning himself with affairs of state should study the chronicles of the Order, he said; they would learn how their great forebears had intervened to make peace and bring about good government: Saint Dominic in Lombardy, and in Florence the Cardinal Latino (a thirteenth-century peacemaker), Saints Peter Martyr, Catherine of Siena, and the Archbishop Antoninus. Besides, who should take the lead in such matters? Certainly not some overzealous partisan, but a moderate who had his feelings under control. He had preached truth to Florence for several years and to be sure he had had to touch on matters of state; why else would he have incurred so much ill will and made so many enemies?[13]

Although those enemies failed to bring him down, they did force him on the defensive. By shifting the burden of the debate from the truth of the prophecy to the legitimacy of the prophet, they exploited a tendency already noticeable in the sermon of January 13. Increasingly, he was obliged to prove that his motives were honorable, his integrity unimpeachable. That this would divert and weaken him might not have been inevitable except that it found his most vulnerable spot: his own private uncertainties about the source and nature of his prophetic inspiration.

As to his proposal for a law of appeal to restrain the Signoria's power of "the Six Beans," he would say no more about it since it had found favor "neither in council, nor in public, nor in private." If the Florentines declined to do what was good for them, he would not insist. Instead, he recommended that they hold a pratica of "good citizens"—Whites, not Grays (no longer was he avoiding those divisive terms), and truth-loving clerics to discuss the matter. Although defenders of truth suffered for it, as the lives of Christ, the apostles, and the saints bore witness, truth was even mightier than the three great motivators: wine, women, and power. Truth would rise to the top like oil on water. Suffering borne with patience and righteous living on behalf of truth was the way to salvation.

Five days later, Savonarola repeated his warning of the coming storm which would turn Rome and all Italy upside down. Then he made a startling announcement: "I want to be a friar; I renounce the state and wish no more to concern myself with the Six Beans. I am going to my cell; don't send for me again. Even if the king of France and the emperor come, I will not [return]. . . . I want to go to Lucca and then maybe even farther. Pray God for me that I may go to preach to the infidel; that's what I very much want to do. As I've told you, they will convert in our time . . . they'll come to baptism like lambs."

Florentines were startled to hear that the Frate was longing to abandon the city and go to the Holy Land to preach to the infidel. Some may have guessed that he spoke out of exhaustion and frustration with the slow pace of reform; some may even have concluded that he was bluffing and that, for the time being, at least, he was going no farther than Lucca. With many Lucchesi eager to see and hear the famous prophet, their elders had obtained a papal brief assigning him to preach Lent there. But even the Priors, Arrabbiati as well as Frateschi, understood that he was crucially needed to preach unity and peace in the crisis-ridden city, and, together with the Ten of Liberty, they appealed to Rome to have the assignment cancelled. In the event, Savonarola did not go to Lucca, much less to the Holy Land. With his program stalled by successive anti-reform governments, he remained quietly in his cell in San Marco and abstained from preaching for the next five weeks. We may leave him there sulking in his tent like Achilles while we catch up with some other events of the previous few months.

On November 17, the day Charles VIII and his troops entered Florence, Pico della Mirandola died at the age of thirty-two. At Pico's Fiesole retreat and in San Marco he and fra Girolamo had read the Bible and Church

Fathers together, at a time when he was working on a commentary on Psalms and studying Hebrew. They had also collaborated to fight the obnoxious and pervasive influence of judicial, or predictive, astrology. Savonarola's *Treatise against Astrology* was a popularized version of Pico's unfinished *Disputations against Divinatory Astrology* (although it was Savonarola, not Pico, who called for defenders of the heretical art to be burned at the stake).[14] How deeply Pico absorbed Savonarola's spiritual and ascetic teachings is a moot point. Pico's ardently Piagnone nephew, Giovanfrancesco Pico, wrote that his uncle often complained to him of the miseries of the human condition and told him of his intention to go barefoot into the world and preach the Gospel. Pico went so far as to sell his possessions and give the proceeds to Giovanfrancesco, setting aside a sum for one of Savonarola's dowerless sisters and alms for the Convent of San Marco.[15] He had resisted Savonarola's pressure that he become a Dominican, but he was buried in the habit of the Order in San Marco's church. Thus was fulfilled, in a kind of ironic parody, Camilla Rucellai's prophecy that Pico would enter the Dominican Order "at the time of the lilies" (the fleur-de-lis).[16]

The story of the Rucellai prophecy is part of the hagiographic aura that surrounds, and inevitably deforms, our picture of this unlikely friendship. Giovanfrancesco's worshipful biographies of the daringly unconventional philosopher and the puritanical Christian reformer constitute our principal source for their relationship, with a few details added by other contemporary admirers, including Giovanni Nesi and Pietro Crinito, but much seems to have been passed over. From the humanist Crinito we have the idyllic story that when Pico smiled indulgently at Savonarola's denunciation of the pagan philosophers the Frate embraced and saluted him as the most learned philosopher and expert on Christianity of the age.[17] What Savonarola thought of Pico's enthusiasm for Kabbalah and magic neither Crinito nor Giovanfrancesco tell us.

Nor do they tell us what stance the Frate took on Pico's sexual vagaries. Savonarola's reassignment to Florence was intended to be part of Pico's agenda of moral rehabilitation after his Arezzo escapade. But it is not at all clear that Pico, even in his new penitential mode, dedicated himself to chastity. The question is further complicated by intimations of homoeroticism. Letters, unfortunately undated, between Pico and Angelo Poliziano contain suggestive images and humorous innuendos about their mutual fondness for boys.[18] It has also been alleged that Pico's relationship with the Neoplatonist poet Girolamo Benivieni had a sexual dimension, although the evidence for this is inconclusive.[19] Benivieni wrote that after he persuaded Pico to compose a commentary on Benivieni's *Song on Divine and Celestial Love,* both men were uncomfortable at having treated love as Platonists rather than as Christians and put the *Song* and the *Commentary* aside.[20] When Benivieni died in 1542 he was buried in Pico's tomb in San Marco with this inscription:

> Here lies Giovanni of Mirandula, famous from the Tagus to the Ganges and perhaps to the Antipodes. Died AD 1494, at barely thirty-three. Here also lies Girolamo Benivieni. Just as love joined their hearts in life, so their bones are inseparable in death.[21]

Savonarola was familiar enough with the writings and reputations of Marsilio Ficino, Angelo Poliziano, Pico, and Benivieni, as well as other members of the Laurentian circle, to know that the tension between sensual and spiritual love, whether of the homoerotic or heterosexual variety, was a constant theme of their poetic and philosophical discourse. It is difficult to believe that this stern crusader against unchastity and particularly against "the unspeakable vice" of sodomy did not suspect that here was more than a theoretical interest. Poliziano's homoerotic preferences, for one, were well known.[22] If sexual license of either variety caused difficulties between Savonarola and his prestigious converts, if he chose to look the other way, or if he was simply naive about such matters, none of the early biographers tell us so. Fra Giovanni Sinibaldi, one of the inner circle at San Marco, wrote that Pico had deceived Savonarola, for even as he pretended to accept the Frate's spiritual guidance he was keeping a concubine.[23]

A week after Pico's death Savonarola ended his sermon with a delphic revelation as ambiguous as the friendship itself. "I want to reveal a secret to you which I haven't wanted to tell until now because I wasn't as certain of it as I have been for the past ten hours. I believe all of you knew Count Giovanni of Mirandola who died a few days ago. I want to tell you that on account of the prayers of the friars and some of the good works he did, as well as other prayers, his soul is in purgatory. Pray for him. He came to religion later in life than had been hoped, and therefore he is in purgatory."[24]

Two months earlier, a sudden fever had also carried away the great humanist scholar Angelo Poliziano at the age of forty. According to Piero Parenti, Poliziano died "in as much infamy and public vituperation as a man could bear," not because of his vices but because of his association with Piero de' Medici.[25] Having been tutor to Piero and Giovanni and dependent for most of his career on Lorenzo's patronage, Poliziano could not easily dissociate himself from the Medici family. Cynics might have pointed out that in responding to fra Girolamo's call to penitence, Poliziano was securing himself against the anti-Medicean backlash of the November revolt, but cynics would also have had to concede the sincerity of his conversion. Unlike his friend Pico, who had faltered on the last step, Poliziano took the vows of a Dominican lay brother before he died. He too was buried in San Marco.

With the deaths of Poliziano and Pico, Savonarola lost his two most important ties to the Laurentian brigade. Marsilio Ficino, the dean of the group, had attended some of his sermons, but soon turned away. Savonarola's relentless attacks on astrology and his disparagement of humanist intellectuals who were more Platonic than Christian must have been intolerable to Ficino, particularly as he watched friends and disciples edge away from him and into the Savonarolan camp.[26]

Between Ficino, brilliant interpreter of the Pythagorean mysteries, and Savonarola, apocalyptic visionary, Girolamo Benivieni chose Savonarola. Benivieni had already undergone at least one religious crisis before he came under Savonarola's spell and abandoned his more adventurous philosophic views.[27] Still, it took Pico's death to convince him that God had spared him so that he would dedicate his life to God.[28] He threw himself into the Piagnone campaign for Christian renewal and composed lyrics for bonfires of vanities, carnival processions, and other spectacles. As an intimate of fra Girolamo he had the freedom of the Convent of San Marco. Benivieni's two brothers— Domenico, a canon of the Cathedral and former professor of logic in the studium at Pisa, and Antonio, a physician—also enlisted in the cause. Domenico's encounter with Savonarola inspired him to formulate a vision of reform even more radical than the Frate's own, impelled on one hand by a conviction of the irredeemable corruption of the historical Church, and on the other by a belief in individual redemption through mystical union with God. In Domenico Benivieni's vision of the Church of the future there was no priestly hierarchy, no distinction between cleric and layman, only between those transformed by divine love and those left behind.[29]

Almost simultaneously with the loss of Pico came news of the death of Elena Savonarola. The infrequent contacts between mother and son had become even rarer in the past few years, his last known letter to her is dated January 1490, and in it the resolve to distance himself from family ties, begun with his flight to Bologna, is still evident. He declares his love for her and his sympathy for her difficult situation (the death of his father in 1485 has left

Elena a needy widow with two dowerless daughters), but he protests that he is unable to help.[30] Most of the letter is about his dedication to preaching and his growing success. When the news of his mother's death arrived, no word of loss or mourning escaped him.[31] To be sure, the news came in the midst of the Florentine crisis when there was little time to dwell on private loss. The French army was just entering the city, and the Florentines, terrified by the king's threats and by reports of the cruelty of his troops, were looking to their prophet for comfort and protection. Over a year was to pass before he made any mention of his mother in public, when he cited her as an example of misplaced affection: families should not lament when one of their loved ones decides to serve Christ by joining a religious order. "My mother wept for years; I let her weep. It's enough that now she knows it was wrong of her to do so."[32]

On March 1 Savonarola returned to the Cathedral pulpit to preach the Lenten sermons. Taking Job for his text he preached almost daily until April 24, revisiting the familiar themes of divine tribulation, penitence, and Florence's destiny and skillfully reworking the theological ground underlying his vision for the city as the New Jerusalem. Through prayer, penitence, and good works, the Florentines had gained God's compassion and avoided the worst tribulations. God had given them prophecy, restored their liberty, and promised them more glory, riches, and power than they had ever known, and they had responded by consolidating this God-given liberty. Woe to anyone who tried to make himself master in Florence! Once again he was obliged to warn them that the devil was drawing Florentines into worldly pleasures and seducing them from their good ways. Soon they would be tempted as Job was tempted, first in small things, then in ever greater ones, and finally they would curse God as evil. Life in the world was a constant struggle against the devil; happiness was spiritual and true felicity and blessedness would come only in the next life, where those who had been raised up would have a vision of God.[33]

On the day Savonarola resumed preaching, March 1, the new Signoria, still hand-picked by the Accoppiatori, took office. As Standard Bearer of Justice (Gonfaloniere) the Priors elected Tanai de'Nerli, a rich, powerful ottimato and a more formidable enemy of Savonarola than the mediocre Filippo Corbizzi. None of these Priors was an enthusiast of popular government or keen to surrender any of the Signoria's prerogatives; still they could not ignore the mounting pressure in favor of the proposed reforms. Nor their logic. As Piero Parenti explained, if the ottimati were to lose their majority in a future Signoria—as they feared was increasingly likely—an amnesty and a law of appeal would protect them against reprisals.[34] With this in mind, they held a series of citizen consultations over the next two weeks to consider the merits of the reform proposals. When a majority vote in the ottimati-dominated Council of Eighty favored a law of appeal, it was decided that the measures must go before the Great Council, although the debate over the proposed reforms continued.

From his Santa Croce pulpit fra Domenico da Ponzo argued that no further constitutional changes were necessary; the Florentines had accomplished great things and their glorious future was assured; any further reforms would wreck their achievement. Not so, Savonarola countered on March 13. Felicity was theirs if they followed his fourfold admonition to fear God, love the common good, make a general peace, and reform their new constitution. With the tide running in favor of fra Girolamo's proposals, da Ponzo made a tearful, almost hysterical attempt to block the passage of the law of appeal. Any weakening of the Signoria's prerogatives would have diabolical consequences—the stink of sulfur and poison would rise to heaven! Savonarola countered in similar vein: peace, concord, and unity were inseparable; the adherents of disunity were wicked—minions of Satan, caring only for their own gain and self-love. He scoffed at the charge that he was the spokesman for the Bigi, or Medicean loyalists, who would profit from a law of amnesty: "You still say that I've been persuaded by others to exhort you to union. I see you take me for a simpleton. . . . Insofar as I preach peace, that's by the persuasion and teaching of the Gospel." And to those who complained of his illicit interference in governmental matters: "As to the rest, I don't interfere; among yourselves do what seems best to you. When you are in disagreement and want to find the truth, first pray God to enlighten you to find it and concentrate on the common good, not on your individual interests. When you find a certain view to be held by men of good conscience and by a majority, it would be praiseworthy of you to adhere to it."[35]

By the overwhelming vote of 543 to 163, the Great Council adopted both reform proposals on March 19. Amnesty was extended to all who had collaborated with the previous regime excepting only the direct male descendants of Cosimo de' Medici. The Signoria's prerogative of the Six Beans was abolished; anyone convicted of crimes against the state was to have the right to appeal to the Great Council, where they might be absolved by a two-thirds vote. This was a major victory for the Frate and his allies in the Great Council. True to the paranoid style of Florentine politics, everyone suspecting everyone of hidden motives, this in turn provoked the old canard that the Frate was secretly serving the cause of the Medici.

Savonarola exulted. Like Jacob, whose name became Israel after a night of wrestling with the angel, the Florentine people have undergone a name change just since yesterday; let them now be called "blessed of the Lord." "See, you have not been able to resist . . . this has been done by God." God himself had changed the white beans ("no" votes) to black ("yes" votes).[36] "You have prayed as I meant you to do and the prayers of the good have had this effect, absolutely." That it had been done so quickly and when hope was failing was due to the intercession of the Virgin; she had been their advocate and in an instant changed many hearts. Therefore, from that day until the Day of the Annunciation, everyone must pray and give thanks to the Virgin; if they did so, perhaps the Lord would pity them and grant other graces they had asked for.[37]

CHAPTER 12

The Virgin and the Republic of Virtue

Savonarola's call to pray to the Virgin Mary was the prelude to one of the more spectacular visionary episodes of his apostolate. On March 24, the vigil of the Feast of the Annunciation, he announced his intention to go to Mary's heavenly throne to ask her to intercede with God on behalf of the city. The next day, Florence's New Year, he reported that the Holy Mother had assured him (by what medium he did not explain) that she would receive him kindly.[1] He gave an account of the journey on April 1, but since we have no adequate text of this sermon (he later complained that it had been taken down "imperfectly and corruptly and sent to various parts of Italy")[2] we rely upon the expanded version (running to almost a hundred pages) in his *Compendium of Revelations*, which he published four months later.[3] The summary that follows offers only a glimpse of its cosmological scope and scarcely conveys the richness of its allegorical imagery.

Setting out on his journey, he refuses the company of Lady Rhetoric and Lady Philosophy or any of "the other kinds of human wisdom inadequate for our embassy"; his companions will be Lady Simplicity, Faith, Prayer, and Patience. An old hermit blocks his way, charging him, among other crimes, with having surrendered the government of Florence to the lowly plebs. After Savonarola refutes him on every point the three ladies expose this antagonist as the devil. Arriving at the gate of paradise, Savonarola shows Saint Joseph the wonderful crown he has been carrying. This crown, he tells Joseph, has been made by the Florentine people as a gift and a set of prayers to the Virgin—not only with words, but with their hearts and deeds. The three tiers of hearts forming the crown represent the three stages of ascent to spiritual perfection—those who have recently come to penitence "in the greenness of their faith," those who have purged their consciences of sin and of earthly desires, and the small number of "the perfect" whose four fiery garnets signify that they are inflamed with the love of God. The tiny hearts at the peak of the crown surmounted by a cross represent the union of love and also the universal peace recently established among the citizens of Florence.[4] (*see Fig. 2*)

Accompanied by Saint Joseph, the travelers make their way through the allegorically rich meadows of paradise until they behold Solomon's splendid throne. On it sits the beautiful woman "more resplendent than the sun" with the Babe in her arms (Rev. 12.1). Savonarola is prostrated by the dazzling spectacle and has to be helped to his feet by Saint Joseph, who explains that this is the mystery of the renewal he has been prophesying. Saint Joseph elucidates each detail of the heavenly company surrounding the throne—doctors and prelates of the Church, laity living the active life in holy simplicity, contemplatives both lay and religious—through which fra Girolamo passes as he continues his ascent. Once in Mary's presence, Savonarola is told to approach and presents the crown. Mary accepts it and places it on her head. At his request she rises and kneels before the Holy Trinity to pray for Florence. Boldly, Savonarola demurs: "Virgin Mother, these are generalities; your blessed hand must be more open." At this Mary reproaches her "beloved people" for their iniquities and lack of faith, but then assures them that what God has promised will be restored: the city will be "more glorious, more powerful, and richer than ever," extending its wings farther than anyone can imagine. The Florentines will not only recover all they have lost but will be protected against future losses and acquire other things that have never been theirs. Four years ago, she reminds them, the Pisans were warned that if they sought their liberty it would be their ruin, and this too will come to pass. As to the coming tribulations, Florence will be scourged more lightly than other places and the renewal—the reform of the Church, the conversion of the Turks, Moors, and other infidels— will take place just as Savonarola has preached, and soon. Many now living will see it.

To illustrate her promises, Mary displays two spheres, the larger depicting the time of tribulations, with Florence suffering less than other cities. The smaller sphere shows Florence bedecked with lilies and guarded by angels. This promise of future glories, she assures him again, is absolute, although how much they will suffer depends on how well they observe good laws, how thoroughly they punish the wicked and the impious blasphemers, gamblers, and those who commit "the unspeakable sin against nature." Still Savonarola persists: when will fulfillment come? The Virgin Mother replies: whether it is in April, July, or September, whether in two years or in six, it will be "quickly and soon." The way will be long and tiring, she tells fra Girolamo, but she and her associates will protect him against his enemies. Soon he too will be of their company and receive the crown of life. Singing psalms, Savonarola and his companions descend the heavenly ladder and the celestial vision comes to a close.

In Savonarola's account of his journey the Virgin Mother not only lent her authority to his campaign for peace and unity in the New Jerusalem, she promised the confusion of the city's enemies, supported Florence's alliance with the French (the union of the lilies), and confirmed the coming tribulations and eventual glory. But how should we understand this interview with the Blessed Virgin? Was it a mystical vision, a prophetic intuition, or an extended homiletic conceit? Savonarola's preliminary announcement to his congregation that he intends to go to the Virgin's heavenly throne suggests prior deliberation rather than mystical spontaneity. The learned and meticulously detailed symbolism of the vision (radically pruned in my summary) also argues for studied preparation. His abundant use of conventional allegory and his borrowings (some acknowledged, some not) from visionary sources, including Pseudo-Dionysius and the Book of Revelation, link the journey to written tradition.[5] One great student of medieval visions thinks it was "probably bogus," but what this means is unclear.[6] Whatever its nature, Savonarola himself presents it as having the same truth value as his other visions.

Florentines were divided about the vision, predictably along party lines. Piagnone Luca Landucci called it a "revelation of the Virgin Mary" tout court and reported that "the majority of the people believed him, especially the righteous who were not influenced by their political passions."[7] Much later, Pseudo-Burlamacchi wrote, mistakenly, that the sermon was so "wonderful" that Savonarola had to deliver it twice, on the Day of the Annunciation and again on the octave of the feast.[8] But Savonarola had to defend himself against those (the tepid, he calls them) who mocked his claim to have traveled to the Virgin's throne.[9] Only a stupid or malicious person would be scornful, he declared, for if what he wrote were carefully examined, it would be seen that it did not mean that he was bodily in paradise but that it was all an imaginary vision, "because in paradise there are no streams nor animals nor trees nor walls nor gates nor stairways nor chairs nor precious stones. Since I described all these things in a spiritual sense, these characters, if they weren't extremely ignorant and thickheaded, or if they weren't so malicious, could have easily understood that everything I saw had been formed in the imagination by angelic agency, just as I described at the beginning of the book and just as I had been given the understanding of all these things. The prophets saw many things in this way. Ezekiel especially often says that in this way he has been many places, to which it is certain that he went with his spirit and not with his body."[10]

What did fra Girolamo mean by "an imaginary vision"? A journey in a dream? An ecstatic or out-of-body experience? As he explained in his *Compendium of Revelations* (and again in the Advent sermons on Ezekiel of the following year),[11] an imaginary vision is something more than the product of human cognition (or, we might add, of human invention); it is nothing less than an infusion of God's supernal light by angelic agency, as he put it in his *Letter to a Friend.* Authenticated by the biblical prophets and guided by angels, visions were considered to be a legitimate, supernatural medium for conveying the divinely guaranteed truths of prophecy. The visionary state was ambiguous by its nature. Saint Paul, "the pioneer of Christian otherworld journeying," as he has been called, was unable to say whether he had been in or out of the body in his ascent to the third heaven (2 Cor. 12).[12] Of his own ecstatic state fra Girolamo said that he had been so inflamed by love and beauty that he forgot he even had a body.

A century and a half earlier, when Dante Alighieri wrote his *Divine Comedy,* voyages to the other world were already "an extraordinarily popular literary genre" with more than sixty examples.[13] Savonarola was acquainted with Dante's great poem, and between it and the *Compendium* vision there are some common features. (One of his antagonists perceived this and compared the vision unfavorably to Dante's.)[14] Mystics and literary travelers to other worlds were typically accompanied by at least one guide and apt to encounter demonic opposition on the way. They traveled as envoys or messengers of the human world and returned wiser, possessed of crucial moral advice and tidings of the future. Whether mystical or literary, paradise had a conventional look. "Heaven is always glowing and white, bright—often so bright that one cannot see for the brightness. There are many people; and there is a focal point of brightness. There are often beautiful clothes and gems, perhaps high walls and flowery fields. Heaven has a fragrant smell, more light, less noise, and perhaps even sweet music."[15] Celestial choirs of angels and saints provided guidance and beautiful music, and the earthly visitor was granted a view of the spheres that made up the hierarchically ordered universe and was frequently allowed to see the entire world, again in the form of a sphere.

As fra Girolamo repeatedly told his listeners, he found his major inspiration in the Hebrew prophets. Ezekiel, God's itinerant thunderer, seer of

sapphire thrones and avenging swords, whisked by spirits from the gate of
heaven to the far-off plain of dry bones, was one of his favorites; Jeremiah,
nemesis of Babylon and prophet of a restored Jerusalem, was another. "Read
the sacred scriptures and have them read to you," he advised his devoted
patron Duke Ercole of Ferrara. "I speak of the prophets and especially Jeremiah and Ezekiel, and you will find almost everything that happened in those
times to be similar to ours."[16]

In the religious culture inhabited by the Frate, visions were a well-known
phenomenon, if less common in the fifteenth century than they had been in
the twelfth or thirteenth.[17] Aquinas, Bonaventura, and other Doctors of the
Church regarded them as a legitimate modality of communicating with the
supernatural.[18] On the relation between visions and prophecy one student of
vision history has written, "It is impossible to draw a real line between the
prophet and the visionary."[19] Savonarola would have agreed: "[The visionary
mode] is the way the prophets saw many things," and "Revelations begin with
an infusion of supernatural light which enables the prophet to see that the
revelations are true and that they come from God." A Savonarola without
visions would have no more been the preacher-prophet than a Petrarch without sonnets would have been the great humanist poet.[20]

In his account of the journey to the Virgin's court fra Girolamo enthroned
Mary in a dazzling aura of near divinity and referred to her as "the Immaculate." Visitors to Dominican churches can see that the Mother of God occupied a leading role in the Order's liturgy, devotions, and iconography. The
friars venerated Mary as their special protectress and associated her with their
founding.[21] San Marco, with its altarpieces and frescoes of the Virgin and
Child, of the Coronation of the Virgin, and of the Annunciation, was rich in
Marian devotion. Yet Savonarola seems to have expected his exaltation of
Mary to raise some eyebrows, for he prefaced his account with a disclaimer:
all praise and veneration was due to the Virgin, but no more than that. Those
who knew his sermons, he said, would note that it was unusual for him to
preach about her, and if they asked him why, he would answer with another
question: "First let me ask you: how is it that in Scripture the Holy Spirit
mentioned her so seldom? And how is it that the apostles wrote about her
rarely or not at all and that the early saints seldom preached her rarely as
well?" His answer was that salvation depends upon faith in Christ and not on
any creature. "A great error has been born in the world in these times; often a
devotion to the Virgin starts up in one place or another and greedy men make
a business out of it. The Virgin has no need of this."

As a student fra Girolamo had taken notes on the lectures of his theology professor, fra Vincenzo Bandelli. Bandelli was a leading spokesman for the belief, widely held among Dominicans, that Mary was conceived in sin like all other human beings and therefore bore the stain (*macula*) of original sin at birth. According to this view, promoted by Saint Thomas Aquinas (*Summa theologiae* III. 27.4), Mary was sanctified, that is, rendered sinless, only after she conceived her son Jesus, Redeemer of all mankind. In a debate before Pope Sixtus IV in 1477, Bandelli argued this so-called maculist view unsuccessfully. Sixtus, like most of his fellow Franciscans, favored the view of Duns Scotus, who held that Mary had been conceived without sin. Although the pope proclaimed an indulgence for the celebration of the Feast of the Immaculate Conception, Bandelli continued to uphold the maculist view in his writings and disputations, as he did in 1481 in a debate in the Ducal Palace of Ferrara where fra Girolamo, lector in Santa Maria degli Angeli, must have heard him. Thus, when Savonarola later celebrated Mary as immaculately conceived, he was in some sense asserting his independence from Bandelli's tutelage as well as from the authority of the Lombard Congregation. This may partly explain why he retained a certain ambiguity about the doctrine. In some of his sermons and in the treatise *Triumphus Crucis* of 1497, as well as in his account of the journey to the Virgin's throne, he described Mary in immaculist terms, although in other sermons and colloquies he refused to take a definite position. "I will leave the question of conception, whether she was conceived in original sin, to be decided in the court of paradise."[22]

Savonarola's mystical encounter with the Blessed Virgin served a dual purpose: Mary endorsed his triple vow to the Florentines while warning them that they would suffer if they failed to live up to their designated redemptive role. This gave him renewed ammunition for the pulpit wars of that spring of 1495. His Lenten sermons on Job and his sermons on Psalms rang with denunciations of the *tiepidi*, the morally slack clerics and laymen who opposed his program of religious and constitutional reforms. With the time approaching for the inaugural session of the Great Council, he pressed for the resignation of the twenty Accoppiatori, whom the oligarchy, in a kind of rearguard action, had empowered to handpick the Signoria in place of election.

Sensitive to charges that he interfered in affairs of state, he stopped short of attacking the Accoppiatori explicitly. Instead he employed another of his pulpit dialogues with an imaginary interlocutor: "Well, what's to be done, Frate?—There's something that needs to be done that I don't want to tell you because it has to do with the state; but God will do it in any case.—O, Frate, what are you saying?—Pray God that he convert these wicked men and if they don't want to convert, it's better that they don't impede good men but make themselves scarce."[23] At the same time he worked behind the scenes to persuade the Accoppiatori to resign. He had little trouble with Giuliano Salviati, one of his most loyal patrician followers, but another member of the commission, Francesco Valori, complained that Salviati's withdrawal meant ruin for the city. Savonarola persisted, and with their solid front broken, Valori and the other members of the commission stepped down. With the formal abolition of the Accoppiatori on June 10, the Great Council came into its own as the sovereign electoral and legislative body of the republic. The new Priors elected Piagnone Lorenzo Lenzi Gonfaloniere of Justice.

Fra Girolamo's moral and political authority now reached into every part of the city's life. When he complained about running horse races on feast days and demanded that they be cancelled with the money saved going to the poor, it was done, although it meant giving up the popular Corpus Christi festivities in August and—even dearer to Florentine hearts—the Palio races on June 24, day of the city's patron, Saint John the Baptist. Fireworks also met with his disapproval and were duly suppressed. "So much did his authority count with us," commented Parenti, who, notwithstanding his growing hostility to Savonarolan populism, was forced to admit that in place of gambling and other abusive practices, people had begun to help each other. A modest resumption of woolen and silk production also provided jobs and lightened the public mood.[24]

Amnesty, the right of appeal, and governo civile he preached incessantly; they were the major steps toward realizing a Christian republic where political life would be inspired by charity in the service of the bene commune. But the New Jerusalem had also to be morally pure. Gambling, tavern drinking, whoring, swearing, provocative dancing were rampant, he complained. Prostitutes openly paraded their wares. "Respectable" women with their low-cut gowns and elaborate hairdos were no less shameless. Young men with shoulder-length hair, tight hose, and intricately worked doublets and capes were still worse, for they erased the God-ordained distinction between male and female.

Always the supreme abomination was sodomy. In his sermon of December 14, 1494, he had urged the Signoria to make a law against "that accursed vice of sodomy for which you know Florence to be infamous throughout Italy. Make a law, I say, without pity, so that such persons are stoned and burned."[25] Two weeks later, on December 31, the two outgoing councils voted 201 to 4 and 170 to 10 to adopt the "harshest law against sodomy in Florentines' living memory."[26] The preamble of the measure was unmistakably Savonarolan: the spread of sodomy is due to "the wicked governors who had [previously] ruled"; Florence must have a moral order worthy of "a Christian and religious republic."[27] Fines were abolished. Offenders under eighteen were to be punished at the discretion of the Council. A sodomist eighteen years or older convicted for the first time was to be publicly pilloried, hands tied behind his back, for at least an hour. Penalties increased with the number of offenses. Repeat offenders were to be bound and paraded through the city to the Old Market where they would be branded on the forehead. Convicted sodomists were ineligible for offices and public honors. Those convicted a third time were to be burned alive.

Sodomy, defined by Saint Thomas as all sexual acts between persons of the same sex, was condemned in Christian doctrine and civil law. Virtually every medieval and Renaissance preacher as well as authors of confessional manuals treated it as a continuing problem. In Florence, as in the rest of Christendom, it was shameful and illegal, yet homoerotic connections between men and boys seem to have been more or less openly tolerated, nor were sexual relations between women unknown. If sodomy was the vice that dared not speak its name, Florentines, as Savonarola complained, talked and joked about it freely. "You know that in all of Italy Florence is infamous for it, maybe this is because you chatter and gossip about it so much that it's said to be worse than it really is."[28] For middle-class Florentine men, who routinely delayed marriage until their thirties, when they were financially established, opportunities for sex with unmarried women of their class were severely restricted. Many, therefore, seem to have satisfied their needs with prostitutes, or with boys, or both. Taverns were known to be meeting places for casual encounters (which helps explain Savonarola's detestation of them), and certain religious confraternities were notorious for encouraging homoerotic liaisons. Policing sodomy had long been the responsibility of the Otto di Guardia, but in 1432 a special Office of the Night had been founded to receive and investigate accusations of sodomy from anonymous informers and to prosecute and punish. The effect was a marked increase in accusations, although few of these resulted in convictions. By far the greatest number were punished with a small fine.

If there is any accuracy to the legend of the era of Lorenzo de' Medici as a time of unbuttoned vice, it applies particularly to the years after the Pazzi conspiracy when, with power well in hand, Il Magnifico promoted lavish

carnivals and other public festivities and patronized the bawdy writings of
Luigi Pulci (himself implicated in homoerotic activity) and others. By granting the Florentines opportunities for indulging and acting out their illicit
sexual instincts Lorenzo may have thought he could divert attention from his
stifling of their political liberty. In any case, even as he lay dying the Eight and
the Officials of the Night were moving to impose new restrictions on sodomy
as well as on gambling and prostitution by limiting access to the usual meeting places and increasing payments to informers.[29]

Savonarola called for war on sodomy without limit. The charity and
forbearance he argued for in connection with his law of political amnesty was
not to be available to sexual transgressors. But to Piagnoni zealots the effects
of the Savonarolan December law on homoerotic activity were still disappointing. Abolishing fines ended a major incentive for informers who had
previously received a share of the monies collected, just as the increased
severity of the penalties seems to have reduced the number of accusations.
The harshness of the proscribed punishments even dissuaded officials from
rigorously enforcing the new law. With fewer cases brought to the attention
of the authorities, there was a sharp drop in prosecutions. When the coun-
cilors tried to remedy this difficulty by restoring fines at least for first offenders, fra Girolamo was furibund: "Are any of the Lords of the Eight present?"
he asked on July 5. "I'd like to see you build a nice fire of these sodomites in the
piazza, two or three, male and female, because there are also women who
practice that damnable vice. I say offer [them as] a sacrifice to God."[30]

A week later he had barely recovered his equanimity, accusing those who
opposed strenuous measures against vice as endangering the city: "Oh, you're
cruel, Frate!"—"[No] you are the cruel one, you who would endanger a city on
behalf of a wretch."[31] His promises of Florentine glory were unconditional he
declared; but how soon glory would come and how many tribulations the
citizens would suffer depended on how quickly and thoroughly they accepted
his four conditions: fear of God, the common good, peace, and the reform of
the Council. They could demonstrate their fear of God by purging vice—and
now he offered a more extensive list: dancing, corrupting young people with
poetry, the effeminate style of dress affected by young men, gaming in the
streets, nighttime drinking (taverns should be closed at sunset), and keeping
open on feast days nonessential shops and businesses.

Still, no vice was as hideous as the sin "against nature." Since it would not
be suppressed by fines or by keeping it secret, Florentines should "make a fire
all Italy will see!" Even though the remedial law of June 25 was restoring

prosecutions to their former higher levels, he was not appeased. When it came to sodomy, pragmatism had to bow to principle. Even though they were counterproductive, he pressed for a return to the drastic penalties of the previous year, and eventually a government dominated by Frateschi gave him what he wanted. The new law of December 19, 1495, announced its intention "to increase rather than diminish the penalties in any way" by allowing the magistrates to choose whatever punishment they saw fit, including death. By this time the issue of policing sodomy had become thoroughly politicized, with Frateschi administrations opting for greater severity and Arrabbiati majorities favoring the older, more permissive methods.

Savonarola's success in turning the Florentine oligarchic coup into a popular revolution and, however imperfectly, translating penitence into continence attests to his power over hearts and minds, a power that he himself attributed to divine inspiration. But it was one thing for a preacher, even a prophet, to show the way, to advise, to warn, to ridicule, even threaten, and another for a cleric and "foreigner" to give law to a divided and troubled people. With his embassies to Charles VIII and his promotion of a *governo civile* Savonarola had long since crossed into the political arena. His political position after the expulsion of the Medici has been likened to that of Lorenzo the Magnificent. The comparison is instructive as much for differences as similarities. As a cleric and noncitizen the Frate was doubly ineligible to hold public office, vote, or take part in government councils. *Consulte* and *pratiche,* the advisory meetings of important citizens, were closed to him. Lorenzo had seldom held public office, preferring to rule from behind the scenes, using his great wealth, family connections, and near-princely status to assert his will through clients, employees, and political allies at home and abroad. None of these resources was available to Savonarola. As a mendicant friar bound by vows of radical poverty and humility as well as obedience to his superiors, he had no access to, nor inclination for, the images of worldly elegance and power that Lorenzo employed to charm, fascinate, overawe, and intimidate his fellow Florentines. Lorenzo's was a charisma of power. Fra Girolamo's was a charisma of grace, a higher form of legitimacy perhaps but more precarious, constantly requiring fresh verification from events and difficult to translate into political reality.

Fra Girolamo was aware of his limits and frequently referred to them, going so far as to express his frustration at the constraints he had put on with his clerical robes: "I am a friar and I have never seen arms, but were I allowed to I would show you reasons to keep you from being afraid. . . . I wish I could (I say 'could' meaning that I wish I were allowed to) put on a *cappuccio* and *lucco* [the magistrate's hood and gown]: I'd show you why you needn't be so afraid." His own political leadership had to be admonitory and prophetic, to teach the Florentines what they must do to protect their God-given liberty and fulfill their role in the coming New Era. His proclaimed ideal was a governo civile in which no one could make himself capo or tyrant. Did the Florentines want a king? Let them take Christ as their king. Publicly, even ostentatiously, he refrained from intervening in specific decisions or supporting particular candidates and he repeatedly disavowed *intelligenze*, as the illegal meetings were called.

Whether, or how regularly, Savonarola transgressed these boundaries is not easy to determine, partly because so little of what was said behind closed doors has survived, partly because such boundaries were even then difficult to define. To his opponents' accusation that he unlawfully interfered in politics, he and his defenders responded with contradictory arguments, on one hand flatly denying the charge that he interfered, on the other citing precedents of other clerics who had done precisely this. Later, to his inquisitors, he would only admit to "half-intelligenze," more or less general political discussions with his sympathizers, and even those, he said, he usually delegated to his lieutenant fra Silvestro Maruffi.

Downplay them as he would, however, those discussions carried over into political action. Guided by such experienced and prominent citizens as Paolantonio Soderini, Giovambattista Ridolfi, Piero Guicciardini, and, eventually, Francesco Valori, the Piagnoni began to form an identifiable bloc in the councils and magistracies, known as the Frateschi, the Frate's men. They were never a majority. Not until 1497, when Valori became their leader, did they follow the consistent agenda and exhibit the tighter discipline of a political party.[32] With the Great Council in place Savonarola relied on the Frateschi to introduce and vote for his proposed reforms and to elect like-minded candidates for office. Although they had leaders of experience, many of these Savonarolan councilmen, being new to public life, were at a disadvantage in debate, tactics, and political judgment. Savonarola chafed at their shortcomings and soon began complaining that too many Council members voted for candidates based on family ties and personal likes and dislikes instead of their ability and dedication to the common good. This led him to reexamine some of his earlier populist and moralistic assumptions. Was it enough that a councilman be virtuous? Should a member of the Great Council vote for a candidate who was "good" if he was foolish or inexperienced? How should voters choose between an able "bad man" and a "good man" who lacked desirable qualities of statesmanship? Although he never gave a definite answer to this dilemma he increasingly emphasized the virtue of prudence, by which he seems to have meant the exercise of good judgment seasoned by political experience.

In that first spring and summer of the new dispensation such questions remained in the background. ("He was held in so much esteem and devotion in Florence at that time," said Landucci, "that there were many men and women who, if he had said to them 'go into the fire' would surely have obeyed him.")[33] But he had always to be aware that his range of political motion had its limits. Viewing his mission in biblical, that is to say, apocalyptic, terms he damned all who hesitated or opposed him as enemies of the fledgling New Jerusalem and complained that the Florentines were less committed to *il ben vivere*, righteous living, than he required. Backsliding, as he saw it, was a recurring temptation as it had been for the Children of Israel. To be sure, the amnesty law had been approved, but law was one thing, spirit another; what the Florentines needed, he believed, was a brotherly union of hearts. Lack of unity was the cause of all their troubles, he insisted; if they said they were truly united, they lied. Love, as Dionysius the Areopagite had written, bound all the orders of creation together, from the angels down to the human and natural worlds. In the Church Christians had found protection in unity, and so too would the Florentines. Once they became truly united, he never ceased to remind them, God would favor them against their enemies, and riches, honors, and empire would be theirs. But coming so hesitantly to concord, they delayed the fulfillment of the promise. Four years ago, he declared, he had predicted that God would send a minister from across the mountains to castigate Italy. If they abandoned their party loyalties and prayed together as a unified body they would have all that was theirs. Thus, the fulfillment of their destiny, at least the timing of it, was in the hands of the Florentines themselves.

Bad news from abroad weakened the fitful unity Florence had achieved. In April it was learned that Pope Alexander VI had formed a Holy League of the major Italian states and the German emperor to drive the French out of Italy. This not only gave the pope new leverage for pressing the city to abandon the French alliance, but it also gave him additional reason to investigate the upstart prophet and his outrageous claim that a French king was

God's instrument for castigating and reforming the Church. Florentines debated. Was it wise to thwart His Holiness (who had so many spiritual and material ways to retaliate)? Was it proper for Italians to support the barbarian invader of their country? Inevitably, the controversy focused on Savonarola, the ideological mainstay of the French alliance, and upon his claim that all this was the will of God. Rumors abounded. Reports of a letter from the pope ordering Savonarola to Rome to explain himself turned out to be false, as were rumors that a group of clerics had met in secret conclave in Rome to decide what was to be done with him.

Savonarola was convinced that plots were being hatched against him. In the growing war of nerves he stepped up his campaign against the tiepidi, that anonymous all-service phalanx of enemies who confused superficial ceremony with spiritual piety and refused to believe in the coming renovation of the Church. Before long he would begin calling for their actual destruction. "I want to tell you something about them this morning [April 4]: in a certain place in this city they have met and taken counsel against me and have arranged to do a lot of things against me, and not only in this city but elsewhere as well." These were the tiepidi, they who were neither hot nor cold, whom the Lamb of God would spit out of his mouth (Rev. 3.15–17); these were collectively the rider of the pale horse whose name was Death (Rev. 6.7), enemies of renewal not only spiritual but, as he now came to believe, political as well.[34]

On May 26 Savonarola wrote to Charles VIII to remind him that God had placed Florence under his protection and to demand that he fulfill his promises. If His Majesty did so, fra Girolamo could tell him with divine authority that he would have victory; if not, punishment. But the king, having heard that the Holy League was organizing most of the Italian powers against him, had already decided to return to France. Leaving a garrison in Naples, he led his army northward. The pope was terrified at his approach and fled Rome. Although Savonarola still clung to the belief that Charles would soon put things in order in the Holy City, reforming the Church was not, at this moment at least, on the king's agenda. Many Florentines even worried that when Charles returned to their city he would put it to the sack and carry out his resolve to readmit Piero de' Medici.[35]

The arrest in Florence on May 16 of two would-be conspirators, Alessandro and Lamberto dell'Antella, appeared to confirm the threat of a Medici takeover. When, under torture, they produced the dubious information that the return of Charles was to be the signal for a rising of Piero's loyalists, weapons were mustered all across Florentine territory and guards were posted throughout the city.[36] The brothers also implicated Lorenzo Tornabuoni, a popular favorite despite being Piero's brother-in-law and one of his defenders in the November revolt. Tornabuoni was questioned but revealed nothing and was released.

Equally unsettling was the news that the Pisans, with the help of their French garrison, had captured Ripafratta, the strategically important town on the road between Lucca and Pisa. After hurried consultations with prominent citizens, the Signoria decided to send ambassadors to the king to request that he respect the people's liberty (that is, withdraw his support for Piero's return) and honor his promises to restore Florence's lost territories. The magistrates also invoked divine aid: in early June they sent for the miracle-working image of the Madonna to be brought to the city from its sanctuary in the nearby village of Impruneta. "The entire populace, male and female, poor and rich, noble and humble, followed the procession," wrote Parenti.[37] A solemn Mass was sung in the Duomo, prayers were offered for the conservation of liberty and protection from hunger, plague, and unfriendly French troops.

Although Savonarola often criticized "ceremony" as the tepid Christian's substitute for deep faith, he could neither prevent nor ignore this citywide outpouring of emotion. Instead he took charge, ordering that alms tables be set up along the route from Impruneta, with half the collection reserved for the Good Men of San Martino, the charity for impoverished citizens who were ashamed to beg.[38] Daily he alternated warnings of disasters with promises of glory and peace. "Well, see if I'm crazy. When things were going well for you I promised you that you would have it bad, and now that things are bad I'm promising you good things."[39] The worst was yet to come, for the Lord was still angry with Italy and would send more barbarians to harrow the land. Men at arms would be crushed by mere boys, jewel-stuffed castles destroyed. Pestilence would be visited upon impenitent, tepid friars, priests, and monks; famine would be the lot of the poor. Yet those who did penance and sought peace would be glorified, for Christ told his disciples to go to Jerusalem and Jerusalem meant peace. Against threats from outside, however, he counseled armed resistance, urging citizens to make themselves ready with weapons and gunpowder. In the coming weeks they undertook to make their New Jerusalem a bristling fortress.

By June 12 King Charles was in Siena, where he met with the hastily dispatched Florentine envoys. His Majesty refused to disclose his intentions toward the city, except to say that because of the growing threat of the Holy League's armies he would keep Pisa and the fortress towns until he was safely back in Asti. Meanwhile Savonarola also prepared to go to the king on the city's behalf. His instructions were to speak to His Majesty at Siena, to assure him of the Florentines' continuing good will, and to insist that Charles fulfill his obligations toward them. Instead, he decided to wait for the king at Poggibonsi, in Florentine territory, some distance north of Siena. He felt safer there, he explained, fearing Sienese wrath for his attempts to take over their Dominican convent and he worried about the French and Pisan soldiers ravaging the countryside. At the same time, by ignoring the Signoria's instructions, he caused the Florentines to lose several critical days in their preparations to prepare the city in view of the French arrival.

Charles arrived in Poggibonsi on June 17 and, according to Savonarola's report, received the Frate with cordiality and respect, inviting him to accompany the royal party to Pisa. Savonarola traveled with His Majesty as far as Castelfiorentino, about halfway to Pisa, during which time they had had two more colloquies, before he returned to Florence on June 20.

Once back in Florence Savonarola was at pains to insist that he had made the trip independently, answerable not to Florence but to God: "So, not having been sent by you I don't have to report to you; I have already reported in full to him who sent me."[40] Seeing that the Signoria had sent him a letter of instructions in which they addressed him as "representative and advocate of the Florentine people" and given him an escort of fifty men at arms, the disclaimer seems both arrogant and disingenuous; he had blundered and used the mantle of divine authority to cover his embarrassment.

The following day Florentines filled the Duomo to hear the report fra Girolamo had insisted he was under no obligation to make: "I've been in the field, which is like being in hell," he told them, but he brought good news. "See, I have so much love for you that I placed myself in peril of my life for you." He had told the king "modestly but spiritedly" that God spoke through him, and the king had listened meekly. He had called upon Charles to treat the Florentines well, warning him that if he did not do so out of love, he would be compelled to do so by God's will. He had also described to the king the punishments God would visit upon him, but these, he said, were secrets which he was not at liberty to reveal to his listeners.

Although Savonarola failed to explain why the king appeared indifferent to fulfilling the messianic role assigned to him, his report was, in practical respects, reassuring: Charles seemed neither to be contemplating an immediate attack on the city nor a restoration of Piero de' Medici. He also appeared to be willing to return the territories he had seized from Florence after he had crossed the border into France. Nevertheless, in a letter of June or early July Savonarola chided the king: the Florentines have been standing "in fire and in flood," yet His Majesty has not returned to them what is theirs. "Most Christian sire, my words are not mine, but from God."[41]

If the king indeed received these letters, Savonarola's appeals and threats influenced him not in the slightest. After leaving Pisa he made his way north through the Apennines. On July 6, finding his path through Lombardy blocked by troops of the Holy League at the Taro River, near Fornovo, he was forced to give battle. Eight hours of bloody fighting left some four thousand dead and many wounded. The army of the League suffered the greater number of casualties and finally gave way, but the Italians' vigorous stand against the mighty French army blasted the aura of invincibility that had surrounded Charles since his easy triumphs of the previous winter.[42] And now those past victories also proved ephemeral: the day after Fornovo, King Ferdinand of Aragon reentered his capital at Naples, and in a battle off the Ligurian coast the Genoese decimated the French fleet.

In Florence the news of the king's retreat further tarnished his image as the New Cyrus. Some insisted that they should cut all ties with this fickle ally and accept the overtures of the League. These arguments were offset by the fear of the League's main protagonists, Milan and Venice, as well as by Savonarola's insistence that Charles would return to Italy to fulfill his pledges and carry out his divinely appointed mission of scourging the Church and going to the East to convert the infidel. Savonarola had his way: the Florentines remained loyal to Charles, but he was now more than ever hostage to the king's intentions toward the city.

CHAPTER 13

The Pope Summons

Pope Alexander VI had tolerated Savonarola's denunciations of immorality in the church hierarchy and the Roman curia. He was even curious about the Frate's prophecies. But the Florentines' refusal to abandon the French alliance alerted the pope to his political influence, and he became more receptive to the warnings of Cardinal Sforza of Milan and fra Mariano da Genazzano. The Dominican was not merely annoying but dangerous.

Savonarola tried to forestall the coming storm by writing to the pope in his own defense. His first letter, now lost, initiated an extended epistolary pas de deux. Alexander's answering brief of July 21, 1495, was at the same time fulsome and subtly menacing.[1] His Holiness rejoiced in fra Girolamo's matchless labor in the Lord's vineyard and was convinced that in disseminating the word of God the friar was inspired by the Holy Spirit. Recently, however, he had learned that fra Girolamo publicly claimed divine revelation, not human wisdom, to be the source of his announcements about the future. His Holiness wanted to hear these things from Savonarola's own mouth. Therefore he urged—no, he commanded—fra Girolamo to come to him as soon as possible and promised that he would be received in paternal love and charity.

Savonarola replied on July 31: he has always wanted to see Rome, to venerate the holy places and pay reverence to His Holiness, especially now that the pope has summoned him, worm that he is. But he regrets that he is unable to comply. For one thing, he has been in poor health. Fever, dysentery, and ailments of the stomach and other organs have forced him to abstain from preaching and study. If he does not do so, the doctors have warned, he might soon die. Ever since God (together with his own labor) restored Florence to peace and holy law and saved it from bloodshed, evil men here and abroad hate him and try to reduce the city to servitude. There have been so many conspiracies to kill him, either by poison or sword, that without guards he may not put a foot outside his door. When he traveled to the camp of the king of France, his loyal guards did not let him go beyond the frontier of Florentine territory. Were he to disdain proper security measures, he would be tempting God. Besides, it is the judgment of prudent and honorable men, and it is God's will, that he not absent himself until the reformation has been completed. He does not believe His Holiness will mind a slight delay.

In the meantime, if His Holiness wants to know what he has been publicly predicting about the scourging of Italy and the renewal of the Church, he may inform himself from a little book Savonarola has just composed. As soon as it appears from the printers he will give a copy to His Holiness's envoy. It will contain everything he is permitted to say (for no mortal being is allowed to reveal what must be kept secret). If the events he has predicted fail to come to pass, everyone will know he is a false prophet.

Savonarola understood the dangers of obeying the pope's summons. If he set out for Rome, there was a good chance he would be waylaid on the journey. If he reached the papal court, he would either be constrained to renounce his claim that he was God's chosen spokesman, thus confessing that he was an imposter, or he would be forced to defend his prophecies against unfriendly judges who would surely condemn him as a heretic, schismatic, or both. In either case he would not have been allowed to leave the Eternal City alive.

Whether he understood equally well the danger of *not* going to Rome is less clear. Apart from the patent insincerity of his regret at not being able to visit the holy places and pay reverence to the pope, he must also have infuriated His Holiness by asserting that his work in Florence was too important to be interrupted by a papal summons. His claim to have secret knowledge, which he was not permitted to reveal even to the pope, could only come across as insufferably arrogant. By refusing to go he only postponed the inevitable confrontation. His prophesying was no longer the sole issue: now it was also a question of clerical obedience and legitimacy as a faithful son of the Church. Forced increasingly on the defensive, he was for the time being protected by the walls of Florence, but only for as long as the Florentines were able—or willing—to resist Rome's pressure to give him up.

Savonarola's plea of ill health was not merely an excuse for putting off the papal summons. On July 28 "all the Magnificent Signori and magistrates" had been present in the cathedral to hear him announce that he was reluctantly taking a brief leave from preaching. Had he taken the advice of his physicians he would already have stopped preaching, he said, "I am persuaded to preach to you this morning not by medicine but by love." Of course, he added, "When I'm up here I'm always well. If I were as well when I am out of the pulpit as I am when I'm up here I'd always be fine, but I think that when I get down from here I'm going to have my troubles."[2] He was talking about more than bodily infirmity. As his audience was well aware, part of his trouble came from Rome; a furlough from preaching might be salutary for that affliction as well.

There would be nothing new or subtle in these parting words, he assured them as he launched into a discourse that veered between complaints about vice to exultant forecasts of the renewal of the Church. Florence's list of moral corruptions was as lengthy as ever: parents who let their children be seduced by poetry; prostitutes ("oh father there are so many!") who must be driven into the open with the blowing of trumpets; gamblers who should be banned from the streets and made to lend the commune double the amount they wager; blasphemers (pull out their tongues!). Dances must be abolished (send spies!); this was no time for dancing. Taverns refused to close at dusk, shops stayed open on holy days. Young men dressed like women. ("Fathers, confiscate their fancy little jackets, lock them away and tell them to have another one made, but then don't give them the money!") Toward the "nefarious vice" citizens were practicing a cruel pity, he complained; with sodomy as with gambling and blasphemy, the wicked few corrupt the whole.[3] Transgressors must be brought into the place of justice and warned that they faced the penalty of death.

Nor could he depart without giving advice on matters both great and small: the taxes on silk and wool should be lowered to give people work; silence must be kept in Council meetings and petitions posted in advance. It worried him that the enemies of freedom might try to bypass the Great Council by manipulating the people into holding a Parlamento: any member of the Signoria who tried to call a Parlamento should have his head cut off!

The poor quality of political judgment in the Great Council also continued to preoccupy Savonarola: members ignore the common good by voting for friends and relatives and voting against qualified men whom they dislike for some irrelevant personal reason. They give votes to incompetent men out of pity for their poverty; thus for a single good deed they ruin the commune. Between two men, one prudent and one good but not prudent, the prudent man should be elected, for as Saint Thomas says, goodness without prudence is not enough in such matters.[4] Men are not angels and their intelligence doesn't increase with virtue as it does in angels. A military commissioner should be a courageous and prudent man, not a fool who when in the field might be afraid to hurt someone. "Oh, is this a sin? I say that to vote for someone whom you know is not competent for the job is a mortal sin." Nor could he part without a note of pathos: "I conclude that I've preached and wearied myself so much for you, Florence, that I've shortened my life by many years and lost a lot."

Although he spent the rest of the summer completing the account of his prophecies for the pope, some of his causes were progressing. In early August the new hall for the Great Council received its vaulting. A new law banned the calling of Parlamento, with a penalty of death for violators. Florentine envoys met in Turin with ministers of Charles VIII and won still another promise that he would restore Pisa and the other territories and grant Florentine merchants a monopoly to do business in his realm. When the pope sent an envoy to Charles ordering him to appear in Rome on pain of excommunication, Piagnoni in Florence were joyful: surely this last desperate papal bid would so anger the king that he would remove Alexander from the papal throne and proceed to the renovation of the Church, just as fra Girolamo had prophesied.[5] That was a pipe dream. Charles VIII showed no disposition to reverse his homeward course and contented himself with a disdainful reply: His Majesty would happily come to Rome if the pope could assure him that he would be there when he arrived and not run away as he had done the first time!

The "little book" Savonarola had promised the pope came off the press on August 18, 1495, now more grandly entitled *Compendium of Revelations*.[6] Conscious of his growing notoriety (word that the sensational Florentine prophet was writing an account of his apostolate had spread far beyond the city), he explained that he had prepared both an Italian and a Latin text so that it would be available to everyone and less likely to be misunderstood. Savonarola's own prince, Duke Ercole of Ferrara, was so impatient to see it that he instructed his ambassador Manfredo Manfredi to have it copied in manuscript if there was to be any further delay in publication. When Savonarola presented Manfredi with a complimentary copy of the Italian edition on fine paper, illustrated with expensive copper engravings, the duke was delighted and full of praise.[7] (Savonarola also sent him a copy of the stylistically improved Latin edition in October, "so that you have it in both languages.") By early October the *Compendium of Revelations* had gone through five printings, with editions in Paris and Ulm the following year.[8]

Part apologia pro vita sua, part polemic, and part graphic replay of his prophetic visions, the *Compendium* is a masterpiece of self-dramatization.[9] God, Savonarola explains, sometimes shares the knowledge of future contingent events with his prophets so they can reveal it to ordinary mortals. He may infuse this knowledge directly, as he did by imparting wisdom to David and Solomon, he may instill it in the human imagination by means of diverse figures and imaginary visions, or he may send it to the exterior senses, particularly to the eyes, as he did when he wrote on the wall at Belshazzar's feast (Dan. 5). He himself, he declares, has received the divine light of prophecy in all three ways.

He then launches into a highly selective account of his prophetic apostolate.[10] So closely has he come to identify himself with Florence that he begins the story with his return to the city in 1489 (rightly 1490), omitting his earlier preaching career and the first apocalyptic stirrings in San Giorgio, San Gimignano, and Brescia. His early uncertainties about his prophetic gift have also disappeared: if at first he did not reveal his prophecies to be of divine origin, he explains, it was not because he lacked confidence but because his audiences were unprepared to hear this. "I always tried to prove these three conclusions [divine scourge, renovation of the Church, and soon] with probable reason and Scriptural figures, and . . . parables based on what is seen today in the Church, not telling [the Florentines] that I had these things in any other way . . . because they did not seem to me disposed to believe [prophecy]. . . . Then, as the years passed and I noted . . . a greater disposition to believe, I sometimes came out with a vision, not revealing, however, that it really was a vision, but proposing it as a kind of parable."

On the second Sunday of the following Lent (1491) after fear made him stop preaching such things, he heard a voice telling him that it was God's will that he continue and he preached "a terrifying sermon." Continuing to expound Genesis, he arrived at the text "Lo, I will bring the water of the flood over the earth" (Gen. 6.17) just as the news arrived that the king of France and his army had entered Italy. Count Giovanni Pico told him that this conjunction of text and event could only have been arranged by God. From that time on he began to reveal that his knowledge of the future came not from explicating Scripture but by "another light." Thus, from heaven came the words: "These things sayeth the Lord God, the sword of the Lord over the earth quickly and soon."

The vision of God's sword and the procession of white-robed angels had appeared to him shortly before Christmas of 1492. "Around then" he predicted that a New Cyrus would cross the mountains and begin the renewal of the Church. Other prophecies, notably the deaths of Pope Innocent VIII and of Lorenzo de' Medici and the revolution of the Florentine state, he had revealed only to intimates. After the French arrived in Tuscany, he was asked by the Florentine government to serve on an embassy to the French king. With "divinely inspired" words he told Charles that he had not identified him by name as "the one who would come" because God had willed him not to do so, although he knew it was he. Others would come after him, he told the king, because it was going to take "more than one barber to shave all of Italy." He also prophesied that the Turks and Moors would convert to Christianity in these times and that "many standing here now will see it." These things had come to him in a vision while he was preaching in San Lorenzo in Lent of 1492. (Here he describes the "imaginary" vision of the two crosses over Rome and Florence that he had first reported in the Reformation Sermon of January 13.)

Other visions and illuminations confirmed his predictions, he says, especially his prophecy of the revolution of the Church and of God's coming scourge. His many predictions that Florence would be reformed and the city more glorious, more powerful, and richer than ever were proven to be God's will, for the city had indeed been reformed and the Great Council established on the model of Venice's Consiglio Grande. When fierce opposition caused the law of amnesty to be postponed the blessings promised to the city were also delayed, although after much more prayer, la pace universale and the law of appeal have been adopted. Thus, on the Feast of the Annunciation, Florence's New Year, he begged the glorious Virgin Mother to be Florence's advocate to the Holy Trinity, and she graciously accepted.

After the account of his journey to the Virgin's throne (see previous chapter) he adds, "I know that many beastly men and others unfamiliar with these things may make sport of me and say that they are human invention and poetic fictions rather than visions or prophecies. They should read the prophets, especially Ezekiel, Daniel, and Zechariah, where they will find similar things wrought in the Holy Spirit. [The prophets] too left it to the holy doctors to clarify the mystery of these things, and much has been left unwritten." He had also intended to keep them hidden, but he decided that in order to remove calumny and console the elect he must explain. Everything he has written is true and no detail will fail to come about. If this little work fails to help well-meaning readers find all the answers, they should apply to him while he is alive or to his disciples and friends after he is dead. They will be completely satisfied. If men believe account books and papers and ancient documents of notaries and other men—of whom it is written, "Every man is a liar [Ps. 115/116.11; Rom. 3.4]"—and if they believe deceitful astrologers and the demons to whom the great maestros go for counsel, and if they believe liars and the fathers and masters of lies, how much more ought they believe these things of which a great part have already been fulfilled and verified by many divine signs? Even when Christ confirmed his teaching with great, stupefying miracles few believed in him and many persecuted him and abandoned him. But the elect of God will not lose themselves, because as the Apostle says, "God's foundation stands firm. 'God knows who are his' [2 Tim. 2.19]."

If Savonarola expected that his "little book" of revelations would persuade Pope Alexander VI of the legitimacy of his prophetic apostolate, it had the opposite effect. Whether the pope read it or learned of its contents from a curial secretary, he treated the *Compendium* as further evidence that the friar was not only a political nuisance but a dangerous heretic. In his breve of September 8 His Holiness dropped all pretense of friendly pastoral concern:

> We have heard that a certain Girolamo Savonarola from Ferrara, of the Order of Preachers, is delighted with the novelty of a perverse dogma and in this same insanity of mind is misled by the shift of affairs in Italy, so that without any canonical authority he attests among the people that he has been sent by God and speaks with God, against the canonical decrees. . . . Moreover [he asserts] that Christ Jesus crucified and God lie if he lies . . . that anyone not believing his vain assertions puts himself outside the state of salvation. . . . Although through our letters we have admonished him by virtue of holy obedience to come to us so that we might understand the truth from him and from his own mouth, nevertheless, he has not only refused to come and to obey us, but even . . . impudently putting forth things . . . to be imbibed in a single sitting which he had previously spouted rashly.[11]

His Holiness appointed fra Sebastiano Maggi, vicar general of the Order's Lombard Congregation, to examine the case, make a judgment, and determine punishment, although in his instruction to Maggi he leaves little room for any decision short of condemnation.[12] In the meantime he suspended the Frate from public preaching and teaching and ordered him to appear when and where the vicar general would summon him. So that no other brothers might be tempted "to imitate him to err and to play the fool" the pope ordered on pain of excommunication that the convents of San Marco and San Domenico of Fiesole be immediately reunited to the Congregation of Lombardy from which Savonarola has "fraudulently" achieved their separation. Finally, he ordered three Savonarolan lieutenants—Domenico da Pescia, Tommaso Busini, and Silvestro Maruffi—to report within nine days to Bologna for reassignment to a convent of the Lombard Congregation outside the Florentine dominion.

The papal breve was addressed to "the Dominican friars of Santa Croce." Was it merely a secretary's error that it was addressed to Santa Croce, a Franciscan house on the other side of the city, instead of to fra Girolamo's San Marco, or was this a tactic to put it into the hands of the Frate's enemies? If the latter, it succeeded; the content of the breve was soon common knowledge. With a letter of September 17 the Signoria protested that the accusations were a calumny; fra Girolamo had brought nothing to Florence but righteous living and peace, and since the separation from the Lombard Congregation, San Marco and San Domenico of Fiesole had blossomed in piety and holiness. The magistrates asked Alexander to rescind both the summons to Savonarola and the order nullifying the separation from the Lombards.[13] But the pope was in no mood for reconciliation.

Immediately after returning from a brief rest in the Tuscan countryside, which included a stop to preach in Arezzo, Savonarola replied to the breve. It was a bold, not to say defiant, letter, a touch grandiose. Echoing the Signoria, he branded all reports of his misconduct as deliberate falsifications by his enemies and pointed to the beneficial effects of his preaching in Florence and to the wonderful changes achieved by separating San Marco and its allied houses from the Lombard Congregation. He countered the pope's complaints about his prophetic preaching with references to Holy Scripture, Church history, the Doctors of the Church, and plain reason. Surely preaching about future events was not new dogma, nor was it forbidden to prophesy. As it was written in the third book of Amos: "The Lord God shall not perform His word, unless He shall have revealed His secret to His own servants, the prophets [Amos 3.7]." Indeed, braving the derision of many, he, Savonarola, had prophesied the coming of the sword; his calls for penitence had brought tranquility to Florence. He would do the same for Italy if she heeded his teaching, and for this all Italy should thank God for him!

Nor was Savonarola above splitting a hair or stretching a point. He had never said that he had been sent "by God alone," he protested, never "expressly" said he spoke with God nor "if I lie, God lies."[14] ("Sometimes when I have said any truth which Christ has spoken, I have subjoined: if I lie, Christ also etc.") As to the charge that he had declared anyone who did not believe his assertions to be outside the state of salvation, he explained: "Since I know that many things I have said are from God, whoever obstinately does not want to believe them, but resolves utterly to contradict them, [shows] that he is outside the state of grace, since as I have said, grace, the light of faith, always inclines to truth." His memory could be selective too: "All know that five years have passed during which I have preached these things, or rather even more than ten. So, I am not misled to do this on account of the shift in Italian affairs."[15] (Anyone who had observed how he had adjusted his vision to the great events of the previous November–December might have disputed that assertion.) Most startling of all, he denied that anyone had ever heard him say he was a prophet.[16]

For disobeying the papal summons to Rome he offered two reasons, a life-threatening illness and the fear that if he set out for Rome he would be attacked by his enemies. He was unable to leave the city without an armed guard, he declared. (A few days earlier he had traveled well beyond Florence, although still within the bounds of the Florentine state, unaccompanied by armed men.) His ailments were real enough, although perhaps not life threatening (in a recent letter to fra Silvestro Maruffi he had passed them off as "the usual stomach infirmity"). Perhaps the most serious reason for his refusal was the one he refrained from mentioning to the pope, although he later explained it to his inquisitors: "I was afraid of being killed on the way, or in Rome, by Piero de' Medici or by the Holy League, because I opposed their offer."[17] Finally, he deplored the pope's decision to put his case in the hands of the Lombard Congregation's vicar general, fra Sebastiano Maggi. Savonarola thought him an "exceedingly suspect" judge; every day Maggi and his friars attacked [the San Marco friars] over the separation. So for the present, Savonarola concludes, he will do nothing. Let His Holiness specify what he should renounce, and he will do it willingly. But he has no wish to sin, not even venially, so if there is no other way to save his conscience but to obey the breve, he declares, he will certainly obey, "even if the whole world comes crashing down." (Two years later he would deny that the pope had actually summoned him.)[18] As to the demand that San Marco and San Domenico immediately return to the obedience of the Lombard Congregation and that his three fellow friars proceed to Bologna for reassignment, he remains silent.[19] Some measure of his concern can be inferred from his call upon influential clerics for help. He sent a copy of his letter to fra Ludovico de' Valenza, procurator of the Dominican Order, a fellow Ferrarese whom he had known since university days.[20] Although he had heard that fra Ludovico had recently criticized him, he hoped that, on the strength of their old friendship, Ludovico would now try to undo whatever harm he may have caused him and speak to the cardinal protector (Carafa). He also sent a copy to another influential sometime friend, Felino Sandei, canonist and auditor of the Sacred Rota in Rome, whom he cited as an expert on the question of papal obedience.[21]

Absent from the pulpit since late July, by early autumn of 1495 Savonarola was anxious to make his voice heard in the city again even if it meant violating the papal ban. Fra Domenico da Pescia, substituting for him in the cathedral, was showing more signs of the naive and reckless enthusiasm that would ultimately lead to their common ruin. To prove fra Girolamo's legitimacy fra Domenico proposed one of two tests: either he would ask Florentines who had been dead for some forty years to rise from their tombs and pronounce the truth, or he would challenge the Frate's enemies to a trial by fire. In either case, presumably, God would intervene on the side of truth.

Another worry was the preaching of fra Marco di Matteo Strozzi who was calling for the expulsion of the Jews, "these enemies of the cross of Christ . . . with their old synagogue, their rites and their usury."[22] Fomenting a new round of anti-Jewish rioting such as had been set off by the rabble-rousing Bernardino da Feltre in 1488 was no more in the interest of the new republic than was fra Domenico's expectation of a miracle. If attention was to be redirected to the main issues of reform and renewal, Savonarola would have to reclaim the cathedral pulpit, and on October 11, he returned.[23]

CHAPTER 14

Obstacles to the Spirit

He comes neither to preach nor to prophesy but "to talk reasonably with the people." Still, he begins on a combative note: he will review his troops and prepare for battle, for what is human life but battle? The true Christian must constantly fight against the obstacles to the spirit. This morning he is concerned with another kind of obstacle to the spirit, the enemy within, the grumblers, malcontents, and Arrabbiati who complain of the new popular government and want to remove him by writing to Rome. As an army must have its captain, Florence has Christ for its king, and already under his leadership the city has overcome its lack of faith and replaced a religion of ceremony with simplicity and its old rulers with Christ —and all without bloodshed.[1]

But blood has now to be spilled, it seems. He calls upon the Otto di Guardia to take strenuous measures against the republic's enemies; they are the enemies of Christ and of himself. They should pass a law of lèse-majesté with a fine of fifty ducats for anyone who speaks badly of this government, for whoever fights this government fights Christ. Under the previous regime those who dared to speak out had been punished; how much more do those who speak out against this new republic deserve punishment! When they hear someone misspeak, they should "give it to him on the ears!" To apprehend grumblers who divide the city and write unauthorized letters to princes and to Rome, the government should place spies everywhere. Do as Rome did against those who tried to restore the tyrant Tarquin the Proud: cut off their heads! Even if they have families: cut off their heads! These grumblers don't really care whether he goes to Rome; their aim is to get him out of Florence. "They say, 'if he obeys the pope we'll have our coup; if he doesn't obey, we'll do it by excommunication. Then everyone will be scandalized and he'll lose their confidence.'" He and his friars would rather die than sin by disobeying, but as Saint Thomas says, we must obey the intention of our superiors, not their words, so we must write to the Holy Father and tell him he is badly informed by the lies that have been told to him in those letters, for example, the charge that he loves new heresies.

Apparently unaware that a papal breve, more moderate in tone than its predecessor but renewing the gag order, had been issued on October 16,[2] fra Girolamo returned to preach on October 18 and 25, continuing to maintain that he was not preaching but "talking." Again he came to rally his troops. Florence was the most beloved of Italian cities and would be exalted, not because of its virtues but Christ's. Christ was the lord of the city and the Council his surrogate. The Council must be nurtured, like a child, for it is young and nothing is perfect from the start. The first task of the government was to finish the great hall; less than a thousand ducats had been spent on it. Everything in the city depended on the Council. They should put up a stone plaque there containing his words: "Whoever wants a Parlamento wants to snatch the government from the hands of the people." If anyone speaks evil of this state and its government, he is to be regarded an enemy and a rebel: "Cut off his head." For this lapse from his usual message of peace and forgiveness he blamed the republic's enemies. ("'Oh, frate, you have preached and continue to preach peace!' O my brother; you are trying to destroy this peace.")

The next task was to examine the Council and decide how it could be improved. You don't want to be like the Sienese or Lucchesans? But God is like everybody. Siena and Venice have good systems for choosing candidates —borrow from them. Magistrates, you must do away with gambling, sodomy, blasphemy, and taverns. Don't let people write anonymous letters to the Signoria or to foreign princes. Everything should be in the open. People who circulate leaflets want to make trouble. Don't believe them. Have spies everywhere and when you discover someone doing wrong, punish him.

Noting that elections for the Signoria were coming soon, he tried again to establish guidelines for political morality and again came to the edge of a dilemma: holiness and simplicity were not qualifications for office. It was one thing to be a good Christian, another to be a good citizen who loves the republic. Of course if one was also a good Christian so much the better—so long as he was no sodomite. And yet a good public servant in the holy republic must be virtuous as well as prudent. Officials who wish to purify the city of vice must not be concerned for their own popularity. Did magistrates avoid displeasing anyone so that they would still be popular when they left office? They should have no fear: if they were righteous, if they followed God's will and acted justly, they would remain popular.

Preaching was fra Girolamo's major weapon in the struggle for the New Jerusalem, his first line of defense against Arrabbiati, tiepidi, Mediceans, rival clerics, and everyone else who wanted to see him gone. But especially during intervals of tactical or forced retreat from the pulpit, he relied upon his other formidable weapon: the pen. After the *Compendium of Revelations* he set to work on a slighter work and finished it before the end of the year. The *Letter to a Friend* is directed mainly at domestic critics and is more polemic than apologia.[3] He is indignant that he still must defend himself against "calumny" at home: those who label him a heretic, he fumed, wouldn't be able to tell you what a heretic was if you asked them. Besides, although many of his critics profess to be clerics, not everyone who wears the habit is a true religious; everyone knows the story of the rapacious wolves who disguised themselves as sheep. As for being a schismatic and disobedient to the Church, he has explained himself to the pope, and His Holiness is perfectly satisfied. (Savonarola seems to take papal silence as approval.)

In defending the new constitution Savonarola repeats the arguments he made to the Tempter on his journey to the Virgin's throne. This is not a regime of the "infima plebe," or lowest class, as some have charged, he insists. Rather it is a government "tutto politico e civile," a broadly representative government in which nobles play a major role (recognizing, apparently, that the ottimati, or as he elsewhere calls them, "important men," have a preponderant share of the regime's public offices). This is a surprisingly candid observation and probably true, as it is also true that members of the old governing class continued to be influential far beyond their numbers in the making of governmental policy. His own social prejudices emerge most clearly in his calls for refining the membership of the Great Council. Important measures are not being acted upon, he complained, because too many "low and foolish people of little judgment are being admitted, some who are not worthy to live upon this earth."

Offsetting this arch and surprisingly vehement observation is his avowal that Florentines of every stamp have benefited from the new regime. Returned exiles, eager for revenge and power, old supporters of the previous regime, citizens who had remained in the city and suffered from tyrannical rule, as well as those who had rebelled against Piero de' Medici—all have been saved from bloodshed and ruin by this government given to them by God.

Even the people who first tried to rule the city after the expulsion of the Medici but had neither the brains nor the good will to manage it have emerged unscathed, he declares. They would have made a crazy mess of it, and the people would have had to give them over to boys (for stoning?).[4] So anyone who speaks ill of this government or tries to do it harm merits heavy punishment by God and by man. Indeed, it is right to put them to death without any need for further testimony by witnesses.

If the city is now going from bad to worse he declares, this is not because the promises have not been fulfilled but because the Florentines lack faith and justice. If they had listened carefully to his words, they would know that the amount of tribulation they will suffer depends on the extent to which they do justice and purge the wicked. The city is full of ribalds who practice all sorts of low vices, speak ill of the government, compose pretty songs, and defame good people—and there is no one to reprove them. We know who is organizing intelligences (political caucuses) to destroy the Council. This is lèse-majesté and counter to what God has wrought, yet no one dares say anything against them, and many people even pretend ignorance in order not to have to make any judgments. He reveals a "secret": if the Florentines had acted justly and purged these wicked men, the tribulations would not have arrived; indeed, the city would already have begun to flourish!

Finally, he attempts to clarify what he has prophesied about the future of the Roman Church. This calls forth some ingenious, doctrinally adventurous, verbal footwork. Some, he says, claim that he is in error in saying that Rome is to be punished (*reprobata*) and Jerusalem elected and given priority (*preposta*). But he has not erred; he does not mean that the form of the Church of Rome will be changed, but that the present Rome, that is, the wicked of Rome, will be reproved and removed, and the flower of Christianity will be found in the region of Jerusalem. "I don't mean by this that the Roman Church will disappear, nor that its faith will change, nor that there will have to be two popes, but that under a single pope the righteous Christian life will flourish more in Jerusalem than here in our region. And in every part of the world where there are Christians they will humble themselves before the Roman Church because all will be correct in the Roman faith under a holy pope (*papa santo*), successor to Saint Peter, the first Roman bishop, [and] whose seat and principal diocese will be Rome, while he will still have fullness of power over all the other churches as all popes have. But even if the pope doesn't reside in Rome, he does not lose his jurisdiction; on the contrary, he is always the Roman bishop and in him the whole Roman Church, indeed, the whole universal Church, is united." Only the wicked, the tepid, the stupid, and the desperate would refuse to be convinced by his doctrine, he concludes, unmindful that a doctrine exalting Jerusalem and predicting the coming of a papa santo might strike even a neutral observer as tinctured with Joachimite millenarianism.

Friends and foes alike snapped up copies of the *Letter to a Friend*, sending it into three quick printings and setting off another round of the pamphlet wars. One antagonist, ironically claiming to be the anonymous friend to whom Savonarola had addressed his letter, taxed him for his many inconsistencies. Although he continually preached peace, the Frate's recent decision to surround himself with an armed guard when he moved between pulpit and monastery was the behavior of a fearful tyrant, not a minister of God. His calls for cutting off the heads of critics were unfitting from a cleric. His complaints that the Great Council admitted many unqualified members was a glaring example of his contradictory stances: "First you strive to demonstrate that you introduced this government as the instrument of the All High, worthy of praise to the heavens, then you chastise it for having admitted so many fools, then you immediately return to excoriating those who criticize [this government] on the grounds that it is your creation." As for his claims to be a prophet: that divine gift had been extinguished with the Incarnation. Indeed, this was no Christian prophet but "another Mahomet who with a scorpion's tail smites the flock of Christ with dreams and visions, seducing the crowd to [believe in] a new sect so that he may be called the originator of great deeds."[5]

The letter of the anonymous friend was quickly answered by Domenico Benivieni, although he avoided some of its most telling points. Domenico found no flaw in the Frate's orthodoxy, nor did he concede that prophecy was impossible in the modern world; indeed, the scourge prophesied by Savonarola had already come to pass.[6] But not even the learned Canon Benivieni could claim the last word. The furious pamphlet war would follow Savonarola to the grave, and beyond.[7]

In the meantime, the Frate's devotees in the government were eager to have him preach for Advent. On November 13, the Signoria wrote to the pope to plead for the lifting of the ban: "This is a good man, Holy Father, of holy life, unimpeachable morals, integrity of faith, wonderful teaching; and, more than everything else, what has drawn and continues to draw our entire people to listen to this man and to obey him is his preaching of the future. . . . We need him, Holy Father, we need this man of God and his preaching!" (The letter was probably written by the humanist Chancellor Bartolomeo Scala, who himself had recently come over to the Piagnone side.)[8] On the same day the Signoria wrote to Oliviero Carafa, cardinal of Naples and Protector of the Dominican Order, so helpful to the Frate in the separation of San Marco from the Lombard Congregation, to ask him to do all he could to persuade the pope to lift the ban so that the Frate could preach during Advent. Four days later the magistrates wrote to Carafa again to press the urgency of their request: Advent was practically upon them; perhaps the cardinal could obtain a verbal order from the pope permitting the friar to preach? On December 5 they wrote to Ricciardo Becchi in Rome, instructing him to remind the cardinal to try to obtain the release either viva voce or with a breve.[9] All these efforts were unavailing. In his diary entry for December 11 Luca Landucci wrote that the pope had sent a reply commanding fra Girolamo not to preach and that the friar "obeyed for some days."[10]

As "some days" stretched into weeks, fra Domenico da Pescia again took over the Cathedral pulpit while the Signoria and the Ten of Liberty worked to have the papal ban lifted in time for fra Girolamo to preach Lent. Besides stressing the friar's sanctity and the spiritual benefits of his preaching, Ambassador Becchi was instructed to convince the pope that in denouncing Rome's worldliness and corruption, the Frate was not criticizing His Holiness personally since these were no more than the conventional moral strictures that were the stock in trade of penitential preachers. The pope was not mollified. Becchi had not only to bear the brunt of papal anger but deal with the frustration of his home government as well. With little personal sympathy for Savonarola, Becchi was aware that questions were being raised in Florence about his diplomatic competence and good faith, forcing him repeatedly to protest that he was doing everything possible. The deeper problem at the curia was not Becchi's lack of enthusiasm nor, annoying as it must have been to Alexander VI, Savonarola's criticism of the immorality at the papal court; the main issue between Florence and the pope was political. What Rodrigo Borgia found unforgivable, and Ricciardo Becchi was unable to finesse, was the Florentines' refusal to abandon the French alliance and join the Holy League for the defense of Italy's "liberty." Convinced that Savonarola was responsible for what he saw as Florence's treacherous loyalty to the French king, Alexander VI repeatedly pressed them to turn the Frate over to the curia.

In this assessment the pope was partially mistaken. Florence's loyalty to the French was not in the first instance due to Savonarola but to the city's calculated political and economic self-interests. Having expelled Piero de' Medici for endangering those interests by refusing to honor the long-standing alliance with the French, the Florentines had found a cosmic justification in the Savonarolan apocalypse with its vision of French Charles VIII as the New Charlemagne, God's agent for protecting their recovered liberty and enhancing their historic exceptionalism. The king's return to France without restoring Pisa and the other lost territories caused some to waiver in their support for the alliance, especially after January 1, when news arrived that the French castellan in charge of the citadel in Pisa had surrendered it to the Pisans instead of to the Florentines as promised.[11] Some—almost everyone according to Parenti—complained that fra Girolamo had deceived them with his promises and that the city would be ruined. Landucci reported on December 9 that "ignorant people" were marching around San Marco at night crying "this pig of a rotten friar ought to be burned up in his house." Hearing that there were many who wanted to kill him, the Otto di Guardia sent two of their officials and a detail of armed men to escort fra Girolamo on his frequent comings and goings between San Marco and San Domenico of Fiesole.

From his pulpit in the Cathedral fra Domenico da Pescia called upon the Florentines to remain steadfast. By recovering their stronghold the Pisans were guilty of controverting God's plan, justifying their eventual extermination! This did little to mollify Savonarola's enemies. Parenti observed that the Florentines were now divided between the party of the French and the faction which wanted to shift allegiance to Milan (that is, to the anti-French Holy League), and that this took the form of a domestic struggle for public offices and territorial magistracies. Moreover, worries about prolonging the war with Pisa had a dampening effect upon commerce, making life so difficult for the populace that there was fear of a new revolt. In effect, said Parenti, the city was divided: one part believed completely in fra Girolamo; the other, fewer in number but more powerful in wealth and reputation, were against him. This, he commented balefully, was how the new year was beginning in their city.

If there was slippage in fra Girolamo's support, the majority of political leaders continued to share his belief that the city's interests were best served by the French alliance and continued to look for the king's speedy return. Aware that the Frate was their most effective spokesman, they continued to press the pope to allow him to resume preaching and to grant the traditional Easter indulgence. Alexander VI's reply was blunt and candid: apart from his personal distaste for Savonarola's preaching, the friar was anathema to the Holy League. With the Lenten season approaching and neither permission to preach nor Easter indulgence forthcoming, the government decided to act on its own authority. On February 11 the Signoria ordered Savonarola to preach the Lenten sermons in Santa Maria del Fiore and wherever else in the city he saw fit. Not to do so would incur their displeasure.[12]

Six days later, Ash Wednesday, the Frate ascended the Cathedral pulpit. Whether he was submitting to the Signoria's order in conscious defiance of the papal ban or believed the rumor circulating in Florence that His Holiness had verbally given his consent, he did not say.[13] If Alexander had given his consent, he seems to have withdrawn it almost immediately: envoy Becchi and others reported that the pope continued to complain that the friar and the city were disobeying his orders. For his part, Savonarola could no longer bring himself to acknowledge the authority of anyone but his heavenly master. He had decided to stop preaching, he told his congregation, only because he needed time for reflection and self-examination (that is, not because the pope had ordered him to keep silent). Had he, he asked himself aloud, erred in speech, in logic, or in philosophy? Was he deficient in his faith? Was there some stain of pride, vainglory, or avarice? Did he talk too much? Perhaps he was moved by anger or by hatred of his adversaries? Having assured himself of his blamelessness in all respects and with a new resolve to be discrete, he had simply decided to return.[14]

Preaching every day during Lent, he was at the top of his form. He took his text from Amos, the shepherd-prophet who excoriated Israel for its injustices and refused the order of the priest Amaziah that he go out of the country.[15] With an almost palpable fervor he speaks directly and intimately across the vast space of the packed Cathedral. He cries out to "My Florence," "my beloved sons and daughters"; he appeals, scolds, protests, and declaims; he forestalls his critics, mimics their forthcoming objections, delivers the crushing rebuke, pauses dramatically ("let me rest a moment, then I'll tell you"), then returns to the fray with new vigor. He pictures the Florentines purified, entering the New Jerusalem like Christ on his donkey entering the Jerusalem of old. He sees three swords in the night sky threatening famine, pestilence, and war. Although each sermon exhibits a determined structure, he moves freely between topics. ("I meander like a river.")

Like the most traditional scholastic preacher, he begins with a scriptural passage, a theological or philosophical principle, a legal or moral precept, or some combination of these; moves to the existential level of faith and morals; then proceeds to expose and condemn the world's corruptions. With no concession to the papal wrath that will surely follow, he excoriates popes, cardinals, and prelates for their concubines and pimps, their mules, horses, and dogs, their pursuit of church benefices for their sons, their neglect of pastoral duties, and their lack of charity to the poor. Friars and nuns who dishonor their vows and mingle too much in the secular world feel the sharp edge of his tongue. Using the familiar "tu," he speaks directly and personally as though to each member of the packed nave, pictures the tribulations they will suffer and the joys awaiting their conversion to il ben vivere, the righteous life of the true Christian. He then moves on to his signature themes: penitence, conversion, tribulation, renovation, and the coming apotheosis of Florence in a future glowing with millenarian promise. Rome will be laid waste, stripped down to its roots, its churches used as horse stalls for invading armies. Jerusalem will be elected once again. Florence has been chosen to lead the world toward renewal. The Turks and other infidels will accept baptism, and Christianity will be unified in a single sheepfold under one shepherd.

Then, in another of his pulpit dialogues:

> God will send a holy pope.—O what do you think, frate? Do you think it is this one or another?—I believe it will be another. I'm not telling you here that a saint[ly pope] is coming immediately after this one. I'm not saying yes or no, nor do I have to.—Have you seen him, frate?—I've seen him and I tell you he's ready.—Do you know him?—I'll tell you the truth; I don't think I've ever seen him again.

And, some days later:

> This is that new pontiff who in these days I said I had seen. It's true that I have seen him, and if I knew how to paint I would paint him as he is, but I wouldn't know how to make it understood in any other way. So don't say that I told you who he is because I don't know this and don't have the ability to tell you.[16]

CHAPTER 15

Mobilizing the Children

In building the New Jerusalem in Florence one of Savonarola's greatest challenges was its children.[1] Gangs of boys (*fanciulli*) and young men harassed passersby, especially women, and fought pitched battles in the streets. Gang rape was not uncommon. Policing was ineffectual—poorly paid and barely professional. Fathers might deplore the rowdiness of their sons but used it when it served their purposes, as they had done in the recent anti-Medicean and anti-Jewish rioting, in which boys had played a prominent role. Savonarola charged that adult men not only exploited the violent tendencies of the city's youth, they were agents of the boys' sexual corruption, introducing them to the "abominable vice" by guile, bribery, and force. If grown men, sunk in their debaucheries, would respond only to harsh punishment, young people (who, Savonarola liked to point out, were the hope of the future) might be rescued and enlisted in the cause of virtue not only on their own behalf but, acting as public police, for their parents. Under the direct supervision of fra Domenico da Pescia a scheme was devised in which boys between six and sixteen were to undergo an intensive regimen of personal discipline and reeducation.

Fra Domenico gave details in a sermon of December 19, 1495. The fanciulli would form companies in the four quarters of the city, each company electing officers to monitor personal behavior. Profanity would be censored, silence in church enforced, quarrels mediated. They would minister to the poor, even keep roadside shrines in good condition. Plain dress would be mandatory: ornamentation, such as the fashionable French pleated pockets banned; hair trimmed to just above the ears. Boys' tribunals were to chastise minor infractions, administer corporal punishment ("fraternal correction") for more severe transgressions, and expel incorrigibles.

Savonarola roundly denied charges that the intent of the reform was to make boys into friars. Whether boys chose the religious life was up to God; by the same token, if a boy decided to become a friar, he couldn't be held back. He even knew some who had been sent off to France but returned to become friars just the same. Send them where you will, they'll come back. He recalled that when he himself was in the world he had said a thousand times that he would never become a friar, but when it pleased God he had to go, and he went around without sleep or appetite until he did.[2]

It has been pointed out that in reforming the fanciulli Savonarola invented nothing.[3] Strictly speaking this is true. Religious confraternities for boys had appeared in Italy early in the century, and Florence had taken them up with enthusiasm. Like their adult models, the confraternity youth did charitable work, celebrated the feast days of favored saints, attended sermons, and even preached. Barefoot, white-robed, carrying candles and singing lauds as they processed, fanciulli were the studied image of angelic innocence. (In Benozzo Gozzoli's Medici palace fresco of the procession of the Magi, the boys of Florence's first family are readily identifiable.) Savonarola's achievement, as in so many other aspects of Florentine life, was to invest traditional ideals and practices with new meaning and urgency. Just before Carnival Savonarola demanded that the boys replace the "foolishness" that usually marked that day's festivities with acts of charity and reverence. Instead of their customary stone-throwing contests and street fires the boys were to plant crosses on every corner and collect alms for the Poor Men of San Martino. He also assigned boys an expanded role in the city's ceremonial and processional life.[4]

On Ash Wednesday, February 16, 1496, the boys assembled in their quarters behind religious banners, each holding an olive branch. Crying "Viva to Christ and the Virgin Maria Our Queen!" and accompanied by the city's drummers, pipers, and mace bearers, boys of all classes proceeded together to the Foundling Hospital in the Piazza de' Servi, then moved to the adjacent church of Santissima Annunziata and from there to San Marco. Leaving San Marco they followed the city's designated processional route, crossing Ponte Santa Trinità, doubling back across the Ponte Vecchio and through Piazza Signoria, ending at the Cathedral already packed with spectators. Entering, the boys deposited the hundreds of florins they had collected for alms, while women in the congregation added their own offerings of personal and household items.[5]

After the sermon, Frate Domenico da Pescia called on the fanciulli to raise the cry against women wearing tiaras on their heads and who solicited for that sin. He then organized them, with a chief for each quarter. . . . They were to come to his sermons, and finally on the day of Carnival, so that they would commit no sin, go in procession. Since it had been their custom to set up barriers [from behind which they demanded money from passersby], he had them continue the practice but now to beg for alms. On almost every street corner were to be seen little altars with crucifixes and other figures where boys begged for alms, which were then distributed to the shame-faced poor [the Poor Men of St. Martin] and others as fra Girolamo saw fit. Finally, on the day of Carnival . . . they gathered in Santa Maria del Fiore and . . . listened devoutly to a solemn Mass . . . they also sang some lauds newly composed for the occasion, then, after dining, they reassembled at la Nunziata [Santissima Annunziata] in order, quarter by quarter. From there they left with the trumpets of the Signoria in the lead, followed by a crucifix, and behind this a scarlet banner with the painted figure of Our Lady, the Child on her arm, all the fanciulli following, carrying olive branches, singing certain litanies and newly composed lauds, walking five abreast, or three abreast, hatless and holding hands, beginning with the quarter of Santo Spirito, then the others in the order designated. . . . It was estimated that there were about 4,000 fanciulli, between noble and commoner, mostly the latter. . . . Noteworthy in this ceremony was the great discipline in everything; even more marvelous was the abandonment of the old custom of stone throwing and the transformation in the use of altars and huts to collect alms to give to God.[6]

The Carnival procession was the dress rehearsal for a still more ambitious event on Palm Sunday, March 27. On that day the children heard the Frate's sermon in the Cathedral from banks of seats installed exclusively for them. Then, dressed in their white robes, singing lauds, many of them written for the occasion by Girolamo Benivieni and Savonarola himself, carrying red crosses, and followed by clerics and laity, they proceeded in their companies along the designated processional route. Girls were also invited to take part in the procession dressed in white, the color of innocence. (They had been raised by their fathers "according to the world, not according to God," the Frate commented, and like their brothers, fallen from purity.) The marchers solicited donations for the recently founded Monte di Pietà, the communal loan fund, a project which, as Parenti observed, Savonarola had taken over from other (that is, Franciscan) preachers.[7]

The squads of fra Girolamo and fra Domenico brought together the two extremes of Florentine youth culture, aggressiveness and spirituality, and fused them into a single mission. Besides their ceremonial role, the fanciulli were to be the shock troops in the Savonarolan war on vice. Landucci describes their baptism of fire: "Some boys snatched from a girl's head the tiara that held her veil, and her family made a great fuss about it. Fra Girolamo encouraged boys to do [such things] in order to censure scandalous behavior and gamblers, so that when someone cries, 'Here come the friar's boys!' every gambler, no matter how bold, runs away, and the women dress more modestly." The boys also harassed drunkards, dandies, violators of the Sabbath, and blasphemers. They continued the pitched battles of former times, but now it was Piagnoni boys fighting *Compagnacci*, sons of the Arrabbiati. These Savonarolan boys, enthused Landucci, had come to be held in such respect that everyone avoided doing bad things, especially "the vice that may not be named."[8]

Respect was far from universal. From Rome Ricciardo Becchi reported that the pope and cardinals were scandalized by Savonarola's "incitement of the passions of the boys" and even more dismayed that the authorities seemed to have given him and the boys a free hand, for this, they contended, dishonored the city and could only lead to its ruin.[9] In Florence angry protests against the boys' arrogant behavior were heard almost immediately, forcing Savonarola to defend what he had created.

"They keep saying we're at the mercy of fanciulli. No, we're not at their mercy; no, what harm are the fanciulli doing? They're stopping people from gambling." And a few weeks later: "Someone says, 'we're in the hands of children!' Tell me, are there children in the magistracy? Are there children in the Eight?"[10]

The disclaimer was disingenuous: if the boys did not have status as official censors of vice it was not for lack of effort by Savonarola. A delegation of them, surely with his blessing if not on his orders, had carried a petition for written authorization and an official seal to the Signoria "so that we may proceed against sodomites, remove streetwalkers, gamblers, and taverners and purge the whole of our city of vice, filling it with the splendor of virtue, thus signifying that this is the will of Almighty God as he tells and shows us every day through his prophets." Not surprisingly, the Priors had misgivings about delegating police powers to children and, despite fra Girolamo's intervention, took no action. In June legislation to grant official status to the boys' companies was introduced repeatedly in the councils and each time defeated. Only in the following year was a compromise measure pushed through, but this would fall far short of what Savonarola was asking for.

Women too were to be marshaled for Savonarola's moral crusade. The challenge was to devise a strategy that would include them without arousing mistrust and hostility. Savonarola shared the general view of women as the inferior sex, poor in judgment, ignorant and voluble, unfit to sit in the councils of government or even to attend a sermon when weighty public business was being discussed, while their vanity made them easy targets for the devil's seduction.[11] At the same time he thought women had at least as much potential for spiritual enlightenment as men; their very simplicity made it easier for them to accept Christ's message. Whether inspired by this paradoxical conviction or frustrated by the failure of his previous efforts to regulate women's conduct, he now proposed that women take responsibility for their own reform. As he outlined it in his sermon of March 18, in each quarter of the city women would elect one or two of their number to a central committee which would devise and administer rules of conduct for the members of their sex.[12]

That very evening in San Marco fra Santi Rucellai received an urgent letter from ser Iacopo Bongianni. The Piagnone Bongianni, who often acted as unofficial ambassador on behalf of Savonarola and San Marco, was a friend and former business associate of fra Santi.[13] (Less than a year earlier the merchant, banker, and civic leader Pandolfo Rucellai, a benefactor both of San Marco and of fra Girolamo's own needy family in Ferrara, had abandoned his life in the world for a vocation in religion, taking the name of fra Santi.)[14] Bongianni had just been talking to Rucellai's sister, Madonna Caterina, widow of Piero di Francesco Vettori, who "told me something that I think I ought to warn you about. As you know, this morning padre fra Girolamo spoke of the reform of women and [said] that each quarter should deputize one or two. Madonna Caterina says that this will cause great trouble among [the women], that by the time they come to agreement they'll have become a laughing stock and that they will do and say a thousand crazy things. Nor does she believe that they will ever carry out anything they enact. She thinks that you should instead summon a woman of your choosing and consult with her, rather than call for the formation of a standing committee." With these sentiments Iacopo himself agreed: laws or statutes made on the advice of women would commend little respect (*riputazione*), he thought. It was all very well to listen to them and note what they say, for they know about certain trivialities. Fra Santi would also do well to give Mona Caterina a half hour of his time so that she could advise him about this and other important things on which she is knowledgeable and which concern her.

Whether Caterina was invited to San Marco to voice her misgivings in person is not known. Two days later, in his sermon of March 20, Savonarola announced that God had inspired him to change his mind. "You women, we want you to reform, but the Lord God has inspired me not to put it into your hands because you would make a mess of it. We must put it into the hands of some worthy men or of some official who will organize it for you."[15] This speedy retreat, so unlike his tenacity in the matter of the Accoppiatori or la pace universale, suggests there were other reasons for abandoning the project besides sudden misgivings about women's capabilities: the support of such influential families as the Rucellai and Bongianni was too important to be jeopardized by what, after all, was no more than an experiment.

Some women complained that Savonarola had raised their expectations with his reform proposal only to leave them in the lurch. The devout, highly literate Margarita di Martino who called herself the Frate's spiritual daughter and quoted not only Scripture but also the *Collationes* of John Cassian, Savonarola's favorite monastic author, rebuked him in her own name and on behalf of others. After inspiring women and especially girls with the zeal to convert to "an honest and simple mode of life," she wrote on May 2, fra Girolamo had proceeded to reform only males, leaving women with the impression that he was no longer concerned with them. If women did not merit as much respect as men, God did not love them the less; indeed, it was of woman that God had willed himself to be born. Fra Girolamo should carry through what he had started; if not, having worked long and hard to sow the seed, his labors might be undone by Satan. Girls would soon be choosing their summer clothes, and they needed to know how to dress properly.[16]

Another letter, unsigned, likewise pressed the need for women's sartorial reform before the arrival of summer, for in warm weather it was the habit of well-dressed Florentine women to wear open-work hose and shirts that revealed "the outline of the parts that incite lust and ought to be hidden." Over these they wore a gown slit on both sides so that every slight breeze "revealed the whole person." Young women lounged about al fresco in garments like these and got up to all manner of sin. Even worse, on holiday mornings in certain churches, "harebrained and silly women," dressed in their finest, planted themselves on the stairways leading to the high altars where they stared directly into the faces of the poor friars![17]

Brazen sexual display by Florentine women had long been on Savonarola's list of vices to be expunged. Women came to church to exhibit themselves to men, he complained. Like whores, their heads uncovered to display their beautiful hair, they crowded into the sanctuary so close to the priest that they attracted his gaze—instruments of the devil.[18] As the anonymous letter writer later noted, the Frate himself had proposed that curtains be attached to the church pillars to be drawn when the friars entered the choir, thus protecting them from the gaze of the laity, but nothing had been done.

Chastened by the debacle of his reform plan, Savonarola returned to less controversial methods. For those who aspired to a deeper spiritual life he had always held up the contemplative vocation. Five years earlier he had confided to fra Roberto Ubaldini that just as God had elected San Marco to be the center of reform for men, so he had chosen the convent of Santa Lucia for women. A medium-sized house of some thirty-four Dominican tertiaries (laywomen living under a rule without taking monastic vows), Santa Lucia was to become a "great monastery," drawing women from "the whole nobility of Florence" to live in spiritual devotion. So many women had responded to the call that they overwhelmed the existing facilities. The problem of housing, organizing, governing, and funding tertiaries continued to be a source of controversy, and fra Girolamo's enemies were convinced that his plans for the convent were further evidence of his lust for power.[19]

While Florentine women were choosing the contemplative life in unexpected numbers, many more remained "in the world" where they persisted in following the dictates of convention and fashion. Stepping up his pulpit efforts to persuade women to accept modest restraints on their public conduct and self-display, Savonarola also redoubled his campaign for new legislation. Four times in the next two years Savonarola-inspired sumptuary laws were introduced and passed in the Council of Eighty, but each time they failed in the more fractious and independent Great Council. Parenti's explanation of this is tinged with his own bias: certain backbenchers, neither Frateschi nor Mediceans, he said, voted against the reforms to show foreigners that Florence was not, after all, governed by a friar.

From Rome Becchi reported that a stream of letters from Florence was accusing Savonarola of leading children in a takeover of the city government; indeed, that the Frate and his fanciulli were now appointing the Signoria, the Eight, the Ten, and the Council of Eighty, and that the boys were roaming the streets policing vice while the citizens were too cowed to speak out or do anything against the friar's will. These reports, said Becchi, upset the pope more than any of Savonarola's other misdeeds, and he complained of them every day to his cardinals and ambassadors. His Holiness was determined to punish the friar and had ordered a search for certain proceedings that had been mounted against him during his time in Bologna. (This must have been the time of the Lenten sermons when he had mocked the Lady Ginevra Bentivoglio, wife of Bologna's ruler.)[20] On March 30 Becchi reported hearing that the pope had also appointed a judicial commission of two cardinals, two bishops, the Dominican general, and some theologians of his order to take up the case of the errant friar. To counteract the "stories and fictions" that troublemakers were sending to Rome, Becchi wrote, it would be very useful if the Ten and the Signoria wrote letters to him expressing the high regard of the Florentine people for His Holiness and the papal court and advising him that they had exhorted fra Girolamo to obey the pope and to speak moderately of him. After the letters had been duly written and received in Rome, Becchi, anxious to demonstrate to his government that he was making headway, reported that the pope was well pleased.[21]

More likely, Alexander was only temporizing while the wheels of Roman justice slowly turned. In the six months since he had ordered Vicar General Maggi to proceed with the case against the Frate there had been no action,[22] and the hastily appointed Dominican commission seems to have broken up without coming to any decision. If there was a softening in papal resolve to have Savonarola condemned, it was, as was usually the case with Pope Borgia, politically motivated. Reports that Charles VIII was seriously preparing to return to Italy were causing Alexander and his ally Duke Lodovico of Milan to reappraise their situations. Alexander VI was said to be considering abandoning the League and making peace with the French. If so, it would be in his interest to ease the pressure on Florence, the one important Italian ally of Charles VIII. The obnoxious Frate could later be taken care of separately.[23] Not to be outdone in treachery, Duke Lodovico had been hinting to the Florentine ambassadors that if he withdrew his troops from Pisa, there would be no obstacle to the Florentines recovering that rebellious city. In exchange, Florence would be expected to help reconcile the French king and the Holy See.[24]

Already in January of 1496 the Milanese ambassador reported to the duke that many influential Florentines were prepared to abandon their support for the French alliance in favor of the Holy League. Parenti added that the more prudent citizens thought it a mistake "to keep hanging on the words of the king of France" or to keep sending envoys to him without at the same time making overtures to the League. Those that clung to the French alliance did so, he thought, either out of simple loyalty, or to court popular favor, or because they believed in the words of fra Girolamo and expected the king to return. On the contrary, Parenti held that everything should be done to prevent the return of King Charles. Experience, the best teacher, showed that the French brought only ruin to Italy.[25]

Ruin was what Savonarola, too, promised Italy. The French, he repeated all that spring, would be followed by other barbarians, barbers who would "shave" Italy, turn her "upside down." The difference, as he continually told them, was that the scourge would also be the instrument of her renewal, the reform of the Church and the Christianization of the world. On March 20, more than halfway through the Lenten sermons, he took up *Zechariah,* the prophet who, together with *Haggai,* exhorted the Jews returning from captivity to Jerusalem to rebuild the Temple.

He began with an unscripted drama: barely had he started to preach when his throat became so constricted that his words came out "all hoarse and choked." Neither a hastily administered drink of water nor the prayers of his listeners, now anxiously on their knees, eased his distress. After several futile attempts to speak he was ready to abandon the pulpit, but first he would try to recite the Pater Noster. At the words "our daily bread" a mighty sound escaped his throat, his voice returned and he was able to finish the sermon.[26] Many believed this was a miracle, wrote the recording scribe. Savonarola seems to have believed it too: the devil had attempted to silence him by removing his voice just now, he declared, but with the grace of God he had recovered it.

On Good Friday, April 1, he described a new vision. On a mountain strewn with flowers above the enormous plain of the world, a revolving crucifix called out, "Come to me all you who labor and are weary and I will give you refreshment [Matt. 11.28]." Blood spurted from the cross into the air, then fell, forming a river. On the left bank stood Christian Rome, on the right pagan Jerusalem. On every Moorish and pagan brow blood described a ruby red cross. As the pagans became aware of the sign on their foreheads they ran to the river, threw off their garments, entered, and drank. Quite drunk with blood, they emerged gentle and sweet, beautiful as angels.

Red crosses also formed on the brows of the Christians on the left bank, but some covered them with their caps or hands or with the masks of wild beasts. To the angels and preachers who came to them repeating Christ's call, they refused to lift their masks or show their crosses. Instead, they ran to don the clothes discarded by the infidels at the riverbank. Although they were deluged by lances, swords, bombardments, and pestilence, they still refused to hear Christ's summons but retreated to their fortresses and took up arms. All who did so died by the sword, while those from the Christian side who ran to the river and drank the blood of the crucifix emerged like angels and were saved. A great number of these were Florentines, and so it would be for them if they returned to God, lived in charity, dispelled their hatreds. All that had been promised them would be theirs. Only, having come so far, they must not turn back.

Breaking into a prayer to the Heavenly Father, Savonarola assumed the person of Christ himself: "Here I am, ready; here I am freely offering myself. Here I am to ascend this wood and be offered as holocaust and host. . . . To you I recommend this Hebrew people, sinners, gentiles and the whole world: all the living and future souls and my city of Florence. O Heavens, stand still for the passion of our Lord! Sun, give no more light! Earth, tremble! Rocks, break! Mountains, split apart! . . . O man, here is your Lord, nailed and dead for you on this wood."

As the congregation cried "Misericordia!" he brought the sermon to a close.[27]

To Rome fra Girolamo gave no ground. He castigated prelates for their corruption and reminded them of the scourge that would soon overtake them, insisted that his prophecies were divinely inspired, and vowed to retract only if Rome showed him wherein he erred.[28] On the Sunday after Easter he reported that his Good Friday vision had returned, this time with more detail, which he was now permitted to interpret (by whom he does not say). There were no surprises: the red crosses signified the contemplation of the passion of Christ, and those who attempted to cover the crosses were the worldly-wise; the tiepidi who put their trust in their works and ceremonies; and the truly wicked—proud prelates, princes, and other raptors. Those who resorted to violence instead of committing themselves to Christ and penitence would go to hell and eternal damnation; those who accept Christ's call would be sheltered from the coming scourge and live in purity and peace.[29] The prelates and princes donned masks of lions and bears. They were the exploiters of their fellows. Dissemblers wore masks of foxes, while gluttons were masked as wolves. But he could now reveal that in the shadow cast by the crucifix were "many of my Florentines," lay as well as cleric, women, men, and fanciulli. Washed in the river, they were happy and content.

With Savonarola unceasing in his prophecy of the renovation of the Church and the ruin of Rome, the pope decided the time had come to complete the judicial proceedings against him, charging him as a "heretic, schismatic, seducer of the people, deceiver, and deliverer of the state of Florence from its well-born citizens into the hands of the plebs."[30] In Florence certain clerics echoed the pope's strictures, most vehemently fra Gregorio of the Observant Franciscan Convent of San Miniato al Monte. Yet it was a great wonder to Parenti that whereas almost all the other religious, both monastic and mendicant clergy, felt enmity to fra Girolamo, the majority of

Florentine citizens regarded him as a saint. Clerical envy was always very powerful, he noted, all the more so at this time when most charitable donations were going to the friars of San Marco.

On the grounds that these renewed pulpit attacks threatened disorder, the Eight of Security announced a two-month ban on unlicensed preaching, citing the danger of infection from plague. The Piagnoni-leaning magistrates may also have thought a cooling-off period would reduce the pressure on Savonarola himself, although he seems not to have shared either concern. In taking his leave on April 10, he pointed out that no one, neither patrician nor woman nor child, who had attended these Lenten sermons had fallen ill from plague; indeed, their prayers had averted "the sword of pestilence." Still, it was important not to tempt God further. He would stop preaching for a little while.[31]

He meant only to shift venue. On April 17 he preached in Prato's convent church of San Domenico. Landucci reported that a crowd of people, many from Florence and the surrounding countryside, descended on that nearby city to hear him.[32] Savonarola promised them tribulation followed by felicity. In the convent rectory he also preached to an assemblage of notables, including Marsilio Ficino and students and professors displaced from the Pisa studium by the rebellion. The theme was faith, and according to hagiographic legend, the Frate spoke for three hours with such power that even his adversaries were captivated ("caught like fish in a net"). The same legend has the distinguished university professor Oliviero Arduini saying, "Let us follow this man; we are scarcely worthy to carry his books." (For an entire winter, according to fra Placido Cinozzi, Arduini was a regular at Savonarola's sermons, remaining for long hours despite great physical discomfort, for he was of an advanced age and fat.)[33]

On the evening of April 25, Savonarola returned to Florence accompanied by two members of the Eight who had gone to Prato to fetch him. With elections to the new Signoria scheduled for the following day, the magistrates, disregarding their own injunction, wanted him to say Mass and preach in the new hall of the Great Council. Instead he passed the assignment to fra Domenico da Pescia, who described a vision of the previous night in which a large crowd of angels and devils gathered in a single place, the devils ranged on the left, the angels on the right.

In the election that followed two Council members were discovered distributing slips listing names of forty-five candidates to be favored. The two men, one described by Parenti as "a man of low status and few brains," the other a cloth weaver, were jailed and tortured. Among the citizens whose names they gave up, the most prominent was the Arrabbiati leader and former Gonfaloniere of Justice Filippo Corbizzi. The so-called intelligenza was found to involve over two hundred citizens committed to vote for anti-Savonarolan and anti-Bigi candidates. Worried that if they revealed the full extent of the plot they would create public turmoil, the magistrates decided to punish only the ringleaders. Although some argued for executing Corbizzi and two accomplices, the Eight compromised on a sentence of life imprisonment. As provided by the new law of appeal the sentences were reviewed and approved in the Great Council. Some who were compromised were fined; about twenty-five others received the *ammonizione*, official warning to refrain from further provocation. The rest were quietly pardoned.

Dedicated searchers for hidden meanings noted that during fra Domenico's sermon and the preelection ceremonies, a preponderance of the conspirators had been seated on the left of the altar while innocent councilmen had been seated on the right. This they took as proof that fra Domenico's vision—angels on the left, devils on the right—had been supernaturally prescient. Others scoffed that this was a coincidence or part of a ruse in which fra Domenico exploited his advance knowledge of the intelligenza.[34] (A disenchanted gloss on the affair would be provided two years later by fra Silvestro Maruffi during his processo. The night before that April election day he had dreamed that the air was filled with good and evil spirits armed with torches and knives who battled each other until the good spirits drove out the bad and took sole possession of the field. The next morning he described this dream to fra Domenico who, as he so often did, included it in his sermon without acknowledging its origin.)[35] Whether Savonarola and his two colleagues knew of the election plot and decided to make political capital of it by hinting at it in fra Domenico's sermon we cannot say. In any case, the scandal helped to ensure the election of a strong Savonarolan partisan, Francisco degli Albizzi, as Standard Bearer of Justice for the next two-month term.[36]

Savonarola had been putting the finishing touches on his *Exposition on Psalm "Qui regis Israel"* (Ps. 79/80), which appeared on April 28.[37] A cry of anguish for a beleaguered Israel, the psalm furnished him with powerful apocalyptic images: the wild boar ravaging the Lord's vineyard; the tepid who pretend to be good Christians while performing no more than the externals of the faith; the rich and powerful who oppress the poor.[38] God, he writes, has removed the true prophets, apostles, teachers, and pastors, the guardians of Israel (that is, the Church) and replaced them with trespassers who know not the way of the Lord or how to serve him. Like Asaph, the priest placed in charge of the Ark of the Covenant (1 Chron. 16.4), he beseeches the hidden God to reveal himself and deliver his scourge. Let him come quickly, for to him we are all little schoolchildren in need of the whip. Afterward God will appear before all his elect, increase the number of his people, and create one sheepfold under a single shepherd (John 10.16). Rome's disapproval has not caused the Frate to soften his indictment of the Roman Church or to disengage from controversy with his superiors. Writing in Latin, he initially intended the work for clerical and educated lay readers, but it was soon translated. Three Italian editions came out before summer's end.[39]

CHAPTER 16

I Can't Live without Preaching

"Well, we're still here; we haven't run away. By now they should be content with all the lies they've told. They say we've carried off a lot of money. Too bad for you, Florentines; you didn't know how to catch me!"[1]

With this verbal snap of his fingers at the latest calumny in circulation, fra Girolamo resumed preaching in the Cathedral on May 8, 1496. He returned in defiance of the papal ban, though apparently with the permission of the Eight, to shore up his "brigade," encourage his followers in their faith, and urge everyone to confess and take communion for Pentecost. His first reason for returning, he admitted, was to defend himself against the slanders of his enemies. His ordering of motives is telling. In years of fending off charges of bad faith, demagoguery, secret ambition, heresy, and diabolic intent, years in which he had also to assure himself that he was truly God's prophet, the message of tribulation and renewal had become virtually identical with the messenger. This was more than a matter of style: in the constant need to affirm the legitimacy of his apostolate he had become his own principal text. Eventually this self-preoccupation would betray him. The audacious "If I lie, Christ lies," caused him endless trouble in Rome. The calls for a miracle to verify his heavenly commission would lead to disaster. Another reason he gave for returning to the pulpit goes to the essence of the man. "I'll tell you the truth, the preaching is for my benefit; I can't live without preaching."

If the papal summons of the previous July had been a mortal warning, the Frate's continued defiance of it was a prescription for self-immolation. Yet the few months following this most recent return to preaching have been described as a period of great calm for him.[2] Rome sent no ultimatums. At home the Arrabbiati could only grind their teeth at the Frate's durable popularity. Most of the Priors elected were favorable to governo civile, if not to him, and the city remained faithful to the French alliance. Duke Lodovico of Milan wrote fra Girolamo honeyed letters, implicitly acknowledging his crucial influence on foreign policy, and the pope sent secret envoys (including, it was rumored, his own son Cesare Borgia) to win him to the Holy League. Another rumor—that Alexander VI, through some back channel, was tempting him with a cardinal's hat—seemed confirmed when the Frate startled his congregation by crying out, "I want no hats, no miters either large or small. I want nothing but what you [God] have given to your saints: death. A red hat, a hat of blood; this is what I want!"[3] A period of calm, perhaps, but martyrdom was never far from his mind.

For his principal text he chose the *Book of Ruth*. He had been reworking his treatise *On the Simplicity of the Christian,* and Ruth, the personification of simple faith, was a convenient model for his ongoing war against the tepid. Simplicity, he declared, was God's gift both to nature and to humans. A preacher who employed elaborate rhetoric was not speaking naturally, from the heart, but from artifice and force; his discourse bore no fruit, for while God was responsible for both simplicity and artifice, he preferred the former because it was spontaneous and direct, whereas the latter was mediated by human effort. Ostensibly attacking his favorite target, superficial Christians, fra Girolamo must also have been thinking of magniloquent orators like fra Mariano da Genazzano, at that moment in Rome urging Alexander VI to action against the insubordinate Dominican.

"You [again using the familiar second person 'tu'] hate good laws, and it seems to me, since you do not want to reform women and boys, that you hate decency. You hate chastity and love sodomy and unchastity. Women, reform yourselves, bring your dresses up to cover your bosoms." You boys, you must wipe the pavements clean where people make water ("I speak with all due modesty") in front of painted crosses and holy images. Wash them down with lime. Boys, the fancy cakes and thousand kinds of junk sold on feast days— confiscate them and give them to the poor. Holidays are for praising God, not for commerce.[4]

Still, piety is sometimes to be tempered with discretion: "On this day of Saint John [the Baptist, patron saint of Florence, June 24] I don't want to tell you to be abstinent or to fast; I absolve you; it's too hot; everyone, fast in the evening; my boys too will fast on the eve of San Giovanni because he's your city's advocate and he'll intercede for you before the Lord." Heat or no heat, however, everyone must go in procession, weeping and barefoot, good people doing penance for the wicked.

At the end of May he exchanged Ruth for a sterner text, the prophet Micah, who attacked the rich and powerful for failing to do justice. Just as Micah had prophesied that Zion would be cast on the ground and plowed over, Jerusalem become a hill of stones and the Temple Mount a forest: "So I say to you, Italy, so I say to you, Rome, that everything will be cast to the earth and your fortresses will be like a mountain of stones, your ground like a forest. Rome, your churches will be made into stalls and horses will be kept in them."[5]

This switch from the peaceful Ruth to the embattled Micah was made amidst a hailstorm of rumors that treated every effort to gain political leverage as a sinister Bigi conspiracy to restore Piero de' Medici and charged that traitorous oligarchs were subverting the effort to reconquer Pisa. The Corbizzi plot was still the scandal of the hour. Savonarola returned to the pulpit just as Filippo Corbizzi and his fellow "conspirators" were appealing their draconian sentences to the Great Council, as the new Law of Appeal entitled them to do. The condemned men with wives and children in tow protested their innocence and begged for clemency. Although Savonarola had passionately called for the Law of Appeal to foster reconciliation and end Florence's politics of revenge, by the spring of 1496 he seems to have concluded that reconciliation had had its day. He now insisted that justice be done, leaving no doubt that he meant the Corbizzi appeals to be rejected. And so they were. But the harsh treatment of the Corbizzi plotters may have harmed more than helped the republican cause. Pro-Medicean Bigi began to congregate and speak out openly. In the next election two of their leaders, Bernardo Del Nero and Francesco di Taddeo, were chosen for the key magistracy of the Ten of Liberty.[6]

Predictably, Corbizzi's party, the anti-Medicean Arrabbiati, countered allegations of collusion for votes and candidates by pointing fingers at the Piagnoni: San Marco, they charged, had become the center of Savonarolan scheming. Savonarola repeatedly denied it. He never discussed politics with outsiders except in the most general terms, he insisted, nor, he insisted from the pulpit, did he have any knowledge of intelligenze in the convent.[7] Conspiracy-obsessed Florentines found this hard to believe. Although it was never proved that full-scale intelligenze took place in San Marco (or anywhere else for that matter), it seemed unlikely that conversations between the friars and their visitors were limited to matters of conscience. In any case, the intimate union of religion and politics in Savonarolan Florence made such compartmentalization difficult. But with both sides vulnerable to charges of collusion (the Savonarola-backed law of August 13, 1495, outlawing Parlamento included a provision against intelligenze), they were at a standoff.

Savonarola's greatest political victory had been the founding of the Great Council, and he continued to hail it as a gift of God. That he would so soon be calling for modifications was perhaps as uncomfortable for him as it was troubling to his followers. The completion of the Great Hall had made it possible for unified sessions, which, he argued, more accurately represented the will of all the people. At the same time, with everyone sitting together, the divisions in the body politic and the inadequacies of some of the new councilmen were more fully on view. Many, he observed, voted in ignorance of the issues; many allowed family ties or personal prejudice to influence their vote. Though he named no names and was vague about the particulars of their performance, he insisted that the Council needed to be "refined." Purge unqualified men and raise the eligibility requirements, he demanded, although he did not specify what new criteria should be adopted or who should be expelled.

In the early days of constitutional reform he had called upon the Florentines "to raise up good men, those who have the virtue of humility." It was just those humble men who fled from exercising power, he had argued, they who should be made to serve.[8] But a year of blistering parliamentary struggle had demonstrated the limitations of humility or, rather, the need for a different virtue, namely, prudence. For the time being, his calls for modifications were stymied in Council. Eventually, with support in some unexpected quarters and with new Frateschi leadership, he would have his way, but the victory proved costly, dimming his aura as a champion of the people and alienating some supporters.

For the city's economic troubles, no solution was forthcoming. The downward spiral that began with the expulsion of Florentine bankers and merchants from France had been slowed but had yet to find bottom. Invasion, war, and local revolts disrupted trade and destroyed harvests. The loss of jobs coupled with the rising price of grain was a formula for widespread suffering. Nor was misery suffered in silence: rioters demanded bread. But treasury balances were depleted by the cost of troops and supplies for the Pisan war, as well as by payments on the huge subvention still owing to Charles VIII.

Savonarola had supported the abolition of *gabelle*, taxes on commodities, which hit the poor especially hard. The adoption of the *decima*, a fixed levy on property, in spring 1495, had been popular but it failed to make up the deficit. This was supplemented by an *accatto*, the traditional interest-free forced loan, of 100,000 florins. Levied on all citizens, "in the name of liberty," it had been greeted with consternation by workers who rightly saw it as a tax and feared it would be ruinous.[9] Tax reform thus became another socially divisive issue, with ottimati doggedly proposing new forced levies and popolani majorities stubbornly rejecting them.

In July the Signoria proposed to ease the city's financial burden by levying an interest-free "loan" on clerical wealth. Fra Girolamo might have been expected to support the move, having already voiced his disapproval of clerical luxuries: "I want to be the first to take a hammer to my monastery's chalices and cross because they're superfluous, and I'd give [the proceeds] to the poor. Saint Gregory gave the silver tabernacle containing the Corpus Domini to the poor for the love of God and put [it] in an ordinary wooden box."[10] But chalices were more expendable than ecclesiastical revenues. Canon law decreed that church property not be taxed by secular governments except in extreme circumstances—an ambiguous principle that invited conflict. A century earlier a Florentine levy on the clergy in its jurisdiction had induced Pope Gregory XI to place the city under an interdict and even to wage war against it.

In this Savonarolan summer of 1496 the proposal to tax the Church was bound to stir up more hostility among clerics already divided between Piagnoni and anti-Piagnoni, to say nothing of its provoking Rome. From his retreat in the upper Arno valley, Angelo Leonora, ex-curialist turned Vallombrosan anchorite and a keen observer of affairs in Florence, called the tax proposal "theft, rapine, and sacrilege." In a letter to the abbot of San Salvi, his Order's monastery in Florence, obviously meant for general circulation, he included the comments of eight of his fellow Vallombrosans. A converso, or lay brother, complained that if the monks had to surrender the poor earnings of their crops and livestock they would starve. A student monk warned of the harm it would do to religion and cited Marsilio Ficino's *On Christian Religion*, which held that religion separated men from brutes. Had not the venerable frate Girolamo, in his *Compendium of Revelations*, warned that God would only punish enemies of the new state as long as it remained pure and just?[11]

The venerable father frate Girolamo was at the moment in the midst of another government-ordered suspension from preaching (officially a precaution against a new visitation of plague). When he returned to the pulpit on

August 20, he protested that although some clergy blamed him for the tax levied on July 23, he was neutral. "If I said a tax should be imposed on the religious. I would be violating canon law unless it were a case of extreme necessity, and I don't want to judge whether it is an extreme necessity. But then if there were some great danger and I said they shouldn't be taxed, they would say 'it was the Frate.' So I left it to God. I'm between Scylla and Charybdis. I don't judge anything, I don't say yes, I don't say no; I'm between one and the other."[12]

Money, how to get it, how to spend it, remained stubbornly at the center of the republic's problems, and however much Savonarola would have liked to remain neutral on taxes, he knew that money was crucial to the success of his apostolate. His credibility as a prophet was tied to the recovery of Pisa and the return of Charles VIII. Both, he insisted, were divinely guaranteed. But both were costly. The military expenses for the first and subvention payments for the second were draining the treasury, ruining the republic's credit, and setting citizens against each other. Even the tax on Church property fell short of a solution.

The high cost of the French alliance was brought home that August when the bishop of Aix, an envoy from Charles VIII, came to request Savonarola's support for an additional subvention. Savonarola refused, pointing out what was at least technically true: that he had no say in these matters. Furious, the bishop protested to the Signoria: he would go into a pulpit and expose the Frate as a hypocrite! If he did that, the magistrates warned, the people would tear him to pieces. The reverend bishop stormed from the chamber and out of the city and applied to Duke Lodovico of Milan for a safe conduct home. Although the duke was no longer an ally of the French, he granted the safe conduct, calculating that the French envoy's departure would leave the Florentines without an official link to the king, their notional protector against the pope and the League.[13]

The comic exit of the bishop of Aix was the prelude to a farce. In the presence of the startled ambassadors of Florence and Ferrara, Duke Lodovico ordered to be read out in council two unsigned letters from Savonarola to Charles VIII, which his agents, he said, had seized en route. The first urged the king to mount a new Italian invasion without delay; the second complained that the French ambassador had been creating disunity in Florence by speaking ill of His Majesty's friends. That Savonarola was urging a new French invasion or that he had fallen out with the French ambassador was news to no one, but Lodovico, having decided to drop the flimsy mask of cordiality he had lately shown to the Frate and eager to drive a wedge between him and his most prestigious supporter, Duke Ercole of Ferrara, seems to have believed that these "secret" communications would cast Savonarola in a sinister light.[14] Instead, Ercole wrote to Savonarola assuring him of his continued esteem.[15] Duke Lodovico had no better success with the pope, who maintained a cryptic silence on matters regarding the Frate.

Savonarola himself denied that he had written secret letters, declaring sarcastically that when he did write to the king, which he had not done for some time, he did it openly.[16] Besides, as far as he and Florence were concerned anything that would bring Charles back to Italy was salutary. "I know you're whispering, 'O frate, letters have been found . . .' I've heard it; they've been brought to me too; I've seen them. Well, what do you think? To me everything seems fine and every Florentine man who isn't an enemy of his country ought to be very glad. So you ought to be obliged to him. . . . Whether it's me or someone else, whoever wrote them you ought to be grateful to him."[17]

Duke Lodovico had somewhat better success with a different sort of intrigue. After months of urging by the League and an offer of a subvention from Milan, Maximilian Hapsburg, king of the Romans and Holy Roman emperor-elect, decided that this was the time to expel the weak French garrison from Naples and assert his imperial lordship over Italy. Before committing a small detachment of horsemen and foot soldiers to the enterprise, Maximilian sent ambassadors to Florence to announce that His Imperial Majesty was coming to drive the French out and extend his protection to all of Italy. The envoys argued that the French had unlawfully occupied Pisa and Naples and brought destruction upon all Italy, including their Florentine allies. Taking aim at that perennial staple of Florentine civic mythology, the Second Charlemagne prophecy, the emperor's ambassadors noted that Charles the Great, the ancient benefactor of their city, was not French, as those "usurpers" claimed, but German. The Florentine officials listened politely and replied that they would respond after further consultation at home.

Though everyone was aware that Maximilian's invitation served the purposes of Duke Lodovico il Moro of Milan, a growing number of Florentines believed it was the wiser course to accept the emperor's offer and end the city's isolation. Famine was threatening, the Venetians were by this time in control of the port of Pisa, and Piero de' Medici was in Tuscany threatening a strike against the city. Since there was no sign of life from Charles VIII it seemed foolhardy to defy the emperor and delay joining the League.[18] Supporters of the French alliance countered, on no evidence at all, that the Florentine envoys in France had sent letters detailing the king's plan of action but that the duke's agents had intercepted them as well as the letters from Savonarola to Charles VIII.[19]

For his part Savonarola reminded everyone that whatever princely promises they might be hearing, the only certainties were those divinely guaranteed: Italy would be scourged, Rome overturned, and the elect receive their ultimate apotheosis. The implication was clear: the Florentines must maintain their faith in Charles VIII and his messianic mission, for these had been ordained by God. These prophetic reassurances seemed to give the pro-French party its margin of victory. The Florentines politely but firmly refused the invitation to join Maximilian, instead calling upon him to declare his intention to restore Pisa to its rightful owners. If he did this, he would achieve his declared goals of peace and justice and the Florentines would gladly entrust him with the restoration of their (other) rights. But Maximilian wanted a more immediate and tangible concession—Florence's entry into the League—and this he failed to obtain.[20]

Shortly after the imperial ambassadors took their leave, Maximilian set sail from Genoa with twelve swift galleys and four ships. The Florentines were unnerved.[21] Was he headed for Livorno? With Pisa already closed to them, a blockade of Livorno would deny them the ability to export their goods and import grain. Advocates of joining the League were quick to point out that these were the drastic consequences of refusing the emperor's offer, but Savonarola urged the city to hold course:

"Come here, poor man and poor woman; if you are afraid of famine, live righteously and God will not let you want for anything. And if you are needy, God will produce bread for you from stones. . . . Do good, and if you do good, don't worry about dying of hunger because God will provide for you—if you are good." He went so far as to declare that between virtue and a full belly there was a direct causal link: "But the wicked poor, blasphemers, and gamblers, are those who will die of hunger. . . . You poor men, look around at who is working. You will see that it's mostly believers who are working."[22]

This improbable and uncharitable thesis met with some indignation and moved the Signoria to consider replacing fra Girolamo with a preacher who would offer more humane and practical advice. It was even rumored that fra Mariano da Genazzano had been approached, but had declined pleading ill health. Fearing this would cause still more controversy, they let the matter drop.[23] In any event, neither nature nor Pisan freedom fighters were bound by

Savonarola's promises of divine protection. For the second straight year the crop of grapes, figs, and grain had been decimated by heavy rains. Food prices rose still higher when a Pisan raiding party captured a Florentine train of thirty mules laden with sugar and leather goods.

Another blow was the news that Piero Capponi had fallen in battle, struck in the head by an arquebus bolt as he led an assault on the castle of Soiana in Pisan territory on October 26. The patrician Capponi had been one of the leaders of the revolt against the Medici and a principal negotiator of the treaty with Charles VIII, although his increasing hostility to Savonarola's populism had strained his commitment to the new republic. Ironically, just as Capponi was giving his life for the recovery of Pisa, the Florentine rumor mill was churning out suspicions that he was "a rapacious friend of the Pisans and a laggard in the war." Whatever the truth about his character and his intentions (both Parenti and Guicciardini were ambivalent), he was given a state funeral. Capponi's death, especially the manner of it, dramatized the seemingly endless frustrations tormenting the city.[24]

While still mourning Capponi the Florentines were dismayed to hear that Maximilian and his fleet were indeed bound for Livorno. The imperial ambassadors returned to warn that unless they changed allegiance they would not only lose Livorno but be forced to look on as the League's army invaded their territory and put their people to the sword.[25] When urgent discussions produced no agreement on a course of action, the Signoria, as Parenti put it, "had recourse to prayer and ordered the image of Santa Maria Impruneta brought to the city in solemn procession so that we could commend ourselves to God that he might aid us in such distress."[26] The Priors also expressly ordered Savonarola to preach. He returned to the Cathedral pulpit on October 28.

In the variety of their styles and content, the three sermons of October 28, November 1, and November 2 traverse the range of Savonarola's preaching modes—moral, political, pastoral, and apocalyptic—and employ the full richness of his preacher's art.[27] For the first his text was Psalm 45/46: "Our God is our refuge and strength, a helper in troubles which have found us exceedingly." Three times he had intervened with the king on behalf of the Florentines, he reminds them, and each time God answered their prayers, freeing them from danger. If they do as he tells them, turning again to God and to prayer, he will again free them, come what may. But wicked persons have been grumbling, saying, "Now it's clear, we've been deceived," so he will demonstrate who is really clear and where clarity is to be found. Then he launches into a pulpit dialogue, bantering, cryptic and peremptory in turn.

"Are you clear?"—"I'm clear, I"—"Oh, you are laughing, frate!"—"I am laughing because I have good news from heaven. . . . I tell you that this is a matter of Christ and that I'm clear about it. Now, consider a little whether you are as clear as I am. . . . I'm clear about the things I've predicted to you and I know they can't fail and I also know something else that I have not told you openly. . . . I've got a secret that I can't tell you, I have to be silent; my secret is mine, my secret is mine."—"Are you clear?"—"I'm clear, I."—"Tell me, what are you clear about?"—"I'm clear that God will confound the mind of Italy. Many will remain deceived. God revealed the mysteries of his Church from the higher angels to the lower, then down to his prophets who passed their light down to ordinary mortals."

But the minds of the wicked remain confused. The Church will be renewed, come what may and, come what may, Florence will have many blessings and more empire than she has ever had. "God wants you to have these temporal benefits of riches and glory to help you maintain your spiritual well-being."—"What should I do, then, frate?"—"First, fear God. Second, support what you have created: love the common good, your city and your country, and don't impede the human measures that must be taken, that is, the financial help, for the city's needs. When you see that the city needs money, help all you can, lend what you have for the good of the commune. I'm not talking about taking usury from the commune, but gratis. . . . And furthermore, unite, all together, leave off your dissensions and if you do this, if you form a true union—note well what I am telling you—I want to give up my [friar's] mantle if you don't drive off your enemies; if you do this I want to be the first to go out to meet [them] with a crucifix in my hand, and we'll make our enemies fly as far as Pisa and even further." The secret remained hidden in his breast for the time being.

The first news that Maximilian's fleet had been wrecked turned out to be false, but word from Lyons that a French relief force was on the way to Livorno proved true. The speedy arrival of seven French ships loaded with grain and soldiers gave the Florentines a respite, widely attributed to the intervention of Madonna of Impruneta. Assurance that Charles VIII would be on the scene in three days proved, as usual, false, but then a sudden storm that did scatter the imperial ships at Livorno seemed further evidence that God had once again come to the city's rescue and verified fra Girolamo's promises.[28] Harassed by the French fleet and "seeing himself without money and without hope, the emperor took the road back and retired ignominiously to Germany."[29]

Fra Girolamo was pointedly casual about the Livorno reprieve. Was this anything more than a verification of what he had predicted? Not until he was well into his sermon of November 1 did he refer to "the good news" the Madonna had brought to the city. "You wicked, you who were saying 'we're all clear' . . . the first thing I told you in my previous sermon was not to proceed with your schemes; then I said, following the psalm [46/47] that God is our refuge and our strength. Does it seem to you that this was the truth? . . . You were already knotting the rope, but the rope didn't slip through the knot. . . . God didn't want you to carry out your scheme. Someone came to spoil it, and so, I say, will the others [be spoiled]."[30]

The main subject of this All Saints' Day sermon was to be the glories of the blessed. Since, as Saint Paul had said, these heavenly glories could neither be seen by the eye, heard by the ear, nor imagined by the heart (1 Cor. 2.9), he would describe them in earthly terms, as Isaiah had done when he pictured God seated on a lofty throne (Isa. 6.1–2). Then he launched into a lengthy account of his own vision much like the journey to the throne of the Virgin of the previous year. He entered a chapel and prayed at a descending succession of altars, beginning with the altar of the Holy Trinity, for new blessings for Florence. At each he received this same response: God will help the city even if the whole world is against it. He will reward the Florentines spiritually and temporally, but those who set their hearts only on worldly riches he will cause to lose both temporal and spiritual goods, lose the blessing of eternity, and go to the house of the devil. The promised temporal rewards are those for the common good of the city, not for personal wealth or power. The Florentines will survive famine, war, and pestilence to become the seed of the renewal of the Church and reap wonderful spiritual and temporal rewards, but first they must rebuild the beautiful city of precious stones which was the primitive Church, now fallen into ruin.

As always, Savonarola's vision of ultimate joy is linked to present events: he is urging the unity of prayer, faith, and patience counseled by the Virgin, not the specious unity currently being urged by wicked men. "But you say, 'Let's make a league.' Make no mistake. No league! There will be no league, only dissension between one lord and another, and between lords and people. . . . But you listen and don't want to understand [Isa. 6.9]. . . . Listen, you wicked person. Three great men of Italy were in the mouth of a fiery serpent, one a cleric. . . . He who was to come arrived and killed those three great men and many others were killed in the tumult in the piazza. Then the bells of glory were sounded and everything became quiet and the renewal began. These men, I tell you, are on the road leading to the precipice. Pray for them, that God may convert them too and that they share in all the glory for which Almighty Lord be praised who is blessed in *saecula saeculorum.*"

From politics and apocalyptic visions fra Girolamo turned in his sermon for November 2, All Souls' Day, to the ultimate pastoral question: how should a Christian face death? He had preached on the theme before, but those earlier efforts had been no more than rehearsals for this masterpiece of the late medieval pastoral genre known as *ars moriendi*.[31] He follows in the doctrinal and homiletical footsteps of such great writers on death and dying as Heinrich Suso, Jean Gerson, Domenico Capranica and Archbishop Antoninus, but in the ability to create emotional intimacy with his listeners and readers and to convey the precarious urgency of preparing for death he was the equal of any. He chides his listeners' self-indulgence and challenges their blind resistance to thinking about their own deaths. He not only tells them what they what must do to make a good death, he shows them: with him they don virtual eyeglasses of the spirit so they may see their own lives rightly and witness the manner of their dying.[32] (*see Fig. 3*)

How many *ars moriendi* scenes hung on the walls of Florentine houses we cannot say. There was a market for cheap religious prints in late fifteenth-century Florence, but even cheap prints may have been beyond the means of many of fra Girolamo's flock—all the more reason for offering them these inspired verbal images. For those who could afford them there was also a growing trade in printed books illustrated with woodcuts. Savonarola was one of the first to understand the power in the fusion of word and image, and he took great pains to select effective pictures for his writings. In that year of 1496 there were five illustrated editions of his *Sermon on the Art of Dying*, three from Florentine printers with whom he regularly collaborated.[33]

On the day of the happy news from Livorno a jubilant Savonarola reclaimed his pulpit. "A little while ago [the wicked] were happily saying, 'Are you clear that we have been deceived?' Now they keep quiet. . . . So, what do you say now? The rope was about to be knotted, but [the cord] didn't slip through. Do you wicked people say that this was due to chance, to fortune?" Taking as his text the second verse of Psalm 47/48 he enlarged on his millenarian vision for Florence: once again God had intervened on behalf of their city, the city of the Lord. If the Florentines trusted no king, no man of this world, but Christ, if they set good governors over their offices and strongholds, they would rule other cities. And on the Fifth Day, when God opened hell and emptied it of all its devils, when out came the ostriches, that is, the tiepidi, who seemed to fly, but the weight of their ceremonialism kept them earthbound, and when all Italy was inundated by strangers, then the Florentines would again confess that God was their refuge. And on the Sixth Day he would say, "Let us see that the Florentine people rule as we do and that [they] have great dominion and create a good, holy government." Then it would be the Seventh Day and they will have their repose.[34]

CHAPTER 17

The Tail Acquires a Head

Whether by divine intervention or the vagaries of Tyrrhenian coastal winds, Maximilian's landing had failed. The Florentines could breathe a little easier. But in Rome a snare was being set for the prophet himself. On November 7, just as the storms were playing havoc with the imperial fleet, Pope Alexander VI issued a breve creating a new province of reformed Roman and Tuscan Dominican convents.[1] In this new Tusco-Roman Congregation there were to be sixteen houses from Rome, Lazio, Umbria, and Tuscany. These would include San Marco of Florence, San Domenico of Fiesole, and the other convents that four years earlier had been united in the Congregation of San Marco. His Holiness took pains to establish that he had no ulterior motive in creating the new province, repeatedly declaring that his sole purpose was to improve religious observance in the sixteen houses. Although Savonarola is not mentioned in the breve, this was clearly a stratagem for ending the stalemate with Savonarola on the pope's own terms. Excommunication was specified as the punishment for noncompliance. No doubt to give the impression that he was not engaged in a personal vendetta, His Holiness delegated Cardinal Oliviero Carafa, Savonarola's old ally in the separation from the Lombard Congregation, to choose the vicar of the new province, in consultation with Dominican Vicar General Torriani, another quondam ally of the Frate. But for Savonarola the identity of the new vicar was irrelevant. Once the Congregation of San Marco had been dissolved into a Tusco-Roman entity the Frate would no longer control the course of reform or even his own destiny. If his superiors in the new Congregation chose to remove him from Florence, he would have to go. If he refused to comply, he faced excommunication as did any of the San Marco friars who remained loyal to him.

Savonarola's only recourse was to claim that the decision on complying with the papal order was not his alone to make. The *Apologeticum* sent to the pope in the name of all 250 friars of the new Congregation of San Marco stated that they had scrutinized and debated the order and unanimously decided not to obey. It was unreasonable, they said, to unite San Marco, a reformed house, with the "deformed" houses of Tuscany. This would do little to improve the poor condition of religious observance in those houses and would certainly do great harm to San Marco's superior way of life, particularly to its younger, less experienced friars. "Reformation," the friars went on to argue, meant returning to original form; if the deformed houses wish to reform, they can do so by resolving to live within the bonds of the three vows and seek perfection through the rule and constitution of the Order. On the other hand, they maintained, citing Savonarola's favorite, John Cassian, that while laymen can easily recover from moral decline, religious who fall from the state of monastic perfection seldom or never return to their original fervor. As to the force of the pope's order: not every command of superiors need be obeyed, only those that conform to the Gospel, the rules and constitution of their Order, and truth. Obedience to orders that ran counter to those standards could only cause great evils to body and soul. Since it could not have been the intention of those who issued the order to cause such evils, their thoughts should be followed, not their words, as "all Doctors [of the Church]" maintain.[2]

What evils the San Marco friars might suffer from compliance with the papal order were never to be known, since their refusal to join the new Roman-Tuscan Congregation left it stillborn. Even if the pope was using the proposal to entrap the Frate, Cardinal Carafa and other prelates seem to have conceived the new Congregation in good faith after "mature consideration," as ambassador Becchi put it, to resolve the impasse and advance the cause of reform. Carafa, through Becchi, advised Savonarola to accept it, "for it was truly God's work," and contended that in the past the friar had wanted just such a union.[3] As they saw it, there was more at stake for the Church than the independence of a single friar, however dedicated he might be. Conflicts within the Dominican Order had to be resolved and papal authority upheld.[4] But to Savonarola submission was not an option; he could only see it as the abandonment of God's work. Carafa and his colleagues judged this to be overreaching by a self-centered friar with an exaggerated sense of his own importance and little regard for the higher good of the Church. Some believed it was the tactic of a charlatan whose claim to prophecy was a device for securing personal influence and fame.

Would a charlatan have been likely to stay the course once it became obvious that it led to excommunication and, very possibly, death? Fra Girolamo again declared that he did not fear martyrdom but welcomed it. "If I stake my life on [God's governance of the world], why don't you want to stake your possessions on it?"[5] The Advent sermons beginning on November 30 show little fear; even the frequent references to the coming persecution of the elect and the constant battle with the tepid are part of his apocalyptic rhetoric of ultimate victory and glory. True to form, he fretted that the moral and political renewal which would bring on that happy time was still incomplete: the reform of women and fanciulli remained a work in progress; sodomites, gamblers, and blasphemers eluded punishment; each citizen pursued his own interest, neglecting the common good. The Great Council had yet to be "refined" through stricter eligibility requirements and the removal of members who did not meet the new standards. With the election to the Eight of Security approaching on December 15, he called for men who were "terrible and rigid" in the cause of justice. "If you don't agree to do justice and love the common good, God will strike you a great blow . . . if you don't go to these magistrates and say, 'Do you want to endanger Florence? Do you want to ruin this city?' . . . you will have tribulations, great ones. If you do it, believe me, you will be the alloy that shines with God-like splendor and you'll be saved from tribulation by him."[6]

Savonarola's call for the selection of "terrible and rigid" men was becoming entangled with another constitutional issue involving questions of power and status. In the first days after the anti-Medicean revolt he had intervened decisively on the side of the people against oligarchical rule and called for filling lesser public offices by lot (*tratte,* or sortition). In this system the names of eligible candidates would be placed in electoral bags and drawn randomly as needed. Instead the constitutional reforms of late December 1494 and early 1495 had established a two-tiered system combining sortition and election, whereby names of rival candidates for an office were drawn from the electoral bags, then submitted to election in the Great Council. Fra Girolamo had endorsed this new system, at first perhaps because it enhanced the importance of the Council, then because he saw that Frateschi candidates, especially the better-known of them, did well in the Council elections. Moreover, as he saw the need for more experience and better political judgment, Savonarola's initial enthusiasm for extending political participation to the previously disenfranchised artisans and shopkeepers had begun to wane. Thus he wanted both to maintain the two-tiered system of sortition-cum-election and to "refine" the Council membership by raising the standards of eligibility.

Conversely, Piagnoni of lesser social standing were losing their enthusiasm for an electoral system that seemed to favor the old ruling elite and began to call for a return to the seemingly more democratic system of sortition. Nor could they have been happy about Savonarola's calls for "refining" Council membership. The dispute was further complicated by Arrabbiati members of the Great Council who now adopted the tactic of casting white beans (nay) for all candidates, not only to obstruct and discredit elections but also to impede the working of the more egalitarian regime they had opposed from the start. As they saw it, a return to sortition would not only remove the Savonarolans' advantage but also restore the mechanism by which oligarchs had controlled Florence for the better part of two centuries. The pro-Medicean Bigi also supported a return to sortition. (Manipulating that system by controlling the names that were drawn from the electoral bags was an old oligarchic practice that the Medici had continued.) Besides, the Bigi saw the random drawing of names from bags to be a more anonymous and impartial method for filling offices than election, thus neutralizing the taint of their Medici loyalty and giving them a better chance of gaining office.

On December 13, two days before the election of new Priors, Savonarola preached before the outgoing Signoria, members of the Great Council, and "almost the whole of our people."[7] Justice was again his theme, the overarching goal of all his moral and political reforms. Again he called for "refining" the Great Council. "Examine it and start refining it, trimming it bit by bit and seeing whether many who are in it ought to be there." Many, he noted, were impatient with this slow procedure and refused to support other legislation, including crucial money bills, until the Council was reformed. "This was foolish; since the thing is good in itself, even though not yet polished to perfection, give it your support; don't let it die because of that; if you do you will help those who want to ruin the Council." Others, he observed, insisted that before the Great Council could be refined the electoral system had to be changed and the method of drawing lots adopted.

"I tell you that anyone who wants this sortition is moved by his passion, not by reason. Confess, confess that you are a sorry Christian, even a wicked one, because knowing the kind of life you are living, you're afraid you won't be elected. . . . Go, read Messer Leonardo [Bruni] d'Arezzo, where it says that the city always went well without sortition and that it was later discovered by ambitious people. It's the same with the evil people who are going around whispering such things in ears. They are the ones who, within and without, hold secret meetings against your city with priests and friars and who make those lovely dinners and breakfasts where their talk is always about the Frate: they practically eat bread and Frate, meat and Frate, wine and Frate. Florence, take measures against these conventicles. But no one thinks about them. Only 'this poor little friar' who must fight the whole world."[8]

"The poor little friar" will defend everything he has said against doctors and prelates and against "that other one" (fra Mariano da Genazzano?) who while accusing him of meddling in affairs of state instead of preaching the Gospel talks more about politics in a single sermon than he himself does in all his sermons. Nor will he fight alone, for God is with him. He is accused of heresy, but the Dominican Order has never had a heretic. Rather, Dominicans have brought much good fruit and reformation of life into Italy, as now. "That other one" charges him with having said the Church should own no property, but this is not true: he has defended the view that the Church may own property many times against those who argue the contrary, which is heresy. (His own friars, not to speak of Vincenzo Bandelli, must have winced to hear it.) He has, however, called upon prelates not to spend the property of the Church abusively.

From this defensive detour he returns to his theme of justice. If the Florentines want peace and consolation, every man, woman, and child must do justice, for this is nothing but rendering to each what is his. Justice means loving the common good and driving out vice. If magistrates refuse to give four turns of the rope to someone who merits it, they themselves deserve that punishment because they are failing to do justice. "When Christ condemned the sinners saying, 'Accursed ones, go into the eternal fire [Matt. 13.42?]!' he did not say, 'I condemn you because you are a thief or adulterer, but because you have not done justice; you have not given food to poor hungry people, not given drink to the thirsty.' By failing to do such works of justice you are ruining the common good. But there is no justice without the sword: let the Signori maintain a force of two or three hundred armed men to render speedy punishment to the accursed sodomites and blasphemers and other wrong-doers." After this startling proposal for summary, violent retribution, he concludes almost feverishly: "Justice, you magnificent Signori! Justice, you lords of the Eight! Justice, magistrates of Florence! Justice, you people! Justice, men! Justice, women! Everyone, cry justice! If you do this your land will render its fruits and the Lord will give you your grace."[9]

Arguments for and against Savonarola's proposal for a new moral police force followed swiftly and furiously. Although some liked the idea of summary justice for errant citizens, others—a plurality, according to Parenti—suspected an ulterior motive: with his situation becoming more difficult and his Franciscan critics compiling new propositions for attacking him in public debate (at the behest of the pope), this was a way to arm his followers and keep his enemies at bay or even, as some charged, to take over the city. In the end fra Girolamo's proposal was defeated. The chronic lack of public funds for arming more police made it too expensive.

The charge that Savonarola was planning a coup was bizarre, but the premise of the conspiracy theorists was correct: his situation was increasingly dire. The papal breve of November 7 with its threat of excommunication was common talk, its implications not only for the Frate but for the city duly spelled out. Theologian Giovanni Caroli, Savonarola's watchful antagonist in Santa Maria Novella, got his hands on a copy of the *Apologeticum* and fired off a refutation. Franciscan, Augustinian, and Dominican preachers learned of it and thundered their own denunciations, and in Rome, fra Mariano da Genazzano called upon the pope to "tear away, tear away this monster from Holy Church."[10]

Fears that fra Girolamo and his party were taking a more aggressive, even violent, turn in the struggle for power were not unrelated to the emergence of Francesco Valori as leader of the Frateschi. The Valori family had been politically prominent since the fourteenth century.[11] Parenti called Francesco *homo di mezo*, locating him somewhere near the political center, but in temperament Valori was anything but moderate.[12] Many of his peers found him domineering, intractable, and overly ambitious. At fifty-eight, Valori was a man of great acumen and experience. Three times elected Standard Bearer of Justice, he had often served in other important magistracies and diplomatic missions. Like Piero Capponi, he was a committed anti-Medicean and served the new republic in various important posts, although he was little more enthusiastic than Capponi about Savonarola's brand of pious populism. Rivalry between Valori and Capponi for the same constituency tended to neutralize both men, but Valori found it intolerable to be kept on the sidelines, and with Capponi's death he moved to claim a more prominent role. His early contacts with the Frate had not been promising; he had been one of the Twenty Accoppiatori forced to resign under pressure from Savonarola. Now he suggested himself as leader of the Frateschi.[13] Savonarola needed a political chief, and confident that Valori would not be able to use the position to gain personal power, he was inclined to accept Valori's offer. When he consulted Giovambattista Ridolfi, his closest political advisor, however, Ridolfi "blurted out certain words" in an effort to dissuade him.[14] He heard similar misgivings about Valori's ambition from others, but as he later told his interrogators, since he worried about his chieftains becoming too friendly with each other and joining forces to rule the city, Valori's personal unpopularity could be an advantage.

Ultimately Valori and Savonarola were drawn together by common interest. Both were unshakeable supporters of the French alliance. (Valori had even refused to join the embassy to the emperor to explore a possible shift to the side of the League.) Both were resolute anti-Mediceans who believed the new republic needed firm leadership. Defeated in the November election for the magistracy of the Ten, Valori "declared himself a partisan of the Frate" and was rewarded by being elected to the Signoria for the January–February 1497 term. The Priors duly chose him Gonfaloniere of Justice. No longer could the Florentines quip that Valori was a head without a tail while the Frateschi were a tail without a head. Still, as Parenti gloomily observed, although the joining of head and tail brought benefits to both, it also deepened the factional split in the city.[15]

The reservations about making Valori the Frateschi leader were offset by his success in advancing the party agenda. Valori knew how to get his way with legislators even in the absence of majorities. One of his favorite tactics was to convene large consultative bodies (*pratiche larghe*) that he stacked with men he trusted to propose measures favorable to his party. When these bills duly came before the Council of Eighty and the Great Council only those known to be in favor were allowed to speak. If a measure faltered, Valori would introduce it again and again until all objections were overcome and its opponents silenced. In this way Valori speedily pushed through much of Savonarola's stalled reform program, including more thorough marshaling of the Florentine fanciulli, more drastic penalties for sodomy and gambling, and tighter regulation of women's dress and ornament.

Clerical detractors of the Frate were made to feel the sting of the civil power. Fra Jacopo da Brescia, one of the most outspoken and tenacious anti-Savonarolan preachers, was summoned to the government palace and subjected to a tongue-lashing by Gonfaloniere Valori himself. When Valori accused him and three other Franciscans of encouraging sedition and threatened to starve out their convents all four fled the city.[16] For writing a sonnet depicting Savonarola and his lieutenants as idolaters and usurpers Francesco Cei was declared a rebel and exiled. Girolamo Muzi, whose *frottola*, or satirical poem, criticized the Florentines for accepting "a guide full of hypocrisy," was heavily fined and sentenced to five years' probation.[17] To interrupt the clandestine flow of letters between Florence and the papal court and prevent dissident Florentines from calling upon Cardinal Giovanni de' Medici in Rome, Valori's government forbade all contacts between Florentines and members of the Medici family. Violators, together with their fathers and brothers, were to be declared rebels and exiled.

If Savonarola worried that Valori's dictatorial style was at odds with his own calls for liberty and peace he voiced no objection. Valori even overcame the Great Council's resistance to "refining" itself. Two years earlier, when it seemed that the basic qualification for the Great Council, the "benefit of the three majors," would yield too few members, it had been decided to relax admission standards temporarily. For a limited period, between January and April 1495, any citizen could qualify for a Council seat by showing that a member of his *consorteria*, or extended family, had served in one of the three major magistracies. This appeared to have liberalized Council membership to some degree and may have precipitated Savonarola's calls for a purge of incompetent members. Valori's initiative not only turned back to the strict interpretation of the "three majors" rule, by which citizens qualified only if they or their fathers or grandfathers had served in one of the three major offices, it also led to the expulsion of members who had been seated under the relaxed interpretation. He also secured a ban on citizens who were in tax arrears, a disqualification more likely to bar people of lesser means than the well-to-do. To make up for the potential loss of membership (finding a quorum was always a challenge) the minimum age for membership was lowered from thirty to twenty-four.[18] Whether these changes would satisfy Savonarola's call for "refining" the Great Council remained to be seen.

CHAPTER 18

Burning the Vanities

Carnival was the time for shedding everyday restraints and flouting moral norms before entering the penitential season of Lent.[1] In Florence giant comic figures and elaborate floats with mythological and satirical tableaux shared the streets with masked citizens who drank, danced, cavorted, and sang licentious songs, the notorious *Canti Carnascialeschi*.[2] Naturally fra Girolamo deplored all this: to him these were pagan antics and the quintessence of the Medici's poisonous legacy. By substituting acts of piety, charity, and reverence, Florentines would transform Carnival into a fitting prelude to holy Lent. Carnival songs, either composed for the occasion or reworked from those of the past two years, expressed perfectly Savonarola's visionary fusion of patriotic chauvinism, popular republicanism, and apocalyptic renewal.

For the Palm Sunday procession of the previous year Girolamo Benivieni had composed a laud celebrating Christ as King of Florence, with the city confidently looking forward to the imminent fulfillment of the divine promise, when Florence would be "richer, more powerful, more glorious than ever."[3] Many things had changed for Florence, for Savonarola, and for the Piagnoni since then, few of them for the better, and Benivieni's new laud for the Carnival of 1497, which he called "a supplication to God for the promises made by him to the city of Florence," expresses the deepening sense of frustration and uncertainty.[4]

> Now that you have elected us, Lord
> Jesus, through grace,
> Inflame our hearts with your love.
> my Lord, summon up
> your might and come,

show yourself as God;
Lord, why more suffering?
Why do you not bind up and muzzle
That insane mob
Troubling the well-being of the city of the flower?

In this mood of embattled virtue and unfulfilled promise Savonarola called for a bonfire of vanities. Seventy-five years earlier, fra Bernardino da Siena had introduced this ritual to Florence to symbolize the destruction of sin, and in 1483 fra Bernardino da Feltre had staged another. Significantly, in Savonarola's version the bonfire of the vanities took place not in front of a church, but in the Piazza della Signoria, center of temporal government, dramatizing the fusion of politics and piety. A great eight-sided wooden pyramid said to be thirty braccia high was built in the center of the square. Each side had fifteen shelves, and on each shelf was heaped "all the accursed stuff of Carnival": shameful pictures and sculptures, gambling devices, musical instruments and music books, masks, costly foreign draperies overpainted with immodest scenes, sculptures of very beautiful and shapely ancient Roman and Florentine women by Donatello and other great masters, gaming boards, playing cards, dice, harps, lutes, zithers, harpsichords, dulcimers, pipes, cymbals, and all the "women's vanities"—hairpieces, diadems, cosmetic cases, polish, mirrors, perfumes, face powder, musk, whigs. Other shelves held "all the lascivious Latin and vernacular books," including not only Luigi Pulci's *Morgante* but also Petrarch, Dante, Boccaccio's *Decameron.* Still another shelf held "beards, masks, wigs, and every diabolic instrument then in use."

The catalogue of vanities was meticulously described by Pseudo-Burlamacchi. "All these things were so varied and unusual as to appear delectable to the eye, and no wonder because they included sculptures of great value, paintings of marvelous beauty, ivory chessmen worth forty ducats, and others of alabaster and porphyry worth even more." Indeed, says the same writer, a Venetian merchant offered the Signoria the enormous sum of 20,000 ducats for the whole, but the offer was rejected. Overall was an effigy of Carnival "so monstrous and deformed" as not to be imagined.

On the morning of Carnival, Savonarola celebrated Mass and gave the benediction. "Many thousands of people" took communion from the hands of fra Girolamo and sang hymns and canticles "in such a way that it was believed angels had come to live among men, and certainly it was true." After breakfast a procession: four beautifully dressed fanciulli "of angelic demeanor" carried on their shoulders a portable platform with a beautiful Donatello sculpture of Jesu Bambino who gave his benediction with his right hand and held the crown of thorns with the nails and cross of the Passion in his left. Twelve fanciulli held a silken canopy over him, and all the other boys, two by two, according to their residential quarters, preceded them while youthful cantors sang psalms and hymns. Others followed soliciting alms, and still others, carrying red crosses, followed. Behind them came young girls and women. After completing the ritual circuit the procession stopped at the Cathedral to sing lauds in praise of the glorious Mary Queen of Florence and to present the alms they had collected to the officials of the Poor Men of San Martino.

Arriving at the Piazza della Signoria, the fanciulli arranged themselves on both sides of the square. As they sang an invective against the figure of Carnival, the towering pyramid was set on fire "with great happiness and joy of the whole people," the burning of so many vanities and snares of the devil causing not only men, women, and children but even "insensible creatures" to celebrate. The palace bells rang out, the Signoria's trumpets, pipes, and cymbals sounded the glory of the great triumph offered to God, and the flames rose to the sky to the honor of God and the ignominy of Satan.[5]

Carnival fervor did not produce cheap grain, however, nor did the symbolic burning of Satan and his minions silence the critics of the regime or scare off Florence's enemies abroad. In the streets people rioted for bread and, Landucci reported, died of hunger.[6] Then, at the beginning of March, just as the arch-Medicean Bernardo Del Nero was assuming office as Gonfaloniere of Justice, came shocking news: on February 25, 1497, Charles VIII had signed a truce with the League. By removing himself as an active force in the affairs of the peninsula, the king left the Florentines isolated among their powerful enemies. Without at least the threat of a new French expedition the city was instantly more vulnerable to the pressure of the pope and the League and its hope of recovering Pisa was severely diminished. Having steadily proclaimed Charles as the New Cyrus, Savonarola's own credibility as a prophet suffered accordingly. Moreover, the pope and the League could feel they had a freer hand to settle accounts with him.

From Rome envoy Becchi reported on March 19 that the League's ambassadors were urging the pope to have no further dealings with the Florentines since they refused "to declare themselves good Italians," and the Venetian envoy had assured him personally that without the good will of his government Pisa would never be restored to them. The pope and the whole court,

Becchi continued, were convinced that fra Girolamo governed everything in the city; thus Florence's obduracy was due to his bad counsel. That he continued to prophesy the destruction and renewal of the Church and of Rome was intolerable. Moreover, if he persisted in refusing to comply with the papal order creating the new Tusco-Roman Congregation, they would initiate proceedings to censure and excommunicate him.[7]

The abandonment by Charles VIII of his alliance with Florence was a cue to Savonarola's clerical enemies to step up their attacks. In San Lorenzo the Franciscan friar Jacopo Grumel spoke against him with such violence that the Eight removed him after a single sermon. But the Augustinian Leonardo Neri da Fivizzano remained firmly in his Santo Spirito pulpit denouncing fra Girolamo as a false prophet and deceiver of the people.[8] Savonarola replied, as usual naming no names. Weakened and easily tired, he said he would be brief this Lent. For seven years he had been saying that they would fight and win, and he would continue to say it. There was great fear, but "we have not drawn a half of our weapons."[9]

Yet he unsheathed no new weapons, disclosed no new revelation, offered no fresh evidence that the New Age was any closer. Nor had he any practical remedies for the people's troubles, while his moral scolding made him appear insensitive to the general suffering.

> You people lament the famine, but you don't say how much you deserve it because of your sins. God is angry with you; famine is in you and in your hands, because if you do good God will help you in everything. Come, you poor of the city and contado, do you go to sermons? What good deeds do you do? Worse, you blaspheme, you gamble. The country girls stay in the contado to dance; on feast days they wear sashes of silk and silver. Florentines, why don't you pass a law that they wear only plain cloth? They want to dress like you [city folk] do and dance all day and then they say, "We're dying of hunger!" That other poor fellow spends all day cursing him who has done him so much good. Poor man, you don't know what you are saying. The [preacher in his] sermon begs for abundance and has put many to work. Those others don't know what they are talking about; they have been incited by evil men who want to stir up turmoil. The turmoil is going to engulf you. If you knew what has been ordered for you up there you'd tremble from head to toe and throw yourself at the foot of a crucifix and weep. The friar is not afraid because he knows very well who is staying his hand.[10]

Less than three years earlier Bernardo Del Nero had ridden his horse through the streets of Florence to rally support for Piero de' Medici. Now he assumed the republic's highest office. This was not so much evidence of a groundswell for the Medici's return (as Piero de' Medici and his supporters seem mistakenly to have believed) as a reaction to Valori's high-handed leadership and of general unhappiness with the condition of the city. It could also be seen as a rebuke to the Frate: as Piero Parenti liked to point out, it was Savonarola who had chosen Valori to lead his party and thus, at least tacitly, approved his methods. Valori continued to lead the Frateschi with energy and skill, although since the end of his term as Gonfaloniere he was finding it harder to advance their interests or outmaneuver the opposition. No longer in control of the legislative agenda, he could not block the issue of relaxing eligibility for offices from being raised again.

On March 18, just over two weeks after Valori stepped down, the Council of Eighty convoked a large pratica to discuss electoral methods. Advocates of sortition linked electoral reform to the fiscal crisis, arguing that citizens who had to pay direct taxes (*gravezze*) should have access to public office—at least the minor magistracies—through selection by lot.[11] The point seemed reasonable but it was disingenuous: a return to sortition was calculated to help the anti-republicans, which explains why Gonfaloniere Bernardo Del Nero himself now argued that the time had come "to choose another method." Valori and his partisans managed to delay action until March 28, but, as he knew, the tide was turning against them. Perhaps hoping at least to have some influence on the inevitable, he agreed on April 4 to serve on a committee with Arrabbiati leader Tanai dei Nerli to study the matter of elections and speedily make a report. The committee's recommendation of a limited change to fill minor offices by lot was endorsed by the Eighty but rejected by the Great Council, apparently because its rank-and-file members thought it did not go far enough. Weeks of reports, proposals, counterproposals, and recriminations followed until both sides were exasperated and at a loss what to do next.

At the same time the election controversy was straining Savonarola's ability to hold his political coalition together he was also warding off one of the more unusual challenges to his leadership. To the east, in the Arno valley, suor Maddalena, a nun at Santa Maria di Casignano, was pitting her own revelations against his. Suor Maddalena was said to have predicted the downfall of Piero de' Medici, after which she gained a following in Florence with prognostications about individual citizens and civic affairs. Now she claimed to have supernatural knowledge exposing Savonarola as a fraud who drew his prophecies from purely human sources. In February, encouraged by the Frate's enemies, suor Maddalena proposed a meeting so that the two prophets could compare each other's visions and decide the best course of action for the city.[12]

Fra Girolamo dismissed the proposal out of hand as the impertinence of an upstart—a woman no less: "There are some women prophetesses who would like to write books and prophecies; but this is foolishness, laughable . . . these prophetesses are simple, but there are other wicked prophetesses who go from house to house all day saying, 'Don't believe those things [that I say].'" The prophet Ezekiel, his main text for Lent, had also inveighed against women who presumed to prophesy, he pointed out (Ezek. 13.17–20).[13]

But Maddalena persisted, writing to the Signoria to demand a meeting. Gonfaloniere del Nero, only too pleased to have this opportunity to embarrass the Frate, sent his chancellor Niccolò Altoviti to bring her to the city (after receiving assurances from her confessor that she was a virgin and lived a blameless life). Lodged in the house of her brother, a priest, on April 5, suor Maddalena held consultations with such important visitors as the Milanese chancellor and the ambassadors of Duke Ercole of Ferrara and of King Charles VIII.

The question of the hour was whether the two prophets should be brought together in a public confrontation. Maddalena wanted nothing better. Neither the Frate nor his supporters would hear of it. In their view he had proven himself many times over, whereas suor Maddalena was a naive country woman manipulated by his enemies. If he shared a platform with her, he not only would be granting her a degree of credibility to which, they insisted, she had no right but would also diminish his own authority. Savonarola's refusal to debate brought the *Paciali* (Florentine officials charged with making peace between disputing factions) into the picture. Taking the long view, they concluded that while Savonarola remained in Florence no peace could be had and they recommended that he be banished. But the Frate's influence proved the stronger. At his request, the Eight of Security hustled Maddalena back to Casignano where, as he saw to it, she was kept in strict cloistered seclusion and forbidden to write anything more against him.[14]

In exiling the prophetess the Eight had acted "in the name of civic peace and unity," particularly critical at that moment because the alarm had sounded: Piero de' Medici was approaching! Persuaded by Bernardo Del Nero's election and by reports of a city in factional turmoil and on the verge of starvation, Piero had decided his hour had arrived. Funded by Venice and his brother Cardinal Giovanni, he marched into Tuscany with a force of four hundred lancers, light cavalry, and foot soldiers. Belatedly the Florentines summoned their mercenary captain Paolo Vitelli to set up a defense perimeter and interned about two hundred citizens as potential Medici collaborators.[15] But heavy rains forced Piero to return to his quarters in Siena, and by the time he was able to make his move again he had lost all element of surprise. Arriving at the walls of Florence at the head of a force swollen to an estimated two thousand men,[16] Piero insisted that a Parlamento be called, then waited for his sympathizers to open the gates. He waited in vain. After several hours he again withdrew to Siena.[17]

Piero's latest attempt had not unleashed a Medicean fifth column in Florence as he had expected, but it exposed the low state of popular morale; leaders who tried to rally the citizenry to take up arms encountered widespread indifference. With reports from Siena that Piero was distributing bread to the peasantry and promising that when he returned to power he would peg the price of grain at thirty soldi per staio, some dared to say that a new Medici regime might be the solution to their troubles.[18] Rumors abounded: Piero was coming on Good Friday to bring bread and beans to the hungry, Piero would lower the price of grain, quell the tumult, and make "wonderful changes."[19]

Fantasies aside, there was reason to believe that Piero would gain the support of Venice and Milan for a return effort. In reaction to these fears the Priors elected for the May–June term were anti-Medici, and they chose the anti-Medicean Piero degli Alberti as Gonfaloniere of Justice. One of their first measures was to appoint a commission of eight to follow Piero's movements as well as to spy upon citizens suspected of Medicean sympathies. Not that this was much comfort to the Piagnoni; most of the Priors, including Gonfaloniere Alberti, were as opposed to Savonarola as to Piero de' Medici and even revived the old canard that the Frate was in league with the Bigi.

When Alberti moved for a two-month ban on unlicensed preaching on the usual grounds that summer plague spread more readily in crowded churches, the Piagnoni understood this to be directed against their prophet. They stirred up so much opposition to the measure that "almost nothing else was talked about in the land but whether or not the Frate would preach." To block the gag measure Savonarola partisans in the Signoria needed five votes but could only muster four, although they did win one concession: preaching could continue through May 4, Ascension Day.[20] Hearing rumors that the Compagnacci were planning a demonstration on that day, Savonarola's friends urged him to pass up this final appearance, but, silent since Lent, he was determined not to cede his pulpit to his enemies. It was God's will that he preach, he declared. In the

streets bets were being made: would the Frate persevere or withdraw? The
Signoria moved swiftly: anyone caught wagering would be fined for violating
the law and good morals.[21]

On the eve of Ascension Day workers in the Cathedral discovered the
rotting, stinking hide of an ass affixed to the pulpit. Nails had been driven into
the lectern to tear the hands of the preacher as he pounded for emphasis.
Feces had been smeared on an adjacent wall. By the time the first worshippers
arrived for the morning service everything had been cleaned and put to rights,
but word of the defilement had spread. Savonarola and his party had left San
Marco accompanied by an armed guard reinforced in the expectation of
trouble. Proceeding down the Via Cocomero, they were met by devotees who
came out of the church to greet him. In his sermon he made no mention of
the desecration, although the psalm he had chosen for his text, "Oh Lord my
God in thee I take refuge" (Psalm 7), had more to do with his own embattled
situation than with the Ascension of Jesus Christ.

> Maybe you thought I would be afraid? But don't you know that faith
> is afraid of nothing? . . . You believed that I wouldn't enter this pulpit this
> morning. See, I've come. Maybe you'll say, 'that's because you've got a big
> escort, frate,' and I'll tell you that I didn't call for this escort and that I
> wanted to come whatever happened, and I'll always come when the Lord
> God inspires me. When that happens no man in the world, whatever his
> rank, can stop me.[22]

After reaffirming his prophecies of tribulation and glory—Rome to suffer
a terrible scourge, God's church to be renewed, Florence to have all that had
been promised, including Pisa—he turned to his personal contest with "the
wicked." "You say, 'Frate, you ought not to have preached this morning.' Oh,
why? 'Because you could cause trouble.' And I answer you that my preaching
has never caused trouble and I trust in Christ that it never will. Believe me, if I
see that it would be better not to preach I won't preach. 'But you had an order
from the Signoria not to preach.' And I say to you, first, that it's not true and
supposing it were, there would be a big disputation as to whether I were
obligated to obey it. . . . But not to enter into that dispute at the moment, I tell
you that if I were afraid there was going to be trouble I wouldn't preach."

A loud crash signaled that the trouble had arrived. Some, apparently the
perpetrators, ran for the exits; others, either to intercept them or to save
themselves, ran in the same direction. Still others made for the pulpit, but
found the way blocked by the Frate's defenders. Bartolommeo Giugni of the

Eight of Security, was pushing forward when Lando Sassolino, apparently thinking that Giugni intended to do harm to the preacher, struck him with the flat of his sword.[23]

"I hear noises!" cried the Frate, startled, but he quickly recovered himself and called out defiance and reassurance: "The wicked don't want to accept their part. You, hold on there! Have a little patience because if you knew what I know, you'd weep. The rest of you, don't be afraid, because God is for us and there are thousands of angels here."

Hearing his appeal for calm, some knelt with him to pray. Drawing a crucifix from his robe, he held it aloft as the worshipers cried "Misericordia!" and "Jesu!" and raised their crosses in response. But when he realized there would be no more preaching that day, Savonarola left the pulpit and made his way out. At the door he was surrounded by a crowd crying "Viva Jesu Christus," some brandishing weapons they had fetched from their houses and forming an escort for the return to San Marco. There he resumed preaching to his friars. The wicked, he told them, have brought forth the iniquity and injustice hidden in their hearts. Secretly plotting the murder of the just, they have made a huge lake, an enormous ditch, but have themselves fallen into it. With praise for the Lord who had rescued him from perils he prayed that justice would come soon.[24]

CHAPTER 19

Excommunicated!

In the Ascension Day imbroglio the Piagnoni had overreacted to a simple prank by two young mischief makers, so thought Piero Parenti. Observing that no Savonarolans had been punished for violating the law against carrying weapons in the street, Parenti concluded that they had lost none of their political power.[1] But the Piagnoni had reason to feel vulnerable. The ban on preaching deprived them of their most effective weapon; Charles VIII's abandonment of his assigned messianic mission left them without earthly protectors; and although Savonarola himself might believe he was answerable to God alone, the order creating the Tusco-Roman Congregation was an ominous reminder that he defied the authority of his earthly vicar at his peril.

"Letter to All the Elect of God and Faithful Christians," Savonarola's long open letter of May 8, was neither a victory claim nor a cry of defiance but an appeal to "the children of God" to remain constant in this time of persecution. As Christ yielded to the Scribes and Pharisees, so he yields to the tiepidi who have ordered him to give up preaching. But tribulation is the prelude to the renewal of the Church. "Just as God reserves a great multitude of demons in this caliginous air of ours and does not make them stay in Hell, as they deserve, in order to test His elect in the faith, so does he allow reprobate men to live and prosper for the same purpose which the demons have; at the last, their judgment will be extremely severe and everlasting. But we await a great inheritance in Heaven, which will never fail, for we shall be children of God."[2]

Whereas he had once labeled as tiepidi the lukewarm Christians who clung to their superficial ceremonies, he now included in this category the magistrates who stopped him from preaching, the writers of secret letters to Rome, the opponents of reform legislation, the advocates of noxious changes in the electoral laws, and the Priors who cast their ballots for hostile Gonfalonieri. All of them were the minions of Satan, enemies of the New Jerusalem—the tepid.

From a sober political perspective, denouncing all his opponents as tiepidi was futile, even counterproductive. Republican politics worked best when adversaries refrained from condemning each others' morals or faulting their political philosophies. With the impasse over a new election law tearing Savonarolans apart and as hostility between parties escalated toward violence, public business was limping toward a standstill, or as Parenti onomatopoetically termed it, a *guazzabuglio*—a mess. Valori, perhaps with the more balanced perspective that came from being out of power, was one of the primati who saw the danger. Contracting with Arrabbiati leader Tanai de' Nerli for mutual support in the coming elections to the Ten, he pressed for compromise and passage of the stalled election reform bill.[3] On May 12, 1497, by a vote of 753 to 354, the Great Council approved the measure it had rejected two weeks earlier. The "three majors" and other prime magistracies, including the Ten of Liberty, Eight of Security, Officials of the Monte (treasury), and Conservators of Law, would continue to be filled by election. Lower level offices, for the most part provincial posts with annual stipends under 600 lire, would now be filled by a more complicated system of election and sortition. For each candidate who received one more than half the votes in Council a slip (*polizza*) bearing his name would be placed in an electoral bag. Slips would be extracted as vacancies occurred. In order to give the new system a reasonable testing period, it was to function until the end of December 1498, at which time it might be renewed or revised.[4]

The new law seems to have had mixed, even contradictory, effects. Guicciardini believed that with the wider distribution of offices the Great Council "had far more friends than ever before." Even the glum Parenti praised the measure, reasoning that by giving more citizens, especially popolani, a greater opportunity to gain minor office it reduced competition and eliminated a major source of resentment.[5] At the same time, as Guicciardini observed, critics of the Great Council now became more outspoken and blocked measures more brazenly, "so that there arose in citizens of all parties a pernicious sense of license leading them to speak ill of the Council publicly and to argue that Florence had been better off under the Medici." This was more than the habitual grumbling in hard times. The upsurge of criticism led Bigi leaders to exaggerate the seriousness of discontent with the republic and encouraged them to open negotiations with Piero de' Medici.[6]

Whether the new election law reduced the Frateschi share of offices as Savonarola and his captains had feared is not clear. Nor is it clear that the greater emphasis on sortition mollified his popolani followers. The growing disparagement of the Council—"my Council," as Savonarola was pleased to call it—weakened popular support for his New Jerusalem campaign, already distracted by hunger, unemployment, recurring plague, and military failures. Every succeeding crisis seemed to mock the promises of Florentine riches, glory, and empire. Calls to have done with a politics that revolved around a foreign friar's claim to the gift of prophecy were angrier and more frequent. How to bring peace to the divided city was the question facing the large pratica convened on May 20. One speaker declared that Florence "should rid itself of these Frate and non-Frate parties that are bringing dishonor and harm to public and private alike."[7] But this was just the problem: the differences between the parties—between Savonarolans and anti-Savonarolans, populists and elitists, republicans and Mediceans—were too ideological and too stark to be willed away in the name of an ill-defined unity. In the meantime, one way to express disapproval of the Savonarolan crusade was to flout it. Piagnone Luca Landucci complained that the Signoria and Eight of Security were allowing gambling and every sort of vice, even the reopening of *el Frascato*, "the Bower," a notorious neighborhood of taverns and brothels.[8]

A surer way to get rid of the Frate than by either politics or ridicule was provided by the arch-tiepido himself, Pope Alexander VI. On May 12, the same day Florence adopted its new election law, the pope issued his long-gestating breve of excommunication. His Holiness complained that "a certain friar" Girolamo Savonarola of Ferrara of the Order of Preachers and at present so-called vicar of San Marco of Florence had continued to disseminate "pernicious dogma" to the detriment of the Florentine people. He had rejected the pope's summons to Rome, ignored his ban on preaching, and refused to comply with the order of November 7 creating the Tusco-Roman Congregation. In the future, the breve continued, anyone, man, woman, cleric, or layman who spoke with him, attended his sermons, or had any other contact with him was also threatened with excommunication.[9]

Copies of the breve addressed to the principal churches of Florence along with a letter to the Signoria were entrusted for delivery to a certain Giovanvittorio da Camerino. Two months earlier Giovanvittorio had been imprisoned in Florence for calling Savonarola a heretic and expelled with a warning not to return. Now, worrying that even official status as a papal messenger might not be enough to override the ban, he dithered in Siena for a month before requesting a safe conduct from the Signoria. When this was refused, Rome's search for a substitute to make the delivery led to still more delay.

Savonarola got wind of the papal action, however, and wrote to Alexander VI on May 20 in an effort to forestall implementation of the sentence. It was impossible that he had slandered the pope, he protested; he regarded His Holiness as standing in the place of God on earth. Accusations had been made against him for the past two years, although a thousand auditors in Florence could attest that they were false. His principal antagonist was "that certain illustrious and elevated orator," meaning of course fra Mariano da Genazzano, chief among those "worthy and learned men" who had convinced His Holiness that his teachings were pernicious. He was the real criminal. This man, as many in Florence could attest, had openly raged against the pope from the pulpit, so that Savonarola himself had had to argue against him and condemn his insolence. As for the allegations that he himself was "a disseminator of heresies," his forthcoming book on the triumph of Christ would vindicate his Catholic faith. In the meantime the pope ought not believe "envious and abusive men" whose wickedness, if human assistance failed, he, fra Girolamo, would make known to all the world. He signed himself "the humble little son and servant of Your Blessedness."[10]

Although the breve carrying the sentence of excommunication was no farther away than Siena, official Florence was apparently reluctant to acknowledge it publicly. Plans for the Corpus Christi celebration of May 25 went forward, and though the festivities were to be more modest than usual, the magistrates granted Savonarola's request that fra Domenico's fanciulli be permitted to conduct their ceremonial procession. They were halfway across the Santa Trinità bridge when at the cry, "Here come Savonarola's boys!" they were set upon by a group of hostile youths who tore the crucifix from the hands of one of the marchers and threw it into the Arno. Such, complained Landucci, was the hatred of the Frate, especially among the youth.[11]

In this climate of embattled and anxious loyalties, in which each public event had become an issue between Arrabbiati and Frateschi, everyone watched for signs of strength and weakness. The revival of the annual Saint Barnabas Day horserace on June 11, after a two-year Savonarola-inspired ban, was justified as a diversion for a city wracked with hunger and fever, but it also said something about Savonarola's faltering influence. "Let the people relax a little; are we all to become friars?" someone asked.[12]

On June 18, 1497, the order of excommunication arrived and was read out, with bell, book, and candle, in five Florentine churches.[13] The next day

Savonarola responded with an "Open Letter to All Christians and Beloved of God against the Recently Issued Surreptitious Excommunication."[14] The Florentines need not obey an excommunication order based on false information he reassures them. He demonizes his critics: soon the tribulations will come that "will weed out the bad plants and renew his Church." The wicked men whose role in the world is to persecute the just are in fact confirming the very prophecies they scorn. It is unreasonable to believe that we are obligated to obey our superiors in everything; rather, we ought to be obedient to a superior only insofar as he represents God, but he who commands what is contrary to God does not represent God and is not our superior. So, it is not only just but necessary that he disobey the papal order.

Another letter, in Latin for the more learned (*sapientes*), followed. Marshaling opinions of theologians, jurists, papal decretals, and decisions of church councils, he demonstrates the limits of papal power, "the power of the keys," to impose an unjust sentence. When such a sentence is null, as in the present case, it is his duty to proclaim this publicly, cost what it may. Moreover, while many blind and rash persons maintain that all those coming to our convent or speaking to us are automatically excommunicated, this is very doubtful since the papal brief only warns them that excommunication may follow. He urges his readers not to believe that such an excommunication has any validity either before man or God.[15]

In their Manichean rhetoric, the letters, circulating throughout the city, polarized the Florentines still further. Piagnoni were determined to resist the pope's order, hopeful that whatever punishment he might inflict on them would bring them closer to the ultimate triumph. Arrabbiati branded a confrontation with the pope as fanatical folly and complained that fra Girolamo and his visions were bringing the city to disaster. As the debates in council halls and streets degenerated into recriminations and threats, members of the Ridolfi, Strozzi, and other leading families met and pledged they would maintain their patriotic equilibrium. In case of trouble, they agreed, it was the duty of citizens to rally at the government palace and, if necessary, take up arms in its defense, but getting involved in "the quarrels of others" was unwise, especially when it meant opposing the pope. Some of Francesco Valori's peers, ignoring his recent efforts at compromise, urged him to reconsider his extreme partisanship and pointed out that he was endangering the city as well as his own safety. They also had advice for the Arrabbiati: stay out of the controversy over Savonarola's ministry; it was not for them to decide whether he was supernaturally illuminated or whether his followers were patriotic or merely ambitious for themselves. Their duty was to concentrate on proper government, not via secret conventicles but at the palace, openly and lawfully. Whatever else happened they must avoid a contest with the pope.[16]

The effort to end factionalism by appealing to the civic good attested as much to political realism as to the patriotism of the leading families all too aware that "this business of the Frate" could ruin the city. If the Florentines had ever been able to draw a bright line between religion and politics, they had great trouble doing so now, when so many believed that they were the people of God, destined to riches, glory, and empire. But several of the city's religious houses notified the Signoria that should Savonarola or any San Marco friars be allowed to take part in the solemn procession of June 24, the day of the city's patron saint, John the Baptist, they would refuse to participate for fear of incurring excommunication. Accordingly, the magistrates ruled that the friars of San Marco and San Domenico must stay indoors lest they "create greater scandal."[17] Hand in hand with this went the decree restoring "the ancient customs of racing and palios in the land." This, claimed Parenti, "made everyone happy except [Savonarola's] partisans, who were very sorry that they were powerless to maintain his pronouncements."[18] So much had changed in the month since Parenti had observed that the Piagnoni had lost none of their power.

With the news of the excommunication the anti-Savonarolan chorus swelled to a clamor. Nighttime demonstrators flung insults and threats at the walls of San Marco. Scurrilous verses and obscene cartoons littered the streets.[19] "Heretic" and "schismatic" were two epithets of choice, especially after it was learned that Savonarola had rejected the papal breve. Francesco Altoviti's polemic combined the two: Savonarola's Ark, he wrote, was a schismatic heresy, which aimed to subject the world to new religious laws of poverty and simplicity.[20] Addressing a pratica, Giuliano Gondi complained that the Frate was the founder of a new sect of Fraticelli (an excommunicated group of Franciscans who embraced absolute poverty and held extreme apocalyptic views) and that he aspired to be the Angelic Pope.[21] Other speakers warned that the city would pay dearly for harboring an excommunicate.[22] Savonarola's onetime admirer, the anchorite Angelo Fondi of Vallombrosa, fired off a spate of letters to the Florentine people, the friars of San Marco, and the canons of Santa Maria del Fiore in which he denounced fra Girolamo as a "hypocritical, lying, and false prophet, a rebel, the enemy and most bitter detractor of the clergy, prelates, priesthood, Roman see, and the one, holy, catholic and apostolic Church," and founder of his own heresy of "Girolamites."[23] As usual, Franciscans were in the forefront of the attack, but they were joined by Augustinians, Conventual Dominicans, and others.

Worried about a papal interdict on the city for harboring an excommunicate, on June 5 the magistrates of the Ten pressed their envoys in Rome to assure His Holiness, via their friends at the curia, that padre Girolamo would always be "*obsequentissimo e devotissimo.*" At first they thought they were successful. On June 14 Ambassador Alessandro Bracci informed the Ten that Alexander VI appeared to be pleased with the Frate's letter of justification of May 21 and perhaps was regretting his breve. Cardinal Carafa, although still displeased with the stalemate over the new Congregation and influenced by General Torriani and his virulently anti-Savonarolan lieutenant Francesco Mei, had candidly admitted to Becchi on May 30 that he thought the excommunication had been instigated by fra Mariano da Genazzano and that it was "badly done." But whatever second thoughts the pope may have had were offset by his anger at hearing that Savonarola had made public his letter of May 21 and by pressure from the Frate's enemies in Florence. He allowed the order of excommunication to take its course.[24]

On the morning of June 15, the body of the pope's favorite son, Juan, Duke of Gandia, was recovered from the Tiber. Bruised and weighted with stones, he was clearly the victim of foul play. Alexander VI was laid low by grief. No culprit was ever found, although Juan's brother Cesare, with whom he had dined the previous evening, was a prime suspect. Inevitably, Piagnoni took the murder as divine retribution for the pope's unjust treatment of their leader,[25] but Savonarola himself rose above bitterness and righteous judgment. In a letter of condolence he lays aside the prophet's mantle and becomes once more the physician of souls, urging Alexander to find consolation in faith and to seek glory in tribulations, for "time is short and we transmigrate to eternity." The sympathy seems manifest and the spiritual counsel genuine, although in selecting this passage from Saint Paul he is obviously reminding Alexander of his own travail: "Therefore let Your Blessedness encourage the work of the faith for all men, on account of which I labor unceasingly even to the point of imprisonment [2 Tim. 2.9]."[26]

The grieving pope did direct his thoughts toward spiritual matters, even to Church reform. While he mourned he refused to concern himself with ordinary business, but he referred the question of reform to six cardinals, one of whom was Carafa. Ricciardo Becchi reported that many were hoping the pope's new resolve would produce good results and so fulfill "the prophecy of padre fra Girolamo, that the Church will be reformed by the sword, etc."[27]

A letter from Ambassador Alessandro Bracci soon dashed those hopes. His Holiness had been moved by Savonarola's letters (was there more than one?) Bracci wrote, and had them read aloud in Consistory. He even went so far as to declare that he had acted hastily in the matter of the excommunication. But just when it seemed he might be ready to suspend the order, if not to rescind it entirely, he had new evidence of Savonarola's contumacious behavior. Secret letters with damning information had arrived from Florence, in addition to which he had seen a letter of fra Girolamo himself attacking the papal breve (this must have been the letter of June 19). The pope also heard that the Frate had celebrated Mass in defiance of his excommunication. Alexander now angrily declared that he would "proceed against him [and] against those disobedient and rebellious to Holy Mother Church in every way permitted by the sacred canons." Still, he added, given his great affection for the Florentine people, and having that very morning received a letter from the king of France commending Florence to him, if fra Girolamo appeared before him to purge himself, he would guarantee his personal safety and give him a fair hearing. If he found him innocent, the pope would give him his blessing; if he found otherwise, he would dispense justice with mercy.[28] A month later Ricciardo Becchi reported that matters stood substantially the same: unless Savonarola consented to the new Tusco-Roman Congregation or within two months humbled himself at the foot of the papal throne, there would be no absolution. If the city of Florence wanted the good will of the pope and his cardinals, Becchi added, it would have to "render some honor and satisfaction" to the Holy See.[29] Presumably the city could do this by turning the Frate over to the curia, or by consenting to join the Holy League, or both.

Savonarola's persistence in defying the supreme head of the Church took its strength from his unshakeable conviction that events were following the divine plan. Writing to friends that spring and summer, he treated the excommunication as a necessary—even welcome—stage in the fulfillment of his apocalyptic vision. "Our affairs," he assures Giovanfrancesco Pico della Mirandola, "are moving along in their proper order, not badly, as some say. These are God's matters, not ours, and God's affairs verify themselves in increased tribulation. [These tribulations] are the lighter to us because we have foreseen and announced them for many years." He says much the same in letters to the Ferrarese functionaries, his friend Lodovico Pittorio and Bertrando Costabili: events are moving in the right way. To Duke Ercole d'Este himself he writes, "Our persecutions don't put me off, nor do they sadden my spirit, because I know they are necessary and will lead to a good end."[30] Whether he viewed the ever greater certainty of his own death as part of the divine plan is difficult to say, but he repeatedly asserted that if he must die, it would be as a martyr. He might go to Rome and abandon his apostolate, but surrender to the pope was not likely to save his life, and if it did not, he would lose the martyr's crown, dying as an abjured heretic or schismatic.

The pope's condemnation made it particularly urgent that Savonarola prove that he was a faithful Christian as well as a true prophet. With his suspension from preaching giving him more time to write, he embarked on one of his greatest works. This is his *Triumphus Crucis*, a celebration of the double victory of the cross over sin and death and over rivals of the true faith or, with a touch of the polemical mode he usually avoided in his doctrinal writings, "against the impious garrulousness of the wise of this world."[31] He dedicated a significant part of the treatise to demonstrating the unique truth of Christianity. For this he was heavily dependent upon the scholastic masters. Reason and the evidence of the senses, he writes, confirm the tenets of Christian doctrine, including the fatherhood of God, the redemption by Christ, and the sacramental efficacy of his true Church; but Christ's redemption is unavailable without faith, and true faith is the gift of divine grace.[32]

After affirming the soundness of his Christian belief (surely with a sidelong glance at the pope and others who branded him a heretic) Savonarola considers what it means to be a Christian. The essence of the *Triumphus Crucis* is here, in its exaltation, in the simple language of human emotion, il ben vivere, the joy and triumph of righteous living. True Christians, he argues, manifest their faith in the way they live, and this can be summed up in a single word, *caritas*. In loving their neighbors they return the love they have received from their Creator and Savior. By following his example they honor and love him and demonstrate their sanctification. Here the intellectualism of Saint Thomas gives way to the passionate existentialism of Saint Paul: "He who through faith is righteous shall live [Rom. 1.17]."[33]

So numerous and so wonderful are Christ's works, Savonarola writes, that humans cannot grasp them by the natural light of reason alone; indeed, many of them are invisible to the human eye. To aid understanding he offers his readers an elaborate image. Let them visualize a four-wheeled cart on which Christ, crowned with thorns, his wounds visible, rides in triumph, holding the cross and other instruments of his passion in his left hand, the Old and New Testaments in his right. Over his head shine the three resplendent faces of the Trinity. At his feet, the chalice, host, and other vessels with oil and balsam and the symbols of the other sacraments. Seated on a step below her son is the holy Virgin Mary surrounded by gold and silver vases decorated with precious stones holding the bones and ashes of the dead. Apostles and preachers pull the cart, preceded by patriarchs and prophets and a throng of Old Testament men and women. Around it swirls a vast number of martyrs, Doctors of the Church, and an innumerable multitude of male and female virgins bedecked with lilies. Bringing up the rear is an infinite number of men and women of every condition—Jews, Greeks, Latins, barbarians, rich, poor, learned and unlearned, small, large, old and young—singing the praises of Christ. In turn they are surrounded by an enormous crowd of enemies of Christ and the Church—emperors, kings, princes, potentates, wise men, philosophers, heretics, slaves, freedmen, men, women, people of every tongue and nation. Strewn about them are their shattered idols, burned heretical books, remnants of their refuted sects contrary to Christ, and every religion that has been overturned and condemned.

This motif of the Triumph had a complex pedigree. Adapted by Ovid and other classical love poets from the ancient Roman welcoming ceremony for victorious generals, it had passed into Christian visionary literature. Petrarch had used it in his celebrated poetic series on love, the *Trionfi*. In the fifteenth century, Triumphs had become an important feature of Italian processional life, serving both religious and political purposes.[34] In Carnival four-wheeled carts elaborately decorated with classical, mythical, and erotic figures and accompanied by Canti Carnascialeschi, the most famous composed by Lorenzo de' Medici himself. Each cart carried elaborate figures and symbols dramatizing the pre-Lenten triumph of the world and the flesh. Savonarola had already made pious lauds out of lascivious Carnival songs; now he worked a similar transformation on the Triumph.[35] The obvious next step would have been to incorporate an actual triumphal cart, suitably Christianized, into the Carnival procession of the next year, but by then time was running out.

As Savonarola was completing the *Triumphus Crucis*, the papal breve tested the loyalty of the Florentines to their prophet. In councils and pratiche citizens reckoned the costs of harboring an excommunicate. In Rome friends and enemies of the Frate jostled for leverage at the curia. Hearing that certain wealthy Piagnoni were offering bribes to cardinals to secure a temporary stay of the papal order,[36] Arrabbiati wrote to the pope urging him to expedite the proceedings. Officially the Convent of San Marco was solid for Savonarola, but some of the friars appeared torn between loyalty and fear for their safety, worrying that if they went out to collect alms while the ban was in effect they might be vilified "like Jews."[37]

When Ambassador Bracci suggested that the friars solicit testimonials on Savonarola's behalf to offset the hostile letters arriving in Rome, Silvestro Maruffi and Roberto Ubaldini began collecting signatures from convent visitors and passersby.[38] (The chronicler Giovanni Cambi was approached by "a youth whom I didn't know, dressed in a mantle and a wine-colored hood, [who] came to me and told me to go to San Marco. I went and talked, I think, to fra Silvestro. I was shown the subscription and signed it.")[39] By such means they collected some 360 signatures, mainly from greater gildsmen and civic leaders, and, according to fra Ruberto, would have had even more if the convent had not just then been hit by plague.

In his covering letter Ubaldini claimed San Marco's unanimous support for padre Girolamo and made the familiar arguments: he was maligned by his enemies; he preached and taught the purest Christian doctrine; he had brought peace and Christian righteousness to the city and to the convent, all with the helping hand of God. Most marvelously, he said (for even in the cloister brotherly love does not seem to have extinguished chauvinism) Savonarola had overcome the stigma of his foreign birth: "we are more than 250 friars, the majority natives of this area, . . . does Your Holiness believe that we would support and defend a foreigner if we were not certain of his life and goodness?"[40]

Arrabbiati leaders cried foul: the petition was a scandal, no more nor less than an "open" intelligenza, an attempt to identify like-minded citizens who would illegally vote en bloc. The Signoria took the charge seriously and deliberated, but the Priors could not agree what to do. Even the hint of reprisal, however, caused some signers to withdraw their names and may have been enough to stifle the petition altogether, for there is no record that it was ever sent.[41]

In June people were falling sick and dying from a mysterious fever.[42] A new visitation of the plague later that month killed more people. Those who could do so fled the city. Fearing contagion, the Great Council suspended its meetings and public business slowed. Imports and distribution of food suffered, and prices, already steep, soared. So many people were falling in their tracks from disease and starvation, wrote Landucci, that every hour the streets had to be cleared, while the hospitals overflowed with the sick and dying.

In early July the plague struck San Marco again, carrying away, among others, fra Tommaso Busini, one of Savonarola's most valued colleagues. Pseudo-Burlamacchi tells us that as Savonarola prayed for divine intervention in his cell together with fra Silvestro and fra Domenico, an angel of God encircled them with a rope and a chain of fire, singing Psalm 132/133, *Ecce Quam Bonus*, "Behold, how good and pleasant it is when brothers dwell in unity." This vision, the Piagnone biographer wrote (a quarter century after their deaths) convinced the three friars that they would not die of pestilence but by hanging and burning. Then, in what he described as a new fervent mode of psalm singing and praying, fra Girolamo led all the friars in procession around the cloister and garden carrying white candles and red crosses and singing *Ecce Quam Bonus*.[43]

The first verse of *Ecce Quam Bonus* was an exhortation to brotherly unity. If there was serious disunity among the friars of San Marco, Savonarola did not acknowledge it in any of the numerous letters he wrote during this difficult time. On the contrary, writing to his brother Alberto in mid-August he said, "Our whole company is living the angelic life in great joy."[44] The relentless spread of the contagion must have been demoralizing, however. His letter to the friars of San Domenico in Fiesole urging faith in adversity suggests that the plague was causing strain, and a letter to fra Pietro Paolo del Beccuto sharply criticized him and other brothers at San Domenico of Fiesole for thinking of fleeing to a safe retreat. Even laymen show less fear than some of you, he spluttered.[45] His two letters to his brother Alberto in Ferrara were efforts to reassure his family that he and his brother Maurelio, who had followed him into the Order, were safe. So far there were relatively few deaths in the city from plague, he wrote, although he acknowledged that another fever was killing between fifty and a hundred people every day and getting worse.

But the pestilence grew more severe and it was decided to send the younger friars into the more salubrious air of the countryside. (Contrarily Landucci noted that the plague was taking heads of households and sparing the youth, and he believed this confirmed the Frate's prophecies of the renewal of the Church and the world.)[46] Savonarola's adversaries put it about that this unusual measure of sending clerics out to live among the laity proved that there was disunity in the cloister, noting, with perverse satisfaction, that having terrified the city by threats of plague, the friars were the first to suffer from it.[47] He had sent away more than seventy friars, mainly the younger and thus more important, while he remained behind with the older brothers to minister to the sick and needy. The friars were being housed in country villas at the expense of the owners, and citizens of Florence were providing for the needs of those who remained isolated in San Marco.[48] For himself he had little fear; he and the brothers were reading Hebrew scriptures, especially the prophets. He asked Alberto to send him "six of those little Hebrew bibles like the one you sent before" as soon as possible and to let him know how much he paid.[49]

To the absent friars he sent letters of comfort and spiritual counsel.[50] They must put their fear of sickness and death in the perspective of eternity, he writes. Bodily remedies may help them postpone death but cannot change the fact that they are mortal, whereas the spiritual remedies of prayer, the Sacrament, compassion to others, and almsgiving can help them gain life everlasting. Still, he concedes, prayer may have some practical utility, for it can be an effective remedy against the ills of the body as well as of the spirit. God commonly sends plague to punish us for our sins, to induce us to turn to him in humility and abandon our evil lives. By removing the cause we may also remove the effect. "If you observe our prescription, you may be certain that the pestilence won't hurt you, since it either won't arrive, or if it does come, you will be healed by God, or, if not healed in the body, you will be healed eternally in the happy 'patria.'"[51]

Whether or not there was unity in San Marco, there was little of it among these younger friars. Free of the convent's tight discipline and established routines, they soon began to wrangle over the conduct of their spiritual and ascetic lives. Savonarola's letter is an inspired lecture on monastic piety. Although he would have them set a judicious course between youthful zeal and veteran caution, he is aware that the via media is not always the best route to communion with God. To be sure, younger brothers must defer to those who are "wiser and have more of God's illumination," but when it comes to piety, wisdom is not always the best guide. Better to be crazy than to try to measure everything with the intellect, he says, citing Paul: "If any among you thinks he is wise in this age, let him become a fool that he may become wise [I Cor. 1.18]." Still, they must exercise reasonable restraint. In this terrible time of suffering some friars hope to placate God by extreme acts of piety, whether of fasting, prayer, or other forms of self-discipline—works of supererogation. But this too is a kind of arrogance. As the Psalmist says, a broken and contrite heart is more acceptable to God than sacrifices (Ps. 50/51). What a great misery that men have left the world in order to humble themselves in the love of Christ and have forgotten what they came to do! In courting the esteem of their peers by performing heroic feats of austerity, friars neglect the more modest acts of devotion and piety that make up the regular course of their monastic obligation and lead most certainly to perfection. Penitence should be carried out discreetly and unostentatiously. On the other hand, devotions must not become routine. Better to pray less frequently but more intensely than to pray constantly but superficially.

The rest of this long letter mainly consists of instructions to the young friars for their day-to-day conduct. They must know when to speak (seldom, and only when given permission), and they must keep their speech within the strictest limits of propriety and wholesomeness, which he spells out in detail. He is particularly insistent that the brothers not complain or listen to the complaints of others; grumbling of any sort is strictly forbidden. Finally, they should read his instructions often, commit them to memory, reflect upon them frequently, and observe them assiduously. This very day and on coming feast days they should gather and read his letter aloud. In this way the friars who do not know how to read may hear and be encouraged to observe these precepts, and those who are able to read will be more likely to remember them.[52]

When not ministering to the sick, reassuring the fearful, reading Scripture with his friars, sending letters to his many correspondents, or monitoring the campaign on his behalf in Rome,[53] Savonarola wrote. He revised his devotional tract *Solatium itineris meum* (*My Comfort on the Journey*),[54] readied the *Triumphus Crucis* for the press, and in response to the papal excommunication, composed a major new work, *De veritate prophetica dyalogus* (*Dialogue on Prophetic Truth*).[55] Leaving aside the flamboyant mysticism of *The Compendium of Revelations* and the vivid imagery of the *Triumphus Crucis,* he enlists the authority of Scripture, the Church Fathers, canon law, and Saint Thomas to defend his claim that he had been divinely endowed with the light of prophecy. To add drama to an otherwise dry scholastic exercise he casts it as a debate with seven mysterious pilgrims whom he meets during a solitary meditative walk. These are the Seven Gifts of the Holy Spirit, and they ply him with questions about his prophecies. When at last he convinces them of their legitimacy he underscores his victory by noting that the first initials of their Hebrew-sounding names (Vrias, Eliphaz, Rechma, Iechimham, Thoralmed, Abbacuc, and Saptham) spell VERITAS.

Unfortunately, these devices fail to enliven arguments that were either technical, stale from repetition, or both. And no argument could disguise the inherent problem, namely, that it was impossible for Savonarola to demonstrate objectively that he had been illuminated by God. Whether he argued from historical cause, that the corruption of the times and the need for the renewal of the Church had made his mission necessary, or from moral effect, that his prophetic enlightenment had made him more righteous and enabled him to convert others to righteous living as well, he could not overcome the subjective nature of his demonstration: ipse dixit was not a proof that skeptics, certainly not this cynical pope, were willing to accept. As Pasquale Villari put: it is a hard case for someone to prove by reason that he is above reason.[56] Savonarola's insistence that whoever refused to accept his demonstration was evil was, in a sense, an admission of the argument's failure. It is hardly necessary to say that the *Dialogue on Prophetic Truth* failed to persuade Alexander VI to reverse his decision.

CHAPTER 20

Defiance

During the plague-ridden August of 1497 the discovery of another plot to restore Piero de' Medici added to the sense of a city under siege. As a ready weapon of political warfare the charge of conspiracy had become dulled through overuse, but this case was extraordinary in the prominence of the accused. It began with Lamberto dell' Antella, the petty intriguer already under the ban for his contacts with Medici exiles. When Lamberto was heard to boast that he had valuable information regarding Piero, he was lured back into Florentine territory and immediately arrested. Under torture he claimed to know of a plot to restore Piero and named the ring leaders, all prominent Mediceans.[1]

Mercenary troops were put on alert. A commission of twenty, drawn from opposing factions, was appointed to investigate and ordered the suspects to appear for questioning. Five presented themselves to the Bargello; others took refuge in their country estates or fled abroad. Lucrezia de' Medici, sister of Piero, was detained in the Pazzi's town house and questioned. The five Medicean leaders held by the Bargello were seventy-year-old Bernardo Del Nero, former advisor to the Medici and three times Gonfaloniere of Justice; Niccolò Ridolfi (brother of Giovambattista Ridolfi, one of Savonarola's closest advisors); Lorenzo Tornabuoni, cousin of Piero de' Medici; and two other leading Bigi, Giannozzo Pucci and Giovanni di Bernardo Cambi. After some turns of the rope each of the five acknowledged they had been in contact with the Medici exiles but revealed little more.

That Lorenzo Tornabuoni had tried to persuade Piero de' Medici to solicit League support for an attempt on Florence was an old story, and it was hardly a revelation that leading Bigi families intended to take over influential and lucrative positions in Florence if Piero were restored to power. Likewise, that Piero would try to win over the populace with cheap grain and bread was already a lively topic of conversation in the street. Niccolò Ridolfi admitted to having talked in Rome with Savonarola's archenemy fra Mariano da Genazzano and to have reported this to Bernardo Del Nero, but Bernardo had done nothing with the information. In fact, Bernardo was not one of those Bigi who wanted to bring Piero back. His preference was for a regime headed by Piero's two cousins, Lorenzo and Giovanni di Pierfrancesco de' Medici, who had returned to Florence after Piero's exile. Lucrezia de' Medici admitted to some contacts with the conspirators but steadfastly refused to implicate her husband, Jacopo Salviati. She was released on the intervention of Jacopo's friend Francesco Valori.

These slim findings notwithstanding, the commission delivered an indictment for conspiracy. The Signoria appointed a committee of two hundred elected officials and civic leaders, a "grande pratica," to recommend action.[2] In the tense, highly charged debates that followed, evidence of guilt or innocence proved less important than party loyalties, and moral scruples were less compelling than the desire for vengeance against Medici partisans. Some speakers observed that the degree of involvement of the five suspects varied; others countered that whoever failed to report a conspiracy was as guilty as the conspirators themselves.

According to Guicciardini, some important men were sympathetic to the defendants, but with the exception of his own father, Piero Guicciardini, they remained silent for fear they would be accused of Medici sympathies. Their timidity allowed the more extreme Frateschi, who had the largest bloc of members in this pratica, to dominate the debate. They were led by the violently anti-Medicean Francesco Valori who regarded Bernardo Del Nero as a personal rival and was impatient to be rid of him. Valori did have qualms about executing thirty-year-old, highly popular Lorenzo Tornabuoni, but he knew that if he made an exception he would weaken his case against the others. As Guicciardini put it, "His passion proved so much stronger [than his sympathy] that he resolved to see them all die."[3]

The committee, individually polled, unanimously declared all five guilty and called for them to be beheaded. When the Signoria ordered the Eight to proceed with the execution, the families of the condemned claimed the right of appeal to the Great Council. The pratica was reconvened to consider their request. Lengthy, acrimonious debates followed, while in the Signoria Piero Guicciardini led a minority of Priors in blocking the motion for execution. After hours of stalemate Francesco Valori pounded his desk, leaped to his feet, and roared: either the conspirators died or he would! In the melee that followed Carlo Strozzi seized Piero Guicciardini by his robe and threatened to throw him out of the palace window. Before he could do so calm was restored and the motion for execution again put to the vote. This time it carried, six to three; the appeal to the Great Council was denied. That same night, August 22, the five condemned men were hurried to the place of execution, told to make their confessions, and beheaded.

Savonarola played no direct part in these deliberations, seemingly content to keep his distance. He sent Francesco Valori a message recommending clemency for Lorenzo Tornabuoni, but (as he acknowledged in his *processo*) he worded it "coldly" so that Valori, whose loyalty he was anxious to keep in the interest of party unity, would understand that his intervention was pro forma. He would, he added, have preferred exile rather than execution for Bernardo Del Nero, but on the whole he was satisfied.[4] This was not the first time Savonarola had condoned or demanded a death sentence for enemies of the republic, but those earlier instances had been rhetorical abstractions. The five men who had invoked the right of appeal were not faceless *tiepidi* but prominent citizens, and the charges against them were vague and partisan. His failure to use his influence on behalf of an appeal was not only a serious mistake of judgment, it was a moral lapse. He had spent a good deal of political capital to secure that right of appeal, arguing that there could be no liberation from the past without it, no civic peace, no universal renewal, and the passage of the Law of Appeal on March 19, 1495, had been a signal personal victory. Nothing in the new republic, not even the Great Council, bore so distinctive a Savonarolan stamp. The previous year it had been successfully invoked in the case of the so-called plot involving ex-Gonfaloniere Filippo Corbizzi. Corbizzi and two of the other ringleaders had been sentenced to life imprisonment, but when they demanded the right to appeal to the Council it had readily been granted.

In the fifteen months since the Corbizzi affair the mood of the Florentines had darkened, and they were more vulnerable to their fears: threats of an incursion by the League, apprehensions of a papal interdict, Piero de' Medici's unnerving sallies at the city walls, and rumblings of internal betrayal. Every charge of *intelligenza*, every plot, real or imaginary, reduced the odds that suspects would get fair treatment. Some said that the prophetess Camilla Rucellai had persuaded Savonarola not to support the appeal by invoking one of her visions. More likely he shared the general malaise and believed that this was not the time for clemency. But Savonarola had not merely absorbed the fearful mood of his followers; he had nurtured those fears with his direst apocalyptic pronouncements and warnings of imminent tribulations. All who opposed him, he now regarded as tiepidi, "the worst men in the world," agents of Satan in the ultimate battle of good and evil.[5]

To the extent that the executions discouraged new plots and kept the city on the alert they served a purpose. The stationing of a permanent security guard in the Piazza della Signoria advertised the regime's determination to protect itself. Savonarolan majorities dominated the Great Council, the Signoria, and most of the major elective offices. Hostile voices were silenced. Fra Mariano da Genazzano, who had been implicated in the conspiracy by Lamberto dell' Antella, was declared persona non grata, in case he should think of returning. Two other clerics, an Augustinian of fra Mariano's old Convent of San Gallo and a lay brother of the Carthusian monastery of the Certosa, were expelled.[6]

The families of the five who died charged openly and loudly that their loved ones had been sacrificed to Valori's personal ambition. Within the Frateschi no one dared challenge Francesco Valori's leadership. (Pierfilippo Pandolfini, his main Frateschi rival, was said to be so aghast at the executions of the five citizens, and so frightened of Valori's power, that he sickened and died.)[7] Other Frateschi leaders, appalled by his action, kept their distance, chief among them Giovambattista Ridolfi, whose own brother had been executed as a conspirator.[8] For Savonarola, maintaining party unity became more difficult, many condemning as opportunism and hypocrisy his failure to invoke his own hard-won appeal measure.[9]

The end of summer brought modest relief to bodies and spirits. In August the price of grain had begun to drop, and in September, although some continued to die from fever, the plague was, briefly, in retreat.[10] The young San Marco friars returned from their rural exile, and on Assumption Day, August 15, the convent was reopened to lay visitors. Events abroad were also working in fra Girolamo's favor. With the armistice between Charles VIII of France, Ferdinand of Spain, and the Holy League due to run its course at the end of October, expectations were high that Charles would resume his interrupted Italian adventure, giving the Florentines hope of support for their stalled campaign against rebellious Pisa.[11] This prospect of the return of the French king to finish what he had begun so alarmed the pope and his allies of the League that they tried to cultivate better relations with Florence. From

Rome the envoys sent encouraging reports: recent statements by the pope could be interpreted as favorable to rescinding the order of excommunication and to certain cardinals giving their support, provided the inducements were generous enough. (Cardinal Carafa recovered some of his good will toward the city, perhaps because the Florentine government had helped him, a dedicated benefice hunter, to acquire some properties confiscated from the Tornabuoni.)[12] Ambassador Manfredi wrote to his master, Duke Ercole of Ferrara, that he was hopeful of an accord, and Ambassador Somenzi glumly complained to the Duke of Milan that the Frateschi appeared to have the government entirely in their hands; at least no one dared offer a contrary opinion.[13]

In mid-September a delegation of fanciulli went to the Palazzo della Signoria with a petition asking that Savonarola be allowed to resume preaching and that their banks of seats in the Cathedral be rebuilt.[14] The petition was not granted, but the delegation had made its point: Florentines were impatient to hear their excommunicated prophet.

Savonarola was impatient to be heard. On October 13 he wrote to Alexander VI casting himself as a son sorrowing over his father's displeasure. He begged to be restored to favor, to have the pope's forgiveness and his blessing, and declared that if the journey were not so dangerous he would have already come to throw himself at the pope's feet. As soon as he could find a safe route he would appear before His Holiness to defend himself against the calumnies to which he has been subjected. In the meantime he prayed that the pope not withhold his mercy, and that he be forgiven for any foolishness inadvertently committed. Once His Holiness has acknowledged him as his own he will find him devoted and sincere.[15]

The letter was either naive or disingenuous. So long as he continued to disobey the pope's summons and refused to cooperate with the order establishing the new Congregation, fra Girolamo could scarcely expect this appeal to soften the papal heart, especially as the Florentine envoys continued to report that Alexander was adamant on both points.

Savonarola himself could be severe with disobedient underlings. Writing on October 13 to fra Benedetto Luschino, who had fled the convent after some infraction, he expressed his grief and disapproval over Benedetto's disobedience and laid down the conditions for his readmission.[16] If fra Benedetto finds them "a bit hard," he should know that he, Girolamo, is acting out of love, to prevent him from "setting out on the road to perdition." He cites Paul, "For whoever keeps the law but fails in one point has become guilty of all of it [James 2.10]." The pope might have said the same of him.

At the same time, in his pastoral role he could be more lenient. Writing to Giovanna Carafa Pico, wife of his great friend and biographer, Gianfrancesco Pico, who had sought his advice on some personal crisis, he cautioned, "Let your conscience not be too scrupulous . . . our Lord is liberal and kind and doesn't pay attention to every minute detail. Charity extinguishes all sins; and with [charity] you ought to live happily, walking the middle way, neither letting fear remove every hope nor having so much hope as to banish all fear."[17]

In November the Florentine government ordered a bronze portrait medal honoring Savonarola. It shows the cowled head of the Frate in profile, over it the inscription: "The Very Learned Girolamo Savonarola of the Order of Preachers." The reverse of the medal shows a hand emerging from a cloud holding a dagger over a city generally taken to be Rome. Around the medal are the words that had become famous: "The sword of the Lord over the earth swiftly and soon."[18] (*see Figs. 4a, 4b*) Given the delicacy of Florence's negotiations with Rome and the possibility of an interdict for harboring, much less celebrating, an excommunicate, the medal might seem untimely, if not an act of outright defiance. But with Charles VIII reportedly poised to return to Italy, the Frateschi-dominated Signoria thought this a propitious moment for declaring the city's faith in its prophet and renewing his warning of the coming scourge of the Church. Savonarola himself evidently concurred; the portrait was the work of one of his own San Marco friars, Mattia della Robbia.[19]

Meanwhile Florentine officials were writing to their envoys in Rome, sometimes twice a day. The Ten's letter of November 7 is typical: "Because our desire [for Savonarola's rehabilitation] is greater than you can imagine . . . we wish and entrust you to call on the Supreme Pontiff and the cardinal of Naples and go wherever you think you can find favor and pound and shout and do everything you can; to achieve this result don't stop or leave out anything."[20]

Cautiously at first, Savonarola began to resume his priestly functions. In San Marco he said Mass and preached, limiting his audience to the friars and other clerics. This congregation was to hear, in a "little sermon" on December 3, an ill-conceived and ultimately fateful proposal. People refused to accept rational arguments for the truth of his preaching, he complained. They wanted miracles; well, perhaps this was the time. If his listeners prayed for a miracle, God would surely grant their request. He cautioned secrecy, although he surely knew that no word he preached would be secret for long. Soon he was reported to be promising that "the lady was already pregnant and the time was approaching for her to give birth." Piagnone Andrea Cambini thought these "very stupendous things" were being talked about all over the territory and renewed both the Frate's personal reputation and that of his party.[21]

On Christmas Day, with about three hundred worshipers present in San Marco Church, Savonarola officiated at three sung masses and offered communion. The congregation then processed into the square led by two friars dressed as angels carrying lighted candles and holding an image of the newborn babe. Two hundred fanciulli followed, then the whole company of friars, dressed in white and carrying lighted candles. Behind them walked lay devotees also carrying lighted candles and an image of the Nativity. After making a circuit of the piazza they reentered the church. Parenti thought many Florentines were shocked by the open defiance of the excommunication. He also noted that Francesco Valori and the other Frateschi heads were prudently absent, preferring to be represented by the "tail," that is, the rank and file.[22]

The Feast of Epiphany, January 6, offered another spectacular occasion for flouting Rome. Reenacting the visit of the Three Kings to the newborn Christ Child had been a specialty of the Company of the Magi, a confraternity based in San Marco and ostentatiously patronized by the Medici who had made the Magi ceremony a regular feature of the family's devotions. Both the confraternity and the ceremony had been suppressed after Piero's expulsion, but now, with the cooperation of San Marco's allies in the government, it was revived.[23] On a day so cold the Arno froze over, the members of the Signoria came to the high altar of the Church with their traditional offering of candles to kiss Savonarola's hand.[24] Seventeen-year-old Jacopo Gucci, the convent's youngest acolyte, dressed as an angel and carrying a pole topped by a shining star, led the procession followed by the entire company of friars in ascending order of seniority: acolytes, subdeacons, deacons, then priests, the liturgical vestments of their rank resplendent in gold and silk. Behind them walked fra Domenico da Pescia, prior of San Domenico of Fiesole, fra Francesco Salviati who had succeeded fra Girolamo as prior of San Marco, and Savonarola himself. Costumed as the Magi in silk chasubles decorated with gold and jewels, the three friars intoned, "Where is he who has been born king of the Jews? For we have seen his star in the East," and the company responded, "In Bethlehem of Judea, as the prophet has written." The kings then searched for the newborn Jesus throughout the convent, performed three stations of the cross, and arranged themselves along the walls of the lower church. After singing matins some young friars dressed as angels took the Baby Jesus from his crib and set him on a portable altar in the middle of the lower church, singing, "Here is the Master you sought and the angel of the testament you wanted." Marveling, the other friars replied, "My God, my God, is it you?"

The Magi presented the Holy Infant to be adored by the friars ranged along the walls of the lower and upper church. First they held forth the babe's feet to be kissed while singing, "My beloved is fair and ruddy, chosen from thousands,"[25] next the hands, while singing, "My beloved is like a bunch of myrrh as he lies between my breasts."[26] The third king then brought the babe to be kissed on the mouth by the friars in the choir, singing, "He kisses me with the kiss of his mouth."[27] After this the whole company went to the refectory to dine and hear a sermon preached by one of the friars.

"Paradise was in those convents [San Domenico of Fiesole and San Domenico of Prato also staged ceremonies]," rhapsodized Pseudo-Burlamacchi, who as a young friar may have been one of the celebrants. "The Holy Spirit descended to the earth and everyone burned with love, so that they were able to say, 'Blessed are the people who know jubilation' [Ps. 88/89.15]."

Ostensibly this was a private ceremony, designed to enhance the solidarity and fervor of the friars and their government friends, although a few citizens managed to watch the pageant through the cracks in the church doors.[28] But it was neither secret nor free from controversy. Arrabbiati were outraged, the more judicious of the Piagnoni astonished.[29] What dismayed friends and foes alike was not so much the ceremony's flouting of the papal ban as the Signoria's official sanction of it. Worthier people did not regard this as a good thing, huffed Parenti; it not only endangered the souls of the celebrants but gave civic sanction to disobeying the pope's commands.[30]

Misgivings of worthier people notwithstanding, the government's endorsement of the Epiphany ceremonies left only one question concerning Savonarola's return to a public pulpit: when would the magistrates sanction it?[31] Opinion favored the Feast of Candlemas, February 2. The fanciulli benches in the Cathedral were hastily rebuilt. On February 1 Savonarola told Ambassador Manfredi he was ready to preach in Lent if not sooner; he was only waiting for a sign from those in command. Did the friar, Manfredi asked, mean the command of the Signoria or of the pope? Neither one nor the other came the answer. The authority he respected was above that of the pope who persisted in his evil life and refused to lift the excommunication. Nor was he waiting for any other creature.[32]

In truth, despite this arch and defiant reply, through January and early

February of 1498 Savonarola continued to hope that Alexander VI would be won over.[33] At last, however, it was clear to him that this was not to be. Domenico Bonsi's letters of February 8 and 12 from Rome reported that the pope had told him there would be no absolution unless "the matter of Pisa" were settled to His Holiness's satisfaction, meaning that Florence had to abandon its alliance with Charles VIII and join the League to keep him out of Italy.[34] This was a price neither fra Girolamo nor the city was willing to pay: not Savonarola, for whom the French king was the New Cyrus, the Second Charlemagne, God's agent of scourge and renewal; not those Florentines who believed in him, nor those who knew how crucial to their economic and strategic interests were good relations with France. And so, no longer able to withhold the use of his most effective asset, his preaching, without which, he was aware, his work was "going to ruin"; pressed by followers complaining that they were "dying of hunger" for their spiritual food; and supported by a friendly Signoria, which ignored warnings of possible disorder and squelched the objections of the episcopal vicar and Cathedral canons,[35] on the morning of February 11, Septuagesima Sunday, Savonarola returned. From San Marco he and his friars walked in stately procession but without his usual armed escort, through streets bordered by the devout, the curious, and the hostile, to the Cathedral. Entering, he made his way along the enormous nave, less crowded than in former times, and mounted to the pulpit. When the congregation had finished singing the *Te Deum Laudamus* he recited the Third Psalm, "O Lord, why are my foes so many?" then took up his text.

CHAPTER 21

Exodus

He expounded Exodus, the story of the liberation of the Israelites from bondage in Egypt. Just as they had escaped Pharaoh's tribulations and persecutions, so, he promised, would the Florentines, the latter-day people of God, be delivered from their enemies. They too would cross the Red Sea unharmed and Pharaoh would be unable to harm them.[1] He was Moses, not only their prophet and lawgiver, but their champion and protector as well. Pharaoh had ordered him to be silent, but to lead his people out of bondage he must preach. His Holiness, he declared, must have been misinformed, for he must know that the excommunication went against truth and charity, that this was a holy mission inspired by God. So he preached, formally acknowledging the pope's authority, denying that it applied to him.

In effect he was preaching to the choir, or what remained of it. The devotees who had braved the threat of excommunication to hear him had not come to hear tedious arguments about the merits of his case but to be comforted in their tribulations and reassured of the ultimate vindication of their common cause. The more fearful and the disaffected stayed away. Some had been disillusioned by unfulfilled prophecies and broken promises, some laid low by hunger and fever, others shocked by the execution of the five conspirators or alienated in the fight over election reform. And Savonarola too was changed. He tired more quickly, interrupting himself to rest more often. He was out of practice, he said; his energy would return. In those moments when he was vindicating his mission or attacking his enemies—that is, when he was defending himself—he seemed the fiery preacher of old, but after a week Landucci observed that still fewer people were going to hear him. ("Although I still believed in him, it seemed a mistake to me," worried Landucci; "I never wanted to take the risk of going to hear him because he had been excommunicated.")[2] Landucci also reported that the young notary ser Lorenzo Violi was assiduously recording the Frate's every word and gesture.[3] Quickly printed and widely distributed, the Exodus sermons were plain evidence of the Frate's defiance of papal authority.

In Rome, Pharaoh, into whose ear was whispered Savonarola's every word and probably many he never uttered, seethed. "Go ahead, let frate Girolamo preach; I never would have believed you would treat me so!" With this petulant outburst the pope waived off the attempts of Ambassadors Bonsi and Bracci to mollify him. The envoys were at a loss what to do, Bonsi reported in his dispatches to the Ten. Papal indignation was not Bonsi's only worry. In the dark of night a band of armed men had scaled his garden wall, opened the gate, and climbed onto the terrace which gave access to his rooms. The commotion woke the household and the intruders fled, leaving behind a man who had hurt his leg in falling from the wall. Bonsi turned this "bold, cunning fellow" over to the police, noting that he wore the device of the Petrucci, Sienese supporters of the Medici. Complaining of the incursion to cardinals and city governors, he gave notice that he would question the man further.[4]

The envoys heard another tirade three days later. No Turk, no infidel, Alexander railed, would tolerate such disobedience. He even had to suffer mockery in sonnets "from there," he complained, and he had them read aloud to the assembled company. He had delayed imposing an interdict on Florence because Lent was approaching, but unless there was a speedy resolution he threatened to proceed. The envoys must immediately dispatch a courier to let their masters know how he felt. Bonsi complied, noting in his message to the Ten that the pope was inflamed by the anti-Florentine insinuations of the Venetian ambassador, and he warned that an interdict was in the offing.

The pope himself intervened. In a breve to the Signoria he demanded that they either send this son of iniquity to Rome forthwith or isolate him from the civic body as a putrid member, keeping him under guard until he could be properly dealt with as a suspected heretic. He sent a second breve to the Florentine Cathedral chapter ordering the canons to deny the use of their pulpit to the excommunicated friar.[5] The Signoria, headed by the Piagnone Gonfaloniere of Justice Giuliano Salviati, refused to intervene.

On Sunday, February 25, 1498, the air thick with epistolary missiles, Savonarola announced that there would be a procession on Carnival Day (*Martedì Grasso,* or Shrove Tuesday), which would be "a great war on the devil," when every fleshly pleasure of Satan would be driven out, replaced by God's spiritual pleasures. On that day too, he promised, they would discover whether his mission was true or false.

> I'll hold the Sacrament in my hand and everyone will pray hard, so that if this is [invented] by me and I am being deceptive, Christ will bring a fire down from heaven over me and draw me into Hell, but if it is from God he will speed up [the fulfillment]. . . . Have all the monasteries pray for it, and tell the tiepidi also to come on that morning and to pray that . . . if I deceive you, a fire will come to consume me. Write to everyone, dispatch couriers to Rome and everywhere, and let prayers be said that day so that if this cause is not from God, evil will come to me, as I've said, but if it's from God, pray that the Lord will quickly show this to be all his work. . . . Believe, I'm not crazy; I know what I'm doing; I wouldn't make myself a target like this if I didn't know that I have God with me. . . . We'll be here, as I've said, with Sacrament in hand. Tell one of these tiepidi to do the same with the Sacrament in hand in presence of the people and have everyone pray that if this cause is not false, God will kill him in the sight of everyone.[6]

On Shrove Tuesday Savonarola sang Mass in the Cathedral and gave Communion, "to about four hundred women and as many citizens," Parenti reported. At the entrance of the church he displayed the Sacrament to the great crowd gathered outside, while his friars sang hymns, including "Bring forth your power, O Lord, and come [Ps. 79.3]." Then, without another word, he went back inside the church.

> A very large number of people had gathered there in the piazza in front of the church, many of whom had come believing that frate Girolamo would perform a miracle but they saw nothing. Left standing there, they began to speak badly of him. He, nonetheless, followed his schedule, and after dining, with many fanciulli assembled behind each quarter's insignia, he had them go in procession through the whole area with garlands on their caps and sprigs of olive in their hands. Behind them followed a good many citizens, his partisans, and a great many women. When the procession was blocked at the Santa Trinità bridge, the usual setting for rock fights, Doctor Luca Corsini was not embarrassed to shed his mantle and fight back against those hindering the procession, saying "he would give his life for the faith." This was seen as very great foolishness, neither necessary nor appropriate.[7]

God not having sent a fire to consume him, Savonarola could have taken this as a sign of approval, as some of his followers thought it was. Fra Benedetto Luschino likened it to Elijah's vindication of his prophetic mission against the priests of Baal (3 Kings 18).[8] Anti-Savonarolans drew the opposite and equally tendentious conclusion. Many criticized Savonarola for not having produced a miracle, commented Parenti. Landucci conveyed the ambiguity of the episode: "A great crowd of people was there thinking they were going to see signs. The tepid laughed and made fun and said, 'He's excommunicated and he gives communion to others.' I thought it was a mistake, even though I continued to believe in him."[9] Savonarola himself made no effort to exploit the incident when he returned to the pulpit, continuing with the events he had scheduled.

Among these events was a bonfire of vanities. Carpenters had built a wooden structure, which Pseudo-Burlamacchi thought even bigger than the one consumed by the flames the previous year. Seated at the top, "on an ancient serpent," was Lucifer, arrayed with symbols of the seven deadly sins. The tower was heaped with the familiar vanities: nude figures and pictures, heretical books, copies of Pulci's *Il Morgante,* looking glasses, and "many immodest and valuable things estimated at many florins." To prevent enemies of the Frate from trying to forestall the proceedings by attacking the structure, or thieves making off with its valuable inventory, the Bargello stationed a night guard in the piazza.

After the procession, twelve boys in white carrying crosses made their way to the Piazza della Signoria despite harassment from the Compagnacci. There they lighted this second and final Savonarolan bonfire of vanities.[10] Returning to the Piazza San Marco, the boys formed a circle around a crucifix with the figure of the Triumphant Savior and four tabernacles, one for each civic quarter.

> Around [the tabernacles] they did three dances, first, all the friars, with great fervor, in this way: removing their cloaks they came out of the convent, every novice paired with one of the fanciulli dressed like an angel, and they did the first round dance [*ballo tondo*]; then each young friar chose a young layman and sang and danced a second round dance; next each of the older priests, abandoning all restraint [*ogni sapientia humana*], with olive garlands on their heads, chose an older citizen and danced the third dance around the first two circles of dancers, so that the first circle was in the middle, the second around the first, and then the third. Everyone, exulted and jubilant, sang lauds to the figure on the cross. In that devout fervor they continued for as long as there was light, then departed.[11]

And what did fra Girolamo think of his San Marco novices and aged friars cavorting with laymen in the streets? The historian Jacopo Nardi, himself a former Savonarolan fanciullo, tells us that the dance was the one remnant of the old Carnival paganism allowed by the Frate and that "friars and citizens often enlivened Carnival by dancing round dances, leaping, and in an excess of sacrilegious devotion, crying out enthusiastically that it was a happy and holy thing to go crazy for Christ."[12] Savonarola often described himself as crazy for Christ, but he was content to watch the dancing from a hiding place, rapt and approving.[13]

After the rapture of Carnival, the prudence of Lent, but mixed with defiance. Comparing his burden of excommunication to the burden of oppression laid on the Children of Israel by Pharaoh, and insisting that he had offended only the Egyptians who hated seeing the Children of Israel increase and multiply every day, Savonarola suddenly announced on March 1 that he would leave the pulpit of the Cathedral. Henceforth he would preach only in San Marco, and only to men, because this is what the times required. The next day in San Marco he explained that like the good shepherd he was ready to die to defend his flock, as he had shown on Ascension Day when despite many threats he had dared to preach. But he had to know when to give way to wrath, as the Savior had done before the Scribes and Pharisees. Prudence taught him that the honor of God, the salvation of souls, the common good all required that he depart from the Cathedral and for the time being preach in this place, leaving the wicked to vent their wrath. From Rome were letters calling him "son of perdition," but it was not he who kept catamites or concubines; he preached faith in Christ and exalted the Church; those writers of letters ruined it. He left the Cathedral, then, "to avoid scandal."[14] Still, if the Florentines were too kind and respectful to reply to them, "Let me answer; I'll sing into their ears a song they'll understand." The time is approaching to open the little chest; when we insert the key a stink, a foulness, will come out of the city of Rome that will spread through Christendom and everyone will smell it. "I will prove what I say both with natural reason and supernatural signs. Don't be afraid of anything. . . . And if you want to drive us away, let me tell you that this tongue will never stop talking as long as my heads sits on my shoulders."[15]

Neither did the hand stop writing. Despite fatigue, pain, the distractions of convent business, politics, and excommunication, Savonarola worked at his desk as assiduously as ever, perhaps sensing that his time was running out.

Even as he prepared his Exodus sermons he polished his long-deferred *Treatise against Astrology,* completed the dialogue *On Prophetic Truth,* and composed his *Treatise on the Government of the City of Florence.*[16] This last, he explained, was at the request of the Signoria although it had long been in his mind, for it was the final part of the agenda he had set himself at the outset of his preaching career. The agenda had four parts: to demonstrate the truth of the Faith, show that the simplicity of the Christian life is the highest wisdom, announce future events (some of which had already happened, some, he insisted, soon to take place), and support this new government of the city. Having already written about the first three, he would now do the same for the fourth, showing all the world that the harmony of natural reason and Church doctrine is sound knowledge (*scientia*).

The theoretical underpinnings of the treatise on government he had already laid down in *De politia,* the school text he wrote fifteen years earlier. Aristotle is represented: government is the natural and necessary solution to the human need for political association and falls into three types, monarchy, aristocracy, and polity (rule of the many), as well as the anti-types: despotism, oligarchy, and democracy or mob rule. Saint Thomas is represented, modifying Aristotelian naturalism by redefining the purpose of government as the cultivation of the moral virtues and the search for eternal blessedness. But here too are Leonardo Bruni and other humanist rhetoricians who celebrated the Florentine genius for liberty and extolled their republican government. Theoretically monarchy is best, since it is most like God's governance of the world and has the greatest ability to promote unity, but too often single rulers promote their private interests and neglect the common good, thus becoming tyrants. Besides, government of a single ruler is especially poisonous for a naturally fractious people. Such people, prone to dissension and regicide, cause infinite trouble to their communities. For them aristocracy may be best. Still, there are other people who can tolerate only a government of the many. This is true of Italians, who, as Saint Thomas observed, have unusual spirit and intelligence and frequently have had trouble living under a single ruler.

It is even truer of the Florentines, a people whose subtle intelligence and bold spirit make it difficult for them to accept any form of rule but a government of the many. Indeed, over the years they have become so devoted to *governo civile* that even tyrants have had to be very astute to maintain their power over them. Although Florentines are merchants, normally peaceful, when they undertake some great enterprise, whether it be civil war or war against a foreign prince or tyrant, they are bold and terrible. Such a government, in which the people express their will through the Great Council, has been sent to them by God. This is more than the truism that every good government comes from God: the government of the Great Council has been given to the Florentines by special providence. Only a blind or stupid person can deny that in the past three years God's hand has saved the city from serious crises and protected it against dangers. Now it is up to the people to make it perfect by protecting their children, particularly vulnerable to corruption because of their imagination and intelligence, and rearing them to righteous living; by enhancing the people's sense of dignity providing them access to civic offices and honors; and by promoting Christian living. Thus will the Florentine people prosper and earn celestial bliss.

> First, they will free themselves of servitude to the tyrant . . . and live in true liberty, which is more precious than gold and silver, and they will be secure in their city, attending to the management of their homes, to honest gain and to their farms in joy and peace of mind. And when God increases their property and their honors they will have no fear that these will be taken from them. They will be able to go to their country home, or wherever they wish, without asking the tyrant for permission, and marry their daughters and sons as they please, and have weddings, be happy and have whatever companions they please, and occupy themselves in virtue or the study of the sciences or the arts as they please and do other such things in a kind of earthly felicity.
>
> This will be followed by a spiritual felicity, because everyone will be able to take up good Christian living without impediment from anyone. Nor will any [magistrate] be constrained by threats so as not to do justice because everyone will be free, nor forced by poverty to make bad deals because with a good government the city will abound in riches, there will be work for everyone, the poor will earn and be able to nourish their sons and daughters in piety because good laws on the honor of women and boys will be made, and this will especially increase divine worship. God, seeing their good intentions, will send them good pastors . . . thus, in a short time the city will attain to such religiousness that it will be like a terrestrial paradise, living in joy and song and psalms, and the boys and girls will be like angels and be nourished on Christian and civil life together. And in time there will be created in this city a government more celestial than earthly, and such will be the happiness of the good that there will be a kind of spiritual felicity in this world.

This vision of a Florentine republic abounding in earthly and spiritual felicities soars beyond Aristotle, Saint Thomas, or Leonardo Bruni. Its inspiration comes from the prophets and the Book of Revelation. And yet it is a very Florentine, a very bourgeois, vision: homes and property will be secure, businesses and farms will prosper, the honor of maidens and boys protected, and marriages will be safe from interfering rulers. Its antithesis is also Florentine: his picture of the tyrant who bans public meetings, imposes punishing taxes, distracts the populace with spectacles and feasts, makes a false show of piety, and sexually abuses highborn wives and daughters (and sons) is a caricature of Medici despotism. But Savonarola has a larger purpose here than merely attacking the Medici. In spelling out the ways in which tyrants subvert the Christian life of a community and, conversely, arguing that good Christians prevent tyrants from coming to power, the *Trattato* is Savonarola's political testament, adding a religious dimension to the discussion of liberty and tyranny that political theorists, jurists, and humanists had been conducting for over two centuries.[17]

By removing himself from the Cathedral to San Marco, Savonarola may have hoped to mollify the pope without surrendering his pulpit. The move was briefly effective. Many who had been afraid to attend his sermons in Santa Maria del Fiore felt safer at San Marco, as if papal fury would not pursue them into Savonarola's "own house," as one observer put it. The observer was Niccolò Machiavelli. Son of an indifferently successful lawyer from a respectable landed family and a student of classical literature and Roman history, at twenty-nine Machiavelli had not yet embarked on his diplomatic career, although he was interested in politics and politicians. Though he was as unmoved by exhortations to penitence as by apocalyptic visions, he was fascinated by the Savonarolan drama and followed it closely, attending the Frate's Lenten sermons despite the pope's disapproval.[18] To his friend Ricciardo Becchi in Rome he wrote an accurate if corrosive account.

He invited all his followers to take communion in San Marco on the day of Carnival. He said he would pray to God to give a very clear sign if the things he had predicted did not come from Him. Some say he did this to unify his party and strengthen it so it could defend him, because he was afraid that the new Signoria that had been elected but not yet announced would be opposed to him. After the new Signoria was announced on Monday [February 26] . . . he figured it to be more than two-thirds hostile to him. Afraid that the [new government] would immediately make him obey the pope's breve summoning him [to Rome] under penalty of an interdict, he decided, either on his own or on the advice of friends, to give up preaching in Santa Reparata and go to San Marco.

Once our friar found himself in his own house you would marvel more than a little if you heard how boldly he began and goes on with his sermons. Feeling himself very unsafe and believing the new Signoria to be bent on doing him harm and figuring that many citizens would be ruined along with him, he began saying terrifying things—very believable to anyone who didn't examine them carefully. . . .

Still expounding Exodus and arriving at the part that tells how Moses killed an Egyptian, he said the Egyptian stood for wicked people and Moses for the preacher who killed them and exposed their vices, and he said: "O Egyptian, I am going to give you a thrust of the knife!" and then he began leafing through the books of you priests[19] and making such a hash of you as was not fit for dogs to eat, adding—and this is obviously what he was getting at—that he wanted to give the Egyptian another wound, a big one, and said that God had told him that there was someone in Florence who wanted to make himself tyrant and was holding meetings and working to bring it about. And he said that trying to drive out the Frate, excommunicate the Frate, persecute the Frate only meant trying to create a tyranny. . . . He said so much that afterwards people openly conjectured about a certain person who is as near to being a tyrant as you are to heaven.[20] But after the Signoria wrote to the pope on his behalf he saw that he no longer had to fear his enemies in Florence. Whereas previously he had sought only to unify his party by bad-mouthing his opponents and to frighten them by using the word tyrant, now that he sees he no longer has to do that he has changed his tune. Exhorting them to unity which is already under way, making no mention of tyranny or of their wickedness, he tries to set all of them against the Supreme Pontiff. . . saying things that you might say of the wickedest man there is. And so he goes, in my judgment, adjusting to the times and coloring his lies.[21]

After a series of Frateschi governments, the Signoria elected for March and April was, as Machiavelli noted, dominated by Arrabbiati. The Priors elected the anti-Savonarolan Piero Popoleschi as Gonfaloniere of Justice.[22] Still, as its instructions to its envoys in Rome show, not even an Arrabbiati government was disposed to accede to the pope's demands. Florentines were jealous of their independence and proud of their long tradition of resisting papal interference. Besides, the new magistrates understood the danger of suddenly depriving the people of their champion and spiritual leader. (The pope himself recognized that by seizing the Frate and hustling him off to Rome they might create a public scandal.) Then there was the problem of Pisa: in the political chess game being played with Alexander and his allies, Pisa was queen. Cardinal Ascanio Sforza, brother of Duke Lodovico of

Milan, and the pope himself were hinting that if the Florentines complied in the matter of the Frate, the Church, Milan, and perhaps other members of the League would help them regain the port city and other lost territories. But the Florentines wanted something more than promises. On the orders of the Signoria and the Ten, Bonsi and the other envoys drew the negotiations out, continuing to extol Savonarola's many virtues, declaring that he had transformed Florence into a truly Christian city, and protesting that contrary to reports from troublemakers he had not attacked His Holiness personally.[23]

Those arguments had worn as thin as Alexander's patience. Waving off the claim that his information had been distorted by ill-wishers, the pope replied that he was perfectly well-informed about Savonarola's slanders and horrified at the aspersions on his personal honor. Among many outrages Savonarola had called him "Pharaoh" and "a broken tool" and made an impertinent reference to his recently dead son. He was not mollified by the Frate's retreat to his convent; that was merely "throwing dust in his eyes." Preaching in San Marco was no less a violation of the ban than preaching in the cathedral. Nor, he complained, did he receive any respect from the Florentine government; the official letters from the city read as though they had been dictated by the Frate himself! Finally, by interfering with the cathedral canons in the discharge of their duty, the Signoria had flagrantly violated clerical privilege. All this left him no choice but to proceed with the interdict.[24]

After further uncomfortable audiences and hearing the latest missive from the Signoria dismissed as "a wretched letter," Bonsi reported that it was no longer a question of whether the pope would impose an interdict on the city but when; the government must act quickly. To his friend, the Piagnone Domenico Mazzinghi, Bonsi wrote from Rome that he was anxious to return home. He no longer believed he could achieve anything useful and therefore could not continue to justify the expense. Besides, one heard only derision and threats, both public and private, and lived in fear of violence from desperate Pisans, Sienese, and other "rebels."[25] Florentine merchants in Rome also wanted protection: they were being harassed and their goods threatened with confiscation. On March 9, a papal breve drew the noose still tighter. Under pain of interdict "or worse," His Holiness demanded that the Signoria shut the obnoxious friar in his monastery and forbid him to preach or speak to anyone until he had been properly absolved. Moreover, absolution was only to be had in Rome. Savonarola must "come to his senses and come here." In Rome he would be benevolently received and, if properly penitent, he would be restored to the Church and to his pulpit to continue preaching the word of God.[26]

The Florentines considered their options. On March 14, another large

pratica brought all important officials together with a hundred leading citizens, twenty-five from each quarter of the city, grouped on benches by
profession and rank. After a reading of Bonsi's letter and the papal breve the
members of each bench chose their speakers. In the hours of impassioned and
heated debate that followed, Florence, to borrow a telling phrase, encountered its own soul.[27]

It was a soul divided. Even colleagues on the same benches could not
agree what should be done. Some insisted they should cleave to the prophet
who had led them out of tyranny and restored them to Christian rectitude—
so holy a man, said treasury official Lorenzo Lenzi, that they should wash out
their mouths before talking of him. Others conceded the Frate's virtues but
argued that they should not meddle in matters of faith and clerical discipline;
these were affairs of the Church and the Holy Father. Speaking for his
Piagnoni colleagues of the Ten of War, Paolantonio Soderini, Savonarola's
collaborator in the founding of the new republic, remained loyal and defiant:
once and for all they should inform the pope that Florence would never join
the League and would protect the honor of God and its own interests.

As for the interdict, let it come! Florence had resisted other interdicts and
would resist this one. Messer Enea della Stufa assured worried merchants
that from interdicts they had nothing to fear. Giuliano Gondi sniffed that
Messer Enea would talk differently if he had anything to lose: as for himself,
an interdict would jeopardize all his wines and goods in Italy and abroad,
leaving him without the means to fulfill his obligations. Starker, even more
cynical realism came from the Arrabbiati lawyer Guidantonio Vespucci (who
the previous May had defended the five condemned conspirators). Of course,
it would be too bad to lose the friar's spiritual consolations for Lent, Vespucci
conceded with patent irony, but all things considered, it would be better to
obey the pope. The Florentines wanted a new decima, they wanted Pisa, they
wanted the absolution of fra Girolamo—all things for which they needed the
pope, but unless His Holiness received satisfaction they would get none of
them. And an interdict would ruin their commerce. Those who say we have
to protect God's honor are not thinking clearly: "we Italians are what we are."
Besides, he added, almost as an afterthought, everyone knew that the pope
had his power from God; whether the Frate had been sent by God was not at
all clear. Unable to arrive at a consensus the pratica disbanded.

Although he had read the alarming dispatches, fra Girolamo stubbornly
preached on. "'Oh, are you speaking ill of the pope?'—Not I!—They who
used to say bad things about the Roman court now are saying that it ought to

be obeyed in everything—'Oh, if he commands you to commit fornication would you obey?'—'Sure I would,' says that one.—'Oh, frate, he is God on earth and the vicar of Christ.'—True, but God and Christ command that one love his brother and act righteously. Maybe you believe that the pope isn't a man? . . . Don't repeat that the head has to be obeyed in everything—only in what is good."[28]

If some thought this imaginary dialogue sallied perilously close to the high wall of papal dignity, it would soon be known that it was a barrier Savonarola had already breached. On March 3 he had written to the pope no longer as the humble, deferential son of the Holy Father, but as his open accuser and prosecutor. Although His Holiness knew "the whole truth of my preaching," he charged, he had withdrawn the assistance he owed to God's cause and allied himself with the friar's detractors. He had failed in his duty and demeaned his office by "giving authority and power to wolves." But the reckoning was already prepared: divine and natural signs would show Alexander and other enemies of God's work the truths which he had been preaching and for which he had been made to suffer. He himself, he declared, looked forward with the greatest desire to death for the sake of Christ. The pope too should be thinking of his salvation.[29]

Refusing to plead for absolution, for which the price would have been the abandonment of his reforming mission, he asserted that Alexander had misused that authority and violated his office by issuing the decree of excommunication. His next move crystallized within days, although it had been forming in his mind for about three months.[30] More than once he had spoken of a "little key" which, when the time was ripe and God willing, he would use to unlock secrets that would stun the world.[31] Fra Domenico da Pescia later told his interrogators that the little key was fra Girolamo's "revelation" that Alexander VI was neither legitimate pope nor a Christian.[32] This was hardly the stuff of mystery; rumors that Rodrigo Borgia was an unbeliever and allegations that he had Moorish, or alternatively, crypto-Jewish roots were common following his election to the papacy in 1492.[33]

Savonarola had not been adverse to using these rumors, but now he had a more important aim than passing on gossip. Working with his secretary, fra Niccolò Serratico, he drafted letters to the Holy Roman Emperor, the king of France, and Ferdinand and Isabella of Spain and planned two more, to the kings of England and Hungary.[34] He charged that the election of Alexander VI had been brought about by simony and that his private life was scandalous. Worse, he was a false pope and a false Christian, indeed, an atheist. And the

Church, suffused with the stink of simony and the selling of benefices, had been corrupted from top to bottom. For the past eight years (that is, even before Alexander's election) he, fra Girolamo, had been preaching that the Church would be scourged and cleansed of its abomination, restored to its former purity, after which, guided by this shining example, the infidel would convert to Christianity. Now God had ordered him to reveal to their Majesties that the time had come: they must convene a council of Christendom that would save the endangered bark of Peter and begin the work of reform. To that assembly, he promised, he would offer proofs of his prophecies, which God himself would verify with miracles.[35]

Calling for a renewal of the Church in head and members was daring; calling upon the Holy Roman Emperor and their Christian Majesties to seize the initiative from an atheistical pope and convene a general council for reform of the Church was a move "to shock the world." At the Council of Basel fifty years earlier, the century-long debate between conciliarists and papalists over Church sovereignty had ended with a victory for papal supremacy. In 1460 Pope Pius II had anathematized anyone other than a pope who presumed to call for a general council. The idea that reform was best achieved via a council had survived papal condemnation, although few were bold enough to assert openly that councils had primacy over popes.[36] Even without that claim, talk of calling a council made popes uneasy, for they recognized that in the hands of political and ecclesiastical enemies Conciliarism could be a dangerous weapon.[37] Alexander VI was aware that he was vulnerable: early in his pontificate proposals for a council were put forward in Italy and abroad, nowhere more seriously than at the court of Ferdinand and Isabella.[38]

Savonarola would have heard this talk of a council from diplomats and foreign visitors as well as from Florentine businessmen who traveled abroad, but as he later testified in his *processo*, the idea of sending the letters was his own.[39] No one remembers what a council is anymore or knows why they are no longer held, he complained. What is a council but a congregation of elders such as Moses summoned when he wished to report the Lord's words and signs? It consists of all good churchmen and worthy laymen, for a true council must have the Holy Spirit. Perhaps this is why people say that councils can no longer be held: the reformers themselves must first be reformed.[40] Meanwhile he was making arrangements, in some cases directly with the relevant Florentine ambassadors, in others through intermediaries, for the reception of his letters at the royal courts.[41] Yet the letters remained locked in Savonarola's writing desk, unfinished and undelivered. The project for calling a Church council was overtaken by events.

Although the pratica of March 14 ended in stalemate, the pressure on Florence to silence the Frate was becoming irresistible. Bonsi's letters were increasingly alarming: the pope, positively splenetic, was threatening to arrest all Florentine merchants in Rome and confiscate their property. To break the deadlock some anti-Savonarolans called for the question to be put before the Great Council. This the Frateschi successfully resisted, arguing that it would only cause more confusion—an ironic departure from their populist ideology and an acknowledgment that their once powerful majority in the Council had dwindled.[42] Whether because they sensed a shift in mood or could not think of an alternative, Gonfaloniere Piero Popoleschi and the Priors reconvened the previously deadlocked pratica. This time the vote went against the Frate. The following day the Signoria and Ten wrote to Bonsi instructing him to inform the pope that they were ordering Savonarola to stop preaching.[43]

Just hours before the pratica met, Savonarola, already sensing the outcome, preached on the text "How lovely is thy dwelling place O Lord of virtues. . . . My soul longs and faints [Ps. 83/84]." For women only, this sermon was non-polemical, devoid of politics, prophecy or self-justification. Reflecting the emotion of his perilous situation and his leave-taking, he returned to the religious essence. He spoke as though in a dialogue with himself, yet his mystical threnody held his audience for a solid hour:

> Now, let's be together; let's be together in love. I want to speak to you, I don't want to speak to you, I want to speak to myself, I don't want to speak to myself.—Oh, you are crazy.—Oh, soul, I want to talk with you, I don't want to talk with you.—Oh, you're crazy, you're drunk.—Oh Lord, my soul wishes to speak with you. *How lovely is thy dwelling place, Lord of virtues.* Oh Lord of virtues, how beloved, how loveable, are thy dwelling places. Oh Lord of virtues, I do not speak to you, earth, who are not lord of virtues; I speak not to you, water, who are not lord of virtues; I do not speak to you, air, you're not lord of virtues; I speak not to you, fire, you are not lord of virtues; I don't speak to you, sky: you are not lord of virtues; I do not speak to you, angels: you are not lord of virtues; I do not speak to you, sun, to you, moon, you are not lords of virtues; I speak not to you, goods of this world, not to honors, not to states, not to worldly things: you are not God of virtues. . . . I seek you, O Lord, who has created the virtues, have created the heavens and this universe. . . . I go searching for you, my love, I search for you who created me, Oh fire of

my heart, where are you? Where will I find you? . . . I go searching for you, my beloved, who have wounded my heart . . . I languish, I burn with love. Remove, lift my soul from this life where it can no longer remain.

After a pause for rest he returns to his twin theme of the soul's longing and his own approaching sacrifice.

My eye no longer wants to stay and see vain things, my ear no longer wishes to hear worldly things, my tongue wishes to speak of nothing but God. The body wishes to die, to stay here no longer without its heart; the heart draws it to itself. . . . Ah, Lord, put me on an altar too. Let me die on one of your altars, let me die on your cross. Here I am with my hands tied, I offer myself and I pray that you don't let me die anywhere but on your altar. And your other altar, of the Sacrament, of the bread, of your body, they are what sustain us. . . . I must die in any case; this world passes away in a breath; these persecutions of the world last only briefly, but in your house, Lord, one lives in saecula saeculorum. . . .

You see that we have become crazy and drunk this morning. . . . I can go on no longer, I no longer know what to say, nothing is left for me but to weep. I want to dissolve, right here in this pulpit. . . . If I am in the way Lord, remove my soul and kill me. What have your sheep done? They've done nothing. I am the sinner. Don't consider my sins, but consider this time your gentleness, your heart, your bowels, and show us your mercy. Mercy, my Lord, *qui es benedictus in saecula saeculorum.* Amen.

Savonarola's scribe writes: "Note that the father preacher arrived at this point in such a spirit, and likewise his listeners in such uncontrollable fervor and weeping, that they broke out in loud cries of 'mercy, God, mercy.' And the father gave his benediction and departed."[44]

About nine in the evening a government messenger officially informed Savonarola that he must cease preaching. The next day, March 18, he preached his last sermon. Soberly, in contrast to what he called "yesterday's intoxication," he likened himself to Jeremiah punished by the priest Pashur for having prophesied the destruction of Jerusalem. Jeremiah had bitterly complained that the Lord's word had become for him "a reproach and derision all day long [Jer. 20.7–8]." Jeremiah had suffered for forty years; he himself only for eight, although he knew there was more to come. Jeremiah, on account of his suffering, had cursed the day he was born. Did this mean that Jeremiah had repudiated his prophetic gift? No, God's prophet could not err; as all the doctors agree, Jeremiah was speaking here not rationally but according to the emotions. God sometimes allowed great men to be greatly confused so that they realize that they are, after all, human. Jeremiah passed this test of his faith and continued to prophesy. Did he himself, then, curse the day he was born? The Lord saw that he was not as strong as Jeremiah and therefore did not let him be tempted in this way; but let the Lord do what he would; the greater the misfortune from above, the greater the crown (of martyrdom) would be down here.

If it were up to him, he declared, he would not leave off preaching. He would resist, just as he had done on Ascension Day, just as he had done when the plague came, and before that, when the five prominent citizens had come to him on behalf of Lorenzo de' Medici and warned him not to say the things he was saying.

> So, what do you say, frate, and what should you do? Are you to preach or not? Let me rest, then I'll tell you. . . .
>
> Now, we were preaching here, and last evening, about 9, since "those who do evil hate the light" [John 3.20], an embassy came from those who rule and said that, for many reasons, I was being asked not to preach. I said to them, "You are doing what your lords tell you to do?" "Yes." "I too have a Lord [I replied] and I will consult his wishes and tomorrow morning I'll give you the answer." So, here, this morning I'll give you the reply. Listen, then, this is what the Lord says: "You are asking me that he should stop preaching. Oh, say you are asking me, not the Frate, because it is I who am preaching, not the Frate, and I have granted it and I have not granted it." I heard this and I was dumbfounded and I tried to understand what this answer meant. [The Lord] said to me, "Don't you remember that text of Job that says, 'If I called upon him and he answered me, I would not believe he was listening to my voice' [Job 9.16]. Do you understand what this means?" I got up early this morning to look at that text because I didn't recall the words very well, but I certainly remembered the exposition, and as soon as I saw it I said to myself, Good, well, now I remember the illustration of this text—the doctor who, when the patient says, "I want some wine," replies, "If you drink wine you'll die," and [the patient] says, "I want some wine," and the doctor says, "I have heard you and I have not heard you," and he yields and gives him the wine. The doctor yields and gives him the wine to satisfy him, but he has not conceded on the principle he had in mind, for [the patient] won't get the cure or the health that he is looking for. . . . So the Lord has heard you here and has also not heard you. He has granted your request to remove the preaching, but he has not granted you health. This preaching has been the health of your city and also the health of the wicked who would have been ruined by now without this firm preaching.

As for himself, there would be no greater pleasure than to remain quiet in his study, but there is much to come. What preaching might have brought about must now be left to prayer. Let the Lord delay no longer to send that which he has promised. Then, reciting the Pater Noster on behalf of everyone, including his adversaries, he departs.[45]

CHAPTER 22

Trial by Fire

Within days of fra Girolamo's farewell sermon, the whirlwind he had loosed reached into the convent of San Marco and pulled him back into the world. It came as a demand for a miracle. On March 25, the Franciscan Francesco di Puglia electrified his Santa Croce congregation by offering to settle the controversy over Savonarola's excommunication with a trial by fire. He had first proposed the test the previous Lent in a sermon in Prato, but when it seemed that fra Domenico da Pescia, also preaching in Prato, would accept the challenge, fra Francesco had hurried back to Florence. With Savonarola silent and the Piagnoni in some disarray, fra Francesco now renewed his call for a heavenly verdict: let the Savonarolans provide a champion to walk through fire with him; he knew he himself would not survive, but the fate of his opponent would show whether the excommunication was valid or not.[1] (Why in this case fra Francesco should have to risk the fire himself he did not explain, but this was a time for miracles, not logic.)

Florentines poured out into the streets to spread the news of the Franciscan's challenge and its acceptance by fra Domenico da Pescia. Fra Francesco protested that he had meant to undergo the fire trial with no one but Savonarola, but the contest was no longer his to control. Fra Giuliano Rondinelli, a fellow Franciscan from Santa Croce, volunteered to take his place. Another volunteer came forward for the Savonarolan side, the San Marco friar Mariano Ughi. Fra Domenico, unwilling to relinquish the initiative, issued a set of "conclusions" he was prepared to defend: this was the generation that would enter the New Age, when the Church would be renewed, when the infidel would be converted, and Florence prosper as never before.

Challenges and counterchallenges volleyed from pulpit to pulpit. Girolamo Benivieni looked on in amazement as clerics, nuns, laymen, and children pushed forward to offer themselves for the trial by fire and women screamed "Me! Me!" as if, he said, someone had proposed marriage to them. Even so, Benivieni believed that once the archbishop's vicar and the Signoria took the affair in hand, it would come to nothing.[2]

To help decide whether and how it ought to intervene the Signoria called another pratica of fifty prominent citizens.[3] Many said they were uneasy taking a position on what both Guidoantonio Vespucci and Luca degli Albizzi dismissed as "a contest between friars." Two speakers pointed out that fire trials were a thing of the distant past; the last one had taken place in the eleventh century when Giovanni Gualberto walked through flames to prove the local bishop guilty of simony and heresy. Carlo Canigiani declared that the pratica was a forum better suited to discuss war and money; saints were canonized in Rome. Giovanni Canacci complained that the affair would make them the laughingstock of the world, and Vespucci, with his usual plainspokenness, reproached his compatriots with a text from the Gospel of Matthew: "It is a wicked and adulterous people that seeks a sign [Matt. 12.39]."

Yet a majority, both Savonarolans and Arrabbiati, agreed: this was an opportunity to free the city from its "intolerable burden" and they should grasp it; in one way or another the matter would be resolved. Even Francesco Valori was of this opinion: "I think what will happen is that either someone will back down, or you'll put [the trial] on and it will result in a miracle or a serious disaster." But he and some of the others urged that before proceeding they seek the authority of the archbishop through his vicar. Girolamo Rucellai spoke for many: "In my opinion we're making too much fuss about this fire; the important thing is to do away with Frate and anti-Frate, Arrabbiato and anti-Arrabbiato, and to think, at last, about making peace among the citizens. If you think a test like this can restore calm to the city, go ahead, not only in fire but in water, in air, on the ground; only let's not concern ourselves with friars, but with the city." With this exasperated, ambiguous warrant, the Signoria moved to take charge of the trial. That same evening a contract incorporating fra Domenico's propositions was drawn up and notarized and the antagonists were called in to affix their names.[4]

CONCLUSIONS TO BE PROVEN BY RATIONAL PROOFS
AND SUPERNATURAL SIGNS
God's Church is in need of renewal
It will be scourged

It will be renewed
Florence also will be renewed and will prosper after scourging
The infidels will be converted to Christ
All these things will take place in our time
The excommunication recently decreed against our Reverend Father
    Girolamo is void.
It is no sin to disregard it

Fra Domenico da Pescia was the first to sign. Challenger fra Francesco di Puglia came next, but reluctantly, explaining that he did so at the request of the Signoria; he had intended to undergo the fire trial with fra Girolamo himself; with fra Domenico he had no quarrel. Noting that this left them uncertain whether they would have a pair of willing champions, the Signoria called the two backup volunteers, Mariano Ughi and Giuliano Rondinelli. Fra Giuliano declared that although he expected to be burned up in the flames he took part willingly "for the salvation of souls." And so, despite ambiguity over the trial's aims, vagueness about its procedures, and even some uncertainty as to who was to participate the event was set for April 7.

Efforts to clarify the terms of the *experimento* introduced more confusion. Fra Francesco di Puglia issued a statement repeating that he had meant to challenge only fra Girolamo, a man "unequaled in learning or goodness." He sensibly observed that if he or fra Domenico died in the fire it would not dispel the confusion—which he then compounded by suggesting that three or four friars should be prepared to undergo the test. When the fire had been lit he (fra Girolamo?) could choose one of them. For its part, the Signoria attempted to clarify the initial contract with a codicil stipulating that if the Dominican champion died in the fire Savonarola and fra Domenico would be exiled from Florentine territory, but if the Dominican survived, the Franciscans fra Francesco di Puglia and fra Lorenzo Corsi (hitherto unnamed) would be the ones to be exiled.[5]

The challenge to a test by fire confronted Savonarola with a dilemma to which he responded with more artfulness than candor. As he later told his interrogators, he was dismayed by the whole business but felt he had no alternative but to endorse it. "I thought it very bad that fra Domenico proposed those conclusions and provoked the affair, and I would have given a lot to have had him not do it. I was also sorry that our friends pressed for it. If it had been up to me I would not have done it. I consented only because I had to defend my honor as best I could. If I had been preaching at the time, when the affair got moving and afterwards when they were pushing for it, I would have thought of a way to squelch it by saying that those conclusions could be proven rationally. I scolded fra Domenico for having got such a big, danger-ous business going. In the end I consented so as not to lose my reputation, always maintaining that we were going through with the trial because we were responding to a provocation."[6]

Though caught unawares, Savonarola deftly reclaimed center stage. On April 5, in a manifesto which seemed both to condone and to deplore this resort to miracle, he tried to explain why he had not personally taken up the challenge to go into the fire.[7] The question, he recognized, was the legitimacy of his prophetic mission, but on this issue his real adversaries were in Rome; if one of them offered to dispute with him, he would himself go through the fiery furnace like Shadrach, Meshach, and Abednego. Since no one from Rome had come forward, however, he would not submit himself to the fire, for that would violate "the proper order of things." For the same reason, he reminded them, Giovanni Gualberto had chosen one of his monks to repre-sent him in a fire test, and he pointed out that all three hundred of his friars as well as other priests, monks, nuns, and citizens, both men and women, had offered themselves. That very morning in San Marco, he noted, thousands had offered to enter the fire for the greater glory of God. But since he and his movement would be destroyed if one of them should die in the fire, the champion should be one God elected from his Order, and that was fra Do-menico. To those who said that he, fra Girolamo, should personally enter the fire or undergo some other miraculous test, he repeated that he had already proved his case by rational arguments, adding that to demand a miracle would be to tempt God. (Why it was not tempting God if he allowed a surrogate to undergo the test, he failed to explain.) As for the secret truths he himself had promised to reveal with supernatural signs, the time had not yet come. When it did, God would not fail to keep his promises.

A day before the trial, in the presence of civic officials and the arch-bishop's representatives, it was finally settled that fra Domenico da Pescia and fra Giuliano Rondinelli would enter the fire on behalf of fra Girolamo and fra Francesco di Puglia. Fra Domenico would uphold the truth of Savonarola's prophecies and the invalidity of his excommunication (as set out in his "con-clusions"). Fra Giuliano would champion fra Francesco di Puglia's proposi-tion that some of these conclusions were false, some dubious, some humbug. These matters, it was noted, were greatly disturbing the city and some of them could only be settled by supernatural means. As for the trial, each of the champions would enter the fire at the same place and continue to the other end. If either refused to enter he would be considered to have failed the test. If fra Domenico entered and emerged unharmed, he would be regarded the victor. What would happen if both champions emerged unharmed the agreement did not specify.

Rome was outraged. "See where this matter is leading!" expostulated the pope to envoy Domenico Bonsi on April 3. "Impermissible without license from their superiors!" interjected the hitherto sympathetic cardinal of Perugia. That a papal excommunication might be nullified or ignored greatly offended the entire curia. Letters from San Marco informing His Holiness that all three hundred friars were solidly behind Savonarola and were ready to go through the fire on his behalf did nothing to ease the general indignation. Could it be stopped? Bonsi replied that the matter had gone too far—unless, he ventured, the pope might be willing to absolve the Frate? But His Holiness was adamant: Savonarola must admit his error and throw himself upon the papal mercy.[8] But now time had run out.

There are many ambiguities about the preliminaries of the fire trial, but no mystery as to its expense. In true Florentine fashion the account books of the Ten record every outlay—for lumber, wood panels, iron fencing, hammers, pickaxes, nails, spikes, wooden chests, and the stacks of firewood and bundles of kindling for the fire. Torches had to be purchased to light the stations of the night guards and cartloads of soil and rocks had to be brought for the raised walkway on which the rivals would pass through the fire. Two knights with their retinues were employed to keep order, carpenters, laborers, and carters hired to prepare the Piazza della Signoria for what everyone was calling "the miracle." The grand total came to just over 662 lire, roughly the equivalent of a year's wages for a dozen guardsmen.[9]

Twice before the great test Savonarola conferred with Giovambattista Ridolfi who shared his opinion that Rondinelli, the Franciscan champion, would balk at entering the fire, and if so, fra Domenico would be released from his obligation. To increase that likelihood fra Girolamo sent fra Malatesta Sacramoro to the Signoria to urge that the fire be made huge. He also arranged that both parties be obliged to enter the piazza from the side opposite the fire and the gate be shut behind them.[10] (Presumably, by the time they had made the long walk toward the blazing fire they would be too terrified to continue.)

On the Saturday morning of the trial, April 7, the gates of the city were shut and a guard posted. Foreigners had been expelled, except for some mercenaries employed as guards; citizens and soldiers patrolled the streets to prevent any demonstration or tumult.[11] In the church of San Marco, packed with the faithful, Savonarola ignored papal excommunication and defied local disapproval to say Mass, give Communion, and exhort the congregation to have faith and courage and pray for a favorable outcome.

Two prophecies were revealed to him the previous night, he says. One is absolute: ultimate victory will be theirs; divine authority and reason told him so. The other is conditional: only God knows whether the test will take place; this is a human decision. He himself believes it will happen, having already gone so far. Some want a miracle; he has no need of it, but even though it tempts God he cannot ignore the provocation. (Did he also say, as reported by fra Benedetto Luschino who had been present, that the guardian angels of fra Domenico, fra Silvestro Maruffi, and himself had appeared in a vision, that they told him fra Domenico had been chosen and would emerge safely if he carried the Host with him? And did he say that challenger fra Giuliano Rondinelli would go to hell for risking the fire despite knowing he would die?)[12] When the prophet Elijah called on the Lord to end a three-year drought the altar of the Israelites burst into flame and a life-giving rain fell upon the parched land (3 Kings 17–18). So will it be this morning. Let their opponents use demonic arts as did the four hundred priests of Ba'al; let them call up all the denizens of hell; no demons will protect their champion from burning in the fire, whereas we will pray to God and he will award us the victory. For seven years they have proceeded righteously in this land, honoring God; how can anyone believe he will allow their work to fail? Let everyone recite the *Te Deum* while he and his friars do what must be done. Women will remain behind praying for a happy outcome.[13]

At this point the mace bearers of the Signoria arrived to announce that all was ready and to escort fra Girolamo and his party to their fateful test.

More than two hundred hooded and robed friars, the youngest in the lead, moved out from San Marco in stately procession carrying red crucifixes and singing, "Let God rise up and dispel his enemies [Ps. 67/68]." Fra Domenico da Pescia, in red velvet cope, carried a wooden crucifix four feet high. Savonarola, who had exchanged his simple habit for an embroidered white velvet cope, carried the Host in an elegant monstrance. Although it was morning, the clerics and laymen who surrounded him carried lighted torches and lamps.[14] Other laymen followed in their train. Through crowd-lined streets the procession made its way to the Piazza della Signoria ringed with armed guards. A large group of Compagnacci were already assembled there, apparently intending to attack the Frate and his party, but they were discouraged by the soldiers.[15] Singing hymns and psalms, the San Marco friars entered, taking their assigned places near the Loggia della Signoria on the east side of the piazza. Fra Girolamo placed the Host in its monstrance on a makeshift altar and said Mass. The Franciscans, separated from them by a temporary barrier, waited in silence—frightened, some said, by the Dominicans' show of devotion and courage.[16] Every space in the piazza as well as the hastily built stands was packed with male spectators, women having been shut out "so as not to give rise to scandal," as Parenti put it. Roofs and windows of adjoining buildings gave access to many more.

From the Palazzo della Signoria a platform about four feet high, sixteen feet wide, built over packed earth, led out to the center of the piazza. Unbaked bricks had been laid over the platform to keep it from catching fire. Over this were heaped pieces of wood to a thickness of about two and a half feet. Willow branches, brushwood, and small twigs were placed on the sides, "very suitable stuff for making a fine fire, arranged very carefully to work well," Parenti noted.

The two parties indicated their readiness to proceed, but hours passed before government officials emerged from the palace to begin discussions on the conduct of the test. When the Franciscans protested that fra Domenico might be concealing magic charms in his robes, he was taken into the palace and strip-searched, then forced to exchange robes with his fellow friar, Andrea Strozzi. More objections were raised and resolved, but when fra Domenico indicated that he intended to carry his crucifix into the fire, the Santa Croce friars objected. Savonarola intervened. He allowed the objection to the crucifix but insisted that unless fra Domenico be permitted to carry the Host, he would not give his consent. The Franciscans professed to be scandalized: this was sacrilege![17] Four lay spokesmen, Giovambattista Ridolfi and Francesco Gualterotti for San Marco, Piero degli Alberti and Tommaso Antinori for Santa Croce, were appointed to argue the question before the government commissioners who decided that fra Domenico would be allowed to carry the Host as far as the fire, but must enter without it. This Savonarola and his men refused to accept.

While rival friars heaped objection upon objection, the spectators waited for the miracle, from time to time their growing impatience and indignation mounting to near riot which had to be squashed by the guards. As the San

Marco friars chanted their prayers and sang their litanies, the skies suddenly darkened and sent down hail, bolts of lightning, and heavy rain. Piagnoni took this as the miracle that vindicated fra Girolamo's prophetic mission and made the fire trial superfluous, but their opponents charged that he was using his demonic arts to abort the trial and prevent the exposure of his lies. By late afternoon, the city officials concluded that no agreement could be reached and halted the proceedings—"without even lighting the wood," as Guicciardini put it. Still squabbling and accusing each other of bad faith, the rival parties marched out, and the guards cleared the square of spectators. The crowd dispersed reluctantly, many complaining that they had been duped by cynical, self-serving friars.

As word spread that Savonarola had blocked the proceedings by refusing to allow fra Domenico to enter the fire without the Host, the blame for the debacle settled on him. Angry spectators mocked and attacked Piagnoni in the streets. Compagnacci toughs pursued the hymn-singing San Marco friars as they made their way back to the convent under protection of an armed escort. If not for the Host, which fra Girolamo held aloft, they would have been torn to pieces, Parenti declared.

When Savonarola reached San Marco he found the church crowded with the faithful, even the women he had left there six hours earlier. In the pulpit he claimed victory for the cause and blamed the cancellation of the test on the Franciscans—a piece of impudence, fumed Parenti, that his adversaries found insupportable and that led to further insults and attacks on Piagnoni. There were also complaints to the Signoria of this latest violation of the papal ban on his preaching.[18]

In the evening some Piagnoni came to San Marco to persuade fra Girolamo to let them take the offensive; if they did not arm and carry the fight to the streets, they pleaded, the convent itself would surely be attacked. Savonarola refused to hear of it. The night passed quietly. The next day was Palm Sunday and worshipers filled the Cathedral. All was calm until the evening vesper service when fra Mariano Ughi arrived from San Marco with a large following and entered the pulpit. Some of the canons raised objections. A certain Antonio Alamanni banged on the seats and railings and shouted that there would be no sermon; the "wretched Piagnoni" and women must leave. A Savonarolan drew his sword, and together with some of his confederates drove Alamanni from the church. Frightened and bewildered worshipers also bolted into the street where a crowd was already gathering. Crying "get the friars!"

and "on to San Marco!" Compagnacci and Arrabbiati agitators quickly took charge, turning the confused and aimless crowd into an angry mob that manhandled fra Mariano Ughi and his party, chasing them back up the Via Cocomoro. A young man singing psalms on his way to Santissima Annunziata was unfortunate enough to be in their path. With the thrust of a lance they left him dead in the street and moved on to San Marco.

As the mob approached, Savonarola was conducting vesper service. Completing his sermon he fell on his knees and addressing the crucifix, gave thanks that Christ was about to grace him with a similar martyrdom.[19] Shouts and the crash of stones on walls and doors announced the arrival of the attackers. Those inside "stared at each other, dumbfounded," said Parenti, most of them too terrified to try to escape. ("I happened to be present," wrote Luca Landucci, "and if I hadn't been able to get out through the cloister and head toward the Porta San Gallo, I would have died there.") Francesco Valori and Giovambattista Ridolfi consulted with Savonarola, and it was agreed that they should go out, rally their followers, and return to defend the convent.

Valori went first. Through a secret exit he made his way out into increasingly dangerous streets and arrived at his family palace just ahead of marauders screaming "get Valori!" and "on to Valori's house!" Hiding himself, he watched helplessly as the palace was ransacked and torched, his nephews attacked and wounded, his wife murdered with a blow to the head. Guardsmen found him and began to lead him away, but he was recognized by some of the rioters who, managing to avoid or dispel the guard, set upon him and killed him. They stripped his body and carried it to the church of San Procolo where Valori-haters came to gloat and take vengeance on his naked corpse. Jacopo Pitti spit on him, crying, "Valori, you'll not rule us any more!" Vincenzo Ridolfi, nephew of one of the five conspirators of the previous summer, cut off his head with a pruning hook. Other Frateschi suffered as well, although none so savagely: the house of Andrea Cambini, a trusted emissary of fra Girolamo, was sacked and burned; the houses of Paolantonio Soderini and Bernardo Nasi narrowly missed the same treatment when government patrols intervened.

As darkness came, San Marco's bell tolled a somber descant to the plight of those barricaded inside. More sympathizers arrived and skirmished with the attackers, leaving one or two dead and several wounded, including Arrabbiati leader Tanai di Nerli who lost an eye. But with the mob close to breaking into the convent, Savonarola began to despair. "Hearing that the number of people [outside] was increasing while none of our friends were coming to help us, I grew frightened and it occurred to me to hold a crucifix and, in the midst of praying friars, move toward the door of the cloister to see if I could resist with my friends or die. But I wasn't allowed to do so by the many laymen who were there, among them Francesco Davanzati and Giovambattista Ridolfi and many others . . . who said, 'We don't want you to go out because without you we are nothing and we want to die with you.' When I saw Giovambattista [Ridolfi] there I was very surprised and frightened because I had believed that he had left with Francesco Valori to do what still could be done."[20]

In constant session since the tumult in the Cathedral earlier that evening, the Signoria at last decided on a course of action. A decree of banishment gave fra Girolamo, fra Domenico da Pescia, and fra Silvestro Maruffi seven hours to leave the territory of the republic, after which they would be declared rebels. Whoever found them after the expired time was free to kill them on sight for a reward of a thousand ducats. All lay persons still in San Marco were ordered to leave. More soldiers were dispatched to the convent, with enough artillery and explosives, observed Parenti, to take a castle, and they assumed control of the assault. Some friars, disregarding Savonarola's orders against violence, had opened the cache of weapons they had been storing in the convent and begun to resist, firing small cannon and crossbows from doors and windows. Fra Benedetto Luschino and others, together with some laymen, climbed to the roof where they ripped up tiles and bricks and hurled them down on the attackers.

Nearly eight hours passed in this way before armed men under command of Giovanni della Vecchia, captain of the guard, broke through the burning doors of the church and convent. The soldiers found most of the inmates huddled in the choir of the church and Savonarola in the library on his knees in prayer. They arrested him and fra Domenico, bound their hands and feet and took them out, leaving a guard to protect the convent from sack. Through streets lined with jeering onlookers, the two friars were taken to the tower of the Palazzo della Signoria and locked in separate cells, Savonarola in the Alberghetto, the "little inn," where sixty years earlier Cosimo de' Medici had been briefly imprisoned. During the confusion of the siege fra Silvestro Maruffi had concealed himself, but he was discovered that same night, arrested, and taken to join his two companions in the palace tower.

On April 7, day of the aborted fire trial, King Charles VIII, Savonarola's New Cyrus, died in his castle at Amboise after striking his head on a doorway. Landucci noted that the day had been filled with celestial disturbances.[21]

CHAPTER 23

Despair and Hope

With Frateschi leaders too frightened to show themselves in public, Savonarola's enemies held the field. But to do what? In a pratica of April 9 Guidantonio Vespucci and Bernardo Rucellai said the three friars should be sent to Rome for trial. Most of their colleagues strenuously disagreed: this was a matter to be dealt with at home and put behind them as speedily as possible. Too much time would be lost waiting for Rome to act. By keeping the investigation in Florence they could control it, with minimum damage to civic interests and individual reputations. As for papal permission, one argued, no special mandate was needed to proceed against clerics already excommunicated. The previous day's order of banishment seems to have been a dead letter. Piero Parenti, newly elected to the Eight, was brutally candid: "Our intention was that [the Frate] not leave here alive so that he would not have another opportunity to cause us trouble."[1]

In fact, the domestic debate over trial jurisdictions was beside the point. With the approval of the archbishop's vicar, fra Girolamo and fra Domenico had already been interrogated on April 8, the night of their arrest.[2] Moreover, the Signoria had already written to Rome for permission to interrogate the friars and for prior absolution in case they violated clerical immunity.[3] The magistrates repeated the request on April 10 and, in a blatantly cynical aside that revealed the political stakes they were playing for, reminded the pope that Florence had not yet recovered Pisa. This letter probably crossed Ambassador Bonsi's from Rome, also of April 10, in which he reported that the pope was satisfied with the arrest of the friars and authorized their interrogation. A breve of April 12 confirmed and expanded his approval: to arrive at the truth of the matter His Holiness allowed the Florentines to examine with torture any clerics or other persons they saw fit, provided that some of the interrogators were clerics. When they had finished they were to deliver the three friars into Church territory, whence they would be brought "to us."

Without waiting for this open-ended license, the Arrabbiati pressed their advantage. So-called emergency elections were called for the two Piagnoni government strongholds—the Eight of Security and Ten of Liberty—resulting in the choice of two Arrabbiati. (Compagnacci leader Doffo Spini was one of the new Eight.) By another dubious tactic these newly elected officials were seated alongside the incumbents and allowed to vote, although their terms had not yet begun. This gave the anti-Savonarolans enough votes to ensure that all seventeen members of the investigating commission (soon reduced to sixteen) would be "fierce enemies" of the Frate.[4] The egregious Doffo Spini also was one of these.

On the same day, April 10, fra Girolamo, his legs in chains, was carried to the palace of the Bargello, and the commissioners set to work. In deference to the pope's wishes, two canons of the Cathedral were included as observers. He was examined according to standard inquisitorial procedures derived from Roman law and medieval practice. Interrogators put questions to the accused who answered viva voce, in writing, or both, as demanded. Questions and answers were recorded by an attending notary. There was no provision for the introduction of witnesses or evidence on behalf of the accused. Torture was allowed, with certain restrictions due to class, gender, and status, clerics generally being exempt unless the ecclesiastical authorities gave express approval. (The authorities had apparently used torture in interrogating him and fra Domenico on the night of their arrest, although they had not yet received permission from Rome.) In inquisitorial procedure judge and jury were one: the commission that conducted the examination also rendered the verdict.

Neither Savonarola's life as a Dominican friar nor his doctrinal views really interested his interrogators. Considering that he was convicted for "heresy, schism, and preaching innovation," these may seem surprising omissions, but the commissioners saw their task as political, not theological. Their aim was to demonstrate that Savonarola was an imposter who had concealed his ambitions for power and fame behind a mask of feigned prophecy and had consistently manipulated the new republican government for his own ends. A second aim was to expose Savonarola's collaborators, both lay and clerical. Nearly a score of them, in addition to fra Domenico and fra Silvestro, were interrogated simultaneously. Most of the Piagnoni leaders were, of course, well known. In addition to the murdered Valori, some of them had been assaulted or their houses sacked. But the interrogators pressed for more names and details, hoping to incriminate, or at least compromise, every prominent supporter of Savonarola as well as to add further evidence of his guilt. These were show trials, staged to convince the Florentine people that their fallen hero deserved neither loyalty nor pity and, should there be a Piagnone resurgence, to deprive it of leaders.

Between April 10 and 19 fra Girolamo was interrogated daily. The inquisitors began with questions (*a parole*), added threats (*con minaccie*), and finally—ostensibly because they were dissatisfied with his answers—moved to *tormento*. The commission's chief notary, Francesco Barone (ser Ceccone), recorded questions and answers, summaries and written statements. The method of torture used was the strappado, also known as *la fune* or more commonly, *la corda,* the rope. The prisoner's hands were bound behind his back with one end of the rope, while the other end was looped through a hook or pulley in the ceiling. At a signal attendants pulled on the rope, drawing his arms over his head and hoisting him off his feet. The stress caused dislocations, a broken arm, and severe pain. The duration of each suspension varied according to the questioners' judgment, the briefest being the time it took "to recite an Ave Maria," the longest probably several excruciating minutes. At the release order the prisoner was dropped until his feet touched the floor or remained suspended just above it for an added shock. Each suspension constituted one *tratta*, or "turn." In a half-turn the arms were stretched above the head without the feet leaving the floor.[5]

On that first day it was recorded that Savonarola twice received three and a half turns. During the days that followed, he gave "different answers to certain things, sometime saying one thing, sometime another."[6] At some point he was given pen and paper, whether because the interrogators were dissatisfied with his answers or, as Landucci reported, because as he hung suspended he cried out, "Let me down and I will write you my whole life story!"[7] Here, in a surviving version, is what he wrote:

> The truth is this. About fifteen years ago, the first time I was in Florence, I was in the monastery of Santo Giorgio with fra Tommaso di Strada, now dead, who was visiting his sister, a nun. I was in the church, thinking about a sermon I was composing, and as I thought about it many reasons occurred to me [for concluding that] the Church was about to undergo some sort of scourge. From then on I began to think a lot about these things and about the scriptural evidence.
>
> And going to San Gimignano to preach, I began. In the two years I

preached there I proposed these conclusions, that the Church was to be scourged and renewed. Since I did not have this by revelation but from reasons derived from Scripture, I said as much. I preached in the same vein in Brescia and sometimes I preached these things in other places in Lombardy where I remained for four years.

Then I returned to Florence—about seven years had passed from that day in San Giorgio described above—and on August 1 I began to expound the Apocalypse; that was in 1490. I propounded the same conclusions described above. Next, in Lent, in Santa Reparata I preached the same things, never saying that they had been revealed to me by God, however, but arguing that the evidence compelled belief and affirming this as emphatically as I could.

Then, after Easter, fra Silvestro, returning from San Gimignano, told me that he had been skeptical of what I was saying and thought I was crazy until, during a vigil, one of our dead friars appeared to him and reproved him, saying, "You should not think this of fra Girolamo, because you know him." After that, as fra Silvestro told me, he had many more apparitions of this kind.

So, as my desire and eagerness to preach such things grew I became more ardent to reaffirm them in some way. Seeing it all go well, and my reputation and favor among the Florentine people grow, I went further and began to say that I had it from revelation, although in fact it was all the invention of my zeal. And so in my great presumption I pressed forward with it determinedly. Many times I said things fra Silvestro related to me, sometimes believing them to be true. Nevertheless, I did not talk with God, nor God with me, in the special way in which he speaks to his holy apostles, prophets, and others of that kind.

I continued to preach with all the force and effort of my ability, presumptuously affirming what I did not know for certain but wanting to believe that what my own mind conceived was true. I became so intoxicated with these things that I ended by saying that I was more certain of them than of standing there in the pulpit, or that two and two make four. All of it was to give more credit to what I was saying and to confirm it all the more in people's minds. I made these things appear to be true with my reasons and similes, maintaining my views ever more forcibly so as to make it seem that I spoke the truth and that this was from God. But I didn't know any of these things; worldly glory carried me along this way until 1494. . . . In 1494, when this government began, I started to push my cause even more, not only for glory but because I wanted to lead the work of Florentine government, partly for my reputation, partly to steer it in my direction, partly to make use of it, as I will explain, and also to achieve standing outside of Florence.[8]

Savonarola had more to say along the same lines in this interrogation and in the two that followed, although the essence of his self-accusation is in these first few pages: he had pretended to divine revelation, deceiving the many who believed in him; his motives were glory, reputation, and influence; his prophetic apostolate was thus based on a lie. Between April 21 and 25, he was examined in a second series of sessions known as the second processo. The official account claimed that torture was not used, although this was contradicted by the Priors themselves in a letter of May 6 to the pope.[9] As in the first processo, the transcript of these sessions was not the usual verbatim record of questions and answers but statements by the prisoner that alluded to the interrogators' questions. There were some damaging admissions: he had lied to fra Silvestro when he told him that the name "Jesu" had been miraculously engraved on his chest together with a crucifix; his visions were fabrications, including the hallmark vision of "the Sword of God, quickly and soon"; he had refrained from confessing his motives, knowing that if he did so he would not be absolved. "When a man has lost his faith and his soul he can do whatever he wants and set himself any great project."

On April 19 he confirmed and signed a lengthy statement. On the same day a transcript containing some version of this statement was read out in the Palazzo della Signoria, in the Great Hall Savonarola himself had done so much to bring into being. Luca Landucci heard it and was dismayed. Many others who had remained loyal to the Frate after the debacle of the fire trial shared his disillusionment. (One of these was fra Silvestro Maruffi, who apparently learned of the "confession" during his own interrogation and concluded that he had been deceived.)[10] Others were skeptical: was the statement they heard on April 19 a faithful version of what the prisoner had actually written or was it the handiwork of malicious editors? How could confessions that had passed through the hands of notaries in the employ of partisan investigators be trusted? For that matter, when all was said and done, how believable was any confession extracted by torture? Suspicions soared when, as if embarrassed by its reception, the government quickly withdrew this version of the first transcript from circulation.

Partisanship aside, every biographer of Savonarola must decide whether the surviving processi records have value as a source by considering two related questions. One, did the recording notaries, either at the interrogators' orders or acting on their own, falsify them wholly or in part? Two, does the fact that Savonarola was tortured make his testimony unreliable, either totally or in part? It may be useful first to know how others have attempted to answer those questions. Pasquale Villari, who discovered and edited the processi records and published them in appendices to his biography, labeled them "apocryphal." Villari's procedure was simple: he dismissed the most flagrantly self-incriminating passages as notarial interpolations and enclosed them in brackets to put readers on their guard. Joseph Schnitzer disallowed many passages of the processi records because they were not consonant with his own highly favorable ideas of the Frate's character and teaching, while, with un-characteristic naiveté, he accepted many of the assertions of the Piagnoni critics.[11] Roberto Ridolfi, third of the great Savonarola biographers, made a fresh, subtle analysis of the surviving transcripts and concluded that the text was for the most part genuine, that is, relatively—but not completely—free of significant notarial tampering. On the other hand, believing that torture forced Savonarola into making false confessions, Ridolfi did not regard the transcripts, genuine or not, to be a trustworthy source. This freed him to pick and choose among possible interpretations according to his own criteria— rarely to Savonarola's discredit.[12]

Recently Paolo Viti, one of the editors of the new edition of the processi, reexamined the question of the validity of the transcript of the first processo and came to even more negative conclusions about its usefulness. Viti notes that the most damning passages tend to come toward the end of sentences where they could have been most easily interpolated, and he thinks that these as well as the formulaic expression in other self-accusatory passages point to malicious editing. He concludes: "These confessions cannot be considered anything but additions and interpolations purposely conceived and inserted in the context of an artificially and predetermined situation."[13] In other words, according to Viti, the record was falsified in the interest of a judicial frame-up.

All the above conclusions have a common problem: they tend to confirm their authors' biases. The same is true of the fiercely unsympathetic assessment of Franco Cordero, for whom the processi confessions proved what he already believed—that Savonarola was a charlatan and a demagogue.[14] Savonarola admirers are confident that torture and notarial interpolations produced false confessions; Savonarola critics and denigrators accept the record as perhaps flawed but confirming his guilt. Such deductive reasoning is difficult, perhaps impossible, to avoid, since we are all prone to be influenced by what we already believe, especially in a case such as this where the objective evidence is weak and the presumption of bias on the part of the authorities strong.[15]

To be sure, torture and tampering complicate the problem. Savonarola himself alluded to interpolations by the notary when he came to sign the second processo transcript (although he did not specify which passages had been altered). As to torture, the authorities themselves recorded several occasions when they ordered the prisoner to be bound and hoisted, and there were probably many other instances they did not care to mention. Was Savonarola's testimony distorted by notarial alterations? Did the pain and fear of the rope "break" him, so undermining his resistance and self-possession that he yielded to his tormentors and told them what they wanted to hear?

Unraveling the puzzle of the transcripts lies as much in what Savonarola did not say as in what he did. A careful reading shows that he did not give the inquisitors everything—or even most—of what they wanted. He confessed to deception over his prophetic inspiration, but there were other instances in which he refused to incriminate himself despite the interrogators' determination to make him do so and despite their readiness to use torture to make him do it. For the most part these refusals concerned his involvement in Florentine, international, and curial affairs—what we may loosely term politics. The commissioners repeatedly tried to get him to admit that he had brokered intelligenze to promote Frateschi candidates for public offices, and that under his leadership the Convent of San Marco had become a venue for those secret and highly illegal meetings. But although he acknowledged his influence on the constitutional reforms of the new governo civile, especially the founding of the Great Council, and on maintaining Florence's alliance with the French —that is, to a general oversight of the principles and policies of the post-Medicean republic—he steadfastly refused to confess that he had unlawfully interfered in its day-to-day workings. As a foreigner he understood little of Florentine politics, he declared, and besides he had to maintain his reputation for impartiality. To be sure, the line Savonarola drew between moral leadership and active political partisanship (not to say direct manipulation) seems overly fine. While he disclaimed any knowledge of intelligenze in San Marco, he admitted to "half" intelligenze, that is, he would sometimes let it be known that he favored a certain citizen for a certain office. He denied that he had induced fra Silvestro to reveal secrets from the confessional, yet he admitted to having occasionally probed him for information he had acquired there. The salient point, however, is that this line of demarcation was meaningful to him, so meaningful that he held to it despite all the efforts of the interrogators, including the use of torture, to make him admit he had transgressed it.

In the third processo the ecclesiastical commissioners would probe him for details of secret dealings with princes and with cardinals and other prelates in the curia on behalf of a general council of the Church. Savonarola freely admitted that he had drafted letters to the emperor and to the monarchs of Spain, France, and England, asking their help in calling a general council of the Church, but he insisted that he had locked the letters away, unsent. To induce their prisoner to expose prelates in the curia who had plotted with him on behalf of a Church council (a particular bête noire of Alexander VI), torturers repeatedly applied the rope, yet apart from reaffirming his well-known contacts with Cardinal Carafa, Savonarola refused to satisfy them by incriminating anyone at the papal court.[16] Neither inquisitorial browbeating nor the terror and pain of the rope could induce him to say what he regarded as untrue. On the other hand, he made certain admissions of moral failure, which, though they show him in an unflattering light, seem to have been unforced. Thus, he volunteered that he had "coldly" refrained from intervening in the matter of an appeal by Lorenzo Tornabuoni, Bernardo Del Nero, and their fellow conspirators, so that they went to their deaths.

A related observation can be made in the matter of notarial forgery. Very possibly, ser Ceccone or a colleague altered and interpolated passages, but for the most part these seem to have been embellishments for greater effect, not wholesale rewritings, and they were largely confined to areas where Savonarola himself had made damaging admissions. There is little in his lengthy written confession of prophetic fraud that can be identified as tampering. Nor did ser Ceccone forge the confession the interrogators most dearly wanted, namely, that Savonarola took part in intelligenze.[17]

How was it, then, that Savonarola confessed to falsifying his divine inspiration but resisted the inquisitors' efforts, even when they tortured him, to force him confess to other sins? Put in this way the question is misleading. The critical point is that what he confessed was not the falsity of his prophecy but the falsity of his claim to divine illumination for it. In my view, the humiliation and pain inflicted by his interrogators forced their way into those areas where his confidence in his prophetic inspiration had already been shaken by the disastrous events of the aborted fire trial and the assault on San Marco, shattering what remained of his belief in his special relationship with God. But the apocalyptic prophecy he derived from Scripture—that Christendom would be scourged, that the Church would be renewed, and soon—this was no invention of his pride and ambition; this he regarded as God's word. The conviction, and its corollary, that he must proclaim this knowledge to the world, never abandoned him. That God had spoken to him, had illuminated him with the light of prophecy, was something he had come gradually, hesitantly, to believe. Propelled by the impetus of a sublime cause and the needy adulation of his audiences, he had been emboldened to claim the title of prophet.

Prophecy was a fragile condition, as the biblical prophets recognized, and Savonarola's frequent denials (*non sum propheta,* I am not a prophet) were more than formulaic.[18] At times, lacking inspiration or troubled by self-doubt, he needed the reassurance of fra Silvestro's visions or the impetus of fra Domenico's credulous enthusiasm. At times, he slipped into equivocation: his mystical transport to the throne of the Virgin had taken place not in body, as he initially suggested, but, as he later corrected, in pious fantasy. Most reckless of all was the millenarian promise: Florence, richer, more glorious, more powerful than ever! In the triumphant aftermath of the republican revolution, when it appeared to him that God had designated Florence the New Jerusalem and, drawing on civic mythology, guaranteed its imperial destiny, that promise rolled easily off his tongue. In the gloomy perspective of his prison cell this must have appeared even to him as brazen demagoguery and unholy presumption.[19]

Long before these terminal self-accusations there had been uncertainty, doubt, and fear. As God delayed fulfilling the prophecies, critics had begun to demand, and admirers to hope, for a sign. Until the previous December he had always resisted that demand. God must not be tempted! But, as we have seen, preaching to a small audience of the faithful in San Marco, he conceded to their weakness: let them all pray for a miracle. With this concession he furthered his own undoing. He was angry with fra Domenico for taking up the Franciscan's challenge to walk through fire, but fra Domenico was his alter ego; if he had ventured too rashly into the province of the supernatural, he was, after all, following the lead of his master. For his part, fra Girolamo, in no position either to block the fire trial or admit to being skeptical about the possibility of a miracle, felt he had no choice but to endorse the trial publicly while maneuvering to put it off. But he miscalculated: when the trial was aborted the blame for failing to produce a miracle inevitably fell on him.

During the terrible unraveling—the retreat to San Marco, the siege, his arrest and imprisonment—no longer in command of the crowd or master of his own actions, he could only feel he was being punished by the God for whom he had presumptuously claimed to speak. In this agony of self-doubt and contrition he faced his judges and, with the first turns of the rope, accepted the cup of penitence he had so often urged upon others, accusing himself of worldly ambition, pride, and glory-seeking. "All that I did or planned to do was in the interest of winning enduring fame, now and in the future, and to have such standing in the city of Florence that nothing of great importance be done unless I wished it. And after becoming thus established in Florence, I aspired to do great things in Italy and outside Italy, making use of the power of the lords with whom I made friends and treating of great matters like that of the Council." No, he continued, he had never aspired to become a cardinal or pope, although he would have accepted the papacy if offered, for the deeds he had set out to accomplish would have made him greater than any cardinal or pope, indeed, "the first man of the world."[20]

With the completion of the second processo the work of the civil commission was at an end. Savonarola was again required to sign off on the accuracy of a transcript, but this time he added a qualification: "although in certain places there are some *postille* [glosses] in the hand of ser Francesco di ser Barone."[21] For the time being no judgment was announced.

Now it was the turn of the Church inquisitors to wring out of him what more they could. Fra Girolamo and his two lieutenants were pawns in a delicate diplomatic game being played out between Florence and Rome; negotiations between the Signoria and the curia over the terms of an ecclesiastical inquest had dragged on. Alexander VI insisted that the prisoners be sent to him in Rome for ecclesiastical trial, and the Florentines, determined to maintain control of the investigation and prevent embarrassing disclosures, had no intention of complying. Still, they were anxious to retain the pope's good will, already sorely tested by the Savonarola affair. They needed papal consent for a new tax on the clergy as well as the Holy League's support for the restitution of Pisa. So they temporized, informing His Holiness through envoy Bonsi and by direct letter that Savonarola was proving a hard case and that they were forced to continue the interrogations.[22]

A compromise was finally reached: the pope would have his ecclesiastical processo, but in Florence, not Rome. On May 8 His Holiness named two commissioners. Two more weeks elapsed before they arrived. In the meantime, alone in his cell as hours stretched into days and weeks, Savonarola was left to his reflections. One mercy was granted him, and to us who want to know what he was thinking during this terrible time: he was allowed writing materials. First from his pen was a brief *Guide to Righteous Living*, which, according to chronicler Simone Filipepi, he wrote for his jailor whose sympathy he had won by gentle patience—and by miraculously curing him of syph-ilis.[23] Hagiographically inspired stories of miracles apart, the highly conven-tional guide (which his devoted jailor delivered into the hands of the Frate's publisher) is evidence that whatever emotions of defeat and shame he may have been feeling, neither his faith nor his sense of pastoral vocation had deserted him.

After the *Guide* he turned to something more evocative of his situation. By May 8, when it was smuggled out of his cell, he had completed an exposi-tion of Psalm 50/51, "Have Mercy on Me, O Lord." Based on the penitential psalm King David was believed to have composed after he had been accused of adultery and murder,[24] Savonarola's great meditation refers only obliquely to his own tribulations but was written "with an intensity that surpasses the *Imitation* [of Christ] and perhaps equals Augustine's *Confessions.*"[25] It was surely inspired by them. He sees himself as a scandal to earth and heaven; he has no refuge; he has loved the world, the flesh, glory, and himself and has feared humans more than he has feared God. Although God created him in his own image, in his misery he has taken on the image of the devil. He recalls Peter who denied Christ and had he seen the whips that were fetched for him, would have denied him again and again. He sees himself as the transgressor in disrepute and in chains. But he is also the prodigal son who pleads for God's pity and forgiveness. He is also Mary Magdalene, the town prostitute who, having washed Christ's feet and dried them with her hair, found divine favor in her sacrifice.

He has lost neither his prophetic voice nor his millenarian hope: once God begins to accept the sacrifices of justice instead of the superficial ones of ceremonies, he predicts, "The people will begin to live in the right way, to keep your commandments, and do justice. . . . Then will the oblations of the priests and clerics be acceptable to you because they have left behind earthly things and girded themselves for a more perfect life. . . . Then will they lay the calves upon your altar, offering their bodies to the cross, that is, to tortures and death, for your name. Then will the Church flourish; then will it expand its borders; then will your praise resound to the ends of the earth, then will joy and happiness take over the whole earth; then will the saints exult in glory and rejoice on their couches [Ps. 149.5] as they await us in the land of the living."[26]

He began working on a second exposition, based on Psalm 30/31, "In You O Lord, I Have Hoped." This meditation, a dialogue between *Tristitia*, Sadness or Despair, and *Spes*, Hope, speaks more directly to his situation. As he grieves over his separation from his cloister and his sins, Tristitia pushes him toward despair. Then Hope comforts him: God will not allow other men to confound and persecute forever. Tristitia appears again to remind him of his wayward life. "[God] guided you from the clatter of the world and the storm of the sea to the quiet port of the religious life; he gave you the habit of a holy community life; he wished you to be his priest; he enrolled you in the school of his wisdom. But you were always ungrateful and performed God's work carelessly despite knowing that it is written, 'the person who did God's work carelessly is cursed' [Jer. 48.10]. Still, the divine kindness did not leave you there but always gently urged you forward to better things (and this is crucial) bestowed on you the knowledge of the Scriptures. It put in your mouth the word of preaching and set you up in the middle of the people as one of the great men. You taught others and neglected yourself. . . . You have become nothing, and you will be nothing forever."

Yet even in near-despondency there is Hope. God is love, he reminds himself; he is infinite goodness and he will complete his work. God provokes the sinner to repentance so that he might make him worthy of his grace and lead him to life everlasting. "These are not your delusions and fantasies but divine inspirations. Suppose they are fantasies. Are they not good? Do they not stem from the virtue of faith? Since every good comes from God, these fantasies are indeed divine illuminations."[27] Even fantasies may be divine illuminations if they stem from faith—it was the most he could rescue from the ruin of his prophetic apostolate. In the midst of these reflections he was called to face the papal inquisitors who had arrived from Rome on May 19.

For his inquisitors Alexander VI had chosen men of high rank and pragmatic temper. Francisco Remolines, a fellow Catalan, was doctor of civil and canon law and a papal auditor (soon to be named bishop, then cardinal).[28] The Florentine rumor mill, always delighted with anecdotes about the peccadillos of Roman curialists, reported that for the length of his stay Remolines was provided with the sexual services of a young woman sent to his quarters in San Piero Scheraggio disguised as a boy. Another story, at least figuratively true, was that on his arrival Remolines boasted that he carried Savonarola's death warrant in his pocket. The other commissioner was Gioacchino Torriani, general of the Dominican Order. He had supported Savonarola's campaign to bring about San Marco's withdrawal from the Lombard Congregation, but in the face-off over the new Tusco-Roman Congregation he had prudently moved to the papal side. In this final chapter of the drama, the circumspect Torriani was satisfied to remain in the background and let Remolines take the lead.

With five Florentine officials, some who had served on the first commission, as observers, the commissioners began their questioning on May 20. Brief, almost cursory, and largely redundant, this third processo served principally to demonstrate that the Church was in charge when it came to dealing with its wayward sons. Remolines traversed much the same ground covered by the previous two processi, making a particular effort to wring more information from Savonarola about his collusion with prelates inside the curia. Although no startling new revelations were forthcoming, the transcript dramatically and meticulously records the debilitating effects on Savonarola of nearly two months of physical and spiritual torment.[29]

It began calmly enough. Asked by Remolines whether he reaffirmed all his previous testimony and whether he had confessed freely and not because of the torture, Savonarola replied that now that he had repented his sins he could say before God that in his confession he had told the truth. Had other ecclesiastical persons colluded with him in matters regarding the Church? None, he insisted, except for fra Domenico, fra Silvestro, and fra Niccolò da Milano, to whom he had confided his great project of a general council. Again he insisted that his contacts with princes and curialists had been limited. He had hoped for assistance from the emperor and the king of Spain whom he knew to be disgusted about the evil conduct of the Roman court. (That the papal commissioners allowed this almost casual reference to corruption at the curia to stand in the record is a testimony to the faithfulness of the transcript, and perhaps to the fact that even curialists knew it was futile to deny what everyone knew to be true.) Had the Frate said, as it had been reported, that the pope was no Christian, that he had never been baptized, and was not a true pope? He had never said these things, he replied, although he had written them in an unpublished letter that he afterwards burned.

What shredded Savonarola's already frayed self-possession was the prospect of more torture. When Remolines abruptly ordered him stripped and prepared for the rope he was seized by panic. Falling on his knees, he cried, "Now hear me God, you've caught me! I confess I have denied Christ. I lied. You, signori of Florence, you're my witnesses; I denied him for fear of the torture: if I'm to suffer I want to suffer for the truth. What I said I had from God. God, you're punishing me for denying you out of fear of torture; I deserve it!" After he was undressed he again fell to his knees and showing his mangled left arm, sobbed, "I've denied you, I've denied you God for fear of the torments, for fear of the torments." Hoisted into the air, his resolve "to suffer for the truth" quickly faltered and he cried out, "Jesus help me, this time you've got me!" Asked why he had spoken thus, he whimpered, "So that I might appear to be good; don't hurt me, I'll tell you the truth, for sure, for sure." Why had he denied (his previous confession)? "Because I'm crazy." Lowered, he explained, "I lose myself when I see the torture [instruments]; I can make more sense when I'm in a room with a few unintimidating people." Had his testimony been true in all respects? "It's true because it's true, and I'll always say so." Why then had he denied it just a moment ago? "I said that because I thought it might make you afraid to lay hands on me, that's why I said those things." After further questioning he was sent back to his cell with instructions to spend the night thinking about telling the whole truth.

The next morning, May 21, he was again asked to say whether all of his testimony, both to the government and papal commissioners, was the truth. He gave this pitiful, rambling reply. "Most Reverend Monsignor, those denials I made yesterday I made as a man terrified; I wanted to avoid that awful experience because I'm more susceptible than other people. Just looking at [the instruments of torture] is for me like getting ten turns of the rope. Everything that has been written—and I signed the first and second time— was true, and I must thank those citizens who treated me gently. If at first I didn't say the whole truth, it was because I was hiding my pride, but seeing that I was treated gently, I decided to tell the whole truth. If it seems that I have said little, don't be surprised: my deeds were important, but there weren't many of them; of great deeds there never are many. What I said yesterday, the denials and retractions, was out of fear. I did wrong and I beg your lordships' pardon. I was wicked; I want to save my soul and unburden my conscience, and therefore I ratify and will ratify everything with my signature. Since previously my answers were brief and restrained, I'm now willing to be more open and clear." He then affixed his signature to the previous day's testimony reaffirming the initial confession.

Still, confession had its limits. Had he ever said that Christ was a man like others, and that he himself could have been like him had he cared to? To this he replied sharply, "That's for crazies; that's an accusation [fra Domenico] Ponzo made. I wanted to be held to be a prophet, learned, holy, and wise; you shouldn't believe I'd have said something so contrary to my aim!"[30] When Remolines again threatened to torture him until he revealed more about his dealings for a Church council, he broke down in tears and self-reproach: "O frate, where have you been led? When I think how I got into this thing, I can only regret it; I don't know how I got into it; I think I'm dreaming."

If it is difficult to tell from this muddle of admissions, recantations, denials, and retractions what Savonarola believed about his prophetic mission at this point, this, it seems to me, is because he himself was no longer certain of its true nature. Failure and humiliation compounded with the fear and pain of the rope had eroded his sense that God had chosen him to be the apostle of the New Era, leaving him with remorse and shame, a penitent naked before his God and his judges. More threats, bindings, hoistings, and lowerings produced nothing new; the well of confession had run dry. Threatened with yet another turn of the rope, he declared, "I can't talk in the presence of so many; I'll say more when there are fewer people." How was it, then, Remolines asked mockingly, that he had spoken so boldly to so many thousands when he was in the pulpit? To which came this poignant reply: "At that time I was signore." Weeks of self-accusation and soul-searching had produced no insight into his own character as telling as this.

Examined, apparently without torture, in two sessions on May 22, Savonarola seems to have recovered his composure, but at the price of resignation. When it was announced that sentence would be pronounced on the following day, he joked, ruefully, "I'm in prison; if I can, I'll show up." Asked again about the reports of spiritual possession among the nuns of Santa Lucia, he replied, "You'll have to ask their confessor." He even chuckled when he recalled that one of these demented nuns had screamed "wretched friar" at him, tore the crucifix from his hands, and seizing him by his cowl, pounded him until he had been obliged to wrench himself free. He hadn't returned *there* for a good while!

In a brief last session, presumably at the request of the two Florentine Priors and other city dignitaries present, Savonarola was obliged to return to the matter of his political aims. With nothing left to lose, his answers were more than usually candid. He and his "sect" had had three main concerns, he said. The first, that they maintain majorities of their partisans in the Council so they could dominate the major offices, including the Signoria, where they needed six votes, the Ten of Liberty, and the Eight of Security. Again he insisted that he kept aloof from details.[31] He had regarded himself as a commander who relies upon a trusted captain. His captain had been Francesco Valori. Second, that they proceed strenuously against their adversaries, exploiting every mistake however small as an issue of justice. Third, that they remain united and furnished with arms—not that they would make the first move, but so that they could respond if their opponents moved against them. (He must have been referring to the weapons stored in San Marco in the last weeks.)

Fittingly, the final question had to do with his three famous promises to

Florence. What, they asked, had he meant to say or do when his material promises to Florence did not come about, and soon? How did he plan to get out of that? "O," he replied, "we weren't lacking in ways; especially because these 'soons' can take a long time to arrive on earth!"[32] This, then, was the wager he had made—whether with God, chance, or, as he feared in his own worst moments, the devil, perhaps he could no longer say.

CHAPTER 24

Silence

That same night fra Girolamo was notified that he had been condemned to die. He received the news in silence, then fell on his knees to pray. Requesting a confessor, he was sent Don Alessandro, a Benedictine monk from the Badia Fiorentina. He was also attended by Jacopo Niccolini, of the Company of the Neri, the fraternity of laymen dedicated to comforting the condemned awaiting execution. Around midnight he asked to be allowed to meet with fra Silvestro and fra Domenico, who had also received their death sentences. After Niccolini had consulted with his jailors the request was granted.

The three friars, each accompanied by his Benedictine confessor and Neri consoler, were conducted to another room where they were reunited. Don Antonio, fra Domenico's confessor, later reported how they passed their brief hour together. Each declared his faith and his hope for life eternal. Fra Silvestro also prayed that he might escape purgatory and that he would be strong when he came to the gallows. Fra Domenico, who during his own trial must have heard reports of Savonarola's recantation, added that everyone, including Commissioner Remolines and General Torriani, should know he no longer believed those reports. Later that evening he wrote to the Convent of San Domenico, where he was prior, urging the friars to keep Savonarola's teachings alive.[1]

Pseudo-Burlamacchi's luminous account of this last night of Savonarola's earthly existence probably owes more to hagiographical legend than to history, but it is practically all we have.[2] Savonarola chided his two disciples for not knowing how they should face death. It had been revealed to him, he said, that on receiving the notice of his condemnation fra Domenico had declared that he wished to be burned alive. But God, not man, the Frate reminded him, chooses the manner of our death. It had also been revealed to him that as he went to his execution fra Silvestro intended to make a public statement declaring their innocence and complaining that the proceedings were unjust. On no account must he do this, said the Frate: Christ was *innocentissimo* yet refused to declare his innocence from the cross; we must follow his example. After these reproofs the two kneeled before their mentor and received his blessing, then were separated again.

By this time fra Girolamo was very tired. Niccolini consented to take his head in his lap and in this way he passed the rest of the night. At daybreak he awoke and asked for a drink of water, which was brought to him in a cup so filthy that he was unable to drink. Someone took pity and brought him water in a clean cup. Then, embracing Niccolini, he said he would repay his many kindnesses by telling him some secret details of Florence's coming tribulations. "You know the things I have pre-announced here and how I predicted many tribulations for this city. Now I want to inform you of the time of its greatest tribulations. Know that it will take place when there will be a pope named Clement." Jacopo was skeptical, but he made copies of the pronouncement for the nuns of the Murate and the friars of San Marco, and in 1524, the year after Giulio de' Medici took the papal throne as Clement VII, he was to recall the prophecy.

Before leaving for the place of execution, the three heard Mass together. Fra Girolamo requested that he be allowed to hold the Host in his hands and when this was granted he recited another confession of faith, prayed that his sins be pardoned, and asked for forgiveness from "this city and this people" for whatever spiritual or temporal offense he may have given them. Then the three took Communion and "like thieves" were led to the place of their sacrifice. As they went down the stairs of the palace, fra Silvestro, who had seemed terribly frightened, suddenly appeared to have been touched by a divine warmth, his face shining with ardor. Now he was the one to rally his companions, and as they continued their descent they sang *Quam bonus*. At some point they were intercepted by fra Sebastiano, prior of Santa Maria Novella, that wellspring of anti-Piagnone sentiment. Claiming that he was acting on orders from General Torriani, fra Sebastiano demanded Savonarola hand over his scapular. Savonarola removed it, but asked that it first be laid on his hands, which seem to have been bound. When this was done he addressed the scapular: "O holy habit, how greatly I wanted you! By the grace of God you were granted me and I kept you immaculate until now, nor would I abandon you, but you have been taken from me."

On day 23

Fra Girolamo, fra Domenico, fra Silvestro at hour 13 were degraded then burned in the Piazza della Signoria.

The above-mentioned general (Torriani) and messer Francesco (Remolines) pronounced sentence notarized by ser Rinieri da San Gimignano.

The tenor of the sentence was that the Apostolic Commissioners having understood that the above mentioned [three friars] had committed the crimes related above in the interrogation of fra Girolamo on the 20th day and found them to be heretics and schismatics and to have preached radical change, etc., they sentenced them to be degraded and turned over to, that is to say left in the hands of, the secular judge. And so it was carried out.[3]

The execution followed immediately. Luca Landucci gave this account.

The sacrifice of the three friars was carried out on Wednesday morning, May 23. They were brought out of the palace and made to mount the scaffolding over the platform where the Eight, the Colleges, the papal envoy, the general [of the Dominican Order], many canons, priests, and friars of various orders, and Bishop Paganotti, who was responsible for performing the degradation (defrocking) of the three friars, were assembled. The ceremony was performed there, on the ringhiera. They were dressed in full clerical robes and then stripped of them one by one as the words of degradation were recited, frate Girolamo continuously declared to be a heretic and condemned to the flames. Their heads and [backs of their] hands were shaved as is done in such degradations. Next, the friars were turned over to the Otto, who immediately decided that they were to be hanged and burned, and in fact they were led out on the platform, to gallows formed like a cross. The first was frate Silvestro; he was hanged on one arm of the gallows, but there was not much tension because the rig didn't pull tightly, the rope not being taut enough, he suffered a long time, repeating *Gesu* over and over as he was hanging. The second was frate Domenico da Pescia, constantly repeating *Gesu;* the third was the Frate, the so-called heretic; he did not speak out loud, only murmuring as he hanged. None of them said anything, which caused great surprise, for everyone was hoping to see signs proving that what fra Girolamo previously told the people was the truth. This was especially so for the righteous people who hoped that God would be glorified, righteous living would begin, the Church renewed, and the infidel converted. So they were not without bitterness and no one made any effort to offer excuses. Many lost their faith.

When all three had been hanged, fra Girolamo in the center facing the palace, the scaffold was disconnected from the platform and the gunpowder previously placed on the circular platform around the cross was set afire, exploding like rockets and bombs. In a few hours they were incinerated, their legs and arms falling off little by little, bits and pieces sticking to the chains. Rocks were thrown to knock these pieces loose because it was feared that the people would collect them. Then the hangman and the other assigned workers cut down the post and burned it on the ground with a lot of brushwood that had been sent for, and they stirred the fire over the bodies to burn up every last remnant. Wagons were brought up and, accompanied by mace bearers, carted off every remaining speck of dust to the Arno, near the Ponte Vecchio, so that nothing would be found. In spite of this, however, some good people had such faith that they collected the ashes floating in the water; but they did it in great secrecy, fearfully, without saying a word about it, for it was as much as their lives were worth, [the authorities] being determined to destroy every relic of him.[4]

That the authorities brought off this theatrical, politically charged execution without hindrance and with scarcely an objection from the crowd was a triumph of Arrabbiati strategy. By dealing with the affair at home, they had been able to control the pace and outcomes of the first two processi and neutralize what remained of the Frate's followers. By holding the executions in the Piazza della Signoria rather than at the edge of the city, where criminals were usually dispatched, and by staging it to mimic the aborted fire trial, they made capital of what was for many Savonarola's ultimate breach of faith.

To be sure, weeks before sentence was pronounced, carefully managed revelations from the interrogation chamber had done their work. Still, some had refused to believe their ears. Even the disillusioned Landucci referred to the execution of the three friars as a "sacrifice." Those hoping for evidence of the friars' innocence continued to find it. In June some fanciulli took a brief visitation of gold-hued caterpillars as a sign that Savonarola's life had also been golden.[5] The partial trial records, printed and circulated, offered further details of his confessed duplicity, but the same material could feed the martyr legend already in the making. Thus it was said that because of his delicate body, further weakened by his well-known austerities, the Frate had been unable to withstand the repeated torments of the rope and given the answers demanded of him. It was also said that ser Ceccone had confessed to doctoring the transcript at the bidding of his employers. Piagnone legend-makers relished stories of the horrible deaths suffered by these Savonarola-haters.[6]

Anti-Savonarolans also resorted to supernatural explanation. In an exculpatory letter to the College of Cardinals written soon after the Frate's execution, Marsilio Ficino explained that it was no ordinary human hypocrite who had deceived the Florentines but an astute demon, servant of malicious astral forces—Antichrist himself. Audaciously simulating virtue and hiding his vices, mixing his prophecies with lies, he had, Ficino said, convinced the crowd of the truth of his predictions until even he himself believed in them and in his own rectitude.[7] For all its paranoia and craven bombast, Ficino's reading of Savonarola's career was psychologically perceptive on a key point which neither crestfallen Piagnoni nor triumphant Arrabbiati seem to have grasped— that the great preacher may have deceived no one more than himself.

CHAPTER 25

Echoes

After the fire had done its work came measures to snuff out the memory of the fallen prophet. Church and state joined in meting out prison terms, banishments, and fines to the most prominent keepers of the flame, both lay and clerical. To possess Savonarola's writings was a criminal offence. His books were to be surrendered, confiscated, destroyed. The San Marco friars were forbidden to discuss his teachings among themselves or with laymen, or even to utter the terms "Piagnone" or "Compagnaccio." San Marco and its allied houses were enjoined from conducting services and ceremonies in memory of their three martyrs or from singing *Ecce Quam Bonus* fra Girolamo's favorite psalm.[1] The very sound that had called to the Savonarolan faithful was stilled: la Piagnona, the great bell of San Marco, was taken down, whipped through the streets by the public executioner, and banished from the city for fifty years.

Still even the most diligent spies could not be everywhere or peer into every heart. If Savonarolan lauds were no longer heard in the streets, they might still be discreetly sung behind closed convent doors.[2] Sentences of banishment ran their course and exiles returned. Even the fifty-year sentence of la Piagnona was reduced; it was returned to San Marco in 1509. Piagnoni began to speak out again and "raise their crest a little," as Parenti put it. Inspired by their "four martyrs"—Savonarola, Domenico da Pescia, Silvestro Maruffi, and Francesco Valori—devotees resumed their campaigns for moral and political renewal.[3]

Arrabbiati and Piagnoni had common interests that pushed them toward a wary political accommodation. One was their determination to prevent the return of the Medici. Another was the recovery of Pisa, which, declared Savonarolan Giovambattista Ridolfi, would give Florence back her soul.[4] To achieve these objectives as well as to protect it against the continuing hostility of the papacy and the Holy League, Florence needed political unity, and this favored the continuation of the governo civile and Great Council with its indelible Savonarolan imprint. Moreover, leaders in both camps were convinced that the time had come to deal with a problem whose solution had eluded the great reformer, namely, the ineffectiveness of a government that limited its chief executive to a two-month term. In 1502 the Great Council voted to make the Gonfaloniere of Justice a lifetime office and elected Piero Soderini, brother of Paolantonio, Savonarola's old political ally and mentor. Piero was neither a Piagnone nor the Frateschi's favored candidate, but he promoted many Savonarolan goals. A skillful politician, he achieved in the next few years the long-deferred reform of the fiscal system, passage of sumptuary laws, and the setting of limits on the size of dowries. He also extended the Piagnone-sponsored Monte di Pietà, or communal loan fund, together with its corollary, the expulsion of the Jews.

Gonfaloniere Soderini also defended the alliance with the French. In 1499 the new French king, Louis XII, invaded Italy, deposed Duke Lodovico of Milan, and sent him to die in a French prison. For the next decade Louis was in and out of Italy, intermittently raising Florentine hopes that he would take up the role Savonarola had assigned to his predecessor. He sent a crusading fleet to the East, contracted—upon payment of a large subvention—to provide Florence with a military force to regain Pisa, and even convened a council in Pisa to reform the Church. Although these undertakings bore little fruit, being subject to the vagaries of Louis' inconstant enthusiasms and changing diplomatic strategies, the Florentines had little alternative but to cling to the French alliance and hope for better fortune or, as Piagnoni preferred to believe, the fulfillment of the divine plan.

In the event, Florence regained Pisa through its own initiative. Backed by Gonfaloniere Soderini, Niccolò Machiavelli, secretary of the Ten, was able to create a citizen militia and reduce the city's dependence on foreign condottieri of uncertain loyalty. The new model army was part of the force that laid siege to Pisa and took its surrender in June 1509. In his victory speech to the Great Council, Soderini declared that Italy now had no more powerful state than Florence, and he admonished his fellow citizens: "It is in your hands to make this republic and its territorial empire great, which can only be done through the observance of justice. . . . If you do this, your liberty and dominion will be very great indeed."[5] Girolamo Savonarola himself could hardly have put it better.

Soderini's chauvinist idealism, with its Savonarolan overtones, fell victim to political realities. After victories over Venice and its allies at Agnadello in 1509 and the Holy League at Ravenna in 1512 (preceded by the terrible French sack of Brescia, which Piagnoni believed to have been prophesied by Savonarola), Louis XII was defeated by the renewed Holy League coalition of Pope Julius II, Venice, and Emperor Maximilian's Swiss, German, and Spanish troops. Florence was left to fend for itself. In August of 1512 soldiers of the Spanish viceroy in the service of Pope Julius and Cardinal Giovanni de' Medici seized the town of Prato, a few miles from Florence, sacked it, and killed hundreds of its inhabitants. When the Florentines learned that six thousand Spanish troops were on their way to the city, they abandoned all thought of resistance. Soderini fled. Cardinal Giovanni de' Medici and other members of his family returned to the city as conquerors. They enlisted the support of leading citizens (many former republicans now becoming good Mediceans); convened a Parlamento, which appointed a balia, or civic commission; and proceeded to demolish the key institutions of the intervening two decades. Great Council and Council of Eighty were no more. They dissolved the militia (for his involvement with the Soderini government Machiavelli was imprisoned and tortured) and trashed the Great Hall of Five Hundred, symbol of the Savonarolan governo civile. Florence would now be ruled from Rome by ministers of Cardinal Giovanni, soon to be elected Pope Leo X (1513–21).

While Soderini and his allies had been trying to save the popular republic, Piagnoni kept Savonarola's apocalyptic teachings alive. San Marco friars spread the word locally, and their exiled brothers were making fresh converts in outlying Dominican houses and lay circles in Tuscany and beyond. Those teachings were received and interpreted in various ways.[6] Some grasped the essential unity of Savonarola's prophetic apostolate in which he fused Christian living (il ben vivere) with liberty, republican government, and civic apotheosis in a single glorious vision. Others developed those devotional, reformist, or political aspects that spoke to their particular inclinations. The mystical millenarianism of a Domenico Benivieni and the Neoplatonic Pythagoreanism of a Giovanni Nesi contrasted with the more conventional path of Church reform favored by friars Vincenzo Mainardi, Bartolomeo da Faenza, and their lay associates. And for every lapsed admirer, every Marsilio Ficino or Ugolino Verino, there was a Giorgio Benigno Salviati or Giovanfrancesco Pico della Mirandola who defied censorship and reprisals to defend Savonarola's memory.

Street preachers stirred the apocalyptic cauldron, claiming a share of Savonarola's prophetic and charismatic gifts. Martino di Brozzi, ragged, self-styled holy madman, appeared in Florence at the end of 1500 to declare that the killing of Savonarola proved that Florence and Rome were about to be scourged and the present Church not merely renewed but exterminated. He was imprisoned.[7] The artisan Pietro Bernardino, dubbed "Bernardino dei fanciulli," having marched in fra Domenico's youth squads, claimed the charismatic succession. Bernardino carried the notion of the redemptive power of youthful innocence beyond anything that had been preached by Savonarola. He adopted a ritual anointing of his followers as ushers of the New Age and barred his followers, the *Unti*, or Anointed, from accepting the sacraments from morally impure priests. This proved too radical for the local clergy, including his counselor Domenico Benivieni, and Bernardino was forced to take refuge with another Savonarolan loyalist, Giovanfrancesco Pico, Lord of Mirandola. In 1502, when Giovanfrancesco was forced to surrender his rule to his brother Lodovico, Bernardino was turned over to the ecclesiastical authorities and burned at the stake for heresy and schism.[8]

Bernardino's fate did not discourage other prophets and visionaries who, like Savonarola himself, took their own sufferings, or "martyrdoms," as proof that the time of tribulations and renewal was at hand. One apocalyptic text attributed to an otherwise unknown Carthusian named Albert of Trent, but probably the work of a Piagnone priest named Giovanni di Miglio, prophesied the coming of the Angelic Pope in 1504 and predicted that poor and humble people would unite to overthrow "every tyrannical sect." The Church would be destroyed in flames, replaced by a new and correct religion "from the islands of the sea" (the New World?).[9] His belief that this religion would be based on the Eternal Gospel linked him to the latter-day followers of Joachim of Fiore. In 1508 Antonio da Cremona, member of a Franciscan sect called the Amadeites, preached a millenarian sermon that centered on Florence as the New Jerusalem. Called before Archbishop Cosimo Pazzi, fra Antonio denied that he had been influenced by Savonarola in any way and pointed out that Florence had had many prophets.[10]

Given continuing social and religious discontents and a deeply rooted faith in the certain arrival of divine justice, Florence was to have many more. In his Advent sermons of 1513, the Franciscan fra Francesco da Montepulciano prophesied the election of a false pope who would be followed by tribulations and a deluge of blood; even nonagenarians would live to see it. He was so terrifying and persuasive, wrote Piero Parenti, that many Florentines, believing the cataclysm was at hand, stopped working. This caused great distress in the city, especially among the poor, although many were pleased, hoping the troubles would bring down the hated government. When the prophet suddenly fell sick and died, "all the people," especially women, came to kiss his hands and feet as he lay in state in Santa Croce.[11] About the same time Francesco da Meleto, a scribe at Santissima Annunciata, published *Convivio,* the first of a number of works in which he blended Savonarolan and other messianic themes with Joachim of Fiore's historical-apocalyptic scheme. According to da Meleto, the conversion of the Jews would take place in 1517, followed by the conversion of the Mahometans; the world victory of Christianity would take place by 1540. Francesco's scholarly pretensions brought him to the notice of influential reformers at the Vatican who were eager for him to have a hearing with Pope Leo X, although there is no record of his having done so. If he did, it did not go well for him: the Synod of Florence, called by Pope Leo in 1517 to deal with Savonarolism in all its manifestations, condemned Francesco's writings and ordered him to retract. He died in 1528, apparently still working on his prophetic theories.[12] By contrast, the renegade monk Don Teodoro di Scutari found his audience in the streets. Teodoro claimed that Savonarola had appeared to him in visions and endorsed him as the Angelic Pastor who would initiate the great reform. In 1515 he was tried, forced to abjure his claims, and sentenced to ten years' monastic detention. Four years later he escaped to an island in Lake Trasimeno where he continued to style himself Papa Angelico.[13]

Despite the efforts of the Synod of Florence, Piagnone republicanism asserted itself again in 1527, when a "barbarian" army nominally under command of the Holy Roman Emperor sacked the Eternal City, desecrated Saint Peter's, and forced another Medici pope, Clement VII, to take refuge in Castel Sant'Angelo. Many in Florence, seeing this as the promised scourging of the Church and a mandate to resume building the republican New Jerusalem, mounted a successful revolt against the harried agents of Medici rule. The restored republic again declared Jesus Christ king of Florence, and Savonarolans and secular republicans, radicalized by their long exclusion from power, joined in legislating against vice and Medici tyranny. Two years later pope and emperor resolved their differences long enough to send a joint force to besiege the city. After ten months, the starving citizens were forced to open their gates, and on August 12, 1530, the republic gave way to its Medici nemesis.

In a last effort on behalf of the Savonarolan vision, seventy-seven-year-old Girolamo Benivieni wrote a long letter to Clement VII.[14] Italy's sufferings, he asserted, confirmed Savonarola's predictions of the coming *flagello*, of famine, pestilence, and barbarian invasions, and this gave a strong presumption of validity to his three other major prophecies: renewal of the Church, conversion of the infidel, and the ultimate felicity of Florence. To be sure, the Frate had said that these prophecies were conditional, depending on human will. That the victorious pope would now accept his destiny as God's agent and fulfill these prophecies was Benivieni's fervent hope, a hope he underscored with Jacopo Niccolini's report that on the last evening of his life Savonarola told him Florence would suffer its greatest tribulations in the time of a pope named Clement.[15] Benivieni himself had confirmed this with Niccolini some weeks before the latter's death in 1526.

For this second Medici pope, however, the humiliations and sufferings of his family obscured any possible vision of himself as the Amos or Zechariah of the Savonarolan New Jerusalem. Instead he moved swiftly to take revenge. Piagnoni friars and laymen were again imprisoned or banished. Some were put to death. Not satisfied with punishing the principal actors, the ironically named Clement moved against their beneficiaries as well, destroying most of the charitable foundations established during this last Piagnone republic.[16]

The definitive restoration of Medici rule sealed the fate of Savonarolism as a viable political movement. One who understood the new reality was the elderly Florentine lay prophet Francesco de' Ricci. In vividly apocalyptic letters to Pope Clement he reaffirmed that Florence was the city of divine destiny, the coming New Jerusalem of Christian reform prophesied in Revelation and other biblical sources. But Ricci no longer urged constitutional reforms or a hearing for Savonarola's prophecies. He now maintained that Florence's destiny was linked to Medici rule: God had given Cosimo de' Medici and his successors custody of Florence for one hundred years in order that the renewal of the Holy Church would begin and be guided there. Seeing further tribulations at hand, Francesco called upon Clement to fulfill the divine charge to the house of Medici.[17] In this new political climate republican liberty had no place, not even on the agenda of Piagnoni.

If the cult of Savonarola himself survived the demise of its political hopes after the accession of the autocratic, relentlessly hostile Duke Cosimo I de' Medici in 1537, it was due in part to the San Marco friars and other devotees who played down the more militant aspects of the Frate's legacy. Under San Marco's sponsorship new biographies in hagiographical mode emphasized

Savonarola's sound doctrine and recorded stories of his miraculous posthumous interventions. As Lorenzo Polizzotto has put it, Savonarola was transformed into "a saintly exemplar of Counter-Reformation piety."[18] In that guise even the friars of Santa Maria Novella, bitter enemies of the Frate in his lifetime, were induced (after great pressure from San Marco)[19] to portray him in a convent fresco among the saints of the Dominican Order. This was too much for Cardinal Archbishop Alessandro de' Medici. In 1583 the cardinal, who had just banished the San Marco artist Bernardo Castiglione for a similar provocation, wrote to his kinsman Duke Cosimo:

> Thanks to the obstinacy of the friars of San Marco, the memory of Savonarola, almost extinguished ten or twelve years ago,[!] is today reviving and spreading everywhere, flourishing as never before. They diffuse his follies among male and female religious and seculars; the most audacious things they do with the young: they secretly recite a martyr's office in his honor; as though he were a saint they conserve all his relics, pieces of his gallows, his vestments, his scapulars, his hair shirt, his ashes and bones that survived the flames; they conserve the wine he blessed and give it to the sick, and recite his miracles; they reproduce his portrait in medallions of bronze and gold, cameos and prints; worse, they inscribe them "Martyr, Prophet, Virgin and Doctor.[20]

To this list Pope Clement VIII (1592–1605), however, considered adding the further distinction of "Saint." With the approach of the hundredth anniversary of Savonarola's death, Clement, a member of the noble Florentine and militantly Piagnone family of Aldobrandini, invited testimonies of Savonarola's holy life and posthumous miracles with a view toward initiating canonization proceedings. But pressed by the Medici grand duke and the Medici cardinal (who became Pope Leo XI in 1605, but died within a month), together with the formidable Jesuit theologian Cardinal Robert Bellarmine, he dropped the matter.[21]

Over three hundred years passed before Savonarolan devotees decided the time was ripe for another try. In 1935 the Dominican Benedetto Lenzetti officially proposed the initiation of a cause for Savonarola's beatification. Private and public testimonies to his life and sanctity have not diminished but rather increased, Postulator Lenzetti wrote, and recent appeals to introduce his cause at the Holy See have multiplied from every direction. In 1952 the publication of Roberto Ridolfi's *Vita di Girolamo Savonarola* and the launching of the so-called National Edition of Savonarola's works with the support of the Italian and Florentine governments were timed to coincide with the fifth centenary of Savonarola's birth and to publicize the Dominican canonization effort. The establishment in 1955 by the General Chapter of the Order of a historical commission to investigate Savonarola's life and works with a view toward introducing a cause of beatification was a major step in that direction. The reaffirmation of this goal by General Chapters in 1983 and 1995 indicated that the cause was ongoing. Still, as Savonarola himself knew, ecclesiastical Rome moves slowly and deliberately.[22]

Notwithstanding heavy surveillance, Florentine printers managed to publish a few of Savonarola's works posthumously, but the main centers of production shifted to Bologna, Pavia, Ferrara, and above all, Venice. In the century that followed his death the treatise *On the Simplicity of the Christian Life* was reprinted ten times, and the *Exposition* of Psalm 30/31, nine. An even more extraordinary afterlife was granted to Savonarola's *Manual for the Instruction of Confessors*, which although left unpublished at his death, in the next two centuries had at least forty-two printings. As with other famous confessors' manuals, including two by Saint Antoninus, the popularity of Savonarola's *Confessional* was undoubtedly due to its sympathetic tone and moderate spirit.[23] To smooth the way for inexperienced priests, he presented a compass for "the uncrossable sea" of writings—papal decretals, conciliar decrees, consilia, and canon laws dealing with sin and its remedies—that they would need in this most difficult task of directing consciences. His sympathy extended to the sinner as well as to the confessor: this was not Savonarola nemesis of the tiepidi, formidable Knight of Christ battling every manifestation of vice, but a kinder, gentler fra Girolamo, Physician of Souls, tolerant of human weakness, generous with the medicines of comfort and mercy. He urged that priests, in meting out punishments, should consider the circumstances in which the sin was committed and adjust the penalties accordingly. True contrition was more important than making satisfaction, but since improvement was a work in progress partial contrition (attrition) should be welcomed. Above all, confessors must send no one away in despair.

The same humane temper characterizes his other devotional and instructional writings, offering gentle corrective for the sins he so harshly denounced in his penitential sermons. Tepidity, or spiritual shallowness, was to be overcome by "inwardness"; lack of charity trumped by justice. Believers who practiced meditation and contemplated the wonder of Christ could no longer be content with outward forms and "ceremonies." Faith, he never tired of repeating, was the grace of Divine Providence, offered as a free gift. Made new by the love of God that accompanies faith, believers are justified, that is, transformed to righteousness. Through the free exercise of will they are able to abandon their lives of sin, devoting themselves to meditation on Christ and to virtuous living. Christian life is a process of spiritual perfection which is only completed in the next world.[24] The sacraments, he taught, are indeed vehicles of grace instituted by Christ, chief among them the Eucharist, but used irreligiously, that is, regarded merely as terminals rather than as portals through which believers can enter into true communion with the Father, they only harden sinners in their sin. Aided by *orazione mentale,* silent, individual prayer and by the contemplation of the crucified Christ, believers nurtured the love and inspiration that made it possible to serve and, ultimately, to imitate him.[25]

In his often-published *Expositions* on Psalms 51/50 and 31/30, the "prison meditations," Savonarola expressed the need for faith and divine forgiveness so poignantly that after reading them Martin Luther claimed him as a fore-runner and martyr of the Protestant Reformation. Calvin and other Protestant theologians concurred. (Savonarola appears on a nineteenth-century commemorative statue erected in Augsburg, Germany, to the heroes of the Reformation.) In their Scripture-based, faith-centered piety and their de-nunciation of a Church calcified in formalism and obsessed with temporal power, as well as in their apocalyptic conviction that divine judgment was imminent, the Italian friar and the German monk spoke a similar prophetic language. Still, I would argue that while fra Girolamo's views on grace, faith, free will, and the seven sacraments were essentially Thomist and Catholic, Brother Martin's doctrines of justification by faith alone and the priesthood of all believers were anti-scholastic and revolutionary.[26] Whereas Luther came to deny the magisterium of the Roman Church, Savonarola reaffirmed it— even when he was most at odds with it over its moral failures. But in the beleaguered conditions of the first Reformation century, Savonarolan and Protestant enthusiasts were likely to submerge differences and emphasize commonalities in their search for allies and precedents.[27]

As early as 1520 Luther's denunciations of Roman corruption and errant Catholic doctrine had been noted by the Florentine historian Bartolomeo Cerretani, who, in his *Dialogue on the Revolution of Florence,* linked him with Savonarola's earlier criticisms and his prophecy of the coming renovation of the Church.[28] But many Savonarolans who dreamed of a renewed Church were horrified by Luther's attacks on the efficacy of good works and his rejection of transubstantiation and priestly power, for he seemed to under-mine the saving grace of the sacraments. Alarmed by the spread of radical Protestant sects into Italy, Savonarolans joined with more conventional Cath-olics in the defense of Romanism.[29] Yet, the affinities, real and imagined, between Piagnoni and Protestants continued to alarm the enemies of each.[30]

In France, where prophecies of a messianic New Charlemagne had a long history, Savonarola's version found ready believers. Huguenots and French Catholics vied over his legacy. In his *Actes des martyrs* of 1564, which had "an enormous diffusion in the Protestant world," the Huguenot Jean Crespin, drawing upon English and German sources, placed Savonarola in the com-pany of such Reformation heroes as John Wycliff, Jerome of Prague, Arch-bishop Cranmer, Gaspard de Coligny, and Martin Luther himself.[31]

Savonarola's teachings of personal, unmediated devotion had particular resonance among women. Convinced that the weaker sex had deep, untapped religious sensibilities, Savonarola had regarded the enrichment of women's spiritual lives as an important part of his pastoral mission. Not surprisingly, his ideas for enhancing female religiosity favored penitence, moral discipline, meditation, and austerity. He had vigorously promoted the monastic life for women, and he and his friars served as directors and preachers in convents and tertiary houses. For their part, women had been a major, vocal presence at his sermons and enthusiastic participants in Piagnone-organized processions and festive celebrations. When the trial by fire was being prepared large numbers of women had clamored to enter the flames as champions of the cause. Consid-ered too emotionally fragile to see, much less participate in, such a harrowing spectacle, women had to be turned away by guards. When Savonarola re-treated with his party to San Marco after the disastrous *sperimento* he found hundreds of women waiting there to reaffirm their faith in him. This largely untapped and underappreciated fount of energy now found an outlet in female mystical devotion. With Savonarola's suffering and death on the gallows, the nature of his spiritual influence took on new dimensions. Enveloped in the aura of holy martyrdom, he now became a supernatural agent of charismatic experience. Women in particular responded to the new inspiration. Male Savonarolans had a variety of options and relative freedom to choose how they would maintain their connection with him, as campaigners for political and moral reforms, penitential preachers, or even prophets. Women were more likely to be drawn to the contemplative opportunities of praying in his name. This was in the spirit of Savonarola's own teaching: suspicious of female prophets, he had believed that the well-ordered cloister, with a male overseer, was the best place for women to develop their religious nature and meditative prayer its most suitable form.[32]

During Savonarola's lifetime women in religious communities in which he took a personal interest had often been restive under his interference. The tertiaries of the Florentine Convent of the Annalena, for example, fretted over his efforts to impose a rule upon them. The mysterious outbreaks of "demonic possession" that swept Santa Lucia may have been the nuns' way of resisting fra Girolamo's demands to increase their ascetic rigor.[33] After Savonarola's death the San Marco friars, believing his legacy was theirs to interpret and protect, encountered similar resistance. The visionary peasant woman Domenica Narducci, of the Florentine suburb of Paradiso, organized a quasi-conventual community under the supervision of San Marco but chafed at the friars' interference. In 1519, after a long contest, she was acquitted of a charge of heresy brought by a leading Piagnone, fra Tommaso Caiani.[34]

Even settled, prestigious female communities, such as the Observant Dominican Convent of San Jacopo di Ripoli, were pressed to accept San Marco's supervision. The sisters evolved a highly individual style of devotion based on Savonarola's teaching that illness and suffering were opportunities to deepen spiritual experience. Having long supported themselves as scribes and book printers, they had a strong sense of their own agency, and they resented the friars' efforts to direct their affairs. Between 1508 and 1512, the convent governor was the arch-Piagnone fra Mariano Ughi (ten years earlier he had been a volunteer for the fire trial). It was fra Mariano who largely worked out the modus vivendi that allowed the nuns a degree of administrative and spiritual autonomy while San Marco retained its prerogatives of oversight. The relatively harmonious system of shared cult helped San Jacopo survive repeated attempts by the authorities to end its veneration of the martyred Savonarola. In 1585 the Dominican General Sisto Fabbri, under pressure from Archbishop Alessandro de' Medici and Grand Duke Ferdinand de' Medici, forbade the very utterance of Savonarola's name by religious or lay persons, but this seems to have been no more effective than previous measures. In the case of the sisters of San Jacopo di Ripoli, fra Girolamo's idea of spiritual suffering may have given them the strength to persevere.[35]

Whereas Savonarola's prophetic message was intimately bound to Florence and its civic myth of power and glory, his mystical legacy went beyond such parochialism and so was more readily received in other cities and regions of Italy and beyond. Moreover, although charismatic Tuscan women in any way connected with Savonarola's cult were likely to be buffeted between the Scylla of San Marco's tutelage and the Charybdis of Medici persecution, elsewhere such women were free of those particular hazards—although seldom free of male interference. Of the several who achieved prominence two outstanding examples will have to suffice here.[36]

Colomba Guadagnoli da Rieti moved to Perugia in 1494 and soon began to manifest typical charismatic behavior including raptures, abstention from food, and visions. Piagnone legend had it that in 1498 she saw in a vision Savonarola and his two fellow martyrs ascending to heaven and wept at the ingratitude of the Florentines toward their prophet. In her advocacy of cloistered houses for Dominican tertiaries Colomba seems to have been following Savonarola's example; in return her ideas influenced fra Roberto Ubaldini, Savonarola's former secretary, who wrote a rule for the convent of Santa Caterina di Siena, a center of Savonarolan piety in Florence from its foundation in 1508.

The Dominican tertiary Lucia Brocadelli was one of the most prominent female charismatics touched by the Savonarolan mystique who flourished outside Tuscany. After she moved from Narni in southern Umbria to Viterbo in 1490, she became famous for her raptures and stigmata, including a vision of the Blessed Virgin modeled on Savonarola's account of his mystical journey to Mary's throne. By 1497 she had come to the notice of Savonarola's former patron, Duke Ercole d'Este, who tried to move her to Ferrara. The Viterbo solons demurred, but Estense determination, money, and influence prevailed. In 1499 Lucia was smuggled out of Viterbo in a laundry basket and took up residence in Ferrara where Duke Ercole built a house for her and her community of contemplatives. She used her prophecies and visions, including miraculous apparitions of Savonarola himself, to promote his cult as far as Spain. The strong Savonarolan imprint of her activities attracted powerful enemies, among them fra Girolamo's old antagonist Vincenzo Bandelli, now master general of the Dominican Order. She also gained the hostility of Lucrezia Borgia, daughter of Pope Alexander VI (although Lucrezia herself had acquired a Savonarolan advisor, the same fra Tommaso Caiani who had brought charges against Domenica of Paradiso). When Duke Ercole died in 1505 Lucia lost her powerful protector. Although helped to continue by the veteran Piagnone count Giovanfrancesco Pico della Mirandola and by Duke Ercole II, she never regained the vigor or effectiveness of those first years.[37]

With Lucia Brocadelli's death in 1544 and the inauguration in the following year of the Council of Trent, the model of the visionary, militantly prophetic woman of a certain degree of autonomy became passé. The new female exemplar of the Counter-Reformation was just as devout, just as likely to feel the mystical stirring of Christ in her heart, but she was more careful to let herself be guided in religious matters, including such vexing questions as the reform and future of the Church, by her male overseers. If some saintly women persisted in expressing themselves on those larger questions, they did so privately, as did Caterina de' Ricci and Maddalena dei Pazzi, two Savonarolan devotees of the later sixteenth century who were eventually supported for sainthood by Piagnoni activists.[38] After a half century of relative freedom, women's spirituality was once more being brought within conventional bounds. On balance this may have been a loss for the propagation of his cult, but Savonarola himself would probably have approved.

Over two hundred years passed before the image of Savonarola shed its Counter-Reformation camouflage and began once again to generate revolutionary idealism. In the nineteenth century, Risorgimento patriots rediscovered him as a hero of liberty, civic virtue, and social justice and, brushing aside the fact that he had always rejected appeals to national unity, repackaged him as a prophet of the new Italy.[39] Under the liberal nationalist banner Pasquale Villari in 1859 published the first volume of his great biography, *The Life and Times of Girolamo Savonarola*, which more than any other single work made the Frate a figure of modern scholarly interest and public inspiration. The Sicilian priest Don Luigi Sturzo (1871–1959) was no apocalyptic prophet, but in founding the Italian Popular Party in 1919 he tried to advance a Savonarola-like doctrine of social justice and Catholic reform. Sturzo too had to cope with a Church that ostensibly disapproved of clerical participation in secular politics, although his advocacy of a common front with the Socialist Party against Mussolini and refusal to countenance the Church's alliance with Fascism incurred the hierarchy's opposition to him and his movement. Lacking Church protection against the dictator, Sturzo was forced into exile in 1924. He returned in 1946, just after the founding of the Christian Democratic Party. Capitalizing on post–World War II sentiment for democratic and moral reform and on the fear of Bolshevism, Christian Democracy became the dominant force in Italian politics and government for almost a half century, drawing upon the Savonarolan legacy for some of its legitimizing, populist symbols. Giorgio La Pira, the mayor of Florence, went so far in his admiration for the Frate as to maintain a cell in San Marco. But the party finally succumbed to the very sins the Frate had inveighed against—greed, worldly ambition, and neglect of the common good.

CHAPTER 26

Afterwords

Listening to Savonarola preach during the embattled days of March 1498, Niccolò Machiavelli decided he was a crafty and dishonest opportunist ("he keeps changing with the times and coloring his lies to suit them"). Machiavelli never softened this withering appraisal and seldom mentioned Savonarola's claim to be a prophet without a verbal wink. In his *First Decennale* of 1504, a verse history of Florence's most recent decade of travail, his depiction of fra Girolamo was just this side of mockery: he was "the capon" whose voice was heard amongst a hundred roosters (*galli*, or Frenchmen), that "gran Savonerola" filled with the divine afflatus whose words sowed so much disunity in the city that his prophetic light had to be extinguished by a still greater fire.

In time, Machiavelli studied Savonarola's political career more seriously, if not more sympathetically, noting the constraints of his situation. But he was primarily interested in using the Frate's spectacular failure to illustrate his lessons in statecraft. In chapter 6 of *The Prince*, which he wrote in 1513, Machiavelli dignified Savonarola by setting him alongside Moses, Cyrus, Romulus, and Theseus, the greatest founders of new states. But where they were successful, the Frate, he pointed out, came to grief, for it is one thing to persuade people of the rightness of a course of action, quite another to keep them steadfast in it; in order to protect his creation a leader needs to have force at his disposal. Moses and the other founders succeeded because they were armed; Savonarola failed because he was unarmed, for when the multitude began to lose faith in him he had no means of holding firm those who had believed, nor could he make the unbelieving believe, and so his new order was ruined.

A few years later, in his *Discourses on the First Ten Books of Livy*, Machiavelli is even more explicit. Founders of new orders will be opposed by envious rivals and must be prepared to use violence against them. Moses and Brutus, for example, were obliged to kill many of their opponents. Savonarola, he perceived, understood that he needed to use force against his opposition, but as a cleric he had no arms at his disposal nor any authority to deploy them. Thus he was reduced to railing against his enemies, to reproach them as "the wise of the world," while hoping that his supporters, who did have the authority to raise arms, would take the cue and do what needed to be done. But they failed to do so and catastrophe followed.

Machiavelli paired Savonarola with another failed statesman, Piero Soderini. Elected Gonfaloniere for Life in 1502 in an effort to strengthen the popular republic, Soderini also understood that he was the object of *invidia* but, being inexperienced, believed that he could overcome it in time with generosity and kindness. Unfortunately, says Machiavelli, time was lacking, goodness was insufficient, fortune was fickle, and no amount of generosity was enough to banish the hatred. So it was that in failing to suppress their enemies both men were ruined: Soderini because he did not understand the need to meet envy with force, Savonarola because, though he understood it well enough, lacked the authority do so. In these examples Machiavelli is less concerned to censure the Frate's demagoguery than to expose his political weakness. Machiavelli too wants a viable state (preferably a republic) and in calling for renewal and in his hopes for a new prince who will redeem Italy he echoes Savonarola's language if not his eschatology. Whereas Savonarola believed that redemption would come from the Almighty, Machiavelli looked for a redeemer-prince who would know how to seize opportunity from Fortune and to act on it. God, he comments, with his inveterate irony, does not wish to do everything for us lest he rob us of our free will and our glory as men.

So, did Machiavelli think Savonarola failed because he mistakenly relied on Providence or because his clerical status disqualified him from using force? Apparently both: since the Frate was prohibited from using force he was obliged to put his hope in Providence—yet another irony. In any case, the figure of the great preacher is always present in Machiavelli's imagination, at least as a negative example and foil. Writing to Guicciardini in 1521, he says he had been imagining an ideal preacher for Florence, although he knew his creation would not please his fellow citizens. *They* want a preacher to show them the way to paradise, while *he* wanted one who would show them how to go to the house of the devil; *they* wanted a preacher who was prudent and sincere, *he* wanted one crazier than Ponzo, craftier than Savonarola, more hypocritical than frate Alberto. A preacher of this sort, having all the excesses of each rolled up into one, would surely teach the Florentines the way to hell, "because I believe that this would be the true way to go to paradise, to learn the way to the Inferno and thus to avoid it."[1]

A decade after the last act of the Savonarolan drama came to its fiery end, Francesco Guicciardini reflected on the Frate's career in his *History of Florence*. Guicciardini was the son of a leading Piagnone and may even have been one of fra Domenico's fanciulli.[2] Not yet thirty, he was already experienced in administrative and diplomatic affairs and showed the capacity for dispassionate analysis of men and events that was to make him one of Italy's greatest historians. On Savonarola's crucial intervention in the post-Medicean republic his judgment was largely favorable, as he was on the qualities of the man himself.

> The work he did in promoting decent behavior was holy and marvelous; never had there been as much goodness and religion in Florence as there was in his time. After his death [these] disappeared, showing that whatever virtue there was had been introduced and maintained by him. . . . When Piero had been expelled and the parliament [i.e., the Parlamento of December 2, 1494] convoked, the city was so badly shaken and the friends of the old regime were in such disfavor and danger that even Francesco Valori and Piero Capponi could not protect them. That many would suffer great harm seemed inevitable. If that had come about, it would have been a great blow to the city, for many of them were good, wise, and rich men of great houses and family connections. Dissension would surely have arisen among those who governed. . . . New upheavals, more parliaments, further expulsions of citizens, and several revolutions would have been the result; and in the end Piero would perhaps have returned, which would have meant disaster and ruin for the city.
>
> It was [Savonarola] alone who made it possible to avoid all this confusion and chaos. He introduced the Great Council, which put a bridle on all those eager to become masters of the city. He proposed the appeal to the Signoria (rightly, from the Signoria to the Great Council), which acted as a safeguard for the preservation of the citizens. He brought about universal peace simply by impeding those who wished to punish Medici supporters under color of establishing the ancient order.

"Without doubt these efforts saved the city and, as [Savonarola] so truly said, worked to the advantage of both those who now governed and those who had governed." But whether Savonarola was a true prophet, Guicciardini was unable to say. "Because the results of his works were so good, and because several of his prophecies were fulfilled, many people continued to believe for a long time that he was truly sent by God and that he was a true prophet, despite the excommunication, the trial, and his death. For my part I am in doubt and have no firm opinion on the matter. I shall reserve my judgment for a future time, if I live that long; for time clears up everything. But I do believe this: if he was good, we have seen a great prophet in our time; if he was bad, we have seen a great man. For, apart from his erudition, we must admit that if he was able to fool the public for so many years on so important a matter, without ever being caught in a lie, he must have had great judgment, talent, and power of invention."[3]

"Time clears up everything." Would that it were so. A quarter century on, Guicciardini wove the insights of a long, distinguished public career into his masterwork, the *History of Italy*. Revisiting the tumultuous years of the French invasion, the overthrow of Piero de' Medici, and the republic of the Great Council, he credited Savonarola for using his putative "divine authority" to save the new republic from the control of a small, self-seeking elite.[4] But whether Savonarola was "good" and a true prophet or "bad" and a great man, he offered no final judgment.[5]

Machiavelli and Guicciardini arrived at different conclusions about Savonarola and his achievement in part because of their different temperaments, in part because they looked at his career from opposite ends. Machiavelli was primarily interested in the reasons for Savonarola's downfall, from which he derived a fundamental lesson in the art of statecraft, namely, that given the natural inconstancy of humankind, polities tend toward entropy. Just as state building requires vision, so the new order must have force at its disposal in order to sustain it. Prophets like Savonarola who do not have force at their command are reduced to hectoring and fakery, symptoms of impotence. Guicciardini, on the other hand, observed the Savonarolan phenomenon from its optimistic beginning rather than its dismal ending. His positive appreciation of Savonarola's intervention in the crisis of 1494 is first of all a lesson in historical objectivity. Setting aside his own preference for government by elites, Guicciardini acknowledged that the Frate had saved the city from chaos and ushered in an extraordinary interlude of peace and Christian living. Although he was fascinated by Savonarola's charismatic personality (he later made a catalogue of fra Girolamo's prophecies), he suspended judgment as to his legitimacy as a prophet. Perhaps this too is a lesson for biographers and historians. Framed in absolute categories of good or evil, divine illumination or unholy pretense, the issue of Savonarola's prophetic legitimacy is better left to theologians and cultists.[6]

As to Guicciardini's dichotomy between the good prophet and the bad man who was a great statesman, the best solution, in my view, is to embrace both alternatives: if prophets are those who in deploring the sinfulness of their time come to believe they have been vouchsafed a vision of a new and better age and are convinced that it is their sacred duty to expound the meaning and consequences of this to their people, Savonarola was surely a prophet. That he drew his energy from the adulation of crowds, evinced greater certainty than he felt, treated the scenarios of his imagination as heavenly visions, and manipulated the political system to the advantage of his partisans (those intelligenze and "half" intelligenze) should be clear to anyone who studies his career without prejudice. If these things mean that fra Girolamo was "bad" in the hagiographic sense, they were also part of what made him "great," as Guicciardini conceded.

In 1863, during the revival of the Savonarola cult, George Eliot completed her novel *Romola*. Set in Florence in the years 1494–98, the central character of the novel is the fictional heroine of the title, but it is Savonarola's presence that shapes its moral universe. It is he who confronts Romola with the issues she must resolve just as he actually confronted Florence. George Eliot was not a professional historian, but she was liberally educated and historically sophisticated, with a knowledge of the classics and modern languages and a deep interest in the history of religion. Aspiring not only to create an accurate picture of Renaissance Florence and its people, but also to understand the nature of their fascination for Savonarola, Eliot read his sermons and writings and immersed herself in the literature and idiom of the time. Her success in bridging the four-hundred-year historical and cultural divide between herself and Savonarolan Florence was remarkable, and her judgment of the Frate himself nuanced and independent.

> In Savonarola's preaching there were strains that appealed to the very finest susceptibilities of men's natures, and there were elements that gratified low egoism, tickled gossiping curiosity, and fascinated timorous superstition. His need of personal predominance, his labyrinthine allegorical interpretations of the Scriptures, his enigmatic visions, and his false certitude about the Divine intentions, never ceased, in his own large soul, to be ennobled by that fervid piety, that passionate sense of the

infinite, that active sympathy, that clear-sighted demand for the subjection of selfish interests to the general good, which he had in common with the greatest of mankind. But for the mass of his audience all the pregnancy of his preaching lay in his strong assertion of supernatural claims, in his denunciatory visions, in the false certitude which gave his sermons the interest of a political bulletin; and having once held that audience in his mastery, it was necessary to his nature—it was necessary for their welfare—that he should *keep* the mastery. The effect was inevitable. No man ever struggled to retain the power over a mixed multitude without suffering vitiation: his standard must be their lower needs, and not his own best insight.[7]

George Eliot was no more able than Machiavelli or Guicciardini—or anyone—to see into the heart of the man, but she perceived his predicament and his contradictions better than most. Persuading himself that he understood the divine plan revealed in the Apocalypse and stimulated by his successes to believe that God had chosen him as his messenger, Savonarola plunged into the affairs of the world to lead it to a better place. Later, disgraced by the failure to produce a miracle and broken by "the rope," he would acknowledge that he had been inspired by ambition for glory and power. The self-accusation was revealing, not altogether forced or misplaced: in proclaiming that he was God's apostle to the Florentines and that the city would be "richer, more glorious, more powerful than ever," he had been more than a little opportunistic, as he acknowledged. Having won credit and fame as a prophet by speaking truth to power, Savonarola found that in his own exercise of power, truth unalloyed by expediency and compromise was a difficult ideal to follow. His post hoc prophecies, ad hoc visions, and claims to divine illumination were all in the service of that truth, but they were also symptoms of increasing megalomania. In demonizing the "tiepidi" and calling for the violent suppression of dissent and the savage punishment of "sodomites," he believed he was leading Florence to the New Jerusalem, but he was also traveling a path of increasing fanaticism that could only take him to desperation, delusion, and disaster. Still, it is unhelpful to dismiss Savonarola as a fanatic or a charlatan; this obscures his noble vision and slights his strenuous efforts on behalf of social justice and political liberty, as well as his repeated calls for the moral and spiritual rescue of a Roman Church sliding ever closer to the brink of ruin. It is equally unhelpful to exalt him as a saint, for this puts

him beyond the reach of human understanding. The challenge is to integrate
—as he himself never ceased trying to do—the irascible puritan at war with his
world, the charismatic preacher who, as Machiavelli would have it, adapted
"his lies" to the times, the ascetic contemplative enraptured by divine love,
and the militant herald of a new age.

Notes

Abbreviations

CHAPTER I. The Making of a Moralist

1. Texts, dating, and analysis of Savonarola's poetry in his *Poesie.*

2. *Prediche sopra i Salmi* I, 256 (May 31, 1495).

3. Contemporary and near-contemporary biographies of Savonarola tend strongly toward the hagiographic, particularly in their accounts of his early years. I have cautiously used the following:

a. Giovanfrancesco Pico della Mirandola, *Vita Hieronymi Savonarolae* and its sixteenth-century Italian translation *Vita di Hieronimo Savonarola.* Giovan-francesco Pico was, like his uncle Giovanni Pico, close to Savonarola, and like his uncle a philosopher. See Charles B. Schmitt, *Gianfrancesco Pico della Mirandola and His Critique of Aristotle* (The Hague, 1967).

b. "Vita Beati Hieronymi, martiris, doctoris, virginis ac prophetae eximii," MS BNF Conventi soppressi I.VII.28.

c. *La vita del Beato Ieronimo Savonarola scritta da un anonimo del sec. xvi e già attribuita a fra Pacifico Burlamacchi.* I shall refer to it as Pseudo-Burlamacchi. Heavily dependent on the *Vita latina* and like it strongly hagiographical. See Polizzotto, *Elect Nation* 324–328; Julia Benavent, "Le biografie antiche di Girolamo Savonarola," *Studi savonaroliani,* ed. Gian Carlo Garfagnini (Florence, 1996) 15–21 and "La cuestión de las biografías antiguas de fra Girolamo Savonarola," in *La figura de Jerónimo Savonarola y su influencia en España y Europa,* ed. D. Weinstein, J. Benavent, I. Rodriguez (Florence, 2004) 161–168; Roberto Ridolfi, "Soluzione di un fondamentale problema Savonaroliano: dipendenza dello Pseudo-Burlamacchi dalla *Vita latina: prolegomeni ed aggiunte alla Vita di Girolamo Savonarola* (Florence, 2000).

d. Benedetto Luschino, *Vulnera diligentis.* On Luschino, see Stefano Dall'Aglio, "Benedetto Luschino, 'biografo' di Savonarola: il *Cedrus Libani* e il *Vulnera diligentis* in *La figura*" 131–150.

4. He is described as "a student of the arts in the city of Ferrara" in a document of June 21, 1473, cited in "Apologeticum Conventus S. Marci Florentiae," ed. A. F. Verde O.P., E. Giaconi, *RN* ser. 2, 37 (1997) 91 n. 45.

5. *Prediche sopra Aggeo* 324–325 (December 21, 1494). On Savonarola's rejection of the Renaissance cult of the family, see Michael Mullett, *Popular Culture and Popular Protest in Late Medieval and Early Modern Europe* (London, 1987) 127–130.

6. On February 14, 1496, Bardo Strozzi would write to fra Girolamo from Ferrara for help in recovering family property so that he could return to live in Florence. *Epistolario di fra Santi Rucellai,* 112–115.

7. Fra Benedetto Luschino said that after Savonarola's death he had this story from fra Mauro Savonarola, then in perpetual exile from Florence (at San Romano di Lucca), *Vulnera diligentis* 3 and n. 24. Maurelio was a younger brother who, after taking orders, followed Girolamo into the Dominican Order, taking the name fra Mauro and joining the San Marco community.

8. "De ruina mundi," *Poesie* 3–5. In an exhaustive critical note Martelli ably refutes theories of a later date and argues convincingly for 1472. Ibid. 201–206. English translation in *Savonarola: A Guide to Righteous Living* 61–63. For fra Girolamo's views on poetry, see

his *Apologeticus de ratione poeticae artis* in Savonarola, *Scritti filosofici* I, 211–272; Eugenio Marino O.P., "Sul trattato *apologeticus de ratione poeticae artis* di fra Girolamo Savonarola," *Frate Girolamo Savonarola e il suo movimento, MD* n.s. 29 (1998) 179–246; idem, "Le poesie del 'Giovane' Savonarola," *Crisi 'Mendicante' e Crisi della Chiesa, MD* n.s. 30 (1999) 375–446.

9. *Poesie* 204.

10. *Lettere e scritti apologetici* 5–6.

11. *De contemptu mundi* in Savonarola, *Operette spirituali* I, 3–7.

12. Pope Innocent III's *On the Misery of the Human Condition,* trans. Donald Roy Howard (Indianapolis, 1969).

13. Mullett argues—somewhat tendentiously I think—that the poem already contains the message of moral renewal that was to become one of Savonarola's main prophetic themes. *Popular Culture* 134.

14. *Prediche sopra Ezechiele* I, 374 (February 28, 1497).

15. Gianfrancesco Pico, *Vita* (Latin version) 114.

16. The incident is reported by Pseudo-Burlamacchi 8.

17. Virgil, *Aeneas* III, 44, trans. W. F. Jackson Knight (Penguin, 1956).

18. *Lettere e scritti apologetici* 3–6.

19. Ibid. 8.

20. The St. Francis story derives from St. Bonaventure's *Legenda maior* II.4. Johannes Jörgensen, *St. Francis of Assisi,* trans. T. O'Connor Sloane (New York, 1913) 47 n. 1.

CHAPTER 2. The Making of a Preacher

1. "This relationship of the outer to the inner person, of the active to the contemplative, lies at the very heart of the Constitutions and was the soul of Dominican life as it was lived in the convents of the Observance." Hood, *Fra Angelico* 46. On the beginnings of the Order and its relation to the Franciscans, Little, *Religious Poverty* esp. 152–169. See also Hinnebusch, *Dominican Order.*

2. On the Dominican educational system in general I have learned much from M. Michele Mulchahey, *"First the Bow is Bent in Study": Dominican Education before 1350* (Toronto, 1998) and her "More Notes on the Education of the Fratres Communes in the Dominican Order, Elias de Ferrariis of Salagnac's *Libellus de doctrina fratrum,*" in *A Distinct Voice: Medieval Studies in Honor of Leonard E. Boyle, O.P.,* ed. J. Brown, W. P. Stoneman, L. E. Boyle (South Bend, 1997) 328–369.

3. "Preachers reached into every nook and cranny of the social world." Peter F. Howard, "The Aural Space of the Sacred in Renaissance Florence," in *Renaissance Florence: A Social History,* ed. R. J. Crum, J. T. Paoletti (Cambridge, 2006) 376–393. Quote on 378.

4. *Prediche sopra Aggeo* 324–325.

5. *Poesie* 10–12. For the question of dating, 211–212.

6. Gianfrancesco Pico della Mirandola, *Vita Hieronymi Savonarolae* 116; Pseudo-Burlamacchi 13.

7. Garzoni, who wrote biographies of Saint Dominic and Saint Thomas Aquinas, willed his library to the Convent of San Domenico and was buried in its church when he died in 1505. Charles Trinkaus, *In Our Image and Likeness: Humanity and Divinity in*

Italian Humanist Thought, 2 vols. (Chicago, 1970) I, 271–2. Garzoni's writings on the human condition, ibid. 272–293.

8. The two letters Savonarola received from Garzoni are published by Gherardi, *Nuovi documenti* 37–39. Since the letters are undated, we cannot be absolutely sure that the correspondence took place in these first convent years. Ridolfi assigns them to 1487 or later, when Savonarola had returned to Bologna after his first unsuccessful stint as a preacher in Florence. Ridolfi, *Vita* 29 and 284 n. 18, but I prefer the earlier dating because Garzoni writes as though Savonarola was newly arrived in Bologna and at the beginning of his studies, that is, between 1475 and 1479.

9. Fra Roberto Ubaldini in "Annalia Conventus S. Marci" fol. 153r.

10. Pseudo-Burlamacchi 12–13.

11. *De Ruina Ecclesiae* in Savonarola, *Poesie* 6–9. For his transcription of the poem together with his line by line annotations, Cattin, ed., *Il primo Savonarola* 210–214. Cattin dates it 1475 or thereabouts. English translation and Savonarola's annotations in *Savonarola: A Guide to Righteous Living* 64–68.

12. I base my discussion of Savonarola's academic career partly on the study by Michael Tavuzzi O.P., "Savonarola and Vincenzo Bandello," *AFP* 69 (1999) 199–224.

13. Ibid. 201.

14. See A. Ferrua, "Bandelli (Bandello), Vincenzo," *DBI* 5 (1963) 666–667.

15. Tavuzzi, "Savonarola and Bandello" 212.

16. Tavuzzi argues persuasively that Bandelli was teaching in the Bologna studium as bachelor of sciences at the time Savonarola was a student there, and that he was one of Savonarola's teachers. The point is important considering the subsequent relations between the two: ibid., particularly 203–205. For the view that Bandelli was not there at the time: Ridolfi, *Vita* 10.

17. Tavuzzi, "Savonarola and Bandello" 210. Although Savonarola already held such views at the beginning of his career, there is no evidence to support Tavuzzi's contention that he "clamoured" for such spiritual reforms while he was at San Domenico. The sermons Tavuzzi cites in evidence are from 1496: *Prediche sopra Amos e Zacchariu* III, 286–314 and *Prediche sopra Ruth e Michea* I, 69–101.

18. Cattin, *Il primo Savonarola* 170–171.

19. Pseudo-Burlamacchi says that to Pico, Savonarola appeared so wonderful in his mode of life, his teaching, and his skill in disputation that he felt he could not live without him. Therefore, when Pico was living in Florence, he persuaded Lorenzo that he would reap honor and glory and do much good for the youth of the city by bringing Savonarola to the Convent of San Marco. Pseudo-Burlamacchi 16–17.

20. Cinozzi, "Estratto d'una epistola," in *Scelta di prediche e scritti di Fra Girolamo Savonarola,* ed. Villari, Casanova 10. Pseudo-Burlamacchi follows fra Placido almost word for word, including the erroneous date and reasons for the move. Pseudo-Burlamacchi 16.

CHAPTER 3. The Making of a Prophet

1. Vespasiano da Bisticci, *Vite* 272–273.

2. Nicolai Rubinstein, "Lay Patronage and Observant Reform in Fifteenth-Century Florence," *Christianity and the Renaissance: Image and Religious Imagination in the Quattrocento* (Syracuse, 1990) 64–82.

3. Isabella Gagliardi, "Firenze e gli eredi spirituali di Silvestro Gozzolini tracce per una storia dall'insediamento silvestrino di San Marco, 1290–1346," *Silvestro Gozzolini e la sua congregazione monastica: atti del convegno di studi tenuto a Fabriano, monastero S. Silvestro Abate, 4–6 giugno 1998* (Fabriano, n.d.) 169–201.

4. On Medici patronage of San Marco: Dale Kent, *Cosimo de' Medici;* Hood, *Fra Angelico;* "La cronaca del convento di San Marco," ed. Raoul Morçay O.P. in *ASI* 71 (1913) 1–29; "Annalia Conventus S. Marci."

5. "Look everywhere in the convents, you'll find them full of the coats of arms of those who built them. I turn my head upwards expecting to see a crucifix over that doorway and there is a coat of arms. Go further, look up, there's another coat of arms. Arms everywhere . . . [even] on the back of vestments, so that when the priest stands at the altar the arms can be clearly seen by the people." *Prediche sopra Amos e Zaccaria* II, 26.

6. "Annalia Conventus S. Marci" fol. 11r.

7. Ibid. fols. 10v–11r.

8. *Scritti filosofici* I, 373–374; Garin, *La cultura filosofica* 209.

9. *Scritti filosofici* I, 208.

10. Ibid. 170–172.

11. Howard, *Beyond the Written Word,* chap. 8.

12. In a marginal note on an autograph manuscript, Cattin, *Il primo Savonarola* 13, 105.

13. Cinozzi, "Estratto d'una epistola" in *Scelta di prediche e scritti,* ed. Villari, Casanova 10.

14. Texts and comments on these sermons in Cattin, *Il primo Savonarola* 106–112, 117–128.

15. Ibid. 262–267.

16. Ibid. 304.

17. *Sermoni sopra il principio della Cantica.* The editor's arguments for assigning these sermons to Lent 1484 are convincing.

18. Ibid. 43.

19. I follow the editor here as in all of my discussion of these sermons (ibid. 225–234). For a different interpretation, see Riccardo Fubini, "Politica e profezia in Savonarola: considerazioni di uno studioso profano," *Frate Girolamo Savonarola e il suo movimento, MD* n.s. 29 (1998) 573–592.

20. "Estratto d'una epistola fratris Placidi de Cinozzis" 11. Assessment of the quality of Savonarola's early preaching and its reception is compromised by the efforts of fra Girolamo himself as well as of Cinozzi and other Savonarola hagiographers to emphasize the contrast with his new, prophetically inspired style.

21. *Prediche sopra l'Esodo* I, 50 (February 18, 1498).

22. *Poesie* 13–15.

23. Scholars have tended to accept Savonarola's recollection (in his first processo) that he initially proclaimed his message of tribulation and renewal of the Church in his San Gimignano Lenten sermons of 1485 and 1486, thus making these sermons a major turning point in his prophetic career. In the surviving sermon drafts, however, I find only generic references to punishment and nothing of the great renewal he was to prophesy after his return to Florence in 1490. See "Girolamo Savonarola: Il Quaresimale di S. Gimignano (1486) 'rationes flagellorum' e rationes fidei," ed. Armando F. Verde O.P., *MD* n.s. 20 (1989) 167–253 and Cattin, *Il primo Savonarola* 42–56, 135–146; Verde, "Et andando a San

Gimignano a predicarvi: la predicazione di Savonarola a San Gimignano," *Girolamo Savonarola a San Gimignano,* ed. S. Gensini (Florence, 2003) 23–57. That Savonarola made no reference to these supposed prophecies when he returned to Florence after Lent of 1486 suggests that at the time he did not regard his preaching as innovative. Cattin notes the absence in the San Gimignano sermons of references to the renewal and observes that the San Giorgio episode "was no bolt of lightning," although the San Gimignano sermons "reveal a process of maturation and deepening, which gradually conducted Savonarola to announce later in a precise way what he had first intuited indistinctly." Cattin, *Il primo Savonarola* 135–144. The notion that this was a "maturation and deepening" of what he had already "intuited" assumes as fact what cannot be known, but apart from this I agree with Cattin's conclusion as to the incremental nature of Savonarola's prophecy.

24. On Joachim and his influence: Reeves, *Influence of Prophecy* passim; West, *Joachim of Fiore;* McGinn, *Calabrian Abbot.*

25. Rab Hatfield notes that more precisely, "Joachim did not believe in the Millennium; his State of the Holy Ghost is intended as an alternative to it." Not Christ but the Holy Ghost would reign for twenty-eight generations, or 840 years, an era of contemplatives. "Botticelli's *Mystic Nativity,* Savonarola and the Millennium," *JWC* 58 (1995) 108. This is to give a very strict definition of the millennium. But it seems to me that the critical element in his preaching is the forecast of an age of earthly spiritual felicity, whether of Christ or the Holy Ghost, before the Last Things. (*see Fig. 7*)

26. Saint Bernardino da Siena, "De fide et mortua," chap. 2, Sancti Bernardini Senensis *Opera omnia,* 9 vols. (Quaracchi-Florence, 1950–1965) III, 109.

27. Giampaolo Tognetti, "Le fortune della pretesa profezia di san Cataldo," *BSI* 80 (1968) 273–317.

28. Cesare Vasoli, "A proposito delle tradizioni profetiche e millenaristiche nella storia religiosa italiana tra la fine del Quattrocento e gli inizi del Cinquecento," *Civitas mundi studi sulla cultura del Cinquecento* (Rome, 1996) 19.

29. Reeves, *Influence of Prophecy* 165, 260–261.

30. Fritz Saxl, "A Spiritual Encyclopaedia of the Later Middle Ages," *JWC* 5 (1942) 84.

31. Celenza, *Piety and Pythagoras* 2.

32. Niccoli, *Profeti e popolo* 21.

33. Claire L. Sahlin, *Birgitta of Sweden and the Voice of Prophecy* (Woodbridge, Suffolk, 2001).

34. *Prediche sopra Ezechiele* I, 274 (February 21, 1497).

35. Stéphane Toussaint, "Profetare alla fine del Quattrocento," *Studi savonaroliani,* ed. Gian Carlo Garfagnini (Florence, 1996) 168.

CHAPTER 4. Florence and the Medici

1. Nicolai Rubinstein, "The Beginnings of Political Thought in Florence" *JWC* 5 (1942) 198–227.

2. Goldthwaite, *Economy* introduction and chap. 1.

3. Sean O' Faolain, *A Summer in Italy* (London, 1949) 102, quoting John Ruskin, *The Seven Lamps of Architecture: The Works of John Ruskin,* 14 vols. (New York, 1885) XII, 141. Thanks to Julia O'Faolain and Lauro Martines for supplying this reference.

4. Excellent overviews by Brucker, *Renaissance Florence,* and Najemy, *History.*

5. *Cronica di Giovanni Villani* III.

6. There is an extensive literature on the history of this French pseudo-prophecy, which, incidentally, foresees the destruction of Florence as well as Rome. See especially Maurice Chaume, "Un prophetie relative a Charles VI" *RML* 3 (1947) 27–42.

7. Fazio degli Uberti, "Firenze"and "Fiesole," in *Poesie minori del secolo XIV,* ed. E. Sarteschi, *Scelta di Curiosità inedite o rare,* vol. 77 (Bologna, 1867) 6–13.

8. Najemy, *History* 151–155.

9. *Cançon del detto Bruscaccio quando fu rotto il duca di Melano a Mantova,* Antonio Medin, "Le rime di Bruscaccio da Rovezzano" *GSI* 25 (1895) 224–226.

10. G. B. C. Giuliari, ed. *Prose del giovane Buonaccorso da Montemagno, Scelta di Curiosità Letterarie e Rare* (Bologna, 1874) 141, 26, 57. Giuliari, xvi–xviii, attributes the orations to another humanist rhetorician, Buonaccorso da Montemagno, but the evidence favors Porcari.

11. The classic treatment of the formation of Florentine civic humanist ideology is Hans Baron's *The Crisis of the Early Italian Renaissance.* I deal with Florence's manipulation of the myths and symbols of Roman imperialism at greater length in my *Savonarola and Florence* chap. 1. See also Alison Brown, "The Language of Empire" in *Florentine Tuscany: Structures and Practices of Power,* ed. W. J. Connell, A. Zorzi (Cambridge, 2000) 32–47.

12. A good introduction to the condottiere phenomenon is Michael E. Mallett, *Mercenaries and Their Masters: Warfare in Renaissance Italy* (London, 1974).

13. Anthony Molho, *Marriage Alliance in Late Medieval Florence* (Cambridge, Mass., 1994). Najemy, *History* esp. 228–231. Pertinent remarks also in Goldthwaite, *Economy* 504–506.

14. Herlihy, Klapisch-Zuber, *Tuscans and Their Families,* chap. 1.

15. The scholarly literature on the Black Death is extensive and views of its nature and impact vary. For specific effects on Florence, see Goldthwaite, *Economy* 77, 138, 363–364 and esp. 547–550. More generally: David Herlihy, *The Black Death and the Transformation of the West* (Cambridge, Mass., 1997); Samuel K. Cohn Jr., *The Black Death Transformed: Disease and Culture in Early Renaissance Europe* (London, 2002); George Huppert, *After the Black Death: A Social History of Early Modern Europe* (Bloomington, 1986).

16. Goldthwaite, *Economy* 541–545.

17. That the Black Death had a major impact on painting is the classic thesis of Millard Meiss, *Painting in Florence and Siena after the Black Death* (Princeton, 1951). Various effects of the Black Death and of subsequent plague visitations examined in *Life and Death in Fifteenth Century Florence,* ed. M. Tetel, R. G. Witt, R. Goffen (Durham, N.C., 1989). Its protracted influence on charity: Samuel K. Cohn Jr., *The Cult of Remembrance and the Black Death: Six Renaissance Cities in Central Italy* (Baltimore, 1992). Fundamental are: Alberto Tenenti, *Il senso della morte e l'amore della vita nel Rinascimento* (Turin, 1957); Jean Delumeau, *Sin and Fear: The Emergence of a Western Guilt Culture, 13th–18th Centuries,* trans. Eric Nicholson (New York, 1983) and his *Le peur en Occident (XIVe–XVIIIe siècles): un cité assiégée* (Paris, 1983). Studies that tend to minimize the specific effects of the Black Death: *The Black Death: The Impact of the Fourteenth Century Plague: Papers of the Eleventh Annual Conference of the Center for Medieval and Early Renaissance Studies,* ed. D. Williman (New York, 1982) and Remo L. Guidi, *L'Inquietudine del Quattrocento* (Rome, 2007).

18. Bizzocchi emphasizes the growing proportion of clergy in Florence, from 1.3 percent just before 1348, year of the Black Death, to 3.7 percent at the middle of the fifteenth century, to 8.7 percent in 1552. *Chiesa e potere* 14. See also P. Battara, *La popolazione di Firenze alla metà del '500* (Florence, 1935).

19. Trexler, *Public Life* 247–248; Maureen C. Miller, "The Florentine Bishop's Ritual Entry and the Origins of the Medieval Episcopal Adventus," *RHE* 98 (2003) 5–28; Sharon T. Strocchia, "When the Bishop Married the Abbess: Masculinity and Power in Florentine Episcopal Entry Rites, 1300–1600," *Gender and History* 19.2 (2007) 346–368.

20. Maria Pia Paoli, "Sant' Antonino 'vere pastor et bonus pastor': storia e mito di un modello," *Verso Savonarola: misticismo, profezia, empiti riformistici fra Medioevo ed Età moderna,* ed. Gian Carlo Garfagnini, Giuseppe Picone (Florence, 1999) 83–139.

21. On Dominici, see "Banchini, Giovanni di Domenico," *DBI* 1, 657–664.

22. Lesnick, *Preaching* passim.

23. Howard, *Beyond the Written Word* 250 and passim.

24. That the Florentines extolled civic liberty while justifying their own territorial expansion is observed by Najemy, *History* 197–198.

25. Raymond De Roover, *The Rise and Decline of the Medici Bank* (Cambridge, Mass., 1963); Goldthwaite, *Economy* passim.

26. On Medici governing methods, Rubinstein, *Government of Florence;* Anthony Molho, "Cosimo de' Medici: *Pater Patriae* or *Padrino?*" *Stanford Italian Review* (Spring 1979) 5–33.

27. Dale Kent, *Cosimo de' Medici* 118–119.

28. On the genesis of the League, see Riccardo Fubini, "The Italian League and the Policy of the Balance of Power at the Accession of Lorenzo de' Medici," *The Origins of the State in Italy, 1300–1600,* ed. Julius Kirshner (Chicago, 1996) 166–199.

CHAPTER 5. The Magnificent Lorenzo

1. Alison Brown, "The Humanist Portrait of Cosimo De' Medici, *Pater Patriae,*" *JWC* 24, 3.4 (1961) 186–221.

2. Alessandra Macinghi negli Strozzi quoted in Rubinstein, *Government of Florence* 139.

3. Ibid. pt. 3. Also, more succinctly, Najemy, *History* chap. 12. On Lorenzo's absorption in, not to say obsession with, Florence and its traditions, past and present, F. W. Kent, *Lorenzo de' Medici* 10.

4. On Lorenzo's patronage networks, ibid. On his cultivation of his image as patron to maximize his visibility both at home and abroad, see Melissa M. Bullard, "Lorenzo de' Medici: Anxiety, Image Making, and Political Realty," *Lorenzo de' Medici Studi,* ed. Gian Carlo Garfagnini (Florence, 1992) 3–40. On Lorenzo's collaboration with fellow ottimati, Michael Mallett, "Lorenzo de' Medici and the War of Ferrara," *Lorenzo de' Medici: New Perspectives,* ed. Bernardo Toscani (New York, 1993) 249–250.

5. F. W. Kent, "Patron-Client Networks in Renaissance Florence and the Emergence of Lorenzo as 'Maestro della Bottega,'" in *Lorenzo de' Medici* 278–313.

6. Poliziano, *Della congiura dei Pazzi* 45. A skillful account of the whole episode can be found in Martines, *April Blood.*

7. Bram Kempers, *Painting, Power and Patronage: The Rise of the Professional Artist in Renaissance Italy,* trans. B. Jackson (London, 1987) 201.

8. Melissa Meriam Bullard, "The Magnificent Lorenzo de'Medici; Between Myth and History," *Politics and Culture in Early Modern Europe: Essays in Honor of H. G. Koenigsberger,* ed. P. Mack, M. C. Jacob (Cambridge, 1987) 25–58. Here and in her work cited in n. 4 above, Bullard provides an analysis of Lorenzo as an historical and mythical figure.

9. Rubinstein, *Government of Florence* 200.

10. Martines, *April Blood* 238.

11. This is largely based on the description by Francesco Guicciardini quoted in ibid. 225.

12. Trexler, *Public Life,* pt. 4, esp. 444; also Najemy, *History* 369–372.

13. Vespasiano da Bisticci, *Vite* 10.

14. Letter to Paul of Middelburg in Marsilio Ficino, *Opera omnia* (Basil, 1576; repr. Turin, 1962) 974.

15. Dale Kent, *Cosimo de'Medici* 110, also citing Cohn, *Cult of Remembrance.*

16. [Charles Avery], "Della Robbia, Luca," *The Thames and Hudson Encyclopaedia of the Italian Renaissance,* ed. J. R. Hale (London, repr. 1989) 113.

17. On the "Medici myth" of singularity and their motivations for artistic patronage, see Dale Kent, *Cosimo de' Medici* and her "Charity and Power in Renaissance Florence: Surmounting Cynicism in Historiography," *Common Knowledge* 9.2 (April 2003) 256. For a discussion of these questions as they relate to Lorenzo, see F. W. Kent, *Lorenzo de' Medici.*

18. F. W. Kent, *Lorenzo de' Medici,* chap. 4, "Lorenzo and the Florentine Building Boom, 1485–92."

19. The charge goes back to the contemporary chronicler Piero Parenti and to Francesco Guicciardini. See ibid. chap. 4.

20. My translation of "Il tempo fugge e vola / mia giovinezza passa e l'età lieta." *Lorenzo de' Medici, Opere,* ed. Attilio Simioni, 2 vols. (Bari, 1939) I, 184. On the poetic theme and Lorenzo's sense of urgency, see F. W. Kent, *Lorenzo de'Medici* 86.

21. Stefano Carrai, "La datazione della confessione e le tracce della polemica fra Luigi Pulci e il Savonarola" *Interpres* (1979) 213–229; Verde, *Lo Studio fiorentino* IV/1, 130–136; IV/2, 504–511. For an overview of Lorenzo's intellectual itinerary and his changing relations to the leaders of Florentine literary and philosophical culture, the works of Mario Martelli are indispensable. See especially his *Letteratura fiorentina* and "La cultura letteraria nell'età di Lorenzo," in *Lorenzo il Magnifico e il suo tempo,* ed. Gian Carlo Garfagnini (Florence, 1992) 39–84. See also Jill Kraye, "Lorenzo and the Philosophers," in *Lorenzo the Magnificent: Culture and Politics,* ed. Michael Mallett, Nicholas Mann (London, 1996) 151–166.

22. The classic statement of this view is Garin, *Italian Humanism.* It has been developed, critiqued, and modified by others, including Mario Martelli, F. William Kent, Arthur Field, Christopher Celenza.

23. Field, *Origins* 6–7, 269.

24. Ibid. 35. Quote 36.

25. Celenza, *Piety and Pythagoras* 15 and n. 62 citing James Hankins, "Lorenzo de' Medici as a Patron of Philosophy," *RN* ser. 2, 34 (1994) 15–53 and the papers in Bernard Toscani, ed. *Lorenzo de' Medici: New Perspectives Studies in Italian Culture* 13 (New York, 1993).

26. Field, *Origins* 3–4. I am much indebted to Field's discussion of "the philosophical Renaissance" in Florence, but see also della Torre, *Accademia Platonica;* Kristeller, *Il pensiero filosofico* and his *Supplementum Ficinianum,* 2 vols. (Florence, 1937).

27. A point made by his (and Savonarola's) admirer Giovanni Nesi, *Oraculum de Novo Saeculo* (Florence, 1497).

28. See the preface to the Italian edition of Ficino's *Pimander* by the translator Tommaso Benci in Kristeller, *Supplementum* I, 98–101.

29. *Commento del Magnifico Lorenzo de'Medici sopra alcuni de' suoi sonnetti, Opere,* ed. Attilio Simoni, 2 vols. (Bari, 1939) I, 14.

30. On Ficino's idea of himself as "a divinely inspired earthly guide," Celenza, *Piety and Pythagoras* 21.

CHAPTER 6. Bologna to Florence

1. In this discussion of Savonarola's studium years and relations with Vincenzo Bandelli I have followed Michael Tavuzzi O.P., "Savonarola and Vincenzo Bandello," *AFP* 59 (1999) 199–224. Less convincing is Alfonso D' Amato, "Fra Girolamo Savonarola e il suo tempo Bolognese e 'Lombardo'" *RAM* (1998) 387–425. D'Amato notes that Savonarola was slated for an academic career but speculates that he left after his first year because he decided that his true vocation was preaching (397–398).

2. Tavuzzi, "Savonarola and Vincenzo Bandello" 210, citing Armando F. Verde O.P., "L'insegnamento della teologia nella Congregazione Savonaroliana di San Marco alla fine dell'400 e all'inizio del '500," *VH* 5 (1994) 495–529.

3. Savonarola, *Lettere e scritti apologetici* 16–20. My translation.

4. In contrast to Roberto Ridolfi who thinks he senses "a greater secret tenderness" under the "pitiless firmness" of this letter as compared to those of five years earlier. See Ridolfi, *Vita* 24.

5. Ridolfi accepts Savonarola's recollection that he continued to preach "in the same manner" as in San Gimignano (ibid. 22), although an attentive reading of the text shows the Brescia sermon to have been a further stage in the friar's prophetic consciousness. Apart from the evidence of the text we might reasonably expect some deepening of prophetic confidence in the four years since his first apocalyptic sermons in San Gimignano.

6. The report is in Pseudo-Burlamacchi (p. 15) who says he heard it from a colleague, fra Bartolomeo da Ragusa, who had it from his former pupil.

7. Ibid. 15–16. This is said to have happened in the early morning after Christmas, which suggests that Savonarola passed more than a few days in Brescia, having preached the famous sermon described here on the Feast of Saint Andrew, November 30. Pseudo-Burlamacchi goes on to give other instances of Savonarola's mystical experiences during that time.

8. Ibid. 19. Pseudo-Burlamacchi's claim that he had this from Pandolfo Rucellai and Piero Berti, two prominent Florentines, gives the story some credibility, if not much. As we shall see, Pandolfo Rucellai later became a friar at San Marco and took the name fra Santi.

9. Ridolfi seems unaware of any difficulties between Savonarola and Vicar General Bandelli, blaming the delay on the cumbersome bureaucratic machinery of the Order as

well as the vicar general's consideration for Savonarola's other commitments. *Vita* 25. Tavuzzi, however, more acutely, assumes that Vicar General Bandelli assigned Savonarola to Mantua rather than to Florence out of ill will, but that at the chapter meeting General Torriani prevented further obstruction. "Savonarola and Vincenzo Bandello" 216–217.

10. Tavuzzi, 217. Documentation of Savonarola voting on other issues at the Como meeting in A. D'Amato, "Sull'introduzione della riforma domenicana nel Napoletano" *AFP* 26 (1956) 260.

11. Excellent discussion of Lorenzo's governing methods in Najemy, *History* chap. 12. On Guicciardini's assessment of Lorenzo's insecurity and his reliance on new men, Najemy, *History*, 364–366.

12. English translation by Renée Watkins, *Humanism and Liberty: Writings on Freedom from Fifteenth-Century Florence* (Columbia, S.C., 1978) 193–223. On Rinuccini, see Rubinstein, *Government of Florence* passim.

13. The phrase is Randolph Starn's in his *Contrary Commonwealth: The Theme of Exile in Medieval and Renaissance Italy* (Berkeley, 1982). See also Christine Shaw, *The Politics of Exile in Renaissance Italy* (Cambridge, 2000).

14. The phrase is from Eugenio Garin, who describes the whole affair in his *Giovanni Pico Della Mirandola* chap. 2. See also *Pico, Poliziano e l'Umanesimo di fine del Quattrocento* (Catalog of an exhibit at the Biblioteca Medicea Laurenziana, December 31, 1994), ed. Paolo Viti (Florence, 1994) 61–62. The standard work on Pico in France and Rome is still L. Dorez, L. Thuane, *Pic de la Mirandole en France, 1485–1488* (Paris, 1897).

15. English trans. of the *Oratio* by Elizabeth L. Forbes with an introduction by Paul Oskar Kristeller in *The Renaissance Philosophy of Man*, ed. E. Cassirer, P. O. Kristeller, J. H. Randall Jr. (Chicago, 1948), 215–254.

16. Letters of Lorenzo de' Medici to Giovanni Lanfredini, his ambassador in Rome, in Lorenzo de' Medici, *Lettere* XI, nos. 1158; XII, nos. 1163, 1185. Ficino's letter in Giovanni Pico della Mirandola, *De hominis dignitate, Heptaplus, De Ente et Uno*, ed. E. Garin (Florence, 1942) 28–29.

17. Lorenzo to G. Lanfredini, Lorenzo de' Medici, *Lettere* XII, 29–30.

18. My main guides here are Martelli, *Letteratura fiorentina* and his "La cultura letteraria nell'eta' di Lorenzo," *Lorenzo de' Medici e il suo tempo*, ed. Gian Carlo Garfagnini (Florence, 1992) 39–84; Martelli, "Politica culturale dell' ultimo Lorenzo," *Il Ponte* (1980) 923–941, 1040–1069; and the papers in *Lorenzo de' Medici New Perspectives*, ed. Bernard Toscani (New York, 1992).

19. Martelli, "Politica culturale" esp. 925.

20. Among these, members of the powerful Valori family who were patrons of Ficino and soon-to-be allies of Savonarola. See Mark Jurdjevic, "Prophets and Politicians: Marsilio Ficino, Savonarola and the Valori Family," *PP* 183 (2004) 49.

21. Italian text in Martelli, "Politica culturale" 929.

22. Landucci, *Diario* 54.

23. Machiavelli, *Lettere* 403 (May 17, 1521).

24. Rubinstein, *Government of Florence* 217.

25. On this and other matters relating to Lorenzo's relations with Pico and Poliziano, including texts of letters and documents: *Pico, Poliziano e l'Umanesimo di fine Quattrocento*, and Garin, *Giovanni Pico della Mirandola*, pts. 1 and 2.

26. *Sermoni del Beato Bernardino Tomitano da Feltre*, ed. Carlo Varischi (Milan, 1964);

Il beato Bernardino da Feltre nella storia sociale del Rinascimento Testo della Conferenza tenuta il 29 settembre a Venezia per le celebrazioni bernardiane, ed. Gino Barbieri (Milan, 1962).

27. In 1484 Mariano preached the Lenten sermons in the Cathedral. An admiring listener was Margherita, daughter of the Florentine patrician Tommaso Soderini, who summarized in her diary what she remembered and understood of each day's sermon. Z. Zafarana, "Per la storia religiosa di Firenze nel Quattrocento," *SM* ser. 3, 9 (1968) 1017–1113.

28. On the condition of San Marco at the time of Savonarola's recall, see Lorenzo Polizzotto, "Savonarola, San Marco and the Reform," *Frate Girolamo Savonarola e il suo movimento, MD* n.s. 29 (1998) 39–49.

CHAPTER 7. Lo, the Sword of God!

1. Pseudo-Burlamachi 18.

2. Ibid. 22.

3. This is my amalgam of contemporary descriptions that are substantially in agreement: Giovanfrancesco Pico della Mirandola, *Vita di Hieronimo Savonarola* 8; Benedetto Luschino, *Vulnera diligentis* 18 and n. 13; "Annalia Conventus S. Marci" c. 153r. (*see Fig. 6*)

4. Text and commentary in "Le lezioni o i sermoni sull'Apocalisse," ed. Armando F. Verde, O.P. 4–108.

5. Cerretani, *Storia fiorentina* 192–193.

6. For two balanced analyses, see Letizia Pellegrini, "La predicazione come strumento di accusa," *Girolamo Savonarola: l'huomo e il frate*, Convegno storico internazionale, Todi 11–14 ottobre 1998 (Spoleto, 1999) 161–189; Roberto Rusconi, "Le prediche di fra Girolamo Savonarola da Ferrara; dai manoscritti al pulpito alle stampe," *Una città e il suo profeta Firenze di fronte al Savonarola*, ed. Gian Carlo Garfagnini (Florence, 2001) 205–6.

7. Valuable remarks by Verde on Savonarola's preaching methods and his citation of authorities in *Il breviario* XXXIX–XLII.

8. Savonarola praised Saint Vincent of Ferrer as an apocalyptic preacher in the margins of his Breviary, his favorite place for keeping notes. Ibid. 376–379.

9. This and the following quotations of the Apocalypse sermons are from the notes published by Verde in "Le lezioni o i sermoni."

10. Ibid. 6–7. Lorenzo Polizzotto, "The Anti-Savonarolan Polemic of fra Giovanni Caroli: An Evaluation," *VH* 9 (1998) 391.

11. Mario Martelli, "La politica culturale del ultimo Lorenzo," *Il Ponte* (1980) 923–950, 1040–1069. Valuable essays on the real and mythic Lorenzo by Melissa Miriam Bullard, "The Magnificent Lorenzo de' Medici: Between Myth and History" in *Politics and Culture in Early Modern Europe: Essays in Honor of H. G. Koenigsberger*, ed. P. Mack, M. C. Jacob (Cambridge, 1987), 25–58, and her "Lorenzo de' Medici: Anxiety, Image Making and Political Reality in the Renaissance," in *Lorenzo de' Medici studi*, ed. Gian Carlo Garfagnini (Florence, 1992), 3–40.

12. "Apologia Marsilii Ficini Pro Multis Fiorentinis ab Antichristo Hieronymo Ferrariense Hypocritarum Summo Deceptis ad Collegium Cardinalium," Kristeller, *Supplementum Ficinianum* II, 76–79.

13. See, for example, his sermon of March 12, 1492. Verde, "Il Quaresimale in S. Lorenzo del 1492" 548.

14. *Prediche sopra l'Esodo* II, 326–327.

15. Guicciardini, *History of Florence* 103.

16. Text of the sermons in *Il Quaresimale del 1491*. See also Armando F. Verde O.P., "Girolamo Savonarola: ideologo e profeta Il Quaresimale del 1491," *Savonarola: democrazia tirannide profezia*, ed. Gian Carlo Garfagnini (Florence, 1998) 127–147.

17. I agree with Mario Martelli that Savonarola was not here attacking Lorenzo as a tyrant and unbeliever, although not with the later date (1495) he assigns to these sermons. Mario Martelli, "Savonarola e Lorenzo," *Frate Girolamo Savonarola e il suo movimento, MD* n.s. 29 (1998) 75–98. Still the issue of Savonarola's relations with Lorenzo is also relevant for these sermons of 1491. That Savonarola feared retaliation for his attacks on the rich and powerful is evident from the letter to fra Domenico cited below. In 1498, in his final sermon, he recalled that he had been critical of Lorenzo but refused to back off, although such retrospective claims cannot be verified.

18. *Il Quaresimale del 1491* 114.

19. *Lettere e scritti apologetici* 21–22 (March 10, 1491).

20. *Il Quaresimale del 1491* 74–83, and Verde's note, 319. Recounting the episode four years later, he called it a "spaventosa," or terrifying, sermon, evidently considering it to have been something of a breakthrough for him. *Compendio di rivelazioni* 9–10 (Italian); 136 (Latin).

21. The month has usually been given as July, but has been corrected by Padre Verde in an endnote added to Ridolfi, *Vita* 405 n. 23.

22. Pseudo-Burlamacchi 24 and rest of chapter on relations with Lorenzo.

23. Ibid. 52–54.

24. Rather less dramatically, Savonarola seems to have already been negotiating for additional space. That June, chronicler Piero Parenti wrote that the Frate had obtained the use of the adjacent unfinished building known as la Sapienza bequeathed to the Merchants Gild by Niccolò da Uzzano. Savonarola proposed to convert it to a study hall or library at a cost of 5,000 florins without altering the original design. Parenti, *Storia* II, 28. Piagnone Domenico Cecchi made various objections to the plan. Mazzone, *"El buon governo"* 123–126. A tunnel connected la Sapienza to San Marco. On the night of April 8, 1498, San Marco's assailants used it to gain entry. Pseudo-Burlamacchi 158. Subsequently the Signoria ordered it closed. Villari, *La storia* I, ccxc–ccxci.

25. Domenico Benivieni, Ugolino Verino, Francesco Guicciardini, and other contemporaries noted Savonarola's discriminating standards and his success in recruiting men of high intellectual caliber. On the other hand, fra Giovanni Sinibaldi (the same who reported that Pico kept a concubine and seems to have been determined to find some humbug in the Frate's apostolate) wrote in the margin of a copy of Domenico Benivieni's treatise in defense of Savonarola that in truth fra Girolamo did everything he could to recruit new friars and rejected very few. Above all, he contended, Savonarola was concerned to recruit men of noble family, although some had to be let go when they proved unsuitable. Armando F. Verde O.P., "La congregazione di San Marco dell' ordine dei Frati Predicatori: il "reale" della predicazione savonaroliana," *MD* n.s. 14 (1983) 153–159. Given the paucity of our information about most of the friars, it is difficult to say whether Sinibaldi's charge has any merit, although, as I note, among his recruits were intellectual luminaries and aristocrats.

26. Some information on friars in ibid.

27. Timoteo M. Centi, "L'attività letteraria di Santi Pagnini (1470–1536) nel campo delle scienze bibliche," *AFP* 15 (1945) 5–51.

28. *Il Quaresimale del 1491* 33.

29. Testimony of fra Roberto Ubaldini, Villari, *La storia* II, cclviii.

30. Fra Silvestro's processo testimony, ibid. II, ccxx–ccxxxi. He talks about Savonarola's claim to have had a crucifix sculpted in his chest; ibid. II, ccxxi. In his own processo Savonarola confirmed that he had told Silvestro of the crucifix but that it "was all a fiction." *I processi* 26. The editors point out that the idea of a spiritual implanting of the crucifix was part of Savonarola's devotional repertoire; ibid. 140 n. 12.

31. Testimony of fra Silvestro, Villari, *La storia* II, ccxxi.

32. *I processi* 26–27.

33. Savonarola had observed fra Silvestro's sleepwalking performances. *Verità della profezia*, ed. C. Leonardi 35, 37.

34. Savonarola's testimony on his relations with these women, *I processi* 16, 38–39. On Camilla herself, ibid. 117–118. For Vaggia and Bisdomini (or Visdomini) and Bartolomea Gianfigliazzi, ibid. 169, 170.

35. Autograph outlines of most of the sermons are in Museo San Marco MS 480. I have consulted them in microfilm. The first eighteen sermons in Verde, "Il Quaresimale in San Lorenzo" 493–605.

36. On the reference to Strozzi, see Verde's remarks, ibid. 516.

37. Ibid. 559 and 561 n. 5.

38. Especially March 15–24, ibid. 562–603.

39. Extract of letter of Niccolò Guicciardini to Piero Guicciardini (April 5, 1492) in Ridolfi, *Studi* 263.

40. Rocke, *Forbidden Friendships* 202 and n. 22, citing a passage of Niccolò Guicciardini's letter omitted from Ridolfi's edition.

41. Ridolfi, *Studi* 262.

42. Ibid. and in Poliziano's letter to Jacopo Antiquari, Latin text and English translation in Poliziano, *Letters*. For some other aspects of the letter, i.e., its kinship to the genre of the "mirror of princes" and the attack on physicians, see the illuminating analysis by Godman, *Poliziano to Machiavelli* 3–30. Godman also notes that Marsilio Ficino was conspicuous by his absence, a sign of Ficino's marginalization in the last period of the life of his chief patron.

43. Landucci, *Diario* 63.

44. Ridolfi, *Studi* 263.

45. Landucci, *Diario* 63–64.

46. Poliziano, *Letters* I, 227–251.

47. Parenti (who also reported Savonarola's deathbed visit, which apparently took place on the same day) wrote that Lorenzo died about a half hour after saying farewell to his son Piero, and that the body, escorted by many relatives and friends, was brought to San Marco at 9 (about 5 a.m.), that the next morning, April 9, Piero received condolences at his house "from the entire people," and that the body remained in San Marco "the whole of the next day which was a Monday" (April 9). Parenti, *Storia* I, 21–22. Landucci agrees, except to say that the body was taken to San Marco about 5 (about 1 a.m.) and remained there in the quarters of "the Company" (i.e., one of the religious confraternities) the entire next day before being taken to San Lorenzo for burial on Tuesday about 20 (4 p.m.). Landucci, *Diario* 64.

48. Poliziano *Letters* I, 227–250; Parenti, *Storia* I, 25.

49. Niccolò Guicciardini to Piero Guicciardini, Ridolfi, *Studi* 264. Savonarola's later recollections of the Lazarus sermon and his vision of the sword of God in the sermon of January 13, 1495, *Prediche sopra i Salmi* 37–62.

50. "Sermo 'In Domino Confido,'" *Scritti vari* 83–94. Editor's notes 310–315.

51. *Libro de vita viduale* in *Operette spirituali* I, 11–62. English translation in *The Book on the Life of the Widow* in *A Guide to Righteous Living* 191–226. On this work, see also Eisenbichler, "Savonarola e il problema delle vedove nel suo contesto sociale," *Una città e il suo profeta: Firenze di fronte al Savonarola,* ed. Gian Carlo Garfagnini (Florence, 2001) 263–271. *Trattato del sacramento e dei misteri della messa,* in *Operette spirituali* I, 63–67. Ibid. 69–75. *Trattato dell' umiltà,* ibid. 129–155. *Trattato in defensione e commendazione dell' orazione mentale,* ibid. 157–185. *Trattato dell' amore di Gesù Cristo,* ibid. 77–127.

52. Cattin, *Il primo Savonarola* 123–128; Schnitzer, *Savonarola* II, 621–623.

53. *Trattato dell'amore di Gesu Cristo* 79–127, 352–356, quote on p. 87.

CHAPTER 8. The New Cyrus

1. In an entry for March 1493 Piero Parenti noted the discovery along with news of a large Turkish attack in Hungary, but he added that some claimed the islands were previously known. *Storia* I, 45.

2. Yvonne Labande-Mailfert, *Charles VIII et son milieu: la jeunesse au pouvoir* (Paris, 1975) 189–191.

3. Comprehensive discussion and bibliography on the French expedition in ibid. and valuable chapters in Abulafia, *French Descent.*

4. Parenti, *Storia* I, 31–32.

5. *Prediche sopra il salmo Quam Bonus.* On the uncertain 1493 dating, see editor's comments p. 236.

6. *Prediche sopra i Salmi* I, 52–54 and *Compendio di rivelazioni* 12–14. On the texts of the sermons, see Ridolfi, *Le prediche* 32–33.

7. "Il Quaresimale in San Lorenzo 1492" 532 and 538 n. 5.

8. Letter to the prioress of San Domenico in *Lettere* 42–51. If the idea arose more than a year before this letter was written (September 1493) as he says, it can be dated to the spring or summer of 1492.

9. Ibid. 24–26 (May 22, 1492). On Savonarola, the Convent of Santa Caterina of Pisa, and fra Stefano Codiponte, see Cesare Vasoli, "Stefano da Codiponte: una breve vicenda savonaroliana," *Frate Girolamo Savonarola e il suo movimento: V centenario della morte di Girolamo Savonarola, MD* n.s. 29 (1998) 261–279.

10. Ibid. 45.

11. Ibid. 30–31. Ridolfi, acknowledging the fanciful elaboration of the story by Piagnoni devotees, makes a creditable if speculative effort to identify its nucleus of truth. *Vita* 49–50.

12. Parenti, *Storia* I, 50–51. Parenti says at this time Savonarola had the support of twenty or twenty-five of the San Marco friars.

13. Michael Tavuzzi O.P., "Savonarola and Vincenzo Bandello" *AFP* 69 (1999) 199–224, esp. 216–223. On Bandelli's and Savonarola's opposing views on communal poverty, 208–210.

14. "Annalia Conventus S. Marci" fol. 13v.

15. *Lettere e scritti apologetici* 41 (May 26, 1493). The separation is described in "Annalia Conventus S. Marci" fols. 13v–14.

16. Text of the letters and other pertinent documents in Lupi, "Nuovi documenti" 41–57.

17. *Lettere e scritti apologetici* 42–51 (September 10, 1493).

18. Pseudo-Burlamacchi 62–71.

19. As fra Domenico called them. G. Niccolini, "Tre lettere di Girolamo Savonarola e una di fra Domenico di Pescia sull'unione dei Conventi di S. Domenico di Fiesole e S. Caterina di Pisa con quello di S. Marco di Firenze," *ASI* ser. 5 (1897) 120–122, quoted by Tavuzzi, "Savonarola e Vincenzo Bandello" 222.

20. Gherardi, *Nuovi documenti* 63 (May 27, 1494).

21. *Lettere e scritti apologetici* 56–62.

22. Letter of the Signoria to the Cardinal of Naples (November 28, 1493), Gherardi, *Nuovi documenti* 58–59. On San Domenico's and Santa Caterina's hopes of emulating San Marco's reforms in communal ownership, "Annalia Conventus S. Marci" fol. 14r–v.

23. Quoted in Ridolfi, *Vita* 62.

24. Gherardi, *Nuovi documenti* 66.

25. *Sermones quadragesimales super archam Noe.* I used a photocopy of a microfilm.

26. Cerretani, *Storia fiorentina* 193.

CHAPTER 9. Liberty!

1. Alison Brown, "Lorenzo de' Medici's New Men and Their Mores: The Changing Lifestyle of Quattrocento Florence," *RS* 16.2, 113–142.

2. For studies on Benigno, see Dall'Aglio, *Savonarola and Savonarolism* 159–160.

3. On the Florentine reaction to the expulsion, Parenti, *Storia* I, 103. On the buildup of revolutionary opposition to Piero among Florentine merchants and others, Alison Brown, "The Revolution of 1494 and Its Aftermath: A Reassessment," *Italy in Crisis,* ed. J. Everson, D. Zancani (Oxford, 2000) 13–39, esp. 13–22.

4. Brown, "Revolution" 15–16.

5. Parenti, *Storia* I, 86.

6. He made use of the sermon outlines he had been preparing for Advent, published posthumously as *Sermones in adventu Domini super archam Noe.*

7. Like the earlier sermons on Genesis, discussed above, we know about these mainly retrospectively, from this account in the *Compendium,* although there Savonarola is more definite about their dating and content. *Compendio di rivelazioni* 10–11. See also Roberto Ridolfi, "Le predicazioni savonaroliane sull'Arca" *LB* 52 (1950) 17–37.

8. *Compendio* 11.

9. *Prediche sopra Aggeo* 1–60. On the relation of these sermons to the sermons on Noah's Ark, see Ridolfi, "Le predicazioni."

10. Parenti, *Storia* I, 114.

11. Ibid. 117.

12. Landucci, *Diario* 72.

13. Pseudo-Burlamacchi 69–70.

14. *Prediche sopra i Salmi* I, 59 (January 13, 1495).

15. The date of his return is not certain. Two years later Savonarola recalled that after

returning from Pisa he preached his first sermon on November 9, and this date is followed by the sixteenth-century editor, but this seems unlikely; given the sequence of events, it was probably one or two days later. For a review of the whole question, see Ridolfi, *Vita* 70 and n. 1, and the editor's comment in Savonarola, *Prediche sopra Aggeo* 499–505.

16. *Compendio* 15–16.

17. Parenti, *Storia* I, 129.

18. *Prediche sopra Aggeo* 61–76.

CHAPTER 10. The Ark and the Flood

1. Descriptions of the king and accounts of the French in Florence: Landucci, *Diario* 80–87; *Ricordanze di Bartolomeo Masi* 26; Parenti, *Storia* I, 133–147; Cerretani, *Storia fiorentina* 212–220.

2. For the treaty: Gino Capponi, "Capitoli fatti dalla città di Firenze col re Carlo VIII, a dì 25 di novembre del 1494," *ASI* 1 (1842) 362–375.

3. *Prediche sopra Ruth e Michea* II, 325–326 (October 28, 1496). Ridolfi believes that Savonarola took part in writing the agreement when he was a member of the earlier embassy to the king, but there is no credible evidence for this. Ridolfi, *Vita* 72–73.

4. Parenti, *Storia* I, 147.

5. Landucci, *Diario* 87–88.

6. *Prediche sopra Aggeo* 105–122.

7. Parenti, *Storia* I, 147–148.

8. The Twelve Companies formed one of the two Colleges advisory to the Signoria. Each company was headed by a Gonfaloniere or Standard Bearer.

9. Quoted by Nicolai Rubinstein, "Politics and Constitution in Florence at the End of the Fifteenth Century," *Italian Renaissance Studies,* ed. E. F. Jacob (London, 1960), 153.

10. *Prediche sopra i Salmi* I, 203–204.

11. *Prediche sopra Aggeo* 166–167 (December 10). Much of what follows is from these sermons on Haggai preached between November 1 and December 28, 1494.

Emphasis added.

12. *Prediche sopra i Salmi* I, 8.

13. Francesco Guicciardini, *The History of Florence,* trans. Mario Domandi (New York, 1970) 102.

14. *Prediche sopra Aggeo* 208.

15. *I processi* 5.

16. Rubinstein, "Politics and Constitution" 164.

17. *Prediche sopra Aggeo* 227 (December 14).

18. Ibid. 226.

19. Ibid. 122.

20. Parenti, *Storia* I, 157.

21. Felix Gilbert, "The Venetian Constitution in Florentine Political Thought," *Florentine Studies: Politics and Society in Renaissance Florence,* ed. N. Rubinstein (London, 1968) esp. 475–477. On the myth of Venice in Florence, see Renzo Pecchioli, "Il 'mito' di Venezia e la crisi fiorentina intorno al 1500," *Studi storici* 3 (1962) 451–492, repr. in Pecchioli, *Dal 'mito' di Venezia all' 'ideologia americana'* (Venice, 1983) 19–73.

22. He referred to it as a government of ottimati in a sermon of February 18, 1496, as

noted by Paolo Prodi, "Gl'affanni della democrazia," *Savonarola e la Politica*, ed. Gian Carlo Garfagnini (Florence, 1997) 32.

23. On this point, see especially Giorgio Cadoni, "Tale stato non può stare così," ibid. 94–95.

24. Parenti, *Storia* I, 159.

25. Rubinstein, "Politics and Constitution" 161.

26. Guidubaldo Guidi, *Ciò che accade al tempo della Signoria di novembre dicembre in Firenze l'anno 1494* (Florence, 1988) pt. 3; Nicolai Rubinstein, "I primi anni del Consiglio Maggiore di Firenze, 1494–1499," *ASI* 112 (1954) 151–194, 321–347.

27. The Signoria consisted of eight elected Priors and the Gonfaloniere (Standard Bearer) of Justice elected by them. The Dodici Buon'Uomini, or Twelve Good Men, was essentially a war and foreign affairs ministry. For the development of these magistracies, see Najemy, *History* passim.

28. *Prediche sopra Aggeo* 319.

29. Savonarola included the Council of Eighty, composed of "the first men of the city" (and chosen by members of the Great Council), as an integral part of the new system, its function to provide expertise for all matters before they were taken up by the Consiglio Maggiore. *Compendio di rivelazioni* 68.

30. Parenti, *Storia* I, 161–162.

31. Roslyn Cooper analyzes officeholding in the Savonarolan republic and concludes that the reforms of December 23 allowed the patricians to maintain their control. See her "The Florentine Ruling Group under the 'Governo Popolare,' 1494–1512," *Studies in Medieval and Renaissance History* 7 (1984/5) 71–181. Giorgio Cadoni argues against this thesis in *Lotte politiche e riforme istituzionali a Firenze tra il 1494 e il 1502* (Rome, 1999) 5–17. Francesca Klein tends to support Cooper in her "Il mito del governo largo: Riordinamento istituzionale e prassi politica nella Firenze savonaroliana," *Studi savonaroliani: verso il V centenario*, ed. Gian Carlo Garfagnini (Florence, 1995) and "Obtenere la provvisione cimentata Cenni intorno al procedimento legislativo nel periodo savonaroliano," *Savonarola e la politica*, ed. Gian Carlo Garfagnini (Florence, 1997). None of these scholars disputes the sincerity of Savonarola's commitment to a governo largo, however.

32. *Prediche sopra Aggeo* 426.

33. Ibid. 349–360.

34. This sermon has not survived. Savonarola mentioned it on January 6. *Prediche sopra i Salmi* I, 9.

35. (December 25, 1494) *Prediche sopra Aggeo* 382. Rab Hatfield, who quotes the passage, notes that in his annotations to the Bible of 1491 (formerly attributed to Savonarola himself) fra Domenico da Pescia talks of the prophecy that Christ will actually be born in Florence. "Botticelli's *Mystic Nativity*, Savonarola and the Millennium," *JWC* 58 (1995) 89–114; esp. 100–101.

CHAPTER 11. Toward the New Jerusalem

1. *Prediche sopra i Salmi*. Citations from the sermons that follow: I, 11, 12–17, 28, 79.

2. Parenti, *Storia* I, 167.

3. *Prediche sopra i Salmi* I, 107.

4. Ibid. 26. In a statement to his interrogators, however, he said that he was careful not

to call his opponents Arrabbiati because he wanted "to maintain my honor." *I processi* 27 (April 23, 1498).

5. Louis F. Marks, "La crisi finanziaria a Firenze dal 1494 al 1502," *ASI* 112 (1954) 40–72.

6. *Prediche sopra i Salmi* I, 27–28.

7. The sermon is in ibid. 37–62. With a few minor modifications I quote from the English translation of the sermon in *Selected Writings* 59–76.

8. *Prediche sopra i Salmi* I, 55. On Savonarola's visions and their illustrations, see Beebe, "Savonarolan Aesthetics."

9. Rubinstein, *Palazzo Vecchio* 40–42.

10. Parenti, *Storia* I, 169.

11. Landucci, *Diario* 129, 131; J. K. Wilde, "The Hall of the Great Council of Florence," *JW* 7 (1944): 68–81.

12. On the palace discussion, Polizzotto, *Elect Nation* 58–61, where Giovanni Caroli is identified as Savonarola's principal antagonist.

13. *Prediche sopra i Salmi* I, 98.

14. On the collaboration and common features as well as differences between the two works, Garin, *Giovanni Pico della Mirandola* 192–193 and passim.

15. *Vita per Ioannem Franciscum illust. principem Pici filium conscripta*, in *Giovanni Pico della Mirandola, Opera omnia* I, no pagination. A partial English translation is *Giovanni Pico della Mirandola: His Life by His Nephew Giovanni Francesco Pico . . . Translated from the Latin by Sir Thomas More*, ed. J. M. Rigg (London, 1890).

16. On Camilla's prophecy, *I processi*, 117–119.

17. Pietro Crinito, *De honesta disciplina*, ed. Carlo Angeleri (Rome, 1955) 104–105.

18. Poliziano, *Letters* I, 27. On Pico's poem, 16–17, Butler says, "The elaborate (and largely untranslateable) erotic and sadomasochistic humor . . . depends on personifying Pico's poems as *Amores* (not simply love-affairs but also 'Cupids')," 322.

19. Chastel, *Art et humanisme* 289–298.

20. More extensive treatment in my *Savonarola and Florence* 205–208; Polizzotto, *Elect Nation* passim. On Benivieni and his writings, see the articles of Olga Zorzi Pugliese, including "Girolamo Benivieni: umanista riformatore (dalla corrispondenza inedita)," *LB* 72 (1970) 253–288; "Il *Commento* di Girolamo Benivieni ai Salmi Penitenziali," *Teologie a Firenze nell' età di Giovanni Pico della Mirandola*, ed. G. Aranci, P. De Marco, T. Verdon, *VH* 5/2 (1994) 475–494; "Benivieni's *Commento* and Bonaventura's *Itinerarium*: Autobiography and Ideology," *RSL* (1994) 347–362. Also Roberto Ridolfi, "Girolamo Benivieni e una sconosciuta revisione del suo Canzoniere," *LB* 56 (1964) 213–234. Excellent sketch of Benivieni's life and work by Cesare Vasoli, "Girolamo Benivieni" *DBI* 8, 550–555.

21. That this proves the relationship to have been homoerotic is less obvious to me than to Chastel, although he is surely right in noting the sexual tensions in those circles. On the *eros socraticus*, or virile love, as a theme of intellectuals and artists and as a theme in the friendship and intellectual collaboration of Pico and Benivieni, see Chastel (n. 19 above). For Benivieni's inscription on their joint tomb, see Isidoro Del Lungo, *Florentia: uomini e cose del Quattrocento* (Florence, 1897) 277–278. The relevant letters of Pico and Poliziano in both Latin and English in Poliziano, *Letters* I, 16–30. Further discussion and texts concerning the relations among Pico, Lorenzo de' Medici, Poliziano, and Benivieni in the catalog of the exhibit *Pico, Poliziano e l'umanesimo di fine Quattrocento*, Biblioteca Medicea Laurenziana, 4 novembre–31 dicembre 1994, ed. Paolo Viti (Florence, 1994).

22. Rocke, *Forbidden Friendships* 198, 202 and passim; Alan Stewart, *Close Readers: Humanism and Sodomy in Early Modern England* (Princeton, 1997) chap. 1.

23. The text of Sinibaldi's note on Pico's concubine in Ridolfi, *Vita* 307–308 n. 11. See also my *Savonarola and Florence* 207–208. The basic study is Garin, *Giovanni Pico Della Mirandola*, but for critical assessments of the received view of Pico as one of the founders of modern thought, see Craven, *Giovanni Pico della Mirandola* and Louis Valcke, "La condamnation de Jean Pic de la Mirandole: rèèvaluation des enjoux," *Le contrôle des idées a la Renaissance*, ed. J. M. M. Bujanda (Geneva, 1996) 49–74.

24. *Prediche sopra Aggeo* 104 (November 23, 1494).

25. Parenti, *Storia* I, 100.

26. In Florence in the 1490s, as Christopher Celenza has said, there was room for only one viatic individual. *Piety and Pythagoras* 33.

27. Girolamo Benivieni, *Opere novissime rivedute ed da molti errori espurgate con una canzone dello amore celeste et divino, col Commento dello Ill: Conte Giovanni Pico Mirandolano distinto in libbri III* (Venice, 1522).

28. Girolamo Benivieni, *Commento sopra a più canzone et sonetti dello amore et della belleza divina* (Florence, 1500) fol. Iv. More extensive discussion in my *Savonarola and Florence* 205–208.

29. Polizzotto, *Elect Nation* 71–75 and passim.

30. Eventually Savonarola did secure some help. From money given to him by Count Giovanni Pico for the purpose he sent his mother forty gold florins and, at another time, to his unmarried brother Alberto, eight florins. His friend, later San Marco friar, Pandolfo Rucellai, gave him 200 ducats toward a dowry of 600 ducats for his sister Chiara. In 1498 another friend, Bartolomeo Lapi, was in Ferrara and gave a gift of grain. Lapi observed that given the family's poverty, fra Girolamo was cruel for not helping. See Savonarola's statement to his inquisitors, *I processi* 25–26 and *Epistolario di fra Santi Rucellai* 9 n. 2

31. Roberto Ridolfi, "Ricerche sopra Elena Savonarola e sopra la sua famiglia," *Studi savonaroliani* 1–18; Elena's will: 268–272

32. *Prediche sopra Ruth e Michea* I, 56 (May 12, 1496).

33. *Prediche sopra Giobbe* I, 188–189.

34. Parenti, *Storia* I, 190–191.

35. *Prediche sopra Giobbe* I, 303–324 (March 19).

36. *Compendio di rivelazioni* 28.

37. *Prediche sopra Giobbe* I, 322–324 (March 20).

CHAPTER 12. The Virgin and the Republic of Virtue

1. The surviving texts of the two sermons of March 24 and March 25, in which he proposed the visionary embassy, are incomplete, especially the second. *Prediche sopra Giobbe* I, 405–423; 424–426 (March 24, March 25).

2. *Compendio di rivelazioni* 4.

3. Ibid. 29–118 (Italian), 155–239 (Latin). English translation in McGinn, *Apocalyptic Spirituality* 211–270.

4. The symbolism is further explained by Mark J. Zucker, "Savonarola Designs a Work of Art: The Crown of the Virgin in the *Compendium of Revelations*," *Machiavelli Studies* 5, ed. Vincenzo De Nardo, Christopher Fulton (1966) 138–141. Rab Hatfield says

the crown is "effectively an elaborate set of prayers," and he describes them in detail, pointing out that they were composed by Savonarola himself, recited in his fanciulli processions, and carried by the angels in Botticelli's painting *The Mystic Nativity*. "Botticelli's *Mystic Nativity*, Savonarola and the Millennium," *JWC* 58 (1995) 89–114, esp. 94–96. See also McGinn, 242–246.

5. The episode has dismayed some of his most admiring biographers, notably Roberto Ridolfi who presumes that a modern reader "can hardly credit that so great a man with so powerful a mind could pursue such fantasies and lose himself in minute descriptions of ingenuous or downright puerile allegories." *Life of Girolamo Savonarola* 114. Ridolfi echoed Pasquale Villari, who also dismissed Savonarola's visions as "puerile."

6. "möglicherweise unecht," Dinzelbacher, *Vision und Visionsliteratur* 21.

7. Landucci, *Diario* 103.

8. Pseudo-Burlamacchi 82.

9. *Lettere e scritti apologetici* 239–255. English translation in Savonarola, *Selected Writings* 280–289.

10. *Lettere e scritti apologetici* 252; *Selected Writings* 287.

11. *Compendio* 6–8; *Prediche sopra Ezechiele* I, 18–22.

12. Carol Zaleski, *Otherworld Journeys: Accounts of Near-Death Experience in Medieval and Modern Times* (New York, 1987) 26–27.

13. Eileen Gardiner, *Medieval Visions of Heaven and Hell: A Source Book* (New York, 1993) xv.

14. "Epistola responsiva a frate Ieronimo da Ferrara dell'Ordine de'Frati Predicatori da l'amico suo," ed. Gian Carlo Garfagnini, *RN* ser. 2, 31 (1991) 113. Its "dantesque flavor" is noted by the editors of "Apologeticum Conventus S. Marci Florentiae," ed. A. F. Verde O.P., E. Giaconi, *RN* ser. 2, 37 (1997) 77.

15. Gardiner, *Medieval Visions* xxix.

16. (August, 1, 1497). Quoted in Cattin, *Il primo Savonarola* 10.

17. For the fifteenth century Dinzelbacher has counted some twenty-one, including Savonarola's.

18. Benz, *Die Vision* 112.

19. Ibid. 131.

20. Three years later he confessed that this vision had been a pretense. "The sermon I gave on the Octave of the Lady 1495, when I showed that I had been in paradise, I did it for reputation and glory. I invented it while standing in the San Marco Greek library. In fact I hadn't been there [in paradise] as I said and invented it to persuade people." *I processi* 18.

21. On Mary as the protector of the Dominican Order and her importance in Dominican spirituality, Pala, *La Mariologia*. Pala marshals the evidence of Savonarola's views on the Immaculate Conception, although oddly, does not discuss the image of the Virgin as Immaculate in the *Compendium* account of the vision. Ibid. 78–87. See also Hood, *Fra Angelico* 60–61 and passim.

22. *Prediche sopra Amos e Zaccaria* III, 264 (April 1, 1496). A half century later fra Ambrogio Catarino Politi, Savonarola admirer turned critic, wrote in a colloquy in San Marco that Savonarola had not only contradicted Church teaching by affirming that the Blessed Virgin had been conceived under original sin, but had claimed to know this by prophetic illumination. Catarino Politi was contradicted by the octogenarian fra Benedetto Luschino who recalled that he had been present at that colloquy on the Feast of the

Immaculate Conception, December 8, 1495, when, after the evening meal, Savonarola had addressed the friars. He did not preach on the issue of the conception, fra Girolamo explained, because it was a dangerous snare which had led many on either side to dishonor Jesus and his most holy mother and to be damned for their pride and arrogance. Concluding, he declared: "You should know that what our Order maintains is the truth, and one day this will be confirmed in the Church. I tell you this in the same light in which I have told you the other things." For fra Benedetto's defense of Savonarola against Catarino Politi, see Stefano Dall'Aglio, "Catarino contro Savonarola: reazioni e polemiche," *ASI* 164 (2006) 55–127.

23. *Prediche sopra i Salmi* I, 198 (May 19); also 224 and II, 19 (June 8). In the statement he wrote for his inquisitors on April 19, 1498, he recalled almost verbatim the words of this sermon and described in some detail his private efforts to persuade the Accoppiatori to resign. *I processi* 8.

24. Parenti, *Storia* I, 245–246.

25. *Prediche sopra Aggeo* 120.

26. Rocke, *Forbidden Friendships* 205 and n. 47. My discussion of sodomy in Florence and of Savonarola's antisodomy campaign draws upon Rocke and Umberto Mazzone, *"El buon governo."* The overview in Najemy, *History* 244–249 is also helpful.

27. Quoted in Mazzone, *"El buon governo"* 100.

28. *Prediche sopra Aggeo,* 220.

29. The policy of Lorenzo's government toward, and policing of, homoerotic activity was complex, even contradictory. The regime's reputation for sexual license and debauche is partly a construct of the Savonarolan regime that followed, as well as of modern Savonarola biographers. Rocke, *Forbidden Friendships* 196–204.

30. *Prediche sopra i Salmi* II, 124–125.

31. Ibid. 147.

32. An argument for conceiving of the Frateschi as a modern political party has been made by Sergio Bertelli, "Embrioni di partiti alle soglie dell'età moderna," *Per Federico Chabod, 1901–1960: lo stato e il potere nel Rinascimento* 1 (Perugia, 1981) 17–35. But see Nicolai Rubinstein, "Politics and Constitution in Florence at the End of the Fifteenth Century," *Italian Renaissance Studies,* ed. E. F. Jacob (London, 1960) 148–183. On the whole issue, see Polizzotto, *Elect Nation* 9–16. On Savonarola's discussion of party governance in his interrogation, see *I processi* 43.

33. Landucci, *Diario* 108.

34. *Prediche sopra Giobbe* II, 138–158. His perception of plots: ibid. 149.

35. Interrogated after his arrest and imprisonment, Savonarola said that in his meeting with Charles VIII in June 1495 at Poggibonsi the king told him he wanted to restore Piero de' Medici as a private citizen but that he had argued against it. *I processi* 16.

36. Parenti, *Storia* I, 221–222.

37. Ibid. 231.

38. Named for Saint Martin of Tours, the knight who gave his cloak to a beggar. On the early history of the organization, see Amleto Spicciani, "The Poveri Vergognosi in Fifteenth Century Florence: The First Thirty Years' Activity of the Buonomini di S. Martino," *Aspects of Poverty in Early Modern Europe,* ed. Thomas Riis (Alphen aan den Rijn, 1981).

39. *Prediche sopra i Salmi* I, 239.

40. Ibid. II, 72–73, 84 (June 21). Parenti, *Storia* I, 238–239.

41. *Lettere e scritti apologetici* 70–71.

42. Many references to the battle of Fornovo in Abulafia, *French Descent into Renaissance Italy.* See also David Nicolle, *Fornovo 1495: France's Bloody Fighting Retreat* (London, 1996).

CHAPTER 13. The Pope Summons

1. *Le lettere* (ed. 1933) 229–230. English translations in *Selected Writings* 261–279.

2. *Prediche sopra i Salmi* II, 152–181.

3. Actually he cites 1 Cor. 5.6: *modicum fermentum totam massam corrumpit,* "a little yeast ruins the whole," referring to the Jewish practice of omitting leaven from all Passover food.

4. Unlike Savonarola, Saint Thomas, in following the discussion of prudence in Aristotle's *Nichomachean Ethics,* does not separate prudence from virtue. *Summa theologica* II. II. 47.10–14.

5. Parenti, *Storia* I, 256.

6. *Compendio di rivelazioni* followed by Latin text: *Compendium Revelationum.*

7. On the costly presentation copies, see Beebe, "Savonarolan Aesthetics" II, 145–147.

8. For its print history, see Ridolfi, *Vita* III and *Compendio* 379–390. Also Beebe, "Savonarolan Aesthetics II," 125–130. For a comparison of the Latin and Italian text, A. Crucitti, "*Il Compendio di rivelazioni,*" *LB* (1972) 165–177.

9. Italian and Latin texts in Savonarola, *Compendio* 3–245. McGinn's introduction in *Apocalyptic Spirituality* 183–191 is valuable.

10. *Compendio di rivelazioni.*

11. I adapt the English translation in *Selected Writings* 265–267.

12. The instruction to Maggi in Luotto, *Il vero Savonarola* 605–606.

13. Villari, *La storia* I, li–lii.

14. "He even used to say that if he was deceiving this people, God was deceiving him." Parenti, *Storia* I, 37.

15. *Lettere e scritti apologetici* 77; English translation in *Selected Writings* 268–277.

16. "Apologeticum Conventus S. Marci Florentiae," ed. A. F. Verde O.P., E. Giaconi *RN* ser. 2, 37 (1997) 67–154.

17. *I processi* 14.

18. *Prediche sopra l'Esodo* I, 37–67, esp. 46–47.

19. The friars of San Marco also sent a reply to the pope on their own behalf with similar arguments. The text has recently been identified and published with valuable notes and comments. "Apologeticum Conventus S. Marci Florentiae."

20. *I processi* 105 n. 90.

21. On Sandei's commentary *Super titulo De rescriptis,* which he may have abstracted and sent to fra Girolamo previously, see Verde, *Lo studio fiorentino* II, 200, 205, IV/2, 680–683 and "Apologeticum Conventus S. Marci Florentiae" 83 n. 47, 101 n. 89. Savonarola seemed to refer to this commentary when he returned to the pulpit on October 11.

As bishop designate of Lucca, Sandei probably had taken part in the effort to have Savonarola assigned to preach the previous Lent there. Later his relations with the Frate became complicated, and ultimately Savonarola was to regard him as his enemy. Luschino, *Vulnera diligentis* 372–373.

22. Najemy, *History* 396.

23. This and the two sermons Savonarola preached on October 18 and 25 in *Prediche sopra i Salmi* II, 182–313.

CHAPTER 14. Obstacles to the Spirit

1. *Prediche sopra i Salmi,* 2 vols., ed. Vincenzo Romano (Rome, 1969, 1974) II, 185–186, 284–313.

2. Text and discussion in Gherardi, *Nuovi documenti* 386–391.

3. *Lettere e scritti apologetici* 234–255 and editor's note 411–412.

4. The meaning of this passage is unclear; he may have been referring to the boys' practice of stoning civic enemies or desecrating their corpses.

5. "Epistola responsiva a frate Hieronymo dell'ordine de frati predicatori da l'amico suo," ed. Gian Carlo Garfagnini, *RN* 31 (1991) 102–120.

6. Domenico Benivieni, *Epistola di maestro Domenico Benivieni Fiorentino, canonico di San Lorenzo a uno amico responsiva a certe obiectione et calunnie contra a frate Hieronymo da Ferrara* (n.p., n.d.). On Benivieni and his several works in defense of Savonarola, see the many references in Polizzotto, *Elect Nation.*

7. On these polemics, see Joseph Schnitzer, "Die Flugschriftenliteratur für und wider Girolamo Savonarola," *Festgabe Karl Theodor von Heigel* (Munich, 1903); my *Savonarola and Florence* chap. 7; Polizzotto, *Elect Nation* passim.

8. Ridolfi, *Vita* 121. Text in Villari, *La storia* I, cxv–cxvi.

9. Text of the letters to Carafa and Becchi in Gherardi, *Nuovi documenti* 130–132. Savonarola later gave his view of Becchi to his inquisitors: "Messer Ricciardo Becchi also wrote to his brother Giovanni about my affairs, but I didn't trust him because he wrote things against us." *I processi* 16.

10. Landucci, *Diario* 120.

11. Reports on the ensuing commotion in the city in ibid. 120–122 and Parenti, *Storia* I, 299–302. By this time Parenti's growing hostility toward the Savonarolan cause is apparent.

12. Gherardi, *Nuovi documenti* 133–134. All nine members of the Signoria, the eight Priors and the Gonfaloniere, voted in favor.

13. Ridolfi's effort to demonstrate that Savonarola did have papal permission is not entirely convincing. *Vita* 123–124, nn. 40, 41. Envoys Becchi on March 3 and Pandolfini on March 24, indicated that the pope continued to withhold consent and to deplore the Frate's disobedience. Gherardi, *Nuovi documenti* 133–134; Vincenzo Marchese, "Lettere inediti" 149–151. The Frate was well aware of this, as these Lenten sermons indicate, and the Signoria and Ten felt obliged to persist in their efforts to secure the lifting of the ban.

14. *Prediche sopra Amos e Zaccaria* I, 8–10.

15. Of forty-eight surviving sermons in this series, twenty-seven are based on Amos, eight on Zechariah, and eight on episodes from the Gospels. See also the editor's remarks in ibid. III, 413–421.

16. These confusing statements suggest that Savonarola was unable to decide whether or not a holy or angelic pope (an iconic figure in millenarian tradition) was about to appear. Domenico Benivieni wrote that in a vision at the time of the death of Pope Innocent VIII (July 25, 1492) Savonarola had learned that someone already living had been chosen to be

the *Sanctissimo Pontefice*. Commenting on this, fra Giovanni Sinibaldi identified the desig-nated person as the Florentine priest Giovanni Vitelli and reported that Savonarola's prophecy caused a great deal of controversy among his associates, as well as distress in Vitelli himself who complained to Savonarola. But the matter ended when Vitelli died. Verde, "La congregazione di San Marco" 156–157.

CHAPTER 15. Mobilizing the Children

1. On children in the life of Florence and Italy: Giovanni Ciappelli, *Carnevale e Quaresima: comportamenti sociali e cultura a Firenze nel Rinascimento* (Rome, 1997); Konrad Eisenbichler, *The Boys of the Archangel Raphael: A Youth Confraternity in Florence, 1411–1785* (Florence, 1998); Ottavia Niccoli, ed. *Infanzie Funzioni di un gruppo liminale dal mondo classico all'età moderna* (Florence, 1993) and Niccoli, *Il seme della violenza putti, fanciulli e mammoli nell' Italia tra Cinque e Seicento* (Bari, 1995); Lorenzo Polizzotto, *Children of the Promise: The Confraternity of the Purification and the Socialization of Youths in Florence, 1427–1785* (Oxford, 2004) esp. chap. 3; Ilaria Taddei, *Fanciulli e giovani crescere a Firenze nel Rinascimento* (Florence, 2001). On Savonarola and the fanciulli: Cesare Puelli-Maestrelli, "Savonarole, la politique et la jeunesse à Florence," *Théorie et pratique politique à la Renais-sance* (Paris, 1977) 1–13; Trexler, *Public Life* esp. chaps. 12, 13; Giovanni Ciappelli, "Il Car-nevale del Savonarola," *Studi Savonaroliani: verso il V centenario*, ed. Gian Carlo Garfagnini (Florence, 1996) 47–59; Ottavia Niccoli, "I bambini del Savonarola," ibid. 279–288; Cecile Terraux-Scotto, "La place des enfants dans la réforme Savonarolienne de la cité," *Savona-role: enjoux, débats, questions*, ed. A. Fontes, J.-L. Fournel, M. Plaisance (Paris, 1997) 81–103; Ottavia Niccoli, "I fanciulli del Savonarola: usi religiosi e politici dell'infanzia nel Italia del Rinascimento," ibid. 105–120.

2. *Prediche sopra Amos e Zaccaria* III, 407.

3. Niccoli, "I bambini." In emphasizing the continuity of the Savonarolan boys' re-form with earlier youth organization I follow Niccoli rather than Trexler who sees the boys' procession of February 16 as a radical departure from past ritual practice. Trexler, *Public Life* 476–480.

4. On this expansion of role, however, I follow Trexler, chap. 11.

5. *Prediche sopra Amos e Zaccaria* III, sermons of March 25, 26, 27. The most complete description of Piagnoni carnival processions, synthesizing the various sources and includ-ing words and music of the songs that were sung, is by Macey, *Bonfire Songs*.

6. Parenti, *Storia* I, 311–312. I translate the word *veliere* as "tiara," since it must refer to the ornate headresses or diadems worn by prostitutes, not the generic veil or head covering worn by respectable women.

7. Ibid. 326. Parenti goes on to give a detailed description of the procession, 326–328.

8. Landucci, *Diario* 123–124 (February 7, 1496). Also Parenti, *Storia* I, 311: "Following fra Domenico da Pescia's sermon the fanciulli were aroused to start taunting women who wore tiaras and sodomites soliciting for that vice."

9. Cited in Niccoli, "I bambini" 284.

10. *Prediche sopra Amos e Zaccaria* (March 13) II, 234; (March 24) III, 97.

11. Two examples of many: *Prediche sopra Ezechiele* I, 305–306; *Compendio di rivela-zioni* 41.

12. The full text of this sermon has not survived.

13. Bongianni's letter and a bio-bibliographical note in *Epistolario di fra Santi Rucellai* 130–132.

14. On Rucellai, ibid.; Raffaella Maria Zaccaria, "Pandolfo Rucellai da mercante fiorentino a frate domenicano e savonaroliano," *Studi savonaroliani: verso il V centenario,* ed. Gian Carlo Garfagnini (Florence, 1996) 99–103; F. W. Kent, *Household and Lineage in Renaissance Florence: The Family Life of the Capponi, Ginori and Rucellai* (Princeton, 1977); Fra Roberto Ubaldini's eulogy of fra Santi Rucellai in De Maio, *Savonarola e la Curia Romana* 224.

15. *Prediche sopra Amos e Zaccaria* II, 433. For the whole incident, F. William Kent, "A Proposal by Savonarola for the Self-Reform of Florentine Women (March 1496)," *MD* (1983) 335–341; Lorenzo Polizzotto, "Savonarola, Savonaroliani e la riforma delle donne" *Studi savonaroliani: verso il V centenario,* ed. Gian Carlo Garfagnini (Florence, 1996) 229–244.

16. Text of letter and commentary in *Epistolario di fra Santi Rucellai,* 173–175.

17. May 3, 1495. Although addressed to fra Girolamo it is included in Rucellai's *Epistolario* 22–23.

18. *Sermones in Primam Divi Ioannis Epistolam* 320, 321; 327–328 (December 5, 12, 1490).

19. Polizzotto, "Savonarola, Savonaroliani e la riforma della donna" 232–234 and *Elect Nation* 188–189.

20. Savonarola refers to the episode in his *Prediche sopra i Salmi* II, 200 and again in *Prediche sopra Amos e Zaccaria* II, 38. See also Ridolfi, *Vita* 332 n. 15.

21. Becchi's letters in Gherardi, *Nuovi documenti* 142–144.

22. Paolo Luotto believed that Vicar General Maggi had rendered a favorable verdict and advised the pope against taking any action. In the absence of any documentation to support this inference from silence, Luotto cited Savonarola's references to having been cleared of "naming the pope" in an investigation, but he was clearly referring to the incident that arose when he preached in Bologna, as I have previously indicated. *Il vero Savonarola* 461–464.

23. Parenti, *Storia* II, 17; Dispatch of Ambassador Manfredi to Duke Ercole of Ferrara, Cappelli "Fra Girolamo Savonarola," *Atti e Memorie* 4, no. 98 (1868); Guicciardini, *Storia d'Italia* I, chaps. 4, 5.

24. Parenti, *Storia* II, 5.

25. Ibid. I, 304–305. Somenzi's report (January 6) referred to in Joseph Schnitzer, *Savonarola nach den Aufzeichnungen des Florentiners Piero Parenti* 87 n. 1. Landucci also notes the ongoing debate. *Diario* 123 (January 19).

26. The choking incident is described by the recording notary. *Prediche sopra Amos e Zaccaria* II, 435–436.

27. Ibid. III, 239–285.

28. Ibid. III, 393.

29. Ibid. III, 396–401.

30. As reported by Parenti, *Storia* II, 5–6.

31. *Prediche sopra Amos e Zaccaria* III, 370–409.

32. Landucci, *Diario,* 129.

33. Cinozzi, "Estratto d'una epistola," in *Scelta di prediche e scritti,* ed. Villari, Casanova 6; Pseudo-Burlamacchi 86–87.

34. Parenti, *Storia* II, 9.

35. Villari, *La storia* II, ccxxi.

36. Parenti, *Storia* II, 7–11; Landucci, *Diario* 129–130.

37. *Operette spirituali* II, 89–124.

38. He repeated the imagery in his sermon of the following August 23. *Prediche sopra Ruth e Michea* II, 193.

39. On the text and its publishing history, ibid. 280–287.

CHAPTER 16. I Can't Live without Preaching

1. *Prediche sopra Ruth e Michea* I, 6–8.

2. Dante described an ephemeral victory by referring to the proverb "come fe il merlo per poca bonaccia," that is, as the blackbird does at the first sign of a little good weather. *Purgatorio* XIII, lines 121–122. Ridolfi refers to it in *Vita* 138. See also the editor's comment in *Prediche sopra Ruth e Michea* II, 480.

3. Ibid. II, 126 (August 20).

4. This and the subsequent passages from the sermon of June 19, in ibid. I, 363, 380, 382–383.

5. Ibid. 384.

6. On the whole affair, see Parenti, *Storia* II, 13–16.

7. *Prediche sopra Ruth e Michea* I, 379; II, 129–130. He continued to deny it after he was imprisoned and tortured. *I processi* 9.

8. *Prediche sopra Aggeo* 137–138 (December 7, 1494).

9. Landucci, *Diario* 97–98 (January 18, 1495); Parenti, *Storia* I, 168.

10. *Prediche sopra i Salmi* I, 92–93 (January 18, 1495).

11. Angelo da Vallombrosa, *Lettere,* ed. Loredana Lunetta (Florence, 1997) 20–30 (August 13, 1496).

12. *Prediche sopra Ruth e Michea* II, 120 (August 20, 1496).

13. Antonio Costabili, Ferrarese ambassador to Florence, to Duke Ercole, in Villari, *La storia* I, cxliii–cxliv.

14. The letters and Costabili's report to Duke Ercole are published in Savonarola, *Le lettere* (ed. 1933) 215–218. They are not included in the more recent edition of Savonarola's letters.

15. Savonarola, *Lettere e scritti apologetici* 135–137.

16. Ridolfi, *Vita* 141 and n. 35. The most recent letters we have are of October 1495.

17. *Prediche sopra Ruth e Michea* II, 234–235. On the affair of the letters: Landucci, *Diario* 137–138; Parenti *Storia* II, 41–42.

18. Ibid. II, 36–37. On Maximilian's expedition, Francesco Guicciardini, *Storia d'Italia* I, bk. 3, chap. 8 and idem, *History of Florence* chap. 14.

19. Parenti, *Storia* II, 37.

20. Guicciardini, *Storia d' Italia* I, bk. 3, chap. 9.

21. Parenti, *Storia* II, 44.

22. *Prediche sopra Ruth e Michea* II, 279–280, 292–293 (September 11, 1496).

23. Parenti, *Storia* II, 46.

24. Ibid. 42–43.

25. Landucci, *Diario* 139. Parenti, *Storia* II, 44.

26. Parenti, *Storia* II, 51.

27. The sermons of October 28, November 1 and 2 in *Prediche sopra Ruth e Michea* II, 298–397.

28. Parenti, *Storia* II, 52–53; Guicciardini, *Storia d' Italia* I, 302.

29. Guicciardini, *History of Florence,* 122; Landucci, *Diario* 140–141.

30. *Prediche sopra Ruth e Michea* II, 359–361.

31. For more detailed treatment, see my "The Art of Dying Well and Popular Piety in the Preaching and Thought of Girolamo Savonarola," *Life and Death in Fifteenth-Century Florence,* ed. M. Tetel, R. G. Witt, R. Goffen (Durham, N.C., 1989), 88–104; Lorenzo Polizzotto, "Dell' Arte del Ben Morire: The Piagnone Way of Death, 1494–1545," *I Tatti Studies: Essays in the Renaissance* 3 (1989) 27–87.

32. On the Italian invention of eyeglasses and their history, see Vincent Ilardi, *Renaissance Vision from Spectacles to Telescopes* (Philadelphia, 2007). Savonarola made frequent use of the metaphor of eyeglasses, different colored lenses determining different moods and views of the world. Ilardi suggests that the metaphor was particularly apt in Florence, a leading center for the manufacture of spectacles. 179–181.

33. The contemporary editions of the sermon are listed by the editor of *Prediche sopra Ruth e Michea* II, 488. Gustave Gruyer, *Les illustrations des écrits de Jérôme Savonarole publiés en Italie au XVe et au XVIe siècle et les paroles de Savonarole sur l'art* (Paris, 1870). Donald Beebe extensively explores the relation between text and illustrations in Savonarola's publications in "Savonarola's Aesthetics." Valuable observations on Savonarola's relations with printers and his impact on the printing of religious books in Paul F. Gehl, "Watermark Evidence for the Competitive Practices of Antonio Miscomini," *The Library,* ser. 6, vol. 15.4 (1993) 281–305. On the history of Renaissance woodcuts, *Origins of European Printmaking: Fifteenth-Century Woodcuts and Their Public,* ed. Peter Parshall, Rainer Schoch et al. (New Haven, 2005).

34. *Prediche sopra Ruth e Michea* II, 398–418 (November 27, 1496).

CHAPTER 17. The Tail Acquires a Head

1. Text in Villari, *La storia* I, cxliv–cxlvii. On the organization of the new Congregation, R. Creytens O.P., "Les actes capitulaires de la Congregation Toscano-romaine 1496–1530," *AFP* 40 (1970) 125–230.

2. There are two versions of the *Apologeticum;* one bearing the stamp of Savonarola's own sharp rhetoric. Both versions in Savonarola, *Lettere e scritti apologetici* 286–308; 422–429. Savonarola's *Proemium* 283–285; important editorial comments 418–421.

3. Becchi to the Ten, March 19, 1497, Gherardi, *Nuovi documenti* 155.

4. Romeo De Maio argues that, contrary to "Piagnone historians," Carafa was in good faith in advising compliance, while Savonarola showed himself in this to be "disobedient and sophistic." *Savonarola e la Curia Romana* 105.

5. *Prediche sopra Ezechiele* I, 14 (November 30, 1496).

6. Ibid. 40–41.

7. On this whole episode, Parenti, *Storia* II, 62–64.

8. *Prediche sopra Ezechiele* I, 96–97.

9. Ibid. 101

10. Nardi, *Istorie della Città di Firenze* I, 101.

11. Documents and information regarding the Valori in L. Polizzotto and C. Kovesi, *Memorie di casa Valori* (Florence, 2007).

12. Parenti, *Storia* II, 28.

13. Guicciardini suggested that Capponi's death was critical. *History of Florence* 123.

14. *I processi* 8. On continuing tensions between Valori and Ridolfi, see the statement of Andrea Cambini to his interrogators (April 27, 1498) in Villari, *La storia* II, cclxxxvii.

15. Parenti, *Storia* II, 66, 71–72.

16. Ibid. II, 74.

17. Ridolfi, *Vita* 149 and n. 21. Parenti commented that Cei was criticizing the partisan activities of Valori and the San Marco friars that transformed "a popular and free regime" into one of bitter partisanship. *Storia* II, 71–72.

18. *Provvisioni*, ed. Giorgio Cadoni, I, 2 dicembre 1494–14 febbraio 1497, esp. 334–352; Cadoni, "Genesi e implicazioni dello scontro tra i fautori della 'Tratta' e i fautori delle 'più fave,' 1494–1499" in his *Lotte politiche* 32–99. Guicciardini remarks on these changes, *History of Florence* 123.

CHAPTER 18. Burning the Vanities

1. Ciappelli, *Carnevale e Quaresima.*

2. For everything that relates to the songs, including texts, Macey, *Bonfire Songs.*

3. *Viva, viva ne' nostri cuori, viva, o Florentia* ("Long live in our hearts, long live O Florence"), ibid. 70–71.

4. Ibid. 73–74. The change in tone from the previous year has also been observed by Macey, *Bonfire Songs.* Translation is my own.

5. Pseudo-Burlamacchi 129–132. Parenti's account of the Carnival and bonfire is compatible. Parenti, *Storia fiorentina* II, 75–76; Macey, ibid. 74–75.

6. Landucci, *Diario* 145–146 and passim.

7. Gherardi, *Nuovi documenti* 154–156.

8. Landucci, *Diario* 145.

9. *Prediche sopra Ezechiele* I, 130–136 (February 8, 1497).

10. Ibid. II, 280 (March 17, 1497).

11. Parenti, *Storia* II, 83–4; Cadoni, *Lotte politiche* 45–49.

12. Parenti, *Storia* II, 89–92; Landucci places the nun's convent in a nearby Arno valley town, Ponte a Rignano. *Diario* 146

13. *Prediche sopra Ezechiele* I, 305–307.

14. In his interrogations Savonarola admitted that he had intervened both with the Otto di Guardia and the vicar of the bishop of Fiesole "to remove this sharp stick from my eyes." *I processi* 26.

15. According to Bartolomeo Cerretani (*Storia fiorentina* 234–235), this was at the insistence of Francesco Valori.

16. Ibid. and Landucci, *Diario* 147.

17. A detailed account in Parenti, *Storia* II, 89–100. See also Guicciardini, *History of Florence* chap. 15.

18. Parenti, *Storia* II, 98.

19. wonderful changes: "grandissima novità." Ibid. II, 84.

20. Text of the measure, which also ordered benches and pews removed from all churches, in Villari, *La storia* II, xxxv–xxxvi.

21. Text of the Signoria's ban on preaching in ibid. II, xxxv–xxxvi. On the threats, see Somenzi's letter to the Duke of Milan, ibid. II, xxviii. The Signoria's ban on the wagers, ibid. II, xxxvii.

22. *Prediche sopra Ezechiele* II, 353–354.

23. Landucci, *Diario* 147–148.

24. *Prediche sopra Ezechiele* II, 351–371; editorial comments on the text of this sermon, 381. Accounts of the Ascension Day tumult in Parenti, *Storia* II, 100–103; letter of Giovanni Borromei to Lorenzo Strozzi in *La storia* II, 23 and xxxvii–xxxviii; Pseudo-Burlamacchi 154–168.

CHAPTER 19. Excommunicated!

1. Parenti, *Storia* II, 101–105.

2. *Lettere e scritti apologetici* 256–264; English translation *Selected Writings* 290–294.

3. Parenti, *Storia* II, 104–106.

4. Cadoni, *Lotte politiche* 54–55.

5. Parenti, *Storia* II, 105.

6. Guicciardini, *History of Florence* 129.

7. Anonymous letter to Lorenzo di Filippo Strozzi, May 20, 1497, quoted in Villari, *La storia* II, 25 n. 1.

8. Landucci, *Diario* 149.

9. Text of the breve of excommunication in Villari, *La storia* I, xxxix–xl.

10. *Lettere e scritti apologetici* 149–151. English translation in *Selected Writings*, 295–296.

11. Landucci, *Diario* 150–151.

12. Ibid. 152.

13. Letters of Alessandro Bracci and Ricciardo Becchi to the Ten, May 25 and 30 respectively, in Gherardi, *Nuovi documenti*, 165–166, 168–169. On the affair, see also Parenti, *Storia* II, 109.

14. Text in *Lettere e scritti apologetici* 271–276; English translation in *Selected Writings* 297–300. I have slightly altered the translation of the title which has been characterized as a clumsy imitation of the salutation of Saint Paul's Letter to the Romans. Cordero, *Savonarola* IV, 46.

15. "Epistula contra sententiam excomunicationis contra se nuper iniuste latam" (June 19), *Lettere* 277–282; English translation in *Selected Writings* 303–307.

16. Parenti, *Storia* II, 112–113.

17. Nardi, *Istorie* I, 112.

18. Parenti, *Storia* II, 113.

19. Ibid. 109.

20. On Altoviti, as well as others on both sides of the Savonarolan polemic, see Joseph Schnitzer, "Die Flugschriften-Literatur für und wider Girolamo Savonarola," *Festgabe für C. Th. Von Heigel* (Munich, 1903) 196–235; idem, *Savonarola* I, chap. 22; Calogero, *Gli avversari religiosi.*

21. Lupi, "Nuovi documenti" 44.

22. Parenti, *Storia* II, 109.

23. Angelo da Vallombrosa, *Lettere* 84–92. See also: Leonora, Angelo.

24. The letters covering the excommunication in Gherardi, *Nuovi documenti* 166–174.

25. Parenti, *Storia* II, 111.

26. *Selected Writings* 301–302; Latin text in *Lettere e scritti apologetici* 101–102.

27. Becchi to the Ten, June 22, 1497, Gherardi, *Nuovi documenti* 169–171.

28. Bracci to the Ten, June 27, 1497, ibid. 171–173.

29. Becchi to the Ten, July 19, 1497, ibid. 173–174.

30. Letters to Ludovico Pittorio (May 23), Bertrando Costabili (June 12), Count Giovanni Francesco Pico della Mirandola (July 2), Duke Ercole of Ferrara (August 1) in *Lettere e scritti apologetici* 152–153, 157–158, 163–164, 170–171, respectively.

31. *Triumphus Crucis.* Book 4 is a refutation of the rivals of the true faith, namely, philosophy, astrology, Judaism, Islam, and heretical Christian sects.

32. Ibid., citing the Italian text, 296–299.

33. For Paul's influence on the *Triumphus,* see Serafino Prete, "Savonarola apologista: il *Triumphus Crucis,*" *Studia picena* 21 (1952) 1–52. Another reputedly valuable study, which I have not seen but is amply cited by Prete, is "Savonarola als Apologet und Philosoph" *Jahrbuch für Philosophie und spekulative Theologie Erganzungsheft* 4 (Paderborn, 1898).

34. Konrad Eisenbichler, "Political Posturing in Some 'Triumphs of Love' in Quattrocento Florence," *Petrarch's Triumphs Allegory and Spectacle,* ed. K. Eisenbichler, A. A. Iannucci (Toronto, 1990) 369–381. The entire collection of papers is relevant here.

35. Joseph Schnitzer's assertion that Savonarola could not have borrowed the image of the triumphal Redeemer from pagan sources since he was completely alien to any form of heathenish pomp is circular. His alternate explanation, that Savonarola formed the image "automatically from the nature of the thing" is unconvincing. Schnitzer, *Savonarola* I, 465.

36. Parenti, *Storia* II, 114.

37. Ibid. 115.

38. In his processo testimony of April 26, 1498, Piagnone Andrea Cambini described the roles of Alessandro Bracci, Francesco Valori, and Giovambattista Ridolfi in persuading the friars to solicit testimonies on Savonarola's behalf. Villari, *La storia* II, cclxxx. In his testimony fra Silvestro Maruffi disclosed that several friars were reluctant to sign because they suspected that this had been engineered by Francesco Valori. They thought fra Silvestro and fra Roberto "were simple and deceived," although once it was under way they signed. Ibid. II, ccxxii.

39. Testimony in ibid. II, lxviii.

40. In his sermon of April 6, 1496, Savonarola claimed San Marco's seventy friars had increased to "some two hundred" with more on the way. Insisting that the citizenry provide the convent with more living space, he threatened, no doubt jokingly: "I know what I'll do; one day I'll dash out and at the head of an angry crowd and go into one of your palaces and say, 'Here is where we want to stay.'" *Prediche sopra Amos e Zaccaria* III, 357–358. Professor Lorenzo Polizzotto has shared with me in a private communication his conclusions on the population of San Marco, which he will publish in a forthcoming article in *MD.* As he says, there continues to be much uncertainty about the number of friars at San Marco during the Savonarolan period, but he believes that in 1496, when Savonarola wrote his letter to the pope, the Convent of San Marco had about sixty friars, with fifty-three novices waiting to be professed the following year. In the figure of "some

two hundred" Savonarola, Polizzotto believes, was including the friars of the other convents in the expanded Congregation of San Marco formed at the time of the separation from the Lombard Congregation. Armando F. Verde discusses Savonarola's claim but does not clarify the matter. "La congregazione di San Marco dell' ordine dei Frati Predicatori: il 'reale' della predicazione savonaroliana," *MD* n.s. 14 (1983) 151–238, esp. 153.

Of the various editions and discussions of the petition, see especially *Scelta di prediche e scritti di Fra Girolamo Savonarola,* ed. Villari, Casanova 512–518, which also has the San Marco covering letter; Guido Pampaloni, "Il movimento piagnone secondo la lista del 1497," *Studies on Machiavelli,* ed. Myron Gilmore (Florence, 1972) 337–347; Polizzotto, *Elect Nation* 13–21. For the list of signatories, their guild affiliations, and residential locations, Polizzotto 446–460. In his interrogation on April 23, 1498, fra Roberto Ubaldini gave a detailed account of how he wrote the letter and obtained the signatures from visitors to San Marco. Villari, *La storia* II, ccliv–cclvii.

41. Parenti, *Storia* II, 115–116. Fra Roberto Ubaldini testified that Francesco Valori, although a signer, said that the letter should on no account be sent to Rome and that all copies should be burned. Villari, *La storia* II, cclvii.

42. Parenti gives a figure of thirty-six deaths per day. Parenti, *Storia* II, 113; Landucci gives different numbers on successive days, although he seems to include deaths from starvation, fever, and then both fever and plague. Landucci, *Diario* 152, 153, 154, 155.

43. Pseudo-Burlamacchi 102, 116, 159. See discussions of the San Marco lauds in Macey, *Bonfire Songs* 26–27 and passim.

44. *Lettere e scritti apologetici* 185–186.

45. Ibid. 186–188; 198–199.

46. Landucci, *Diario* 155.

47. Parenti, *Storia* II, 118.

48. The letters to his brother and the other San Marco and San Domenico friars during this plague crisis in *Lettere e scritti apologetici* 175–199.

49. Ibid. 168–169 (July 24); 185–186 (August 14). As noted, he advised scriptural reading to Duke Ercole. "Read and require to be read, the Sacred Scriptures, I'm talking about the prophets, especially Jeremiah and Ezekiel, and you will find that almost everything that happens in those times is similar to [what is happening in] ours." Ibid. 171.

50. Ibid. (July 15) 165–167; (August 5) 175–181; (August 14) 188–198.

51. Ibid. (August 5) 175–181.

52. Lorenzo Polizzotto, in a communication to me, surmises that the brothers who could not read were conversi, lay brothers of modest social origins who took vows but could not aspire to the priesthood and were expected to perform the menial tasks of the convent.

53. As in his letter of August 13, 1497, to Ludovico Pittorio, *Lettere e scritti apologetici* 184.

54. On the complicated history of the two versions of the *Solatium,* neither of which was published in his lifetime, see Ridolfi, *Vita* 352 n. 23.

55. Published together with Girolamo Savonarola, *Compendio.*

56. Cited in Ridolfi, *Vita,* 353 n. 24.

CHAPTER 20. Defiance

1. Documents of the investigation of Lamberto dell' Antella in Villari, *La storia* II, iii–xxv. See also Parenti, *Storia* II, 119, 127, 133–134.

2. Parenti, *Storia* II, 121–122. He gives a total of 160.

3. Guicciardini, *History of Florence* 132.

4. In the third processo (*I processi* 36) his statement was reported as follows: "As to the death of the five citizens who were executed in August, he says he was satisfied that they would be put to death or driven out, but didn't particularly interfere. He knew that Francesco Valori was keen on it and he sent to recommend Lorenzo Tornabuoni to Francesco Valori, but coldly, so that Francesco would understand that he didn't care."

5. "A tutti li Cristiani e diletti di Dio contra la escomunicazione surrettizia nuovamente fatta," *Lettere e scritti apologetici* 275.

6. A. F. Verde supplies some further archival information in his additional notes to Ridolfi, *Vita* 419 n. 75.

7. Guicciardini, *History of Florence* 136; Parenti, *Storia* II, 126.

8. Processo of Andrea Cambini in Villari, *La storia* II, cclxxvi.

9. Cambini's testimony gives some evidence of this, ibid. II, cclxxxii, as did Savonarola in his first confession.

10. Landucci gives the price of grain as three lire (per staio) considerably down from its former highs of four and five lire. He reported the fever as killing male heads of households, but not women or children, and new cases of plague on October 19. *Diario* 156, 158.

11. On the end of the truce, Parenti, *Storia* II, 127.

12. Texts of letters between the envoys, Carafa, the pope, and the Signoria and Ten in Marchese, "Lettere inediti"153–173. On Carafa's interest in benefices, see De Maio, *Savonarola e la Curia Romana* 119.

13. In Villari, *La storia* II, xxxv (September 10, 1497).

14. Landucci, *Diario* 157.

15. *Lettere e scritti apologetici* 204–205.

16. Fra Benedetto was one of the friars who tried to defend the convent on the fateful night of April 8, after the aborted fire trial. In 1509 he killed a man and was imprisoned in the dungeon of San Marco where he began to write about the Frate. Eventually released, he continued to champion the Piagnone cause as late as the 1550s. Stefano Dall'Aglio, "Riflessioni sulla figure di Benedetto Luschino," *Frate Girolamo Savonarola e il suo movimento: V centenario della morte di Girolamo Savonarola e il suo movimento*, *MD* n.s. 29 (1998) 453–483 and *Vulnera diligentis* xxvii–liv. See also Mario Ferrara, *Per la storia del proverbio nel sec. XVI: Fra Benedetto da Firenze e la sua divisio proverbiosa* (Lucca, 1925); Donald Weinstein, "A Lost Letter of Fra Girolamo Savonarola," *RQ* 22 (Spring, 1969).

17. *Lettere e scritti apologetici* 214–216.

18. "Fra Ieronimo's reputation reviving here in the land, a naturalistic effigy of him was cast in bronze medals. One part shows his head, around it the inscription: 'The very learned Hieronimus Savonarola of the Order of Preachers.' On the other side Rome was carved and over it a hand with a dagger and the words, 'the sword of the Lord over the earth quickly and soon,'" Parenti, *Storia* II, 128. Parenti's identification of the threatened city as Rome has been generally accepted. For the iconography of the medal and those that followed, see Sebregondi, *Iconografia* 47–52, 395–396; George Hill, *Corpus of Italian Medals of the Renaissance before Cellini*, 2 vols. (London, 1930) I, 276–279; II, 1790–80. Beebe disputes the standard identification of the city as Rome and offers a more generalized interpretation of the symbolism of the medals in "Savonarolan Aesthetics" II, 189–202.

19. Of the famous della Robbia family of artists, his secular name was Marco. Sebregondi, *Iconografia* 47–52.

20. Marchese, "Lettere inedite" 163.

21. On Savonarola's "little sermon" (sermoncello) and secret call to his followers to pray for a miracle, see the statement of Andrea Cambini to his interrogators (April 27, 1498) in Villari, *La storia* II, cclxxxi. The metaphorical prophecy of the gravid woman reported in Parenti, *Storia* II, 130.

22. Parenti, *Storia* II, 133.

23. Rab Hatfield, "The Compagnia de' Magi," *JWC* 33 (1970) 107–161.

24. Landucci, *Diario* 161. The ceremony is described in Pseudo-Burlamacchi 117–118. English translation in Trexler, *Public Life* 189–200.

25. "Dilectus meus candidus et rubicundus, electus ex millibus" (Song of Songs 5.10).

26. "Fasciculus myrrhae dilectus meus mihi, inter ubera mea commorabitur" (ibid. 1.12).

27. "Osculetur me osculo oris sui" (ibid. 1.1).

28. Hatfield thinks they were closed. It is interesting to compare these motives with the functions of the ceremony under the Medici, which, he says, was intended "to distract men's minds from unpleasant realities" and to serve as "an emblem of Medici dominance." "Botticelli's *Mystic Nativity*, Savonarola and the Millennium," *JWC* 58 (1995) 138.

29. On the amazement of "the more comprehending" of Savonarola's friends, Landucci, *Diario* 161.

30. Parenti, *Storia* II, 135.

31. Parenti describes the return as a step-by-step process, with fra Domenico da Pescia's sermons in San Lorenzo as the final testing of the waters. *Storia* II, 138.

32. Manfredi to Duke Ercole quoted in Ridolfi, *Vita* 174–175.

33. As he stated to his inquisitors. *I processi* 15 and nn. 109–112.

34. Texts in Gherardi, *Nuovi documenti* 176–177.

35. Somenzi to Duke of Milan Feb. 13 reports the vicar published an order to all the parishes of the city excommunicating any who attended Savonarola's sermons and the Signoria's reaction, barring the vicar from functioning in his office. Somenzi concluded that the Signoria, or the greater part, must have been "the cause" of Savonarola's resuming his preaching. Villari, *La storia* II, li–lii.

CHAPTER 21. Exodus

1. *Prediche sopra l'Esodo* I, 73.

2. Landucci, *Diario* 162–163 (February 18, 25).

3. Ibid. On Lorenzo Violi, his transcriptions of Savonarola's sermons and his recollections of the Frate, see editor's introduction to Violi, *Le Giornate*.

4. Correspondence between Bonsi, Bracci, and the Ten as well as the relevant papal breves in Gherardi, *Nuovi documenti* 174–213. On the break-in, 178–179.

5. This breve has been lost. Accounts differ as to how the canons were to comply with this order.

6. *Prediche sopra l'Esodo* I, 95–96.

7. Parenti gives an extended account of the whole episode, including the confused reaction of the Cathedral canons, Savonarola's resort to miracle, and the ensuing fight at the bridge. *Storia* II, 140–145.

8. On Luschino's defense of Savonarola, a half century after the event, see Stefano

Dall'Aglio, "Catarino contro Savonarola," *ASI* 164 (2006) 124–125. Fra Benedetto failed to note that in Elijah's demonstration God's fire did arrive and consumed the offerings.

9. Landucci, *Diario* 163.

10. This is a composite account based on the report of the Milanese ambassador Somenzi to the Duke of Milan (Villari, *La storia* I, li–liiii), Landucci, *Diario* 163, Parenti, *Storia* II, 144–145, and Savonarola himself (*Prediche sopra l'Esodo* I, 111–112).

11. Pseudo-Burlamacchi 134.

12. Nardi, *Istorie* I, 99–100 and note (a).

13. On "holy madness" as a mystical state, see Olga Zorzi Pugliese, "Girolamo Benivieni: umanista riformatore (dalla corrispondenza inedita)," *LB* 72 (1970) 253–288; Pseudo-Burlamacchi says that Savonarola commended the dancers in his sermon of the next morning. This cannot be verified from the abbreviated surviving text of the sermons. Savonarola, *Prediche sopra Ezechiele* I, sermons IX, X. On the texts, Ridolfi, *Le prediche* 68–74.

14. To his interrogators he gave this more explicit explanation: "The reason I withdrew from Santa Reparata on the second day of Lent was not out of obedience to the pope, but for fear of being killed." *I processi* 15.

15. *Prediche sopra l'Esodo*, I, 145.

16. *Prediche sopra l'Aggeo* 435–487; nn. 519–527.

17. Still the most comprehensive study of this discussion is von Albertini, *Das Florentinische Staatsbewusstein*. For an overview see Quentin Skinner, *Foundations* vol. 1. Whether and how the *Trattato* made an original contribution to the discussion on tyranny is debated by several scholars in *Savonarola: Democrazia Tirannide Profezia*, ed. Gian Carlo Garfagnini (Florence, 1998).

18. On Machiavelli's interest in Savonarola's preaching and developments in Florence during the years of his ascendancy, see especially Innocenzo Cervelli, "Savonarola, Machiavelli e il libro dell' Esodo," in *Savonarola*, ed. Garfagnini 243–298.

19. As well as serving as a Florentine envoy Becchi had a curial post, although whether he was in clerical orders is not clear. See "Ricciardo Becchi," *DBI* 7 (1965) 494–496.

20. In his first interrogation Savonarola identified the man whom he accused of aspiring to become tyrant as Lorenzo di Pierfrancesco de' Medici. He did so, he said, to shake his followers from their apathy although he had no evidence (thus confirming Machiavelli's assertion). Indeed, he had a high regard for Lorenzo although he worried that he was too close to the Duke of Milan. Lorenzo left Florence shortly after this, never to return. *I processi* 19 and n. 145.

21. Machiavelli, *Lettere* 29–33.

22. The three Savonarolan Priors were Lanfredino Lanfredini, Alessandro degli Alessandri, and Filippo Cappelli. *I processi* 147 n. 37.

23. Texts of the correspondence in Gherardi, *Nuovi documenti* 174–213; Cappelli "Fra Girolamo Savonarola" 301–406; Villari, *La storia* II, xlviii–lxvi.

24. Bonsi to the Ten, March 7 in Marchese, "Lettere inediti" 92–93.

25. Bonsi to Domenico Mazzinghi, March 19, 1498, Villari, *La storia* II, cclxvi–cclxvii.

26. Gherardi, *Nuovi documenti* 194–195.

27. "Florence's encounter with Savonarola was a meeting with much of its own soul: with its piety, anticlerical attitudes, patriotism, eloquence, republicanism, and even its rationalism." Martines, *Fire in the City* 287.

28. *Prediche sopra l'Esodo* II, 180 (March 14).

29. *Lettere e scritti apologetici* 226–227; alternate version 404; English trans. in *Selected Writings* 310–311. See editor's discussion of the two texts in *Le lettere* (ed. 1933) clxxiv–clxxviii and in Ridolfi, *Vita* 359 n. 35.

30. "This matter of the Council, I had been working on it for three months, not more." *I processi* 39. See also editors' commentary, ibid. lxxviiii–lxxix.

31. Sermons of February 23, March 4, March 24, 1496, in *Prediche sopra Amos e Zaccaria* I, 201, 417, III, 98, respectively. See editors' discussion in *I processi* 125 n. 33. "As for the little key and chest, which I mentioned many times and that I said belonged to the Church, I said it to terrify and threaten and tie the hands of those who wanted to do harm. They were, after all, words with no other special secret or revelation in them." Ibid. 18, also 125 n. 133.

32. Villari, *La storia* II, ccxvii–ccxviii.

33. On allegations of unbelief connected with his Catalan nationality, Parenti, *Storia* I, 34 (August 1492). On Rodrigo Borgia's alleged Marrano connections, Schnitzer, *Savonarola* I, 118. Tamar Herzig says Savonarola called the pope a Marrano in his letters to the princes. *Savonarola's Women* 135. I find no passage in which he was so explicit, although calling Alexander an unbeliever and atheist was surely coded language for that charge.

34. Savonarola discussed his plan for a Church council in his first inquest and, in more detail, in the third. *I processi* 20–21, 39–41.

35. *Lettere e scritti apologetici* 227–236. Robert Klein has written that having given up hope of a political solution, Savonarola now lived between expecting to be sacrificed and impatiently awaiting a miracle. *Le procès de Savonarole,* 70. For the text of letters to Florentine envoys in Spain and France regarding the Council, see Villari, *La storia* II, lxviii–lxix.

36. A doctrinaire defense of Savonarola's call for a council was made by Jourdan Hurtaud, "Lettres de Savonarole aux princes Chrétiens pour la réunion d'un concile," *Revue Thomiste* 7, no. 44 (1900) 631–674. The substance of Hurtaud's argument is that in calling for a council to consider his charge that Alexander was a heretic Savonarola was not asserting that councils were superior to popes.

37. For a brief summary of the history and issues, Hubert Jedin, *Ecumenical Councils of the Catholic Church: A Historical Outline,* trans. E. Graf (Edinburgh-London, 1960). Text of *Execrabilis* in Carl Mirbt, *Quellen sur Geschichte des Papsttums und des Römischen Katholizismus,* 4th ed. (Tübingen, 1924) 242–243.

38. De Maio, *Savonarola e la Curia Romana,* chap. 10.

39. The Piagnone chronicler Giovanni Cambi testified that in mid-March he had shown Savonarola the draft of a letter in which he appealed to the emperor to call a council. The Frate, he said, had approved of the letter but proposed to make some changes in it before forwarding it to the emperor. Cambi said he had left it with him for forwarding. Cambi's testimony (April 23, 1498) in Villari, *La storia* II, cclxvii–cclxviii. Savonarola's testimony in his first deposition (April 19) *I processi* 20–21.

40. *Prediche sopra l'Esodo* II, 50–51 (March 9).

41. The letter to England, for example, was to be consigned to fra Francesco Pugliese who had an English friend in Florence who in turn undertook to send it to a friend at court who would show it to King Henry VII.

42. Parenti, *Storia* II, 148–149.

43. Gherardi, *Nuovi documenti* 201–203.

44. *Prediche sopra l'Esodo* II, 255–288.

45. Ibid. 289–329.

CHAPTER 22. Trial by Fire

1. Landucci, *Diario* 167. Landucci's account, which has the initial challenge coming from fra Domenico on March 26, is not always accurate. Pseudo-Burlamacchi's account is more detailed but the usual cautions against hagiographical embellishment apply. Pseudo-Burlamacchi 140–154.

2. Letter to Francesco Fortunati, parish priest of Cascina, March 29, 1498, Gherardi, *Nuovi documenti* 216.

3. Text of the speeches in Lupi, "Nuovi documenti" 54–72; Gene Brucker provides a shrewd, informed analysis of the pratica in "Savonarola and Florence: The Intolerable Burden," *Studies in the Italian Renaissance: Essays in Memory of Arnolfo Ferruolo*, ed. G. P. Biasin et al. (Naples, 1985) 119–133, reprinted in Gene A. Brucker, *Renaissance Florence: Society, Culture and Religion* (Goldbach, 1984) 333–347, esp. 342–343.

4. Roberto Ridolfi, "Due documenti Savonaroliani sopra la prove del fuoco," *LB* 38 (1936) 234–242. Text on 240–241. I have translated "rationibus" as "rational proofs," although I am not clear what the Signoria meant by this. Readers will recall that Savonarola himself originally predicted the coming renewal of the Church on the basis of "reasons" derived from Scripture, but the proposal of a trial by fire was based on the expectation of a miraculous sign.

5. Texts of these statements in Villari, *La storia* II, xci–xciii.

6. *I processi* 21–22.

7. "Risposta di fra Hieronymo da Ferrara dell'ordine de' Predicatori a certe obiectione facte circa lo experimento dello intrare nel foco per la verità profetica da lui" in Savonarola, *Lettere e scritti apologetici* 310–313.

8. Bonsi to the Ten and to the Signoria April 4, 7, 8, and the San Marco friars to the pope, April 3, Gherardi, *Nuovi documenti* 217–222.

9. Ibid. 222–225.

10. As Savonarola himself testified. *I processi* 22. These maneuvers were also attested to by the Piagnone Francesco Davanzati, interrogated on April 26. Villari, *La storia* I, ccxlvi–ccxlvii.

11. Parenti, *Storia* II, 159–160.

12. Fra Benedetto wrote this account about a quarter century later. He also asserted that Savonarola did not tell his audience that the vision was fra Silvestro's, passing it off as his own. *Vulnera diligentis* 111 and n. 107.

13. Savonarola, *Lettere e scritti apologetici* 314–325.

14. "The others wanted to hold the affair at three in the afternoon; I said no, because it should be done more soberly." Ibid. 323.

15. Their leader Doffo Spini told the Piagnone sympathizer Simone Filipepi that they had been plotting to "to tear fra Girolamo and his people to pieces." Filipepi, "Estratto della Cronaca" 481.

16. Guicciardini, *History of Florence* 140.

17. "Horrendous, wicked" to try for a miracle with the body of Christ for a matter of

state, fumed one observer (Giovan Batista di Messer Antonio), Raffaella Maria Zaccaria, ed., "Due nuovi documenti savonaroliani," *Letteratura, verità e vita: studi in ricordo di Gorizio Vita* (Rome, 2005) 234–244.

18. In addition to Savonarola's exhortations in *Lettere e scritti apologetici* 309–325 and his trial testimony in *I processi* 3–44, my account of the preparation and proceedings of the aborted fire trial and its aftermath is based on the reports of Parenti, *Storia* II, 159–168; Landucci, *Diario* 168–171; Redditi (in Schnitzer *Quellen und Forschungen* 65–68); Filipepi, "Estratto della Cronaca" 487–490; Cerretani, *Storia fiorentina* 244–247; Violi, *Le Giornate* 75–91; Luschino, *Vulnera diligentis* passim; Giovan Batista di Messer Antonio, see n. 17, above; Nardi, *Storia* II, 127–135; Guicciardini, *History of Florence* 139–140; reports of Milanese ambassador Paolo Somenzi in Villari, *La storia* II, xcv–c; Pseudo-Burlamacchi 155–163. See also the reference to the letter of April 9 of Giovan Battista di Antonio to Giovanni di Bernardo Iacopi in *I processi* 50. Important testimonies of friars and citizens present in San Marco at the time of the assault include: fra Silvestro Maruffi, Villari, *La storia* II, ccxxv–ccxxxvi; fra Luca della Robbia, ibid. II, ccxxxix–ccxlii; fra Girolamo Gini, ibid. II, ccxlix–cclii; Francesco Davanzati, ibid. II, ccxliv–ccxlix; Bartolommeo Mei, ibid. II, cclxxxiii–cclxxxvi.

19. Filipepi, "Estratto della Cronaca" 487.

20. *I processi* 30–31.

21. Landucci, *Diario* 172.

CHAPTER 23. Despair and Hope

1. Parenti, *Storia* II, 175.

2. Evidence for this preliminary questioning and torture is based on accounts by the Milanese ambassador in Florence, Paolo Somenzi, and Francesco Tranchedini, the Milanese envoy in Bologna. Both indicated that the archbishop or his vicar gave his approval. See their letters to the duke in Villari, *La storia* II, xcv–cviii.

3. Letters and papal breves pertinent to these developments in Marchese, "Lettere inedite" 175–181; Gherardi, *Nuovi documenti* 226–268.

4. Guicciardini, *History of Florence* 143–144. Names of all the commission members in *I processi* 3–4; for modifications and the "absolutely extraordinary procedure" adopted, see ibid. 52–53 nn. 3, 4.

5. On torture, Fiorelli, *La tortura giudiziaria;* Giorgio Zordan, *Diritto e la procedura criminale nel Tractatus de maleficiis di Angelo Giambiglioni* (Padua, 1976).

6. Villari and Ridolfi cite contemporary accounts indicating that Savonarola was tortured much more extensively than the official version admits, although these accounts vary among themselves and none of them are based on personal witness. Villari, *La storia* II, 189–190; Ridolfi, *Vita* 203–206 and nn. 46, 59.

7. Landucci, *Diario* 172 (April 10).

8. *I processi* 4–5.

9. Marchese, "Lettere inedite" 188. Also Landucci reported hearing from several citizens that Savonarola "suffered martyrdom" on April 23. For this and the following reference: *Diario* 174, 173.

10. That Savonarola's confession was shown to fra Silvestro as part of his own interrogation (dated April 25) is suggested by fra Silvestro's replies, although this is not definitive. He

is twice recorded as saying that he was deceived by fra Girolamo (Villari, *La storia* II, ccxxi, ccxxxi) although these may be notarial interpolations. The second, in the final sentence of the transcript, is especially suspect since it follows a very favorable comment and may have been tacked on to make fra Silvestro's testimony end with an anti-Savonarolan remark. Text of fra Silvestro's processo in ibid. II, ccxx–ccxxxi. Fra Domenico da Pescia's processo is dated April 16, hence he seems not to have known of Savonarola's so-called confession, not released until April 19. Despite repeated torture, fra Domenico remained unshaken in his belief in Savonarola's prophetic apostolate as well as in fra Silvestro's dream visions and in his own charismatic experiences. He regarded the objections to his carrying the Host into the fire as inspired by the devil. Two versions of fra Domenico's transcript in ibid. II, cxcix–ccxix.

11. Schnitzer, *Savonarola* I, chap. 27.

12. Roberto Ridolfi, "I processi del Savonarola," *LB* 46 (1944) 3–41 and "Ancora i processi del Savonarola," *LB* 47 (1945) 41–47.

13. Paolo Viti, "La traduzione latina del primo processo di Girolamo Savonarola," *Girolamo Savonarola l'uomo e il frate: atti del XXXV Convegno storico internazionale* Todi, 11–14 ottobre 1998–9 (Spoleto, 1999) 247–260.

14. Cordero, *Savonarola* IV esp. chap. 5.

15. Acute observations about Savonarola's testimony have been made by four French scholars. With none of them do I agree completely, but each is helpful: Klein, *Le procès*; Georges Mounin, *Savonarole* (Paris, 1960) and Jean Delumeau (review) "Roberto Ridolfi, *Savonarole*, Robert Klein, *Le procès de Savonarole*," *RH* 221.1 (1959) 161–165; Jean-Louis Fournel, "Le procès de Savonarole: Manipulation et Bilan," *Actes du colloque organisé par le CIRRI*, ed. A. Fontes, J.-L. Fournel, M. Plaisance (Paris, 1997) 223–241; and Jean-Louis Fournel, "Profetismo e dubbi della storia giudizi contemporanei e logica dei processi savonaroliani," *Savonarola: Democrazia Tirannide Profezia* ed. Gian Carlo Garfagnini (Florence, 1998) 213–229.

16. Threatened with another round of torture, Savonarola implicated Carafa in his efforts to have a Church council called, but he later explicitly retracted, explaining that he had named Carafa out of fear. *I processi* 39–42.

17. As Georges Mounin points out, important opportunities for damaging the Frate's reputation in the course of the processi were passed over. Thus, the first processo contains nothing about the Frate's role in the death of the five conspirators nor his involvement in the armed resistance from San Marco on April 9, two areas where it would have been easy to invent compromising admissions by him that would have been widely believed. *Savonarole* (Paris, 1960) 170.

18. Gian Carlo Garfagnini, "Savonarola e la profezia: fra mito e storia," *SM* 29 (1988), 175–201.

19. Savonarola's self-accusation and humiliation is noted both by Schnitzer, *Savonarola* II, 136–137, and Ridolfi, especially in his "I processi," 35–37; but they argue that this reaffirms Savonarola's sense of himself as a prophet.

20. *I processi* 21 (first processo). Savonarola discussed virtue and vices in his *Compendium philosophiae moralis* books IV–VII.

21. *I processi* 31.

22. Signoria to Bonsi, April 8, 11, 18, 21, 1498, Marchesi, "Lettere inediti" 175–184.

23. *Regola del ben vivere* in *Operette spirituali* II, 187–194 and nn. 331–335. English

translation, *Girolamo Savonarola: A Guide to Righteous Living* 187–190. Editor Eisenbichler rightly likens it to Savonarola's sermon on the art of dying well. For the story, see Filipepi, "Estratto della Cronaca" 501.

24. *Operette Spirituali* II 197–234, 237–262. I quote from the English translation in Girolamo Savonarola, *Prison Meditations*.

25. *Prison Meditations* 17. Editor Donnelly's comments on the two works are very helpful.

26. Ibid. 93–95.

27. Ibid. 133–141.

28. On the biography of each, see *I processi* 152–154.

29. Text of third processo in ibid. 33–44.

30. Ibid. 38.

31. Ibid. 43. "Per la mia superbia" looks suspiciously like a notarial interpolation. It conflicts with his previous explanation that he did not interfere in details of government because as a foreigner he did not know much about it and because he wanted to maintain his reputation.

32. Getting the exact sense of this revealing response is critical. Fournel quotes part of it, but he leaves out the first phrase ("O, we weren't lacking in ways") and thus misses its cynicism. "Le procès" 236.

CHAPTER 24. Silence

1. For a discussion of sources, including Girolamo Benivieni's previously unknown account of that last night, see Olga Zorzi Pugliese, "A Last Testimony by Savonarola and His Companions," *RQ* 34.1 (1981) 1–10.

2. Pseudo-Burlamacchi, chap. 45, esp. 177–181.

3. *I processi* 44.

4. Landucci, *Diario* 176–177. (Cerretani and others reported that when the good bishop, a great admirer of the Frate, mistakenly, and no doubt nervously, declared that he was separating him from the Church Militant and Triumphant, Savonarola corrected him: "Monsignore, you are mistaken; you may only say separated from the Church Militant. What regards the Church Triumphant is up to God." Cerretani, *Storia fiorentina* 251.

5. Anna Benvenuti Papi, "I bruchi di Frate Girolamo l'eversivo anacronismo del Savonarola," *Savonarola e la politica*, ed. Gian Carlo Garfagnini (Florence, 1997) 163–167.

6. See, for example, Filipepi, "Estratto della Cronaca" 488–489, 492–493.

7. "Apologia Marsilii Ficini pro multis Fiorentinis ab Antichristo Hieronymo Ferrariense hypocritarum summo deceptis ad Collegium Cardinalium," *Supplementum Ficinianum* II, 76–79. No date.

CHAPTER 25. Echoes

1. Relevant directives by Francesco Mei, procurator of the Tuscan Congregation, Master General Torriani, and his successor Vincenzo Bandelli in Gherardi, *Nuovi documenti* 329–337. The Signoria order to remove and whip la Piagnone in Villari, *La storia* II, ccxci–ccxcii.

2. On the diffusion, performance, and collection, as well as content, of Savonarolan music in all parts of Europe as well as Italy, Macey, *Bonfire Songs*.

3. On the politics of the republic until its overthrow in 1512, see Najemy, *History* 375–413. For the survival of Piagnonism in this period, see especially Polizzotto, *Elect Nation* 206–238 and passim. More on the politics of the period in Butters, *Governors.*

4. Polizzotto, *Elect Nation* 226.

5. Najemy, *History* 413, quoting from Cerretani, *Storia* 380–381.

6. On the divergent tendencies and directions inspired by Savonarola's teachings, see especially Polizzotto, *Elect Nation* passim.

7. Ludwig von Pastor, *History of the Popes,* 40 vols. (London, 1938–61) vol. 5, trans. F. I. Antrobus 213–216.

8. Polizzotto, *Elect Nation* 128–138.

9. Edition of the text and commentary in my "The Apocalypse in Sixteenth-Century Florence: The Vision of Albert of Trent," *Renaissance Studies in Honor of Hans Baron,* ed. A. Molho, J. H. Tedeschi (De Kalb, Ill., 1971) 311–331.

10. Giampaolo Tognetti, "Un episodio inedito di repressione della predicazione post-Savonaroliana (Firenze, 1509)" *BHR* 24 (1962) 190–199; Polizzotto, *Elect Nation* 200–201. The Amadeites were inspired by the *Apocalypsis Nova* and devoted to its supposed author Amadeus Menendez de Sylva, although they read his work in Giorgio Benigno Salviati's decidedly Savonarolan version. Ibid. 204–205.

11. Schnitzer, *Savonarola nach den Aufzeichnungen des Florentiners Piero Parenti* 302–303.

12. Dall'Aglio, *L'Eremita e il Sinodo* passim; Dall'Aglio, "L'altra faccia dello pseudo profeta Francesco da Meleto scrivano dell' SS. Annunziata di Firenze," *BHR* 67 (2005) 343–351.

13. Cesare Vasoli, "L'attesa della nuova èra in ambienti e gruppi fiorentini del Quattrocento," *L' Attesa dell'età nuova nella spiritualità della fine del medioevo, Convegni del Centro di Studi sulla Spiritualità Medievale* III October 16–19, 1962 (Todi, 1970) 370–432, esp. 425–426. Parenti says he was born in Florence, of Greek nationality, and was "a man of evil life." Schnitzer, *Savonarola nach den Aufzeichnungen Piero Parenti* 305–307.

14. Published in Varchi, *Storia* III, 307–330.

15. See chap. 24.

16. On Clement's harrowing of Piagnoni and his efforts to efface all their works, Polizzotto, *Elect Nation* chap. 8.

17. Discussion and texts of the letters in Polizzotto, "Prophecy, Politics and History in Early Sixteenth-Century Medicean Florence: The Admonitory Letters of Francesco d' Antonio de' Ricci," *Florence and Italy: Renaissance Studies in Honour of Nicolai Rubinstein,* ed. P. Denley, C. Elam (London, 1988) 107–131; additional discussion in Polizzotto, *Elect Nation* passim.

18. Ibid, 439–445. Other letters of Ricci in Marco Cavarzere, "Un savonaroliano tra I Medici e la repubblica: tre lettere di Francesco d' Antonio de' Ricci," *RSC* 2 (2006) 505–518. Savonarola's sixteenth-century legacy has also been discussed by Joseph Schnitzer, Roberto Ridolfi, Eugenio Garin, Cesare Vasoli, Domenico di Agresti, and most recently Dall'Aglio, *Savonarola and Savonarolism* chaps. 10, 11, with excellent bibliography.

19. Polizzotto, *Elect Nation* 443–444.

20. Schnitzer, *Savonarola* II, 892. Schnitzer quoted this from Ceslao Bayonne, presumably his *Études sur Jérôme Savonarola* (Paris, 1879), which I have not seen.

21. Ibid. II, 893–896. See now also Miguel Gotor, *I beati del papa: santità, Inquisizione e obedienza in età moderna* (Florence, 2002) 1–25.

22. The most recent published information on the efforts toward beatification that I have seen is Innocenzo Venchi O.P., "Iniziative dell'Ordine Domenicano per promuovere la causa di beatificazione del Ven. fra Girolamo Savonarola O.P." *Studi savonaroliani: verso il V centenario,* ed. Gian Carlo Garfagnini (Florence, 1996) 93–97.

23. See my "The Prophet as Physician of Souls: Savonarola's *Manual for Confessors,*" in *Society and Individual in Renaissance Florence,* ed. William J. Connell (Berkeley, 2002) 241–260; Gilberto Aranci, "Il Savonarola tra pulpito e confessionale: *l' introductorium confessorum* nel progetto di riforma della chiesa e della città," *VH* 10 (1999) 265–294.

24. Savonarola expounded these views in various writings and sermons, including his two most comprehensive doctrinal works, *De simplicitate Christianae vitae* (e.g., I. VIII) and *Triumphus Crucis* (e.g., I. *Proemium*).

25. The influence on Domenico Benivieni and Pietro Bernardino, if not on Savonarola himself, of *The Imitation of Christ* was posited by Massimo Petrocchi, *Una "Devotio Moderna" nel Quattrocento italiano?* (Florence, 1961). Lorenzo Polizzotto finds further evidence that *The Imitation* was among Benivieni's sources and surmises that he was led to it through his admiration for Jean Gerson's mystical writings. "Domenico Benivieni and the Radicalisation of the Savonarola Movement," *Altro Polo: A Volume of Italian Renaissance Studies,* ed. Conal Condran, R. Cooper (Sydney, 1982) 99–117.

26. Simoncelli, *Evangelismo italiano,* esp. 6, and his citation of Giorgio Spini, "Introduzione al Savonarola," *Belfagor* 3.4 (July, 1948) 414–428. Josef Nolte argues that Savonarola's prison meditations influenced Luther in the formulation of his doctrine of justification by faith: "Evangelicae doctrinae purum exemplum: Savonarola's Gefängnismeditationen im Hinblick auf Luthers theologische Anfänge," *Kontinuität und Umbruch Theologie und Frömmigkeit in Flugschriften und Kleinliteratur an der Wende vom 15. zum 16. Jahrhundert* (Stuttgart, 1978) 59–92. But as I understand him, Savonarola held that while the gift of faith was necessary to justification, the Christian believer proceeds, through penitence, charity, and righteous living to achieve the beatific vision which is salvation. I do not find in Savonarola an explicit doctrine of sola fides nor any foreshadowing of Luther's idea of imputed righteousness.

27. Paolo Simoncelli terms it "a sentimental link, cemented and justified by an obvious and common anti-Roman, but not yet doctrinal, position." *Evangelismo italiano,* 5.

28. Cerretani, *Ricordi* 369–371 and his *Dialogo* 7, 17–18.

29. Simoncelli, *Evangelismo italiano* esp. chap. 1.

30. A still useful survey of anti-Savonarolan sentiment in the sixteenth century is provided by Schnitzer, *Savonarola* II, chap. 36.

31. Dall'Aglio, *Savonarola in Francia.*

32. For example, in his exchange with the Tempter, Savonarola said he did not trust in women's prophecies since women were naturally weak in judgment and prone to deception by the devil. *Compendio di rivelazioni* 41. Also Herzig, *Savonarola's Women* 21–22. Ironically, the *Compendium,* as Herzig points out (p. 75) was one of the main sources of Savonarolan inspiration for charismatic women.

33. Lorenzo Polizzotto, "When Saints Fall Out: Women and the Savonarolan Reform in Early Sixteenth Century Florence," *RQ* 46 (1993) 508–509.

34. Ibid., 486–525.

35. Sharon T. Strocchia, "Savonarolan Witnesses: The Nuns of San Jacopo and the Piagnone Movement in Sixteenth-Century Florence," *SCJ* 38.2 (2007) 393–418.

36. Herzig, *Savonarola's Women* is a comprehensive survey and analysis with a good bibliography of recent scholarship.

37. On Brocadelli's role in the propagation in Spain of stories of Savonarola's miraculous apparitions, ibid. 108–111; Julia A. Benavent, *Savonarola y España* (Valencia, 2003) 130. On Lucrezia Borgia's religion: Gabriella Zarri, *La religione di Lucrezia Borgia: le lettere inedite del confessore* (Rome, 2006).

38. Herzig, *Savonarola's Women* 186–187 and nn. 156–157.

39. Giovanni Gentile, *Gino Capponi e la cultura toscana nel secolo decimonono,* 2d ed. (Florence, 1926).

CHAPTER 26. Afterwords

1. The comparison with Moses and the other statesmen in Niccolò Machiavelli, *Il Principe,* ed. Luigi Firpo (Turin, 1961) chap. 6 (English: *The Prince with Related Documents,* trans. and ed. William J. Connell [Boston, 2005]). The passage comparing Savonarola and Piero Soderini in Machiavelli, *Decennale primo* III. 30, *Il teatro e tutti gli scritti litterari, Opere,* ed. Franco Gaeta VIII (Milan, 1965) 242. The letter to Guicciardini on an ideal preacher for Florence, *Opere* VI (May 17, 1521) 403. The "crafty Ponzo" he refers to is surely fra Domenico da Ponzo, Savonarola's tenacious pulpit rival and putative Milanese spy. Fra Alberto may have been fra Alberto da Orvieto, an emissary to Savonarola from Pope Alexander VI. For more on Machiavelli's views on Savonarola, see my "Machiavelli and Savonarola," *Studies on Machiavelli,* ed. Myron Gilmore (Florence, 1972) 253–264; Alison Brown, "Savonarola, Machiavelli and Moses a Changing Model," *Florence and Italy: Renaissance Studies in Honor of Nicolai Rubinstein,* ed. P. Denley and C. Elam (London, 1988) 57–72; John H. Geerken, "Machiavelli's Moses and Renaissance Politics," *JHI* 60 (1999) 579–595; Marcia Colish, "Republicanism, Religion and Machiavelli's Savonarolan Moment, *JHI* 60 (1999) 597–616. Geerken says Machiavelli thought Savonarola failed because he "could not confront the need for violence," which is to misunderstand both Machiavelli and Savonarola. He also believes Savonarola continued to believe a state could be ruled by paternosters, a view fra Girolamo discarded. Colish seems to assume that Savonarola was master of Florence and therefore that the loss of Pisa, Montepulciano, and other possessions was due to his failures. But Savonarola was never master of Florence and had nothing to do with the loss of Florentine possessions. He certainly supported the military campaigns to recover them.

2. Roberto Ridolfi, *Vita di Francesco Guicciardini* (Rome, 1959) 9.

3. Guicciardini, *History of Florence* 146–148.

4. Guicciardini, *Storia d'Italia* I, 151, 293; decline and downfall 333–337. For more on Guicciardini's views of Savonarola: Enrico Gusberti, "Il Savonarola del Guicciardini," *NRS* 54 (1970) 581–604; 55 (1971) 21–89. Athanasios Moulakis's contention, in his *Republican Realism in Renaissance Florence* (Lanham, Md., 1998) 83, that the mature Guicciardini in the *Storia d'Italia* expresses "nothing but contempt for Savonarola" is without foundation. Perhaps he had in mind Guicciardini's comment: "This overabundant benevolence of our [friars] of San Marco is either hypocrisy or, when not simulated, perfectly suitable for a Christian, but it is of no help for the well-being of the city." Guicciardini seems to have written this around 1527, at the time of the last, disastrous phase of the Piagnoni revival in San Marco, in his *Ricordi,* ed. Mario Fubini (n.p., 1971) no. 179, p. 246.

5. Guicciardini may have been echoing Savonarola's own words in his sermon of October 11, 1495. Speaking of the danger that the pope might excommunicate him, he said, "If you believe that [my words] are from God, you are foolish not to also believe that God will give me a way out without scandal; if you don't believe they're from God, you must also believe I am an evil man, and therefore you are foolish, because if I don't fear God I would also not fear excommunication." *Prediche sopra i Salmi* II, 200–201.

6. As Adriano Prosperi has recently put it, it is not up to the historian to say whether Savonarola was a saint, a religious prophet as Roberto Ridolfi believed, or a civil prophet as Giuseppe Villari maintained. "Il carisma di Savonarola," *La Repubblica* (December 6, 2008) 41.

7. George Eliot *Romola,* ed. Andrew Brown (Oxford, 1994) 223.

Selected Bibliography

Savonarola Published Works

Apocalyptic Spirituality: Treatises and Letters of Lactantius, Adso of Montier-en-Der, Joachim of Fiore, the Franciscan Spirituals, Savonarola, ed. Bernard McGinn (New York, 1979).

Compendio di rivelazioni e Dialogus de veritate prophetica, ed. Angela Crucitti (Rome, 1974).

De simplicitate christianae vitae, ed. Pier Giorgio Ricci (Rome, 1959).

"Fra Girolamo Savonarola e Lorenzo de' Medici: il Quaresimale in S. Lorenzo del 1492," *ASI* Anno 150. 552. II (1992) 493–605, ed. Armando F. Verde O.P.

Il breviario di Frate Girolamo Savonarola, ed. Armando F. Verde O.P. (Florence, 1999).

Il primo Savonarola: poesie e prediche autografe dal Codice Borromeo, ed. Giulio Cattin (Florence, 1974).

Il Quaresimale del 1491: la certezza profetica di un mondo nuovo, ed. A. F. Verde O.P., E. Giaconi (Florence, 2001).

Le lettere di Girolamo Savonarola, ed. Roberto Ridolfi (Florence, 1933).

Le lettere di Girolamo Savonarola: nuovi contributi, ed. R. Ridolfi (Florence, 1936).

Lettere e scritti apologetici, ed. R. Ridolfi, V. Romano, A. F. Verde O.P. (Rome, 1984).

"Le lezioni o i sermoni sull'Apocalisse di Girolamo Savonarola (1490) 'nova dicere et novo modo,'" ed. Armando F. Verde O.P., Imagine e Parola, Retorica Filologica-Retorica Predicatoria (Valla e Savonarola) *MD*, n.s. (1988) 5–109.

Operette spirituali, ed. Mario Ferrara, 2 vols. (Rome, 1976).

Poesie, ed. Mario Martelli (Rome, 1968).

Prediche sopra Aggeo con il Trattato circa il reggimento e governo della città di Firenze, ed. Luigi Firpo (Rome, 1965).

Prediche sopra Amos e Zaccaria, ed. Paolo Ghiglieri, 3 vols. (Rome, 1971–72).

Prediche sopra l'Esodo, ed. Pier Giorgio Ricci, 2 vols. (Rome, 1955–56).

Prediche sopra Ezechiele, ed. Roberto Ridolfi, 2 vols. (Rome, 1955).

Prediche sopra Giobbe, ed. Roberto Ridolfi, 2 vols. (Rome, 1957).

Prediche sopra i Salmi, ed. Vincenzo Romano, 2 vols. (Rome, 1969–71).

Prediche sopra Ruth e Michea, ed. Vincenzo Romano, 2 vols. (Rome, 1962).

Prison Meditations on Psalms 51 and 31, ed. and trans. John Patrick Donnelly, S.J. (Milwaukee, 1994).

Savonarola: A Guide to Righteous Living and Other Works, ed. and trans. Konrad Eisenbichler (Toronto, 2003).

Scritti filosofici, ed. G. Garfagnini, E. Garin, 2 vols. (Rome, 1982–88).

Scritti vari, ed. Armando F. Verde O.P. (Rome, 1992).

Selected Writings: Religion and Politics, 1490–1498, ed. and trans. A. Borelli, M. P. Passaro (New Haven, 2006).

Sermones in adventu Domini super archam Noe (Venice, 1536).

Sermones quadragesimales super archam Noe (Pietro Nicolini da Sabio, 1536).

Sermoni sopra il principio della Cantica, ed. Silvia Cantelli Berarducci (Rome, 1996).

Sermoni sopra il Salmo Quam Bonus, ed. Claudio Leonardi (Rome, 1999).

Solatium itineris mei, ed. Giulio Cattin (Rome, 1978).

Triumphus Crucis, ed. Mario Ferrara (Rome, 1961).

Verità della profezia: De veritate prophetica dyalogus, ed. Claudio Leonardi, trans. Oddo Bucci (Florence, 1997).

Documents

Capelli, Antonio, "Fra Girolamo Savonarola e notizie intorno il suo tempo," *Atti e Memorie delle RR Deputazione di Storia Patria per le Provincie Modenese e Palmensi,* vol. 4, no. 98 (1868).

Gherardi, Alessandro, *Nuovi documenti intorno a Girolamo Savonarola,* 2d ed. (Florence, 1887).

I processi di Girolamo Savonarola (1498), ed. I. G. Rao, P. Viti, R. M. Zaccari (Florence, 2001).

Lupi, Clemente, "Nuovi documenti su Girolamo Savonarola," *ASI,* ser. 3 (1866) 3–77.

Marchese, Vincenzo, "Lettere inedite di frate Gerolamo Savonarola e documenti concernenti lo stesso," *ASI* 8 (1850) 73–203.

Passerini, Luigi, "Nuovi documenti che concernono a frate Girolamo Savonarola e ai suoi compagni," *GST* 2 (1858) 79–101, 193–238; 3 (1859) 46–65, 111–120.

Portioli, Attilio, "Nuovi documenti su Girolamo Savonarola, *ASL* 1 (1874) 325–354.

Provvisioni concernenti l'ordinamento della Repubblica Fiorentina, 1494–1512, ed. Giorgio Cadoni, 2 vols. (Rome, 1994).

Ridolfi, Roberto, *Studi savonaroliani* (Florence, 1935).

Contemporary and Near-Contemporary Biographical Accounts

Cinozzi, Placido, "Estratto d'una epistola . . . de vita et moribus reverendi patris fratris Hieronimi Savonarole de Ferraria," in *Scelta di prediche e scritti di fra Girolamo Savonarola con nuovi documenti intorno alla sua vita,* ed. P. Villari, E. Casanova (Florence, 1898) 3–28.

Filipepi, Simone, "Estratto della Cronaca di Simone Filipepi," in *Scelta di prediche e scritti di fra Girolamo Savonarola con nuovi documenti intorno alla sua vita,* ed. P. Villari, E. Casanova (Florence, 1898) 453–518.

La vita del Beato Ieronimo Savonarola scritta da un anonimo del sec. xvi e già attribuita a fra Pacifico Burlamacchi, ed. Piero Ginori Conti [Roberto Ridolfi] (Florence, 1937).

Luschino, Benedetto, *Vulnera diligentis,* ed. Stefano Dall'Aglio (Florence, 2002).

Pico della Mirandola, Giovanfrancesco, *Vita Hieronymi Savonarolae,* ed. Elisabetta Schisto (Florence, 1999).

——, *Vita di Hieronymo Savonarola,* ed. R. Castagnola (Florence, 1998).

Pico della Mirandola, Giovanni, and Gian Francesco Pico della Mirandola, *Opera omnia,* 2 vols. (Basel, 1557; repr. Hildesheim, 1969).

Vespasiano da Bisticci, *Vite di uomini illustri del secolo XV* (Florence, 1938).

Violi, Lorenzo, *Le Giornate,* ed. Gian Carlo Garfagnini (Florence, 1986).

"Vita Beati Hieronymi, martiris, doctoris, virginis ac prophetae eximii," MS BNF Conventi soppressi I.VII.28. Anonymous. Usually referred to as *Vita latina.*

Diaries, Histories, Letters

Angelo da Vallombrosa, *Lettere,* ed. Loredana Lunetta (Florence, 1988).

Cerretani, Bartolomeo, *Dialogo della mutatione di Firenze,* ed. Giuliana Berti (Florence, 1993).

——, *Ricordi,* ed. Giuliana Berti (Florence, 1993).

——, *Storia fiorentina,* ed. Giuliana Berti (Florence, 1994).

Cronica di Giovanni Villani, ed. F. G. Dragomanni, 4 vols. (Florence, 1844–45).

Guicciardini, Francesco, *History of Florence,* ed. and trans. Mario Domandi (New York, 1970).

——, *Storia d'Italia,* ed. Silvana Seidel Menchi, 3 vols. (Torino, 1971).

——, *Storie fiorentine dal 1378 al 1509,* ed. Alessandro Montevecchi (Milan, 1998).

Landucci, Luca, *Diario fiorentino dal 1450 al 1516,* ed. Iodoco Del Badia (Florence, 1883). English trans. *A Florentine Diary from 1450 to 1516,* Alice De Rosen Jervis (London, 1927).

Machiavelli, Niccolò, *Lettere,* ed. Franco Gaeta (Milan, 1961).

Masi, Bartolomeo, *Ricordanze di Bartolomeo Masi calderaio fiorentino dal 1478 al 1526,* ed. Giuseppe Odoardo Corazzini (Florence, 1926).

Medici, Lorenzo de', *Lettere,* ed. Nicolai Rubinstein et al., 12 vols. (Florence, 1977–2007).

Nardi, Iacopo, *Istorie della città di Firenze,* ed. Lelio Arbib, 2 vols. (Florence, 1838–41).

Parenti, Piero di Marco, *Storia fiorentina,* ed. Andrea Matucci, 2 vols. (Florence, 2004–5). (Vol. 1: 1476–1478 and 1492–1496, vol. 2: 1496–1502. Partial coverage of years 1502–17 in *Savonarola nach den Aufzeichnungen des Florentiners Piero Parenti,* ed. Joseph Schnitzer [Leipzig, 1910].)

Poliziano, Angelo, *Della congiura dei Pazzi (Coniurationis Commentarium),* ed. Alessandro Perosa (Padua, 1958).

——, *Letters,* ed. and trans. Shane Butler, vol.1 (Cambridge, Mass., 2006).

Redditi, Bartolomeo, and Tomaso Ginori, *Quellen und Forschungen zur Geschichte Savonarolas I: Bartolomeo Redditi und Tomaso Ginori,* ed. Joseph Schnitzer (Munich, 1902).

Rucellai, fra Santi, *Epistolario,* ed. A. F. Verde O.P., E. Giaconi, *MD,* n.s. (2003).

Varchi, Benedetto, *Storie fiorentine,* ed. G. Milanesi, 3 vols. (Florence, 1858).

Modern Biographies

Cordero, Franco, *Savonarola,* 4 vols. (Bari, 1986–88). I have not seen the new edition.

Martines, Lauro, *Fire in the City: Savonarola and the Struggle for the Soul of Renaissance Florence* (Oxford, 2006).

Ridolfi, Roberto, *The Life of Girolamo Savonarola,* trans. Cecil Grayson (New York, 1959). Based on first Italian edition of *Vita* 1951; notes omitted.

——, *Vita di Girolamo Savonarola,* 6th ed. with additional notes by Armando F. Verde O.P. (Florence, 1997).

Schnitzer, Joseph, *Savonarola: Ein Kulturbild aus der Zeit der Renaissance,* 2 vols. (1924); Ital. trans. *Savonarola,* trans. Ernesto Rutili (Milan, 1931).

Villari, Pasquale, *La storia di Girolamo Savonarola e de' suoi tempi,* 2d ed., 2 vols. (Florence, 1930).

——, *Life and Times of Girolamo Savonarola,* trans. Linda White Mazini (New York, 1890).

Book-Length Studies

Abulafia, David, ed., *The French Descent into Renaissance Italy* (Aldershot, Hamps., 1995).

Beebe, Donald P. R., "Savonarolan Aesthetics and Their Implementation in the Graphic Arts," 2 vols. (Ph.D. diss., Yale University, 1988).

Benz, Ernst, *Die Vision: Erfahrungsformen und Bilderwelt* (Stuttgart, 1969).

Bizzocchi, Roberto, *Chiesa e potere nella Toscana del Quattrocento* (Bologna, 1987).

Brucker, Gene A., *Florentine Politics and Society, 1343–78* (Princeton, 1962).

——, *Renaissance Florence* (Berkeley, 1969).

——, *Renaissance Florence: Society, Culture, and Religion* (Goldbach, 1994).

Butters, Humfrey C., *Governors and Government in Early Sixteenth Century Florence, 1502–1519* (Oxford, 1985).

Cadoni, Giorgio, *Lotte politiche e riforme istituzionali a Firenze tra il 1494–1502* (Rome, 1999).

Calogero, Cassandra, *Gli avversari religiosi di Girolamo Savonarola* (Rome, 1935).

Celenza, Christopher, *Piety and Pythagoras in Renaissance Florence: The Symbolum Nesianum* (Leiden, 2001).

Chastel, André, *Art et humanisme a Florence au temps de Laurent le Magnifique: études sur le Renaissance et l'Humanisme Platonicien* (Paris, 1961).

Ciappelli, Giovanni, *Carnevale e Quaresima: comportamenti sociali e cultura a Firenze nel Rinascimento* (Rome, 1997).

Craven, William G., *Giovanni Pico della Mirandola Symbol of His Age: Modern Interpretations of a Renaissance Philosopher* (Geneva, 1981).

Dall'Aglio, Stefano, *L'eremita e il sinodo: Paolo Giustiniani e l'offensiva medicea contro Girolamo Savonarola, 1516–1517* (Florence, 2006).

——, *Savonarola and Savonarolism,* trans. John Gagné (Toronto, 2010).

——, *Savonarola in Francia: circolazione di un' eredità-religiosa nell' Europa del Cinquecento* (Turin, 2006).

della Torre, Arnaldo, *Storia dell' Accademia Platonica di Firenze* (Florence, 1902).

De Maio, Romeo, *Savonarola e la Curia Romana* (Rome, 1969).

Dinzelbacher, Peter, *Vision und Visionsliteratur im Mittelalter* (Stuttgart, 1981).

Field, Arthur, *The Origins of the Platonic Academy of Florence* (Princeton, 1988).

Fiorelli, Pietro, *La tortura giudiziaria nel diritto comune,* 2 vols. (Milan, 1953).

Garin, Eugenio, *Giovanni Pico Della Mirandola: Vita e Dottrina* (Florence, 1937).

——. *Italian Humanism: Philosophy and Civic Life in the Renaissance,* trans. Peter Munz (New York, 1965). Orig. pub. in German, 1947.

Gilbert, Felix, *Machiavelli and Guicciardini: Politics and History in Sixteenth-Century Florence* (Princeton, 1965).

Godman, Peter, *From Poliziano to Machiavelli: Florentine Humanism in the Age of the High Renaissance* (Princeton, 1998).

Goldthwaite, Richard A., *The Economy of Renaissance Florence* (Baltimore, 2009).

Guidi, Guidubaldo, *Ciò che accadde al tempo della Signoria di novembre dicembre in Firenze l'anno 1494* (Florence, 1988).

Herlihy, David, and Christiane Klapisch-Zuber, *Tuscans and Their Families: A Study of the Florentine Catasto of 1427* (New Haven, 1987).

Herzig, Tamar, *Savonarola's Women: Visions and Reform in Renaissance Italy* (Chicago, 2008).

Hinnebusch, William H., *The History of the Dominican Order*, 2 vols. (New York, 1966).

Hood, William, *Fra Angelico at San Marco* (New Haven, 1993).

Howard, Peter Francis, *Beyond the Written Word: Preaching and Theology in the Florence of Archbishop Antoninus, 1427–1459* (Florence, 1995).

Kent, Dale V., *Cosimo de' Medici and the Florentine Renaissance: The Patron's Oeuvre* (New Haven, 2000).

Kent, F. W., *Lorenzo de' Medici and the Art of Magnificence* (Baltimore, 2004).

Klein, Robert, *Le procès de Savonarole* (Paris, 1957).

Kristeller, Paul Oskar, *Il pensiero filosofico di Marsilio Ficino* (Florence, 1953).

Leftley, Sharon Ann, *Millenarian Thought in Renaissance Rome with Special Reference to Pietro Galatino (c. 1464–c. 1540) and Egidio da Viterbo (c. 1469–1532)* PhD Thesis, University of Bristol, 1995.

Lesnick, Daniel R., *Preaching in Medieval Florence: The Social World of Franciscan and Dominican Spirituality* (Athens, Ga., 1989).

Little, Lester K., *Religious Poverty and the Profit Economy in Medieval Europe* (Ithaca, 1978).

Luotto, Paolo, *Il vero Savonarola e il Savonarola di L. Pastor* (Florence, 1909).

Macey, Patrick, *Bonfire Songs: Savonarola's Musical Legacy* (Oxford, 1998).

Martelli, Mario, *Letteratura fiorentina del Quattrocento: il filtro degli anni Sessanta* (Florence, 1996).

Martines, Lauro, *April Blood: Florence and the Plot against the Medici* (Oxford, 2003).

Mazzone, Umberto, *"El buon governo": un progetto di riforma generale nella Firenze savonaroliana* (Florence, 1978).

McGinn, Bernard, *The Calabrian Abbot Joachim of Fiore in the History of Western Thought* (New York, 1985).

Mulchahey, M. Michele, *"First the Bow Is Bent in Study": Dominican Education before 1350* (Toronto, 1998).

Najemy, John M., *A History of Florence, 1200–1575* (Oxford, 2006).

Niccoli, Ottavia, *Profeti e popolo nell' Italia del Rinascimento* (Rome, 1987).

Pala, Gavino, *La Mariologia del Fra Girolamo Savonarola* (Cagliari, 1975).

Polizzotto, Lorenzo, *Children of the Promise: The Confraternities of the Purification and the Socialization of Youths in Florence, 1427–1785* (Oxford, 2004).

——, *The Elect Nation: The Savonarola Movement in Florence, 1494–1545* (Oxford, 1994).

Reeves, Marjorie, *The Influence of Prophecy in the Later Middle Ages* (Oxford, 1969).

Ridolfi, Roberto, *Le prediche del Savonarola* (Florence, 1939).

Rocke, Michael, *Forbidden Friendships: Homosexuality and Male Culture in Renaissance Florence* (New York, 1996).

Roth, Cecil, *The Last Florentine Republic, 1527–1530* (London, 1925).

Rubinstein, Nicolai, *The Government of Florence under the Medici,* 2d ed. (Oxford, 1997).

——, *The Palazzo Vecchio, 1298–1532: Government, Architecture, and Imagery in the Civic Palace of the Florentine Republic* (Oxford, 1995).

Sebregondi, Ludovica, *Iconografia di Girolamo Savonarola, 1495–1998* (Florence, 2004).

Simoncelli, Paolo, *Evangelismo italiano del Cinquecento: questione religiosa e Nicodemismo politico* (Rome, 1979).

Skinner, Quentin, *The Foundations of Modern Political Thought,* vol. 1: *The Renaissance* (Cambridge, 1978).

Taddei, Ilaria, *Fanciulli e giovani: crescere a Firenze nel Rinascimento* (Florence, 2001).

Trexler, Richard C., *Public Life in Renaissance Florence* (New York, 1980).

Verde, Armando F., O.P., *Lo Studio fiorentino, 1473–1503,* 5 vols. (Florence, 1973–94).

von Albertini, Rudolf, *Das Florentinische Staatsbewusstein im Übergang von der Republik zum Prinzipat* (Bern, 1955).

Weinstein, Donald, *Savonarola and Florence: Prophecy and Patriotism in the Renaissance* (Princeton, 1970).

West, Delno, ed., *Joachim of Fiore in Christian Thought,* 2 vols. (New York, 1975).

Index